AGRARIAN RADICALISM IN SOUTH INDIA

AGRARIAN RADICALISM
IN SOUTH INDIA

MARSHALL M. BOUTON

PRINCETON UNIVERSITY PRESS

Library of Congress Cataloging in Publication Data will be
found on the last printed page of this book

ISBN 0-691-07686-3

This book has been composed in Linotron Baskerville

Clothbound editions of Princeton University Press books
are printed on acid-free paper, and binding materials are
chosen for strength and durability

Printed in the United States of America by Princeton University Press
Princeton, New Jersey

TO THE MEMORY
OF MY FATHER AND
TO MY MOTHER

CONTENTS

THIS BOOK is a study of the conditions and forces that give rise to and shape the development of agrarian radicalism. It addresses several questions central to a growing body of comparative literature on peasant rebellion and revolution while also seeking to shed light specifically on the role of agrarian mobilization in Indian political development. The focus and comparative advantage of this study is the analysis of the *local* conditions and forces in which agrarian politics is peculiarly rooted, particularly those structural characteristics that vary so much in adaptation to the geophysical ecology of agriculture. These sources of agrarian radicalism are best revealed through the examination of a significant case—here the district of Thanjavur in Tamil Nadu State, India.

This study had its origins in my experience as a development intern with the Ford Foundation in India in 1968-1969. It was during that year that Thanjavur District attracted national and even international attention as the site of violent clashes between Communist-led agricultural laborers and landowners. These and other incidents were soon being interpreted as evidence that India's new growth-oriented agricultural strategy was causing economic polarization, social breakdown, and political radicalization in the countryside—that the "Green Revolution" was turning "Red." I resolved to make this then popular and simplistically Marxist hypothesis the subject of a later study. But when I returned to India and to Thanjavur District in 1972 to carry out my field research, I soon discovered that this explanation of the events of the late 1960s was grossly inadequate. It did not take into account either Thanjavur's history or the complexity and variability of the present. Thus I found myself engaged in a much broader effort to understand the multiple sources of agrarian radicalism in Thanjavur and to relate them to general explanations of how peasant societies respond to or achieve modernization.

My work was substantially completed in 1977. Unfortunately publication has been all too long delayed for a variety of personal and professional reasons. However, despite the fact that the data on which much of this study is based were collected ten years ago, I remain fully confident of the continuing validity and relevance of my findings. This never was an effort to provide an up-to-date account of agrarian politics in Thanjavur. Rather its purpose was to focus on those periods and events most significant to an understanding of agrarian radicalism, the most recent of these being the events of the period 1967 to 1972. Furthermore, I was able to confirm my findings in a brief return visit to Thanjavur in 1980. I traveled to all parts of the district, interviewed a large number of officials and political leaders, and met with groups of farmers and laborers. My observations and discussions uncovered no evidence to challenge the major conclusions of this study.

My research was supported at various times by the Foreign Area Fellowship Program of the Social Science Research Council and the American Council of Learned Societies, the National Science Foundation, and the United States Agency for International Development. In addition, a consulting relationship with the Development Research Centre of the World Bank, arranged through the good offices of T. N. Srinivasan and Clive Bell, made possible analysis of a part of the extensive survey data collected. I am grateful to these organizations and to the individuals involved for their interest and support.

In the process of completing such an excessively ambitious and lengthy study I have become deeply indebted to many individuals for intellectual guidance and moral support. I am most indebted to Lloyd I. Rudolph for his constant encouragement, thoughtful criticism, and faith in the outcome at every stage. How much I had been influenced by his remarkable understanding of India and politics I did not fully realize until my project was complete. Sidney Verba and Norman Nie inspired my search for unusual ways of measuring agrarian radicalism and advised on strategies for data collection and analysis. Francine Frankel first helped me to make sense of Indian politics and later produced widely read interpretations of agrarian politics in India that have, as the pages to come will reveal, greatly influenced me. The gentle prodding and warm support of Robert F. Goheen, Phillips Talbot, and A. A. Johnson moved this project forward at critical junctures.

My debt to individuals and institutions in India is enormous. Not all can be mentioned but some deserve special acknowledgment. First, the hundreds of farmers and laborers and scores of officials and political leaders in Thanjavur and Madras who took the time to talk with me or my assistants, to fill out my questionnaires, and to search out the most obscure information have my great gratitude. Without the assistance of Pradip Mehendiratta and the staff of the American Institute of India Studies at a difficult time it would not have been possible for me to carry out my research. Dr. C. A. Perumal was an understanding guide and a source of friendship. Mr. C. Muthiah shared with me his remarkable insights into the Thanjavur situation. S. V. Krishnan and M. Kumaran, principal research assistants throughout my field work, played loyal, invaluable roles in organizing the massive data collection effort on which the study is based. C. T. Ramasamy, R. Singaravelu, S. Thyagarajan, and T. K. Palanisamy all demonstrated great skill in interviewing the farmers and laborers of Thanjavur. Finally, I am grateful to A. Venkataraman and P. K. Sivasubramaniam, then of the Madras Department of Agriculture, and their staffs for their special efforts in helping me to locate and assemble much needed data.

In the United States also many individuals and institutions provided assistance for data and manuscript preparation. In Chicago: Susan Hull, Norman Hurd, Rosemary Garrison, Kokila Roche, Pratibha Rao, Bonnie Hahn, and Betty Leiderman. In New York, Ainslie Embree made possible research affiliation with Columbia University, Paul Heikkila did a brilliant job of organizing the survey data coding, and Seetha R. Kauta gave expert data-processing assistance. Special thanks are due to Andrea Marquez for preparation of maps and graphs. I am also very grateful to Debby Rosenman and Elisabeth Matheson for their superb skill and persistence in typing and retyping the manuscript.

My greatest debt and appreciation go to my wife, Barbara, without whose unfailing patience, encouragement, and sacrifice this study would surely never have been completed. For this, and for so much else, my gratitude is too deep to express.

Despite these numerous debts all responsibility for whatever faults are revealed in these pages is of course my own.

LIST OF ABBREVIATIONS

ADT. 27   Aduthurai 27
AIKS   All-India Kisan Sabha
CPI   Communist Party of India
CPM   Communist Party of India (Marxist)
DK   Dravida Kazhagam
DMK   Dravida Munnetra Kazhagam
HRCE   Hindu Religious and Charitable Endowments
HYVP   High-Yielding Varieties Programme
IADP   Intensive Agricultural District Program
MLA   Member of the Legislative Assembly

AGRARIAN RADICALISM IN SOUTH INDIA

CHAPTER 1

Introduction

DURING the 1970s, agriculture and agrarian society became increasingly central to explanations of political development in the Third World. Until late in the 1960s, however, political development theory rested heavily on the assumption that industrialization and urbanization were the principal engines of political change in the Third World, as they had been in the West. Economic development theorists concentrated on the urban-industrial processes or stages through which economic growth would take place. Political development theorists focused on the political requisites for and processes through which rapid industrial growth and orderly urban growth could take place. "Modernization" was defined as the transformation of a primarily agricultural and rural society into a primarily industrial and urban society, and political development was generally conceptualized as the political response to modernization. This response had two related components: the capacity of the political system to meet the demands placed upon it by the processes of industrialization and urbanization, and the effect of these interrelated socio-economic changes on the nature of politics in these societies. Some writers concluded that democracy was the inevitable political consequence of socio-economic change and the hallmark of political development.[1]

[1] The seminal studies include: Walt W. Rostow, *The Stages of Economic Growth: A Non-Communist Manifesto* (Cambridge: Cambridge University Press, 1960); A.F.K. Organski, *The Stages of Political Development* (New York: Knopf, 1965); and C. E. Black, *The Dynamics of Modernization* (New York: Harper and Row, 1966). For a study that refutes the "dichotomous" view of modernization and political development, see Lloyd I. Rudolph and Susanne Hoeber Rudolph, *The Modernity of Tradition: Political Development in India* (Chicago: University of Chicago Press, 1967). See also Gabriel Almond and G. Bingham Powell, Jr., *Comparative Politics: A Development Approach* (Boston: Little, Brown, 1966); S. N. Eisenstadt, *Modernization: Protest and Change* (Englewood Cliffs, N.J.: Prentice-Hall, 1966); Karl Deutsch, "Social Mobilization and Political Development," *American Political Science Review* 55 (September 1961): 493-511; Samuel P. Huntington, *Political Order in Changing Societies* (New Haven: Yale University Press, 1968); Seymour Martin Lipset, "Some Social Requisites of Democracy," *American Political Science Review* 53 (March 1959): 69-105; and Phillips Cutright, "National Political Development: Its Measurement and Social Correlates," in *Politics and Social Life*, ed. Nelson W. Polsby et al. (Boston: Houghton Mifflin, 1963), p. 571.

Beginning in the late 1960s, events forced a gradual reorientation of political development theory. The emphasis on industrialization, urbanization, and democratic politics were increasingly in conflict with Third World realities. The Vietnam War and a growing awareness of China's political development focused attention on the role of the peasantry in Asian political change. The emergence of the so-called "Green Revolution" suggested that agricultural development rather than industrialization might be the main source of economic growth in Asia. Later, concern over the distributional consequences of the Green Revolution added emphasis to the importance of the rural agrarian sector in socio-political change.[2] Finally, the poor survival rate of democratic regimes in the Third World suggested that whatever the locus of economic growth or the nature of modernization, competitive democracy was not the inevitable outcome.

In response to these challenges, development theory began to pay greater attention to the role of agriculture in economic development, to agrarian socio-economic change, and to the significance of peasant-based revolution in political development, especially in Asia.[3] Barrington Moore's *Social Origins of Dictatorship and Democracy*, published in 1966, was the first major comparative work to

[2] See Eric R. Wolf, *Peasant Wars of the Twentieth Century* (New York: Harper & Row, 1969), pp. ix-x; Jeffery M. Paige, *Agrarian Revolution: Social Movements and Export Agriculture in the Underdeveloped World* (New York: The Free Press, 1975), p. xii; Lester R. Brown, *Seeds of Change: The Green Revolution and Development in the 1970s* (New York: Praeger, 1970); Clifton R. Wharton, Jr., "The Green Revolution: Cornucopia or Pandora's Box?" *Foreign Affairs* 47 (April 1969): 464-476; Lester R. Brown, "The Social Impact of the Green Revolution," *International Conciliation*, no. 581 (January 1971), pp. 5-61.

[3] On the role of agriculture in economic development, see John W. Mellor, *The New Economics of Growth: A Strategy for India and the Developing World* (Ithaca: Cornell University Press, 1976). On agrarian socio-economic change, see Keith Griffin, *The Political Economy of Agrarian Change: An Essay on the Green Revolution* (Cambridge, Mass.: Harvard University Press, 1974), and George Rosen, *Peasant Society in a Changing Economy: Comparative Development in Southeast Asia and India* (Urbana, Ill.: University of Illinois Press, 1975). On peasant revolution, see Wolf, *Peasant Wars*; John Wilson Lewis, ed., *Peasant Rebellion and Communist Revolution in Asia* (Stanford, Ca.: Stanford University Press, 1974); Joel S. Migdal, *Peasants, Politics, and Revolution: Pressures toward Political and Social Change in the Third World* (Princeton, N.J.: Princeton University Press, 1974); Paige, *Agrarian Revolution*; James C. Scott, *The Moral Economy of the Peasant: Rebellion and Subsistence in Southeast Asia* (New Haven: Yale University Press, 1976); and Samuel L. Popkin, *The Rational Peasant: The Political Economy of Rural Society in Vietnam* (Berkeley, Ca.: University of California Press, 1979).

provide this focus on the role of peasant revolution in modern political development.[4]

This new concern with agrarian society and with its relationship to political change gave rise to a considerable body of literature that attempts to explain the "origins" or "sources" of peasant or agrarian radicalism. Two central questions are addressed in this literature. First, what kinds of agrarian social structure, or what changes in that structure, are conducive to radical political mobilization? Second, what forces produce such types of or changes in agrarian structure?

The first question may be broken down into several components. Is it certain positions or relations within a given social structure, or structural changes within the agrarian sector, that open the way to radical political mobilization? If it is a certain type of structure, it may then be asked which positions or strata (middle peasant, poor peasant, landless laborer) or which type of relations (patron-client, "class-type") are conducive to radical mobilization? If change is the key, then the question is what kind of change leads to agrarian radicalism (if primarily economic, for instance, is it negative or positive, relative or absolute)?

With respect to the second central question—what factors account for a particular structure or change in structure—factors must be identified that are responsible either for the existence of a given structure or for changes in that structure. For instance, "ecological explanations" usually refer to existing agrarian systems and explain radicalism as a response to one or another of them, while "technological explanations" usually explain radicalism as a response to marked change in agrarian relations.

The present study addresses these several questions by examining the sources of agrarian radicalism in an area of south India, Thanjavur District in Tamil Nadu State, with particular reference to the period 1960 to 1972. Through careful analysis of this significant case I intend to contribute to the critical evaluation of the new literature on agrarian radicalism—Has it posed the right questions in the right way?—and to add to our understanding of why and how under a variety of circumstances agrarian radicalism does or does not emerge.

I have chosen India and Thanjavur District as the focus of this study for several reasons. First, I hope to shed some light on the

[4] Barrington Moore, Jr., *Social Origins of Dictatorship and Democracy: Lord and Peasant in the Making of the Modern World* (Boston: Beacon Press, 1966).

question of why in India agrarian radicalism has not been expressed in revolution, attempted revolution, or revolt that threatened the state.[5] Most of the literature on agrarian radicalism is concerned with its more extreme consequences—rebellion, revolt, revolution, or war—and little attention has been given to explaining what Barrington Moore terms "Indian exceptionalism." Moore himself suggests several possible explanations, including the survival of India's peasant economy and society into the modern period.[6] My study provided an opportunity to examine the factors identified by Moore and to extend the analysis of the relationship between agrarian radicalism and wider political forces in the Indian situation.

Thanjavur District was selected for this study because it is one of few areas of rural India with a lengthy history of agrarian unrest and related political mobilization. This history goes back to Communist efforts just before World War II to organize Thanjavur sharecroppers and farm laborers. These efforts led to agrarian disturbances in 1948 that Kathleen Gough has identified as one of seventy-seven peasant revolts in modern India.[7] Parts of Thanjavur remained a relative stronghold for India's Communist parties through

[5] This question has been the subject of some debate. Moore argues that in contrast to China "peasant rebellions" in India "in the premodern period were relatively rare and completely ineffective," and implies that in the modern period there was only one "substantial attempt at peasant revolt in India, that in Hyderabad in 1948" (Moore, *Social Origins*, pp. 202, 457). Kathleen Gough sharply contests Moore's assertion, claiming to have identified at least seventy-seven instances of peasant revolt over the period from the last decades of Moghul rule to the present. See Gough, "Indian Peasant Uprisings," *Economic and Political Weekly* 9 (Special number, 1974): 1,391-1,412.

The debate is in part due to definitional confusion. For instance, Gough uses the terms *peasant revolt* and *social movement* interchangeably. But it seems to me that the weight of the evidence favors Moore. Crucial to this judgment is the fact, which even Gough does not openly dispute, that these peasant uprisings never posed any real possibility (by spread effects or aggregation) of leading to revolution at the national or even regional level. For studies of the important Telengana case, see Carolyn M. Elliott, "Decline of a Patrimonial Regime: The Telengana Rebellion in India, 1946-51," *Journal of Asian Studies* 34 (November 1974): 27-47; Barry Pavier, "The Telengana Armed Struggle," *Economic and Political Weekly* 9 (Special number, 1974): 1,413-1,420; Mohan Ram, "The Telengana Peasant Armed Struggle, 1946-1951," *Economic and Political Weekly* 8 (June 9, 1973): 1,025-1,032; and P. Sundarayya, *Telengana People's Struggle and Its Lessons* (Calcutta: Communist Party of India [Marxist], 1972).

Other recent relevant studies of peasant movements in India include: D. N. Dhanagare, *Peasant Movements in India, 1920-1950* (New Delhi: Oxford University Press, 1983), and M.S.A. Rao, ed., *Social Movements in India*, vol. 1, *Peasant and Backward Classes Movements* (New Delhi: Manohar Publishers, 1978).

[6] Moore, *Social Origins*, p. 460.

[7] Gough, "Peasant Uprisings," p. 1,403.

the 1950s and 1960s, and in the late 1960s there were renewed outbreaks of Communist-led agrarian unrest in the district. While I cannot agree fully with Gough's classification of Thanjavur as an area of peasant *revolt*, the record clearly warrants selecting the area for a study of agrarian radicalism.

In Thanjavur District agrarian radicalism has been less sustained and intense than comparable movements and events in rural areas of West Bengal and Kerala states. The 1967 peasant rebellion in Naxalbari, West Bengal, was certainly a more significant incident[8] and Communist mobilization of tenants and agricultural laborers in Kerala has been more widespread and effective.[9] In both the West Bengal and Kerala cases, however, the local development of agrarian radicalism has been very heavily influenced by, indeed almost inseparable from, Communist predominance in state-level politics. In Thanjavur, on the other hand, although the development of agrarian radicalism has been shaped in part by Communist fortunes at the state level, the Communist parties have never dominated politics in Tamil Nadu (formerly Madras) State. Thus, the Thanjavur case tends to focus attention on the local sources of agrarian radicalism that this study seeks to highlight.

A second consideration in the selection of Thanjavur District relates to Barrington Moore's explanation of Indian exceptionalism. The most important factor in Moore's explanation was that "modernization has but barely begun in the (Indian) countryside."[10] Yet by the time this study was launched (1971), many observers believed that as a result of the Green Revolution, agricultural modernization was well under way and already having a "radicalizing" effect on rural society.[11] Thanjavur has been closely identified with the Green Revolution and earlier intensive agricultural develop-

[8] Two good studies of the Naxalbari movement and "Naxalism" are: Biplab Das Gupta, *The Naxalite Movement*, Centre for the Study of Developing Societies, Monograph no. 1 (New Delhi: Allied Publishers, 1974), and Sankar Ghosh, *The Naxalite Movement: A Maoist Experiment* (Calcutta: Mukhopadhyay, 1974).

[9] Among the many studies of agrarian relations and Communist politics in Kerala, see especially Robert L. Hardgrave, Jr., "The Kerala Communists: Contradictions of Power," in *Radical Politics in South Asia*, ed. Paul R. Brass and Marcus F. Franda (Cambridge, Mass.: The M.I.T. Press, 1973), pp. 119-180; Donald S. Zagoria, "The Social Basis of Communism in Kerala and West Bengal: A Study in Contrast," *Problems of Communism* 12 (1973): 16-24; and T. J. Nossiter, *Communism in Kerala: A Study in Adaptation*, published for the Royal Institute of International Affairs (Berkeley, Ca.: University of California Press, 1982).

[10] Moore, *Social Origins*, p. 460.

[11] For a major statement of this hypothesis, see Francine R. Frankel, *India's Green Revolution: Economic Gains and Political Costs* (Princeton, N.J.: Princeton University Press, 1971).

ment efforts. It was thus frequently cited as a prime example of the alleged relationship between agricultural modernization and agrarian radicalism and so offers a meaningful test of this hypothesis.[12]

Finally, while Thanjavur District is only one of about three hundred fifty districts in a country known for its great economic, social, and cultural diversity, it has two characteristics that will enable me to relate the findings of this study to other areas of India. First, as will be fully detailed in Chapter 3 and Chapter 4, Thanjavur is significantly heterogeneous in terms of physical and agro-economic conditions. Analysis of covariation between these characteristics and agrarian radicalism will help to identify factors that may facilitate or impede the development of agrarian radicalism in other areas. Second, because large parts of the district are ecologically and socio-structurally similar to other areas of India in which agrarian radicalism has emerged, there will be opportunities for specific comparison and generalization.

The concept of "radicalism" is central to this study and requires further definition.[13] By radicalism I mean an orientation of action that is "extreme" with respect to either means or ends. In defining radicalism as an "orientation of action" I am drawing on Weber's formulation of the linkages between the objective and subjective dimensions of human behavior.[14] That is, I wish to recognize that radicalism is an orientation that arises out of the interaction of objective circumstances and subjective values and attitudes. Take the very relevant example of "class action," usually so closely associated with radicalism. I share Weber's view that class action (in Weber's terms, "communal action by members of a class") results from the combination of objective conditions (individuals sharing a "market-situation" and thus economic interests) and the subjective recognition that the "class situation" affects "life chances." In other

[12] See Brown, *Seeds of Change*, p. 77. Thanjavur is one of five case studies in Frankel, *Green Revolution*, pp. 81-108. The apparent connection between agricultural modernization and agrarian unrest in Thanjavur in the late 1960s also attracted Indian national and international press attention. See Ashok Thapar, "Warning From Thanjavur," *Times of India*, January 20, 1969, and the *New York Times*, October 27, 1967, p. 10.

[13] Webster defines *radical* as relating to "extreme change in existing institutions and/or conditions" and *radicalism* as "the will or effort to uproot and reform that which is established."

[14] See Max Weber, *The Theory of Social and Economic Organization*, trans. A. M. Henderson and Talcott Parsons, ed. Talcott Parsons (New York: The Free Press, 1947), esp. pp. 112-118.

words, class action is "linked to the *transparency* [Weber's emphasis] of the connections between the causes and consequences of the 'class situation' " Or shifting to Marxist terms, "consciousness" of the salience of class interests is a prerequisite to class action.[15]

My study will analyze both the objective and subjective sources of agrarian radicalism. Because systematic data on geographic, agro-climatic, demographic, and agro-economic conditions were more widely and readily available, I have been able to analyze these objective factors in greater depth than the subjective factors. However, survey data collected from over four hundred cultivators and three hundred agricultural laborers in Thanjavur District, which are analyzed in Chapter 8, allow me both to examine the attitudinal dimensions of agrarian radicalism and to compare aggregate correlates of radicalism with individual evidence.[16] In addition, I have probed the role of class consciousness by focusing special attention on the objective conditions most likely to affect it. For instance, I have examined closely those aspects of the agro-economic structure most likely to affect the "transparency of the connections between the causes and the consequences of the class situation." Thus, to the extent we find that economic interests are divergent and sharply defined, we can conclude that a basis for communal action, or class consciousness, is likely to develop.

Turning to the second part of my definition of radicalism, I have stated that an orientation of action is radical if it is "extreme" with respect to means *or* ends. Extreme means are those extralegal actions, such as strikes, agitations, or "land-grabs," that are violent or pose a direct threat of violence. Extreme ends are those that would fundamentally alter the agrarian economic and political structure, especially the control over the use of land and its products. Radicalism oriented to *extreme means only* may (but does not necessarily) result in revolt or rebellion. Revolt and rebellion express and seek redress of grievances but do *not* seek system change

[15] Max Weber, *From Max Weber: Essays in Sociology*, ed. and trans. H. H. Gerth and C. Wright Mills (New York: Oxford University Press, 1946), pp. 181-185. On the role of individual and group awareness in class formation, see also T. H. Marshall, *Class Conflict and Social Stratification* (London: LePlay House Press, 1938), pp. 103-104.

[16] This survey was carried out during my field research in India in 1972 and 1973 and is more fully described in Chapter 3. Unfortunately, due to limits of time and funding, only a small part of the data collected in the survey could be analyzed and included in this study.

or state power.[17] Rather they express the desire that the existing system work up to established norms. Radicalism oriented to *extreme ends only* seeks transformation of the economic and political system through orderly and peaceful means. This orientation has been espoused by different segments of Indian communism at different points in time.[18] Radicalism oriented to extreme means *and* ends is, of course, revolutionary. There are, however, many intervening variables between revolutionary radicalism and revolution. For instance, there is much historical evidence—Russia, Yugoslavia, China, Vietnam—that war is a crucial precipitant of revolution.[19] In other words, radicalism is a necessary but not a sufficient condition for revolution.

By defining radicalism in terms of positions along two axes, orientations to extreme means and orientations to extreme ends, I have adopted a concept that encompasses a range of phenomena; a narrower definition would not reflect the complexity and variability of the reality. The orientations to means and ends are continuous, not dichotomous, variables, and the mix of the two is changeable. As this study will demonstrate, radicalism is manifested in different ways at any given time and over time.

To measure radicalism, therefore, I have used an indicator through much of this study that in the context of the Indian situation reflects an underlying propensity to radicalism rather than an unchanging commitment to particular means or ends. Specifically, I have operationalized radicalism in terms of Communist electoral strength at the local level. While not the most precise, this measure is powerful because it is the lowest common denominator of radicalism across considerable space and time. The several reasons and precedents for my choice of this measure are described in detail in Chapter 3.

The variability of agrarian radicalism reflect its close dependence on local conditions. For this reason the primary mode of expla-

[17] See Mark N. Hagopian, *The Phenomenon of Revolution* (New York: Dodd, Mead, 1974), p. 10.

[18] For a thorough review of Indian Communist ideology, strategy, and tactics, see chaps. 1 and 2 in Bhabani Sen Gupta, *Communism in Indian Politics* (New York: Columbia University Press, 1972). See also Chapter 3 below.

[19] See Hagopian, *Revolution*, pp. 163-165, and Donald S. Zagoria, "Peasants and Revolution," *Comparative Politics* 8 (April 1976): 323-324. Zagoria lists several ways in which the impact of war helps to precipitate agrarian revolution: 1) the breakdown of authority leads to spontaneous peasant uprisings; 2) the vacuum of authority created by war facilitates the raising of a revolutionary army; 3) the government aids revolutionary organization; and 4) isolation encourages collective action.

nation in this study, which I shall later describe as "comparative micro-ecology," emphasizes local geographical, technological, and agro-economic factors. At the same time a full explanation of agrarian radicalism requires consideration of the relationship of the agrarian system to the larger society or to its own past.[20] Thus, throughout the study I shall describe how history has shaped the sources of agrarian radicalism in Thanjavur District and, in Chapter 10 particularly, how external economic and political forces have affected its evolution.

Finally, a word about terminology is in order. In much of the literature the term "agrarian" is used interchangeably with the term "peasant."[21] I intend hereafter to drop "peasant" as a general term in order to avoid its misuse in describing a much more general and complex reality. According to Andre Beteille, the term peasant is best used to describe a "more or less homogenous and undifferentiated community of families characterized by small holdings operated mainly by family labor."[22] Because in India village communities are very often highly differentiated in terms of the ownership, control, and use of the land and the disposal of its products, it is misleading to use the term peasant in a general sense with respect to its rural society. Whether radicalism in India is associated with peasant or other types of agrarian structure is an empirical question I intend to examine. For these reasons I prefer the term agrarian, which refers more generally to the main structural principle of rural agricultural society and thus encompasses the range of variation that may exist in the actual structure.

[20] According to Webster, the noun *peasant* means "one of a chiefly European class that tills the soil as small, free landowners or hired laborers," the adjective *peasant* means "of or relating to simple agricultural economy," and the adjective *agrarian* means "of or relating to land or landed property."

[21] For Eric Wolf the role of agents linking the peasant class to the larger society is one of the most important factors in explaining the political mobilization of the peasantry (Wolf, *Peasant Wars*, p. xii). Similarly, Mattei Dogan places great emphasis on the *historical roots* of political cleavages in his study of agrarian communism in France and Italy. See Dogan, "Political Cleavage and Social Stratification in France and Italy," in *Party Systems and Voter Alignments: Cross-National Perspectives*, ed. Seymour M. Lipset and Stein Rokkan (New York: The Free Press, 1967), pp. 183-184.

[22] See Andre Beteille, *Studies in Agrarian Social Structure* (New Delhi: Oxford University Press, 1974), pp. 24-25. Eric Wolf makes the point that in reality peasants are a differentiated lot but retains the term and speaks of types of peasants: "rich peasant," "middle peasant," "poor peasants," etc. (Wolf, *Peasant Wars*, pp. x-xi).

CHAPTER 2

The Sources of Agrarian Radicalism: Theoretical Considerations

OVER THE LAST DECADE the shifting focus of political development theory has resulted in the publication of several major studies of agrarian change and agrarian radicalism in the Third World. This important new body of literature serves as a guide to important concepts and problems in the explanation of agrarian radicalism and as a basis for discussion of the wider implications of the analysis of agrarian radicalism in Thanjavur District.

Any attempt to summarize the literature must take note of its variety. First, the contributions come from different disciplines: Barrington Moore from history; Eric R. Wolf from anthropology; Keith Griffin from economics; Joel S. Migdal, Jeffery M. Paige, Samuel L. Popkin, James C. Scott, and Donald S. Zagoria from political science.[1] Second, the precise phenomenon under study varies. For Moore and Wolf it is revolution; for Scott, rebellion. For Popkin it is the response of peasant society, including revolutionary action, to outside forces of change. Migdal's focus is peasant political involvement, although he extends his argument to involvement in revolutionary movements. For Zagoria it is Communist mobilization of the peasantry. Paige examines a range of agrarian movements. Finally, these authors examine the problem

[1] Barrington Moore, Jr., *Social Origins of Dictatorship and Democracy: Lord and Peasant in the Making of the Modern World* (Boston: Beacon Press, 1966); Eric R. Wolf, *Peasant Wars of the Twentieth Century* (New York: Harper & Row, 1969); Keith Griffin, *The Political Economy of Agrarian Change: An Essay on the Green Revolution* (Cambridge, Mass.: Harvard University Press, 1974); Joel S. Migdal, *Peasants, Politics, and Revolution: Pressures toward Political and Social Change in the Third World* (Princeton, N.J.: Princeton University Press, 1974); Jeffery M. Paige, *Agrarian Revolution: Social Movements and Export Agriculture in the Underdeveloped World* (New York: The Free Press, 1975); Samuel L. Popkin, *The Rational Peasant: The Political Economy of Rural Society in Vietnam* (Berkeley, Ca.: University of California Press, 1979); James C. Scott, *The Moral Economy of the Peasant: Rebellion and Subsistence in Southeast Asia* (New Haven: Yale University Press, 1976); Donald S. Zagoria, "Asian Tenancy Systems and Communist Mobilization of the Peasantry," in *Peasant Rebellion and Communist Revolution in Asia*, ed. John Wilson Lewis (Stanford, Ca.: Stanford University Press, 1974), pp. 29-60.

in different (though sometimes overlapping) geographic and historical contexts.

Despite these variations it makes sense for several reasons to treat these works as a class and to try to identify commonalities and differences in their approaches and findings. First, the identification of the sources of agrarian radicalism clearly requires an interdisciplinary approach. Second, radicalism as defined in Chapter 1 underlies most, if not all, of the phenomena explored by these studies. Finally, in spite of their empirical limitations, most of these works lay at least a limited claim to general explanation.[2] Each concludes that one factor or set of factors is universally important in defining revolution or rebellion or Communist mobilization, and by my inference, radicalism.

Two general observations can be made about the relevance of much of the literature to the present study. In the first place, most of these studies are primarily concerned with the role of long-range historical forces in the development of agrarian radicalism. Although there are differences in terms and in the nuances of interpretation it is at this level of "distant causes" that these studies are most in agreement. In general, they conclude that everywhere the stage was set for radical mobilization of the peasantry by the direct and indirect effects of the related forces of capitalism and imperialism. Most of the authors, the so-called "moral economists," find that the disruptive impact of the commercialization of agriculture, the intrusion of the state, and population growth on the precapitalist "moral economy" of peasant society causes peasants to seek restoration of that order through collective involvement in political action, rebellion, and revolution. Popkin takes the only notable exception to this general argument, disputing the view that precapitalist villages provided guarantees of subsistence and welfare and arguing for an interpretation of peasant responses to market forces based on individual, rational decision making.

As a general proposition the link between capitalism, imperialism, and radicalism seems undeniable: in many, but not all, cases it is possible to trace the genesis of agrarian radicalism directly to the impact of these forces; in other cases the circumstantial evidence is quite strong. Regarding the proposition in general, however, two

[2] The wide range of empirical reference in these studies strengthens the argument that most of them have in common, the importance of long-range historical forces, particularly the spread of capitalism and imperialism, in explaining agrarian radicalism. On the other hand, the diversity of contexts makes it difficult to perceive how these forces eventuate in agrarian radicalism.

reservations may be expressed. First, much of the literature tends to take a highly undifferentiated view of premodern agrarian social and economic organization. Popkin notes, for instance, that contrary to the implied moral economy view stratification did exist in precapitalist villages.[3] A more differentiated view would of course make it harder to predict the impact of external forces, such as the growth of the market economy and the modern state, on agrarian society. As a case in point, Migdal recognizes that the impact of marketing penetration will be somewhat different in "freeholding" (less stratified) and "lord-and-peasant" (more stratified) villages, but he does not relate this difference clearly to political effects. Therefore, as Donald Zagoria has observed, "although it is true that certain long-range historical forces have all contributed to peasant unrest, it is difficult to establish any direct connections without considering a host of intervening factors." If this were *not* the case, if, as James Scott has written, "anger born of exploitation were sufficient to spark a rebellion, most of the Third World (and not only the Third World) would be in flames."[4]

A second general observation is that the arguments in this literature diverge and are less convincing when they seek to explain why the impact of commercialism or population growth or taxation is radicalizing at some places and times and not at others. That is, they say little about the "proximate" causes of agrarian radicalism, and what they say about them differs more than what they say about "distant" causes. This is perhaps understandable because we might expect more variation in the proximate causes. In fact, some might argue that it is impossible to identify a single determinant combination of long-range and short-range factors in explaining agrarian radicalism. However, without some understanding of the range of variables that may intervene to bring a radical result out of the disruption of agrarian society, the "distant causes" lose much of their potency. As mentioned briefly in Chapter 1, the proximate causes of agrarian radicalism, particularly (but not exclusively) factors internal to agrarian economy and society, are the primary focus of this study.

One consequence of the focus on distant causes in the literature on agrarian radicalism is a heavy emphasis on the relationship between agrarian society (the village) and *external* forces. Contrary

[3] Popkin, *The Rational Peasant*, pp. 61-62.

[4] Migdal, *Peasants, Politics, and Revolution*, pp. 156-189; Donald S. Zagoria, "Peasants and Revolution," *Comparative Politics* 8 (April 1976): 326; Scott, *Moral Economy*, p. 4.

to this trend my study will emphasize the role that *internal* agrarian conditions and forces play in the emergence of agrarian radicalism. The most important of these, one that is recognized by most authors but explored in depth by only a few, is *agrarian structure*, here defined as the dominant configuration of economic and social linkages and cleavages that characterizes the agricultural village. Barrington Moore recognized the importance of agrarian structure when he wrote:

> In this complex of related changes [modernization] three aspects are important politically: the character of the link between the peasant and the overlord, property and class divisions within the peasantry, and the degree of solidarity or cohesiveness displayed by the peasant community.[5]

A different set of internal factors, short-run changes in agricultural technology, is emphasized by Keith Griffin and Francine Frankel.[6] They both argue that the Green Revolution has contributed directly and indirectly to radical mobilization of the peasantry because its skewed income effects create new or accentuate existing economic cleavages and thus facilitate "horizontal mobilization." Because the impact of technological change in Thanjavur has received much attention, this argument will be described in more detail later in this chapter.

The possible proximate causes of radical agrarian mobilization include external factors too. The most important of these is the constellation of political forces in the wider society that determines in great part the character of political organization and leadership available for mobilization of the peasantry. As Moore points out, "whether or not this [revolutionary] potential becomes politically effective depends on the possibility of a fusion between peasant grievances and those of other strata. . . . The peasants have to have leadership from other classes."[7] The same is true for nonrevolutionary mobilization. For instance, Migdal concludes that "in practically all cases of effective organization of peasants, the initiative is from above, from those outside the peasant class."[8] Few studies of agrarian radicalism attempt a close examination of the inter-

---

[5] Moore, *Social Origins*, p. 468.

[6] Griffin, *Political Economy*, pp. 210-219; Francine R. Frankel, *India's Green Revolution: Economic Gains and Political Costs* (Princeton, N.J.: Princeton University Press, 1971), pp. 191-215.

[7] Moore, *Social Origins*, p. 479.

[8] Migdal, *Peasants, Politics, and Revolution*, p. 209.

action between local conditions and external political and economic events and forces, a subject that will receive considerable empirical attention in Chapter 10. To provide a context for examining the impact of such events and forces in Thanjavur, I will conclude the present chapter with a review of a major study of India's national political economy by Francine R. Frankel.[9]

CAPITALISM, IMPERIALISM, AND AGRARIAN SOCIETY

All of the authors just cited, especially Moore, Wolf, Migdal, Scott, and Paige, share the fundamental thesis that the ultimate sources of agrarian radicalism are to be found in the worldwide spread of capitalism and imperialism during the nineteenth and twentieth centuries. The diffusion of these systems gave rise to economic, social, and political forces, such as commercialization, population growth, and increased state power, that undermined the existing agrarian order. According to Barrington Moore, whose highly influential book actually seeks to explain why the transformation from agrarian to industrial society results in different regimes (democratic, socialist, and fascist), there are two main conditions under which the peasantry has become a potentially revolutionary force: when the structure of premodern society was centralized rather than segmented (compare China and India), and when the landed upper class failed to commercialize successfully, thus allowing peasant society to survive weakened but intact into the modern period (compare Russia and Germany). The second condition may at first glance seem to be at odds with the general argument that commercialization contributes to the emergence of revolutionary forces. This apparent contradiction is explained by making a distinction between early and late commercialization. The failure of the landed upper class to commercialize at an early point leaves peasant society vulnerable to commercialization and other forces of modernization at a later point in the transformation. At that later point the intrusion of the market and the spread of state authority place greater stress on an established peasant social order.[10] Whether this stress results in peasant revolution depends on several other factors.

For Eric Wolf, "peasant wars" (he examines the Mexican, Russian, Chinese, Vietnamese, Algerian, and Cuban cases) are at the most general level attributable to the "worldwide spread and diffusion

[9] Francine R. Frankel, *India's Political Economy, 1947-1977: The Gradual Revolution* (Princeton, N.J.: Princeton University Press, 1978).
[10] Moore, *Social Origins*, pp. 457-460, 467-468.

of a particular cultural system, that of North Atlantic capitalism."[11] The spread of capitalism resulted in the redefinition of land and human labor as commodities for sale and cut "through the integument of custom, severing people from their accustomed social matrix in order to transform them into economic actors, independent of prior social commitments to kin and neighbors." At the same time commercial expansion created a rapid acceleration in population growth, confronting the peasant with a widening gap between population and resources. Moreover, the dislocations created by capitalism "de-stabilized" the distribution and exercise of power and invited a greater (but inherently weak) centralization of power. According to Wolf, another effect of these economic and political crises was the disruption of "the networks which link the peasant population to the larger society, the *all-important* structure of mediation intervening between center and hinterland." The breakdown of these networks gave rise to political movements directed against the new centers of economic and political power. It was the "fusion" of such movements with the "defensive reactions" of the peasantry that ultimately resulted in revolution.[12] Whether such a fusion occurred depended upon the structure of peasant society and the availability of outside leadership.

The main thrust of Joel Migdal's argument is quite similar to Wolf's. Both highlight the interaction between the peasant village community and the wider environment.[13] For Migdal the premodern village, whether of the "freeholding" or "lord-and-peasant" type, was dominated by "inward-oriented forces." In the freeholding village this inward orientation was an adaptation to the insecurities of dealing with the larger society; in the lord and peasant village, it was enforced by the lord as a means of economic and social control. In both, the inward orientation was embodied in social and economic mechanisms that provided subsistence needs and restricted outside involvement. These mechanisms and restrictions produced a fixed technology and constant levels of income and expenditure.

The spread of "worldwide imperialism" gave rise to several forces that created sustained economic crisis for the village.[14] Market intrusions, rapid population growth, and the loss of craft income upset the balance of income and expenditure. These forces had a

[11] Wolf, *Peasant Wars*, p. 276.
[12] Ibid., pp. 279, 285, 289.
[13] Migdal, *Peasants, Politics, and Revolution*, p. 15.
[14] Ibid., pp. 92-111.

differential impact on peasant society. Those with the greatest resources successfully increased their involvement with the outside world. Others were forced to participate in a market "fraught with danger . . . due to corruption, monopoly and structural incompleteness."[15] Furthermore, sustained economic crisis created new, more rigid patterns of stratification.

As a result of this crisis, peasants increasingly sought participation in a new political community, either as a means of reaching an accommodation with outside forces or in hopes of finding some solution to their specific problems. According to Migdal, peasant involvement in political movements usually begins at the level of securing individual material or social gains. But where movements with revolutionary leadership are able to institutionalize this exchange, peasant involvement might eventually become more class oriented.[16] Migdal's argument suffers from a rather loose theoretical connection between the disruption of the inward-oriented village community and the development of revolutionary potential among the peasantry. He seems to place all the burden of whether a radical movement develops on the presence or absence and the organizational capacity of revolutionary leadership.

Although attempting to explain peasant rebellion, not revolution, James C. Scott differs from Migdal in the degree of emphasis he places on the role of peasant beliefs in the development of radical potential. Precapitalist peasant society was governed, he argues, by a "subsistence ethic." The subsistence ethic had its roots in peasant economics. Peasant households, living close to the subsistence margin, sought to minimize risk rather than to maximize income. This "safety-first principle" lay behind "the technical, social and moral arrangements of the pre-capitalist agrarian order" and regulated relations between the village and outside elites. The desire for subsistence security was "socially experienced as a pattern of moral rights or expectations" that formed the "normative roots of peasant politics."

According to Scott, two major transformations occurred during the colonial period (his analysis is based on the Southeast Asian experience) that radically undermined the pre-existing social insurance patterns and violated the "moral economy of the subsistence ethic": the imposition of capitalism (following Wolf), and the development of the modern state under colonialism. The first dis-

[15] Ibid., pp. 141-153, 230.
[16] Ibid., pp. 237-252.

rupted the agrarian order by transforming land and labor into commodities for sale, the second by enforcing the imposition of the market economy and by laying new claims on peasant income. Like Wolf, Scott concludes that the peasant rebellions that he examines (in Burma and Vietnam) were basically "defensive reactions" based on appeals to past norms and practices.[17] Scott points out, however, that rebellion was not a characteristic expression of peasant politics. While he gives some consideration to the conditioning effect of social structure on the response of the peasantry to exploitation (defined as violation of the subsistence ethic), he argues that the failure to revolt is mainly due to repression.[18]

In his influential book, *The Rational Peasant*, Samuel L. Popkin takes strong exception to the generally shared views of Wolf, Migdal, and Scott, whom he collectively terms "moral economists." Popkin agrees that colonialism, the expansion of markets, and the formation of central states had a major impact on peasant society. Where he differs, and sharply so, is in his assessment of the nature of the precapitalist peasant order and of peasant reactions to external forces of change. This difference stems from widely varying views of the sources of peasant behavior. Whereas the moral economy approach stresses social and normative behavior, Popkin adopts a political economy approach that emphasizes individual and rational behavior.

Thus, according to Popkin, the moral economists are wrong in their depiction of the precapitalist peasant institutions, especially the village and the patron-client relationship, as providing welfare and security. They are also wrong therefore in arguing that peasants had nothing to gain and everything to fear from market forces, the intrusion of the state, and population growth. For instance, the expansion of markets and of state authority may offer alternative resources and alliances to subordinate groups in the stratified precapitalist village.[19] How peasants respond to these opportunities will be determined principally by individual calculations of short- and long-term gain and loss. According to Popkin's political economy view, "peasant struggles are frequently battles to tame markets and bureaucracies, not movements to restore traditional systems."[20] Whether individual peasants contribute to such collective actions depends on individual, not group, benefits.

[17] Scott, *Moral Economy*, pp. 5-11.
[18] Ibid., pp. 201-240.
[19] Popkin, *The Rational Peasant*, pp. 63-68, 79-81.
[20] Ibid., p. 35.

While most of the studies so far examined focus on the establishment of internal markets as disruptive of traditional agrarian economic and social organization, Jeffery Paige emphasizes the direct and indirect effects of the "world market in agricultural commodities which developed in response to the demands of the industrial economies of Europe and North America" during the nineteenth and early twentieth centuries. In Paige's own words, "the demands of the industrial economies led to specialized forms of agricultural organization adapted to production for world markets and created profound changes in traditional patterns of land tenure and rural class relations." The effects of export agriculture were not spread evenly over the entire rural population but instead tended to be concentrated in commercial enclaves. While Paige recognizes that this was not the only source of political change in rural areas (he also credits the development of internal markets), he contends that "the relationship of the rural population to the new forms of class cleavage and class conflict introduced by the agricultural export economy is essential in understanding the origin of this agrarian unrest in the developing world." Paige goes on to argue that export agriculture gave rise to distinct patterns of agricultural organization in various parts of the world, each associated with a particular crop or set of crops. Each of these patterns tends, in turn, to give rise to distinctive forms of agrarian social movements.[21]

Paige is also unique in his attempt to trace the impact of long-range external forces through the intervening factor of agrarian structure. In so doing he places greater emphasis on the importance of agrarian class formation as a prerequisite of agrarian radicalism than do the other authors examined here. Especially in the works of Wolf, Migdal, and Scott peasant mobilization, whether radical or not, is generally conceived as a reaction of the peasantry *against* the forces of wider social and economic change. For instance, Wolf concludes that peasant rebellions are "but the parochial reactions to major social dislocations, set in motion by overwhelming societal change."[22] In this respect these authors seem influenced by the classical Marxist tenet that peasants lack the conditions for class formation and action, and thus peasant mobilization takes place only through the incorporation of the peasantry in the class struggles of urban-industrial society.[23] Paige, on the other hand, finds

[21] Paige, *Agrarian Revolution*, pp. 1-12.
[22] Wolf, *Peasant Wars*, p. 295.
[23] See Karl Marx, *The Eighteenth Brumaire of Louis Bonaparte* (New York: International Publishers, 1963), p. 128.

that in one type of agrarian system, decentralized sharecropping, there are conditions for class formation precisely analogous to those in the urban-industrial sector and thus that there exists a potential for agrarian class conflict independent (except perhaps in a tactical sense) of industrial class conflict.

AGRARIAN STRUCTURE AND AGRARIAN RADICALISM

Most of the authors under review here do not systematically treat the role of agrarian structure in the development of agrarian radicalism; therefore much of the discussion to follow has to be extracted from their more general arguments. Still it is possible to discern in this literature two or three fairly distinct positions on the question of what type of agrarian structure is most conducive to the radicalization of the peasantry.

Although Barrington Moore does not clearly identify any particular type of agrarian structure with radical peasant mobilization, he suggests that a number of structural considerations are highly important. The first we may infer from Moore's general argument that the failure of the landed upper class to commercialize successfully at the onset of modernization is a precondition for peasant revolution. Implicit here is the continuation into the modern period of a rigid and sharp cleavage *within* agrarian society. Successful commercialization or departure into nonagricultural occupations by the landed upper class would change the character of or eliminate this cleavage. Moore seems to suggest that conflicts within the agrarian social structure, as opposed to conflicts between agrarian society and external forces, favor the emergence of radicalism. This impression is strengthened by his observation that the quality of the lord-peasant relationship is likely to deteriorate as the upper class seeks "to maintain its style of life in a changing world by extracting a larger surplus out of the peasantry."[24]

Indeed, Moore goes on to suggest that the character of the link between lord and peasant is one of three closely related structural variables conditioning the political response of the peasantry to the disruptive impact of modernization.[25] If the link remains strong, the tendency to radicalism is weak. Moore cites several factors affecting the strength of the link between peasant and lord. The first

[24] Moore, *Social Origins*, p. 460. In addition, Moore observes that "the failure of commercial farming to take hold on any very wide scale made the situation worse, since it meant that there was scarcely any alternative to squeezing the peasant" (p. 472).

[25] Ibid., p. 468.

of these, competition for land, tends to undermine the lord-peasant relationship and is often the consequence of accelerated population growth. According to Moore, the political effects of population growth, or, for that matter, any other type of economic or social change, will be conditioned by the timing, scope, and context of that change. The more sudden, rapid, and widespread the change, the more likely it will generate a radical response.[26] Similarly, certain ecological contexts may absorb these changes more readily, thus lessening the likelihood of a radical political response. (For instance, the tendency of irrigated paddy regions to absorb population increases has been superbly described by Clifford Geertz.)[27]

It is clear, nevertheless, according to Moore, that increasing pressure on the land is likely to negatively affect the link between peasant and lord in two ways. First, the demand for land would make it easier for the lord to impose more exploitative terms on the peasants. In this connection, Moore argues that another condition for maintenance of a strong lord-peasant link is that "the contributions of those who fight, rule and pray must be obvious to the peasant, and the peasants' return payments must not be grossly out of proportion of the services received."[28] In other words, the peasant must not be exploited. Second, increased pressure on the land might also be expected to reduce, both objectively and sub-

[26] Moore writes: "Economic deterioration by slow degrees can become accepted by its victim as part of the normal situation" (ibid., p. 474). Scott agrees that the scope and suddenness of change directly affect the potential for a radical response, but he takes issue with Moore's suggestion that slow changes will be "accepted" by peasants, if acceptance is taken to mean that the changes are not considered exploitative (Scott, *Moral Economy*, pp. 193-194). Migdal argues that the timing of change determines the selection of the means to relieve the stress it imposes on the peasant community. Thus, rapid change, such as the imposition of taxes, is more likely to result in short-term out-migration and changes in the distribution patterns of agricultural products, while slow change, such as population growth, is more likely to lead to long-term out-migration and changes in *both* distribution and productive patterns (Migdal, *Peasants, Politics, and Revolution*, pp. 125-128).

[27] Clifford Geertz, *Agricultural Involution: The Processes of Ecological Change in Indonesia* (Berkeley, Ca.: University of California Press, 1963). Scott notes that such "passive adaptation" is one reason why peasants fail to revolt more often than they do (Scott, *Moral Economy*, p. 205).

[28] This raises the complicated question of "false consciousness," or whether exploitation is primarily an objective or subjective phenomenon. Moore argues that the gap between objective exploitation and subjective awareness of it is not meaningful (Moore, *Social Origins*, pp. 470-471). Scott basically agrees, arguing that the failure of the peasant to protest violation of the subsistence ethic is not the result of false consciousness but is instead due to coercion (Scott, *Moral Economy*, pp. 225-240).

jectively, economic distinctions *within* the cultivating peasantry and thus to contribute to solidarity among them.

The other two closely related structural variables that have "an important bearing on political tendencies" are property divisions and solidarity in agrarian society. In this connection Moore notes that "property arrangements vary a great deal in the way they tie the peasants to the prevailing society and hence in their political effects." Solidarity may be of two kinds: that which ties "those with actual and potential grievances into the prevailing social structure" (vertical integration), and that which ties the peasants themselves together (horizontal integration). Moore suggests that where both types of solidarity are either absent or weak political action of any kind is difficult. He attributes such a situation to the breakdown of cooperative relationships under the impact of capitalism but does not clearly identify it with any specific set of property relations.[29] I would suggest that weak solidarity could derive from one of two different property structures: one in which politically salient property divisions (i.e., those that exacerbate conflicting interests) are absent altogether, and one in which property divisions are so complex and cross-cutting as to nullify each other's political tendencies. In either case the net effect of weak solidarity is conservative.

According to Moore's analysis, if vertical integration is strong, the effect is also conservative. This occurs because there is a "humble niche for those with little property." The conservatism of those possessing even a small plot of land has been recognized in many studies. Thus we would expect agrarian structures in which small owners are a major component, or at least numerous enough to be a strong countervailing force to radical elements, to be less likely to produce radical movements.[30] Horizontal integration, on the other hand, tends to be radicalizing as it promotes the spread of grievances and hostility to the lord. Here we would expect "radical solidarity" to emerge where property divisions *within* the cultivating peasantry are small relative to property divisions *between* the cul-

[29] Moore, *Social Origins*, pp. 475-477. Moore cites the "amoral familism" found by Banfield in southern Italy as an example of such breakdown. See Edward C. Banfield, *The Moral Basis of a Backward Society* (Glencoe, Ill.: The Free Press, 1958).

[30] See Paige, *Agrarian Revolution*, pp. 26-32. In his very perceptive analysis of peasant communism in Europe Juan Linz notes that small peasant owners tend to vote center or conservative, except where, as in France, they are proletarianized by a very low standard of living in the context of a highly polarized agrarian structure. See Linz, "Patterns of Land Tenure, Division of Labor, and Voting Behavior in Europe," *Comparative Politics* 8 (April 1976): 385-396.

tivating peasantry and the lord. Although Moore does not lay down any firm rules for the relationship between agrarian structure and agrarian radicalism, an overview of his analysis suggests that the dyadic lord-peasant relationship, where weakened and polarized by competition for land and increasing exploitation and where characterized by a propertyless and relatively homogeneous, and thus cohesive, peasantry, is most likely to foster radical movements.

Although Eric Wolf's treatment of agrarian structure is less explicit and less detailed than Moore's one of his major findings grows out of structural considerations. Drawing heavily on Marx, Wolf notes the constraints on political participation by the peasantry. First, he points to the isolation entailed by family-oriented subsistence production. For Marx it was precisely this lack of more than local communication that prevented peasants from forming a class (thus, he likened French peasant society to a "sack of potatoes").[31] Of course, in making this observation both Marx and Wolf had in mind a rather undifferentiated view of peasant society in which cultivation is carried out primarily on small owner-operated or tenant-operated holdings. They did not include in their analysis the possibility that some modes of agricultural production might foster rather than inhibit communication among those who cultivate. Additional constraints on political participation include the peasant's heavy workload, ability to retreat into subsistence production, multiple alignments, and ignorance. (Note that the next-to-last point is the same condition that I have suggested leads to weak solidarity.)

But for Wolf the decisive factor is power: "The poor peasant or the landless laborer who depends on a landlord for the largest part of his livelihood, or the totality of it, has no tactical power . . . ," and "poor peasants and landless laborers, therefore, are unlikely to pursue the course of rebellion." In the absence of some external power, concludes Wolf, the only component of the peasantry likely to be a source of rebellion is either the "middle peasantry," those peasants with "secure access to land" and family labor, or the peasants located in peripheral areas outside landlord control.[32] The economic independence provided by landownership and the political independence provided by geographic isolation are said to give these groups the "tactical freedom" with which to challenge their overlords.

[31] Marx, *Eighteenth Brumaire*, pp. 123-124.
[32] Wolf, *Peasant Wars*, pp. 290-291.

As Wolf himself recognizes, there is a paradox in his argument, for the middle peasantry are precisely those "whom anthropologists and rural sociologists have tended to see as the main bearers of the peasant tradition," and are thus the most conservative. Reiterating his emphasis on peasant mobilization as an extension of wider economic and social change, however, Wolf argues that it is the middle peasant's *position between agrarian society and developing urban-industrial society* that makes him most potentially radical. He is, according to Wolf, most exposed to influences from the developing urban proletariat while still retaining ties to the village and land.[33]

We can infer from Wolf's argument the view that an agrarian structure in which the middle peasantry is prominently represented is most conducive to radical mobilization. This is, of course, in direct contrast to Moore's suggestion that radical mobilization is most likely where the agrarian's structure is polarized. My analysis of Thanjavur District offers one opportunity to test the two hypotheses.[34]

[33] Ibid., p. 292. Wolf's position on the radical potential of the middle peasantry is shared by Hamza Alavi, who argues that the middle peasants were the leading peasant element in both the Russian and Chinese revolutions. (See Hamza Alavi, "Peasants and Revolution," in *Imperialism and Revolution in South Asia*, ed. Kathleen Gough and Hari P. Sharma [New York and London: Monthly Review Press, 1973], pp. 291-337. For an interesting attempt to synthesize the "middle peasant theory," see Eduarado Archetti et al., "Agrarian Structure and Peasant Autonomy," *Journal of Peace Research* 3 [1970]: 185-195.)

Interestingly, Alavi's account of the role of the middle peasantry in the Chinese revolution differs from Mao's own analysis of their role:

Such people are very eager about getting rich and . . . they constantly desire to climb up to the position of the middle class. . . . They are timid, afraid of government officials, and also a bit afraid of the revolution. Since their economic status is quite close to that of the middle class, they more or less believe in the latter's propaganda and adopt a sceptical attitude towards the revolution.

(Anne Fremantle, ed., *Mao Tse-Tung: An Anthology of His Writings* [New York: New American Library, 1962], p. 54.)

Alavi argues that the middle peasantry has been initially the most militant in India but lays the failure of Indian peasant revolts to this class's later withdrawal. (Alavi, "Peasants and Revolution," pp. 332-334.) This view is challenged by Kathleen Gough, who takes the position that mobilization of the Indian peasantry has suffered because Communist leaders have "never accorded sufficient weight to the poor peasants and laborers." (Gough, "Peasant Resistance and Revolt in South India," *Pacific Affairs* 41 [Winter 1968-1969]: 526-544.)

[34] Roy Prosterman suggests that constraints on political participation by poor peasants and landless labor are violated more often than not. See Prosterman, " 'IRI': A Simplified Predictive Index of Rural Instability," *Comparative Politics* 8 (April 1976): 345-348.

As mentioned above, Wolf also argues that peasants located on the periphery of state control, in frontier areas for example, "will have greater tactical freedom" and thus are likely to be more easily mobilized. Donald Zagoria, on the other hand, argues that peasants in densely settled areas are more open to change and more likely to develop "class consciousness."[35]

Finally, Wolf argues that ethnic distinctions are conducive to radical mobilization where they enhance "the solidarity of the rebels." This view is shared by other scholars but raises a difficult question: Where ethnic distinctions overlap economic distinctions, how do we know whether we are witnessing ethnic or class mobilization? This question is especially important in the Indian context and will be addressed in my analysis.[36]

Of the authors reviewed so far, Joel Migdal affords the least attention to the relationship between agrarian structure and agrarian radicalism. This is perhaps because he seems to take a basically Leninist view of peasant radicalism. Migdal is in basic agreement with the other authors when he argues that peasants become involved in political movements because of their economic circumstances (their vulnerability in a corrupt, monopolistic, and structurally incomplete market). He departs from the others in his belief that at the outset peasant involvement is motivated by a desire for accommodation with prevailing political forces, or, at the most, a desire for individual material or social gains. The development of radical consciousness among the peasantry is slow to mature, according to Migdal, as it is entirely a function of their involvement in the movement.[37] Implicit in this view is a de-emphasis of the role of structural conditions, which are credited by others with either facilitating or impeding the development of radical consciousness. For instance, Moore argues that property arrangements affect solidarity patterns that in turn affect the "spread of grievances" and hostility to the lord. Both Paige and Zagoria argue that family-size tenancy and decentralized sharecropping systems respectively are associated with radical movements because they fa-

---

[35] Zagoria, "Asian Tenancy Systems," pp. 43-44.

[36] Wolf, *Peasant Wars*, p. 293. See also Donald S. Zagoria, "The Ecology of Peasant Communism in India," *American Political Science Review* 65 (March 1971): 145. Kathleen Gough has noted the "partial isomorphism" of agrarian classes with ethnic groups in Indian peasant revolts. She concludes, however, that these revolts were basically class struggles. See Gough, "Indian Peasant Uprisings," *Economic and Political Weekly* 9 (Special number, 1974): 1,391-1,412.

[37] Migdal, *Peasants, Politics, and Revolution*, pp. 248-250.

cilitate the development of class consciousness among the rural proletariat.[38] The "spread of grievances," hostility to the lord, and class consciousness are of course not to be equated with revolutionary consciousness in the sense of the intent to transform the existing socio-economic order and/or to seize state power. All the authors under review here agree, as do I, that revolutionary ideology, leadership, and organization is necessary to the adoption of those aims by the peasantry. However, Moore, Scott, Paige, and Zagoria might all be expected to disagree with the Migdal's exclusive emphasis on the role of the outside organization as a radicalizing force and to assign a greater role to agrarian economic and social organization.[39]

Despite this de-emphasis of agrarian structure Migdal entertains some interesting views on the subject. He argues that the impact of economic crisis on traditional peasant society results in three types of more polarized, rigid stratification patterns: 1) the mechanized and extensive agriculture pattern, 2) the intensive agriculture pattern, and 3) the marginal-land agriculture pattern. The first pattern, which Migdal likens to Arthur L. Stinchcombe's "ranch" type, develops where agriculture is amenable to capital inputs and is created in part by high out-migration.[40] It is organized around two classes, capitalist farmers and a rural proletariat. The intensive agriculture pattern (Stinchcombe's "family-size tenancy") develops where economies of scale are limited, as in paddy cultivation, and is not accompanied by large displacements of the peasantry. Rather there is a deepening of existing divisions among several classes, including small capitalist farmers, poor peasants, and landless laborers. The marginal land pattern develops where poor soil and water conditions prohibit both extension and intensification of cultivation. Those who can leave agriculture; stratification is increasingly based on access to nonagricultural work, and prior gaps in resources and power are accentuated.

Although Migdal argues that a theory of peasant participation in revolutionary movements must be based on "the specifics of the

[38] Paige, *Agrarian Revolution*, p. 62; Zagoria, "Asian Tenancy Systems," p. 31.

[39] In a review of Migdal, Scott makes precisely this point and charges that Migdal perpetuates "a Leninist vision of the peasantry." See James C. Scott, "Peasant Revolution: A Dismal Science," *Comparative Politics* 9 (January 1977): 240-242.

[40] Migdal, *Peasants, Politics, and Revolution*, pp. 157-167. See also Arthur L. Stinchcombe, "Agricultural Enterprise and Rural Class Relations," in *Political Development and Social Change*, ed. Jason L. Finkle and Richard W. Gable, 2d ed. (New York: John Wiley & Sons, 1971), pp. 359-371.

interaction of outside forces and peasant needs" (and peasant needs surely vary with the stratification patterns just described), he does not make any systematic attempt to relate these patterns to revolutionary mobilization. As previously noted, however, he argues that one prerequisite of peasant participation in revolutionary movements is involvement in a market characterized by monopoly, corruption, and structural incompleteness. He goes on to say that these market conditions are most likely to exist in marginal and frontier areas *and* that the stratification patterns most likely to be associated with peasant radicalism are those of the intensive agriculture type. Yet by Stinchcombe's and Migdal's own criteria the intensive agriculture pattern is least likely to occur in marginal and frontier areas (Migdal uses irrigated paddy cultivation in India as an example of this pattern). A further inconsistency emerges when Migdal later adopts the Wolfian view that the middle peasants are the most readily mobilized sector of the peasantry.[41] Stinchcombe argues that the radical potential of the "family-size tenancy" pattern lies in the poor peasant (the tenant), not the middle peasant.[42]

For James C. Scott variations in agrarian structure are less a factor in the "explosiveness" of agrarian society than in the "nature of the explosion," and he therefore accords structural considerations little attention.[43] Like Wolf and Migdal he argues that the economic crisis of the peasant brought on by demographic change, market penetration, and the spread of state authority makes possible the creation of radical potential. However, Scott's emphasis on the "subsistence ethic" lends greater weight to the role of the internal dynamics of agrarian society in the amassing and activation of this potential (in contrast to Wolf, for whom economic linkages to the outside are critical, and to Migdal, for whom political linkages are crucial). This position is reflected in Scott's overriding concern with the impact of economic change on the tenantry and in his placing of the tenant at the center of radical agrarian tendencies. Scott does not share Wolf's view that the middle peasantry are most susceptible to radical mobilization. He quite clearly takes the position that the primary source of agrarian radicalism is agrarian class conflict between landowners and "poor peasants" (defined primarily as tenants). It is apparent that he believes that the economic dependence of the poor peasant ceases to be an effective constraint on mobi-

[41] Migdal, *Peasants*, pp. 230-231, 247-248.
[42] Stinchcombe, "Agriculture Enterprise," pp. 365-366.
[43] Scott, *Moral Economy*, p. 203.

lization when the peasant comes to believe the relationship is no longer reciprocal.[44]

Furthermore, other aspects of Scott's analysis contain the suggestion, if not the conclusion, that the radicalization of the tenant is most easily accomplished in the context of a polarized agrarian structure. First, he argues that the commercialization of agriculture has a polarizing effect on agrarian class relationships (primarily between landowner and tenant). Second, he finds that at least one of the areas of peasant rebellion that he examines closely, Nghe-An and Ha-Tinh provinces in the northern Annam region of Vietnam, was characterized by a polarized pattern of land ownership.[45]

Finally, Scott does devote a short section in his book to a discussion of the relationship of *peasant* social structure (by this he means the degree of economic differentiation *within* the cultivating community) to peasant revolt, although he is reluctant to conclude that there is any clear relationship. However, following Moore, he suggests that a peasant community which is less internally differentiated along economic lines will be more explosive because it will experience economic change more uniformly and will have greater solidarity and therefore a greater capacity for collective action.[46] Scott's reservations about this conclusion stem from consideration of two contravening tendencies: first, less differentiated peasant communities tend to be less exposed to economic change; second, they are more able to "redistribute the pain" of such change.

It is Scott's failure to differentiate between types of "poor peasants" that weakens his analysis. Whether or not a tenant is completely landless is likely to be an important factor in his political behavior. This is of course suggested by Moore's general observation that property divisions affect solidarity. A poor peasant who owns as well as rents some land is more susceptible to identification with landowners and thus to "conservative solidarity." For instance, Mao Tse-tung observed that the "revolutionary qualities" of the "semitenant peasants" (part owners, part tenants) were inferior to

[44] Ibid., pp. 170-171. For Scott's view of the impact of economic change, see chap. 3 in ibid., pp. 56-90; on the role of tenants in Southeast Asian rebellions, see chap. 5, pp. 114-156. From time to time Scott discusses the situation and role of the landless laborer, but his emphasis on the tenant is clear.

[45] Ibid., pp. 66, 130-131. Moreover, the polarization was even greater in the "heartland" of the rebellion, the districts of Thanh Chuong and Nam Dan (pp. 139-141). It is instructive to note that Juan Linz found that French and Italian tenants were more likely to be "leftist" where they were surrounded by a large landless labor force (Linz, "Patterns of Land Tenure," pp. 402-405).

[46] Scott, *Moral Economy*, p. 202.

those of the "poor peasants" (pure tenants).[47] In addition, and perhaps more important, is the question of what the actual *rights* of the tenant are. Juan Linz has suggested that tenancy rights, such as security of tenure, rather than position in the production process and economic status, are the key to the tenant's political behavior.[48] The nature of these rights will directly affect the tenant's attitude toward the landowners and the agrarian system.

In spite of Scott's reluctance to be more specific about structural factors his analysis is an important step away from the classical Marxist position in which, for structural reasons, the peasantry is viewed as inherently conservative (because by themselves they cannot form a class) and towards the Maoist position in which the potential for agrarian class formation and radicalism is a question to be answered through careful analysis of structural considerations (where structure means more than position in the property structure or production process).

Agrarian structure figures importantly in Samuel Popkin's analysis of the political economy of rural society of Vietnam only insofar as he seeks to demonstrate that precapitalist villages were not generally characterized by equality and normative consensus. Popkin's assumption of individual motivation for gain leads him to emphasize conflict of interest, variable access to resources, and stratification within the village. "Stratification occurred before production for markets," observes Popkin, "because peasants were interested in individual security and approached villages as sources of gain, just as they did markets."[49] Landlords capitalize on competition and conflicts among peasants to maintain their "monopoly position," and peasant responses to commercialization and the spread of state authority are of course conditioned by their resources and relations with other village groups.

Implicit in this argument is the conclusion that agrarian structure affects the individual's decision concerning involvement in revolutionary movements, but Popkin does not develop it. His very heavy emphasis on individual decision making leads him away from such considerations. He briefly observes that the division between tenants and small owners on the one hand and laborers on the other affects the ability of either group to organize against landlords, but he does not extend this line of analysis to other situa-

[47] See Fremantle, *Mao Tse-Tung*, p. 55.
[48] Linz, "Patterns of Land Tenure," p. 397.
[49] Popkin, *The Rational Peasant*, p. 61.

tions.[50] In general, Popkin's political economy approach contributes more toward a critique of the generalized moral economy view of peasant behavior and less toward an alternative view of why peasants sometimes become involved in collective radical actions.

Turning to the work of Donald S. Zagoria and Jeffery M. Paige, both of whom place greater emphasis on structural factors in the development of agrarian radicalism, we find that both also owe an intellectual debt to Arthur L. Stinchcombe. In a 1961 article Stinchcombe constructed a highly suggestive typology of commercialized agricultural enterprises and rural class relations.[51] He concluded that one type of agrarian structure, which he termed "family-size tenancy," is most likely to produce revolutionary movements. Zagoria and Paige extend and modify Stinchcombe's arguments, but, more importantly, they share his basic conclusion and provide further evidence and arguments in support of it.

Stinchcombe begins by arguing that Marxist class analysis is particularly relevant to agriculture because "agriculture everywhere is much more organized around the institutions of property than around those of occupation."[52] An "agricultural enterprise" is a social unit that allocates control over the use of land and the distribution of its products. Different types of agricultural enterprise give rise to different types of agrarian class systems. Agrarian class systems vary 1) in the extent to which classes are differentiated by legal privileges; 2) in the degree of differentiation of style of life among the classes; 3) in the "distribution of the technical culture of husbandry"; and 4) in the degree of communication and political activity and organization within the classes.

Employing these variables, Stinchcombe distinguishes five types of agricultural enterprise: 1) the manorial or hacienda system; 2) the plantation system; 3) the ranch system; 4) the family-size tenancy system; and 5) the family small-holding system (see Table 1 for the characteristics of these systems). According to Stinchcombe, in the first three systems the lower classes tend to be politically incompetent, apathetic, or dispersed and therefore difficult to organize. In the fourth type, family small-holding, the lower classes tend to be united with the upper classes in opposition to urban interests. In the family-size tenancy system, however, the potential for organization is great.

[50] Ibid., p. 256.
[51] Stinchcombe, "Agricultural Enterprise."
[52] Ibid., p. 357.

TABLE 1
Stinchcombe's Typology of Agricultural Enterprise and Rural Class Relations

Type and Characteristics of Enterprise	Class Structure
Manorial	Division of land into domain land and labor subsistence land, with domain land devoted to production for market. Lord has police power over labor. Technically traditional; low cost of land and little market in land.	Classes differ greatly in legal privileges and style of life. Technical culture borne largely by the peasantry. Low political activation and competence of peasantry; high politicization of the upper classes.
Family-size tenancy	Small parcels of highly valuable land worked by families who do not own the land, with a large share of the production for market. Highly labor- and land-intensive culture, of yearly or more frequent crops.	Classes differ little in legal privileges but greatly in style of life. Technical culture generally borne by the lower classes. High political affect and political organization of the lower classes, often producing revolutionary populist movements.
Family small holding	Same as family tenancy, except benefits remain within the enterprise. Not distinctive of areas with high valuation of land; may become capital-intensive at a late stage of industrialization.	Classes differ neither in legal privileges nor in style of life. Technical culture borne by both rich and poor. Generally unified and highly organized political opposition to urban interests; often corrupt and undisciplined.
Plantation	Large-scale enterprises with either slavery or wage labor, producing labor-intensive crops requiring capital investment on relatively cheap land (though generally the best land within the plantation area). No or little subsistence production.	Classes differ in both style of life and legal privileges. Technical culture monopolized by upper classes. Politically apathetic and incompetent lower classes, mobilized only in time of revolution by urban radicals.
Ranch	Large-scale production of labor-extensive crops on land of low value (lowest in large units within ranch areas), with wage labor partly paid in kind in company barracks and mess.	Classes may not differ in legal status, as there is no need to recruit and keep down a large labor force. Style of life differentiation unknown. Technical culture generally relatively evenly distributed. Dispersed and unorganized radicalism of lower classes.

SOURCE: Arthur L. Stinchcombe, "Agricultural Enterprise and Rural Class Relations," in *Political Development and Social Change*, ed. Jason L. Finkle and Richard W. Gable, 2d ed. (New York: John Wiley & Sons, 1971), p. 365.

Stinchcombe finds that the family-size tenancy system is most likely to occur where five conditions are met: 1) land has very high productivity and a high market price; 2) the crop is labor intensive, and mechanization is not developed; 3) labor is cheap; 4) there are no appreciable economies of scale in factors other than labor; and 5) the cropping period is one year or less. These conditions are most fully met in the case of irrigated rice or cotton.[53]

Although under this system the cultivating unit is the family, property rights rest with "*rentier* capitalists," an arrangement Stinchcombe finds politically unstable for several reasons. First, the issue in conflict between the *rentier* and the tenants is clear: the lower the rent of the *rentier*, the higher the income of the tenant. Second, there is severe conflict over the distribution of risk. The *rentier* tries to shift as much of it as possible to the tenant, making the tenant's income highly variable.[54] Third, there tends to be little social contact between the *rentier*, who usually lives in the city, and the tenant. Fourth, the tenants may be led by the "rich peasant" who owns all or most of the land he cultivates and is therefore more independent of the *rentier*. Finally, the tenants are not ignorant about operation of the enterprise and therefore pose more of a threat to the landowner.

In most respects the agrarian structure that Stinchcombe finds most conducive to agrarian radicalism parallels most closely the characteristics suggested by Moore: property arrangements serve to weaken the link between lord and peasant and to promote peasant solidarity. And although Stinchcombe also seems to be taking the non-Marxist position that agrarian radicalism can emerge out of the internal dynamics of agrarian class formation, two of his observations would seem to run counter to this interpretation. First, he notes that the social distance between *rentier* and the tenant is a result of the fact that the *rentier* usually is an absentee and has taken on an urban life style. However, he does not take into account the possibility that social distance may be great for other reasons, such as status distinctions. Second, Stinchcombe seems closer to Wolf when he argues that the leadership of the rich peasant, Wolf's middle peasant, is an important factor in mobilization of the tenantry. And while he argues that the middle peasant's interests are not opposed to those of the tenant, he does not explain what would

[53] As we shall see, Thanjavur is an almost perfect illustration of these conditions.
[54] As Moore, Migdal, and Scott have all argued, this is particularly the case as the commercialization of agriculture proceeds.

make the middle peasant turn radically against the *rentier*. The middle peasant might have a variety of grievances against the *rentier*, but as several studies mentioned here have suggested his attachment to the land is likely to prevent those grievances from being transformed into an organized violent assault on the agrarian property system. Third, Stinchcombe neglects the possibility that the poor peasant may achieve some independence of the landowner through other than economic means, such as political organization itself.

Donald S. Zagoria begins his own argument linking tenancy systems of "Monsoon Asia" with Communist mobilization by accepting Stinchcombe's conclusion that family-size tenancy is most conducive to radical mobilization.[55] However, Zagoria goes on to add some new considerations and emphases. First, he alters somewhat Stinchcombe's explanation of why family-size tenancy tends to be radicalizing. He argues that this system is usually associated with heavy pressure on the land and, partly for that reason, with insecurity of tenure. Under these conditions, Zagoria notes, it is easier for class consciousness to emerge. In addition, Zagoria does not see the leadership by the rich peasant as a necessary ingredient of radical mobilization. Rather, he argues that because of the social distance between lord and peasant and the peasant's knowledge of cultivation in the family-size tenancy system, the poor peasant has greater independence of the lord than in the manorial, plantation, or ranch systems.

In explaining under what conditions such a system emerges, Zagoria adopts a primarily *ecological* approach. He therefore tends to emphasize the role of *landlessness per se* rather than of *relations* between lord and peasant imposed by a particular structure in fostering agrarian radicalism. Zagoria agrees that Stinchcombe's five conditions are associated with family-size tenancy and adds a sixth to the list: population pressure. He argues that these six conditions are most likely to be found in the "wet-rice areas" of Monsoon Asia. Such areas have four related characteristics: 1) heavy pressure on the land (a function of high population density), inequitable land distribution, and low per capita output; 2) a concentration of landless households; 3) increasing "proletarianization" due to population growth; and 4) "parasitic landlordism." Under these conditions, Zagoria argues, the peasantry has a proclivity for radical movements. He offers one test of this hypothesis with Indian

[55] Zagoria, "Asian Tenancy Systems," pp. 29-31.

data. In these data he finds a correlation between Communist vote and various indicators of landlessness, such as the "agrarian density" (the number of agricultural workers per unit of cultivated area) and the proportions of "dwarf owners," tenants, and laborers in the agricultural work force.[56]

Unfortunately, these data do not provide a complete or clear picture of the relational implications of agrarian structure that are at the heart of Moore's and Stinchcombe's arguments. Such data tell us only about the "bottom" of the structure, not about its "top." It is risky to infer, for instance, that a high degree of landlessness results in a clear opposition of interests between the poor peasantry and the "landed upper class." Also, Zagoria's "landlessness" is a composite of three possibly distinct types of poor peasants and may therefore hide relational factors that would inhibit rather than facilitate the development of radicalism. For instance, as has been previously suggested, there is good reason *not* to assume that small owners have radical proclivities. Such a conclusion would seem to require closer inspection of the agrarian structure.

Zagoria concludes, with others, that structural factors establish a radical potential and that other factors must be included in a full explanation of radical mobilization. In particular he focuses on one factor that does not receive much attention elsewhere: literacy. He argues that education in general and literacy in particular are important in overcoming the effect of isolation on the perception by peasants of their conditions and the possibility for change. He supports this argument with Indian data. But studies by Parkes Riley and Robert L. Hardgrave have found that the correlation between Communist vote and literacy in India does not stand up to close inspection.[57]

Zagoria identifies three additional factors that facilitate radical mobilization. First, he contends that family-size tenancy areas near to urban areas are most susceptible to radical movements because

[56] Ibid., pp. 32, 40-41, 45. See also Zagoria, "Ecology of Peasant Communism," passim.

[57] Zagoria, "Asian Tenancy Systems," pp. 41-44. See also Donald S. Zagoria, "A Note on Landlessness, Literacy and Agrarian Communism in India," *European Journal of Sociology* 13 (1972): 326-334; Parkes Riley, "Poverty, Literacy and the Communist Vote in India," *Asian Survey* 15 (June 1975): 543-558; Robert L. Hardgrave, Jr., "The Communist Parties of Kerala: An Electoral Profile," in *Electoral Politics in the Indian States*, vol. 4, *Party Systems and Cleavages*, ed. Myron Weiner and John Osgood Field (New Delhi: Manohar Book Service, 1975), pp. 204-206.

they are more exposed to change.[58] Second, he argues that in densely populated areas poor peasants are more likely to become aware of the power of their numbers (this is really a structural argument). Third, he concludes that the sheer difficulty of the work that poor peasants perform affects their proclivity to radical action.

While all these factors create the potential for radical mobilization, Zagoria concludes that actual mobilization, leading to rebellion or revolution, is likely to occur only when the rural elite is weakened or state authority breaks down. However, like Scott, Zagoria is mainly concerned with explaining, in Scott's words, "the creation of social dynamite rather than its detonation." Unlike Scott he lays heavy emphasis on ecologically derived structural factors.[59]

In his wide-ranging book on agrarian revolution Jeffery M. Paige attempts to specify and systematize the interaction of variables implied by the Stinchcombe typology into a theory of rural class conflict. His argument rests on the proposition that "fundamentally the actions of peasants, sharecroppers, and agricultural laborers depend on their relationship with other agricultural classes, with whom they must share the proceeds of their labor.[60] According to Paige, the relationship between the cultivating and noncultivating classes is defined by their relationships to the factors of production as indicated by their principal sources of income. Noncultivators, typically the upper class, may draw their income from land or capital, or some combination of the two. Cultivators, typically the lower class, may draw their income from land or wages, or some combination of the two. Paige argues that although noncultivators and cultivators may draw income from capital and wages respectively it is the relative importance of land as a source of their income that sets the direction and intensity of rural class conflict. And it is the interactions of the economic and political behavior of noncultivators and cultivators as determined by their sources of income that structures rural class relations.

With respect to the noncultivating classes, Paige argues that the land-capital dimension reflects the transition from a landed upper class to a commercial elite resulting from the penetration of the market into subsistence areas. (This is one major difference be-

---

[58] Here Zagoria's argument runs both with and against Wolf's. On the one hand, he is agreeing with Wolf that wider economic and social forces play a role in agrarian radicalism. On the other hand, by implication he rejects Wolf's argument that frontier areas are more likely to produce radical movements.

[59] Zagoria, "Asian Tenancy Systems," pp. 50-54; Scott, *Moral Economy*, p. 4.

[60] Paige, *Agrarian Revolution*, p. 9. Paige's theory is described on pp. 9-71.

tween Zagoria and Paige: whereas Zagoria emphasizes the ecological determinants of structure, Paige seems to give equal weight to ecological factors, which determine the type of crop grown, and to the impact of the commercialization of agriculture.) The wealth and power of the landed upper class depend not on the efficiency of its estate but on the area of land controlled. Thus, the presence of a landed upper class tends to lead to concentration of land in and economic dominance by a few estates and to the reduction of small landowners to dependent laborers. Where market forces are stronger, the landed upper class will likely be replaced by an agricultural upper class based on commercial or industrial capital.

These changes produce, according to Paige, two different types of agricultural organization, the plantation and the small-holding system. In the latter type, Paige admits, there is no agrarian upper class, but there is a substantial commercial and industrial class whose power and income are based on control of processing machinery, storage facilities, transportation, etc. The small holder is thus a worker in a system controlled by urban financial interests (note the correspondence of this system to the Marxist-Wolfian view of the peasantry). And because the upper class dependent on commercial or industrial capital enjoys a distinct competitive advantage over the landed upper class, the continued existence of the landed upper class depends on its ability to restrict the operation of free markets in land, labor, and capital. This difference accounts for the divergent political behavior of the two types of noncultivating classes. Note that Paige's argument is similar to Moore's proposition that peasant revolution is more likely where the landed upper class *failed* to commercialize successfully.

Paige's three propositions are illustrated in Figure 1. First, because it is economically weak, the landed upper class must rely for its survival on political restrictions on land ownership and control, thus focusing conflict on this issue. In contrast, the strong economic position of the commercially based upper class focuses conflict on the distribution of income from property. Second, the landed upper class must depend on servile or semiservile labor and cannot therefore permit the extension of economic or political rights to cultivators, with the result that labor conflicts are more likely to be politicized. The commercially based upper class usually depends on free labor, and so labor conflicts tend to be economic rather than political. Third, the landed upper class is associated with a static agricultural product, creating a zero-sum conflict between cultivators and noncultivators. A commercially based upper class can increase production through capital investment and thus expand the sum of agricultural income to be shared with cultivators. In Paige's words, "the expanding profits from technological change can be used to buy off rural social movements and divert them into reformist channels."[61]

Turning to the cultivating classes, Paige once again argues that the fundamental distinction lies in the source of income, here land versus wages. In general, land will be used as payment where it is extensively cultivated or where the small holding is the most efficient mode of production. Where land is valuable or where industrial-type organization is efficient, laborers will be paid in wages (cash or kind). Note that this proposition is consistent with Stinchcombe's argument that family-size tenancy will be found in areas of high land productivity and value and of high labor intensity. The importance of payment in land versus wages is summarized by Paige in three propositions (see Figure 2). First, the greater the importance of land as a source of income for cultivators, the greater their avoidance of risk and the greater their avoidance of radical political movements. Conversely, the greater the importance of

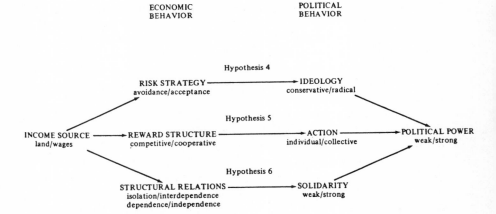

FIGURE 1. Diagram of Paige's Hypotheses on the Effects of Principal Sources of Income on the Economic and Political Behavior of Noncultivators

SOURCE: Jeffrey M. Paige, *Agrarian Revolution: Social Movements and Export Agriculture in the Underdeveloped World* (New York: The Free Press, 1975), p. 21.

[61] Ibid., p. 24. The main lines of Paige's arguments with respect to the noncultivating and cultivating classes are found on pp. 12-25 and pp. 25-40 respectively.

wages (whether cash or kind), the greater the acceptance of risk and the greater the receptivity to radical political movements. This first proposition corresponds to Moore's observation that ownership of even a small plot of land tends to promote "conservative solidarity." Paige argues that payment in land leads to an avoidance of any risk that might precipitate landlessness or lead to gains for the landless at the expense of property owners. Wage earners, on the other hand, have little, if any, property to lose.

Second, Paige postulates, the greater the importance of land as a source of income, the stronger the incentives for economic competition and the weaker the incentives for political organization, and conversely where wages are more important. This is true, Paige argues, because upward mobility is possible through individual efforts in agrarian systems based on income from land. Wage payment (in agriculture) creates incentives for collective political action.

Third, the greater the importance of land as a source of income for cultivators, the greater their structural isolation or dependence on noncultivators and the weaker the pressures for political solidarity, and the greater the importance of wages as a source of income, the greater the structural independence and the greater the pressure for political solidarity. These observations are attributable to the fact that small cultivators tend to carry on their productive activities in relative isolation, while laborers are usually

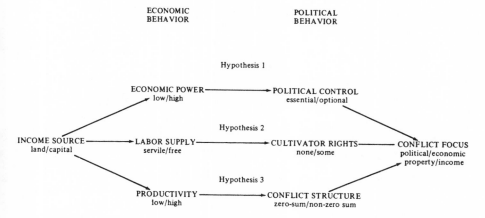

FIGURE 2. Diagram of Paige's Hypotheses on the Effects of Principal Sources of Income on the Economic and Political Behavior of Cultivators

SOURCE: Paige, *Agrarian Revolution*, p. 29.

brought together in common work groups. Again, we are reminded of the conditions for radical solidarity suggested by Moore.

By combining income sources for the upper and lower classes, Paige derives four types of agricultural organization, each associated with a particular type of agrarian social movement (see Figure 3). Both small-holding and plantation systems tend to produce reform movements because in each case conflict is focused on economic issues, the former on the control of the market in commodities, the latter on the price of labor. In the small-holding system the lower class (cultivators) tends to be politically conscious and organized, but because of its reliance on capital the upper class tends to be willing to compromise.

However, in those systems where land is the principal source of income for the noncultivating class, political movements, when they arise, tend to be radical. Such movements are relatively rare in the commercial hacienda system because the lower class's relationship to the land inhibits political consciousness and organization. However, Paige points out that it is possible for conflict to become politicized where external forces bring about a weakening of landlord control and/or political organization among the peasantry. Because the internal sources of mobilization are weak, such conflicts tend to be short-lived. Thus, the characteristic movement in the commercial hacienda system is the agrarian revolt.

	CULTIVATORS	
	LAND	WAGES
LAND	COMMERCIAL HACIENDA ——— REVOLT (Agrarian)	SHARECROPPING MIGRATORY LABOR ——— REVOLUTION (Socialist) (Nationalist)
CAPITAL	SMALL HOLDING ——— REFORM (Commodity)	PLANTATION ——— REFORM (Labor)

NONCULTIVATORS

FIGURE 3. Paige's Typology of Agrarian Social Movements
SOURCE: Paige, *Agrarian Revolution*, p. 11.

   Radical political movements are more likely to arise in the share-cropping/migratory labor system, where the upper class is generally uncompromising and the lower class politically conscious and organized. The issue tends to be structural and political: control over the means of production, land. Within this classification Paige differentiates two types of revolutionary movements, revolutionary nationalism and revolutionary socialism. This distinction need not be recounted in detail because it is not very relevant to the present study. Briefly, Paige finds that because of structural differences between the sharecropping and migratory labor systems (for instance, there is less work-group interdependence in the latter), migratory laborers must rely more on external political ideology and support. Often this comes from the traditional agrarian elite and takes a nationalist form. The structural characteristics of sharecropping ("a homogeneous landless peasantry with strong incentives for collective action and intense pressure for group solidarity"), on the other hand, produce a strong internal radical potential that invites mobilization by Socialist parties.
   Paige finds the origins of such sharecropping systems in both historical forces and ecological conditions. They develop, he argues, through the gradual growth of markets in stratified peasant societies and where ecological conditions inhibit successful commercialization. A formerly paternalistic upper class becomes increasingly "parasitic" under pressure from market forces. Paige agrees with Zagoria that these conditions are most likely to be met in areas of "wet-rice cultivation" characterized by high land values, pressure on the land, and labor intensity.[62]
   In Paige's theory of rural class relations many of the structural considerations raised by others are systematically examined and interrelated. The result is a strong hypothesis relating agrarian radicalism to agrarian structure that presents an interesting paradox. On the one hand, Paige's assertion that the sources of the most potent agrarian radicalism are located *within* the agrarian system takes us farther away from the classical Marxist position on the peasantry than any of the other studies reviewed here. On the other hand, the theory he has constructed is clearly the agrarian analogue of Marx's theory of industrial class conflict. As Paige himself points out:

   The homogeneous poorly paid, concentrated mass of workers that Marx saw as the vanguard of the revolution are found not

[62] Ibid., pp. 59-66.

in industrial societies, but in commercial export agriculture in the underdeveloped world. It is in such societies that the greatest incentives for class-based organization and class conflict exist.[63]

Paige's theory is of special interest in the context of this study, for as I have suggested in Chapter 1, the structural conditions that on first glance characterize Thanjavur District clearly resemble closely those that Moore, Stinchcombe, Zagoria, and Paige agree play an important role in the emergence of agrarian radicalism.

TECHNOLOGICAL CHANGE AND AGRARIAN RADICALISM

I now wish to turn my attention briefly to an interpretation of contemporary agrarian radicalism that is clearly less far-reaching than those just discussed but nevertheless worthy of some consideration. This is what I term the "technologial explanation" of agrarian radicalism. Actually, it is an extension of the by-now very familiar "commercialization" argument in a form that emerged and attracted interest in the wake of the so-called Green Revolution.

Francine Frankel's study, *India's Green Revolution*, is one important example of this approach. Frankel argues that the introduction of new agricultural technology in India has led to: 1) an increase in economic disparities and ultimately to economic polarization in agrarian society, 2) the accelerated erosion of traditional norms and the collapse of vertical integration in agrarian society; and 3) an increase in political mobilization along class lines.[64] Basically, Frankel is arguing that technological change is now having the same effect on agrarian society that the introduction of markets had in the nineteenth and early twentieth centuries. Other studies have come to similar conclusions, although the details of interpretation may vary. For instance, Keith Griffin agrees that technological change is likely to lead to growing inequality, but he argues that this is not so much the independent effect of the technology per se as it is the result of the constraints on the access to new technology inherent in the existing agro-economic structure.[65]

Several questions are raised by this explanation. First, what exactly is meant by the "Green Revolution" or technological change? The impact of mechanization on the agrarian structure is likely to

[63] Ibid., p. 34.
[64] Frankel, *India's Green Revolution*, passim. For other relevant studies by Frankel, see the Bibliography.
[65] Griffin, *Political Economy*, pp. 209-219.

be very different from the impact of high-yielding varieties and fertilizer. Second, even if technological change does tend to benefit the agrarian upper class, is it possible, as Paige's analysis suggests, that the increases in agricultural income brought about by technological change will inhibit the growth of radical movements by facilitating compromise settlements between landowners and tenants or laborers? Third, is it possible to generalize about the impact of technological change across a wide variety of ecological and agro-economic conditions? I shall attempt to deal with these and other questions when I address the subject of technological change in Chapter 9.

THE WIDER POLITICAL ECONOMY AND AGRARIAN RADICALISM

The emergence and development of agrarian radicalism at any given time and place are influenced by economic and political conditions and forces outside the agrarian sector. Economic policies and performance at the national and regional levels affect the growth and distribution of the agricultural product, the relative well-being of different agrarian groups, and thus the issues around which agrarian conflict can occur. The ideologies of the national regime and of competing political forces shape the agrarian agenda and its articulation. The nature of the party system and of party organization, the capacity of the state to carry out its policies and of interest groups to resist them, and the quality of political leadership constrain or enlarge the possibilities for agrarian mobilization.

A major study by Francine R. Frankel of India's political economy from 1947 to 1977 provides a broad context for assessing the impact of key external events and forces on the mobilization of agrarian radicalism in Thanjavur District.[66] Frankel's work is particularly relevant to my study because she views the problem of agrarian mobilization as central to India's economic and political development. A brief review of her analysis and conclusions will be useful in understanding the Thanjavur experience and relating it to the wider political economy of India. Although Frankel's work covers the years 1947 to 1977, I shall focus on her account of events up through 1972, the period covered in this book.

Frankel focuses her study on what she views as the central and unresolved dilemma of Indian political economy: How can the radical social change necessary to economic growth and political

[66] Frankel, *India's Political Economy.*

stability, at least in the long run, be accomplished without a frontal assault on the social order that itself would threaten social chaos and national disintegration? The contradiction between the commitment to accommodative politics and the need for radical social change has, according to Frankel, produced an impasse. Despite swings in national policy over the thirty years since Independence, no way has yet been found to achieve necessary economic progress without social change that might undermine the democratic order. This failure is due largely, argues Frankel, to the separation of politics and social reform—in particular, to the absence of a national *political* effort to organize India's poor, especially the poor peasantry. Without such an effort, and in the face of continuing economic distress among the poor, the growth of political consciousness that has resulted from universal suffrage and open electoral process contributes to disillusionment with the democratic system.

Frankel argues that the tension between accommodative politics and the need for rapid social change had its roots in India's Independence movement, particularly in Mahatma Gandhi's conviction—which prevailed over socialist alternatives in the 1930s—that the process of eliminating inequalities had to proceed gradually in order to avoid fragmenting India's highly segmented society. The result was a development strategy which separated politics from social reform. The Congress party sought to function as an aggregative mechanism, embracing all interests rather than actively seeking to mobilize any group or class. (The only party committed to class-based politics, the Communist Party of India (CPI), was severely hampered by its isolation from the nationalistic mainstream.) Social change was to be pursued through nonpolitical means, beginning with Gandhi's "Constructive Program."

In the early years of Independence, Congress party commitment to gradual social change came under increasing attack from both the left, represented by a more assertive CPI, and the right, largely represented by state party leaders who drew their most powerful support from rural and urban propertied elites. Jawaharlal Nehru, India's prime minister from 1947 to 1964, responded by continuing to follow an accommodative party ideology aimed at reassuring the conservative forces while pursuing an economic strategy designed to build popular organization and political consciousness outside the party system. Through institutional reforms, such as village cooperatives, *panchayat-i-raj* (popularly elected village councils), and the community development program, Nehru hoped to weaken the economic and political dominance of the landed castes and to create new solidarity and leadership among the peasantry. But without the political organization and links to outside centers of power that could only be provided by committed party cadres, argues Frankel, these institutional reforms were misused by dominant local elites, thus reinforcing rather than undermining vertical mobilization of the peasantry along caste and factional lines.

The strategy of gradual, democratic social transformation came under increasing pressure in the late 1950s as the result of a perceived leftward shift in the 1959 general elections and the resource requirements of the Second Five-Year Plan's ambitious industrialization goals. Nehru moved toward a more active agrarian policy based on cooperativization of farming and state trading in food grains. But strong conservative opposition, including the formation of the Swatantra party, forced concessions that, according to Frankel, precluded carrying out institutional reform on any meaningful scale. Meanwhile the capacity of the one-party dominant system to accommodate diverse interests was increasingly strained, as reflected in growing factionalism within the Congress party, including the formation of the Congress Forum for Socialist Action dedicated to ending the tactical separation of political and social issues. Nehru's death in 1964 precluded any possibility of reconstructing Congress party consensus for the strategy.

The period of Lal Bahadur Shastri's prime ministership (1964-1966) saw a clear shift in economic policy towards greater reliance on private investment and initiative. This was most apparent in agriculture, where a new strategy emphasizing technological change, individual enterprise, physical inputs, and selectivity took hold. According to Frankel, however, this strategy "failed to accelerate the process of economic growth even as [it] increased disparities and eroded the legitimacy of Congress."[67] Evidence of these trends was found in the success of the Communists in organizing peasant agitations in the late 1960s and in the dramatic Congress party losses in the 1967 elections. They were also reflected in growing tension between Shastri's successor as prime minister, Indira Gandhi, and the Congress state party leaders, which finally erupted in the Congress party split of 1969. With the separation came a polarization and a radicalization of the Indian political economy that seemed in the early 1970s to be leading towards a fusion of politics and radical social reform.

The thrust of Frankel's analysis is that the wider Indian political

[67] Ibid., p. 247.

economy since 1947—accommodative politics and an economic strategy that has on the whole favored incremental change through growth rather than redistribution—has impeded radical agrarian mobilization even while it has contributed to growing economic disparities and political disillusionment conducive to such mobilization. She concludes that competitive electoral politics have tended to strengthen the power of the dominant forces in the countryside over a fragmented and dependent peasantry despite their superior numbers. In the absence of radical institutional reform, growth-oriented policies have resulted in a further concentration of productive assets and incomes in the rural sector. Similarly, the party system has not provided the leadership or organization necessary for the poor peasants to achieve political power or economic gain. Frankel recognizes that such class-based political organization, in her view the key to social reform and political stability, is inhibited by economic and social divisions within the peasantry but seems to believe that these divisions can be overcome as traditional vertical loyalties are severed and political awareness grows.

Whether or not Frankel's characterization of the Indian political economy is reflected in the emergence and development of agrarian radicalism in Thanjavur District is a question that I shall examine in some detail in Chapter 10.

CHAPTER 3

Approaches to the Study of Agrarian Radicalism

EMPIRICAL STUDIES of rural politics in modern India generally fall into four broad categories: 1) the one- or two-village case study;[1] 2) the district or state case study;[2] 3) the multidistrict aggregate (socio-economic and electoral) data analysis;[3] 4) the single or multivillage survey data analysis.[4] These types are listed roughly in

[1] For two book-length studies, see F. G. Bailey, *Politics and Social Change: Orissa in 1959* (Berkeley, Ca.: University of California Press, 1963), and Andre Beteille, *Caste, Class and Power: Changing Patterns of Stratification in a Tanjore Village* (Berkeley, Ca.: University of California Press, 1965). For an overview of such studies, see Ralph W. Nicholas, "Structures of Politics in the Villages of Southern Asia," in *Structure and Change in Indian Society*, ed. Milton Singer and Bernard S. Cohn (Chicago: Aldine Publishing Co., 1968), pp. 243-284.

[2] Notable examples include Myron Weiner, *Party Building in a New Nation* (Chicago: University of Chicago Press, 1967); Myron Weiner, ed., *State Politics in India* (Princeton, N.J.: Princeton University Press, 1968); Paul R. Brass, *Factional Politics in an Indian State: The Congress Party in Uttar Pradesh* (Berkeley, Ca.: University of California Press, 1966); Baldev Raj Nayar, *Minority Politics in the Punjab* (Princeton, N.J.: Princeton University Press, 1966); Marcus F. Franda, *Radical Politics in West Bengal* (Cambridge, Mass.: The M.I.T. Press, 1971); and Marguerite Ross Barnett, *The Politics of Cultural Nationalism in South India* (Princeton, N.J.: Princeton University Press, 1976).

[3] The number of such studies is quite limited. The most comprehensive is the volume by Biplab Das Gupta and W. H. Morris-Jones, *Patterns and Trends in Indian Politics: An Ecological Analysis of Aggregate Data on Society and Elections* (New Delhi: Allied Publishers, 1976). Four volumes edited by Myron Weiner and John O. Field have added substantially to this literature. However, the data (assembled by the M.I.T. Indian Election Data Project) on which these studies are based have a major flaw—they are electoral only. The project chose not to try to match the electoral with socio-economic data on an all-India basis. See Myron Weiner and John O. Field, eds., *Studies in Electoral Politics in the Indian States* (New Delhi: Manohar Book Service, 1974-1977), vols. 1-4. Other significant national and regional aggregate data analyses include Paul R. Brass, "Political Participation, Institutionalization, and Stability in India," *Government and Opposition* (Winter 1969): 38-72, and David J. Elkins, *Electoral Participation in a South Indian Context* (Durham, N.C.: Carolina Academic Press, 1975).

[4] The number of major studies based on survey data is very limited, especially at the national level. Election studies conducted by the Centre for the Study of De-

order of their frequency, with the village and district or state case studies heavily predominant. The use of quantitative aggregate and survey data to analyze Indian politics is relatively recent.

Each of these methodological categories is generally associated with a particular substantive focus. The village case studies have been carried out mostly by anthropologists and have thus usually focused on the relationship between caste and other "traditional" forms of social organization on the one hand and politics on the other.[5] Many village studies approach the subject with the assumption that caste is the principal "independent variable" in explaining village-level political behavior. Attempting to account for the impact of wider socio-economic and political change on village social structure and politics, some studies introduced important modifications in the concept of village social structure and organization, such as M. N. Srinivas's "dominant caste,"[6] or placed greater emphasis on the role of "neo-traditional" relations, particularly factionalism.[7] Still, the predominant view has been that conflict within the village is politicized and contained through "adaptive" forms of traditional social organization, in particular, caste, and there is little support

veloping Societies, New Delhi, have resulted in several articles and two books: Rameshray Roy, *The Uncertain Verdict: A Study of the 1969 Election in Four Indian States* (Berkeley, Ca.: University of California Press, 1974), and Samuel J. Eldersveld and Bashiruddin Ahmed, *Citizens and Politics: Mass Political Behavior in India* (Chicago: University of Chicago Press, 1978). Two major surveys have dealt with political and administrative leadership at the local level: *The International Studies of Values in Politics: Values and the Active Community—A Cross-National Study of the Influence of Local Leadership* (New York: The Free Press, 1971), and Shanti Kothari and Rameshray Roy, *Relations between Politicians and Administrators* (New Delhi: Indian Institute of Public Administration and Centre of Applied Politics, 1969). For a state-level study employing survey data, see Iqbal Narain et al., *The Rural Elite in an Indian State: A Case Study of Rajasthan* (Columbia, Mo.: South Asia Books, 1976). There have been numerous survey analyses, especially elite studies, at the district or village level.

[5] See Andre Beteille, *Studies in Agrarian Social Structure* (New Delhi: Oxford University Press, 1974), pp. 21-24.

[6] See M. N. Srinivas, *Social Change in Modern India* (Berkeley, Ca.: University of California Press, 1967). Lloyd and Susanne Rudolph have argued that caste has "adapted" to function effectively in modern democratic politics through the "caste association." See Rudolph and Rudolph, *The Modernity of Tradition: Political Development in India* (Chicago: University of Chicago Press, 1967).

[7] For a thorough discussion of the factionalism thesis, see Norman K. Nicholson, *Panchayat Raj, Rural Development and the Political Economy of Village India*, South Asia Occasional Papers and Theses, no. 2 (Ithaca: Cornell University Rural Development Committee and South Asia Program, 1973). A study that provides an economic interpretation of factionalism is Mary Carras, *The Dynamics of Indian Political Factions: A Study of District Councils in the State of Maharashtra* (Cambridge: Cambridge University Press, 1972).

for the view that economic cleavages are becoming more important than caste as the basis of village structure or that class is replacing caste or faction as the principal group actor in village politics.[8]

The general bias of the village case study method toward an interpretation based primarily on adaptive forms of traditional social organization can be explained in a number of ways. First, because the dominant paradigm in anthropology is committed to the study of "indigenous" social categories and to structural-functional analysis, anthropologists have focused on caste, kin, and faction as the roots of village integrity and stability. Second, the study of a single village tends to focus attention on the "wholeness" of the village.[9] Third, the selection of only one or two villages does not permit comparative analysis of the relationships between geophysical, agro-economic, and political factors at the village level. Given that ecology and agro-economic structure can vary even from village to village, this approach is not well suited to the systematic analysis of the sources of agrarian radicalism.[10]

District and state level case studies have tended to focus on the role of institutions, particularly political parties, in mobilizing, socializing, and aggregating diverse interests and groups in Indian society by emphasizing the relative autonomy of party leadership and organization. In other words, the party system, in particular the long-dominant Congress party, has been the principal "independent variable" in explaining political behavior.[11] And inasmuch as many early studies of this type have emphasized the *aggregative* nature of the Indian party system, they, like the village case studies, have tended to conclude that conflict based on economic cleavages and ideology has not been very important in Indian politics.

In this approach also the method of study has shaped the sub-

[8] Two exceptions to this rule are Kathleen Gough, "The Social Structure of a Tanjore Village," in *Village India: Studies in the Little Community*, ed. McKim Marriott (1955; reprint ed., Chicago: University of Chicago Press, Phoenix Books, 1969), pp. 36-52, and Dagfinn Sivertsen, *When Caste Barriers Fall: A Study of Social and Economic Change in a South Indian Village* (Oslo: Universitets Forlaget, 1963).

[9] It is interesting to note that even those studies of Thanjavur villages more attentive to the sources of conflict are based on villages that are spatially and socially compact. There have been no comparable studies in areas of the district where the village is typically more spread out and heterogeneous. See Chapter 5 for a full discussion of such differences within Thanjavur.

[10] See Beteille, *Studies*, pp. 26-27. For one study that almost as an afterthought attempts to relate ecology to social structure and politics across a number of different villages in the same region, see Alan R. Beals, *Gopalpur: A South Indian Village* (New York: Holt, Rinehart & Winston, 1967), pp. 84-97.

[11] See Weiner, *Party Building*, esp. pp. 1-16, 459-496.

stance. First, the choice of a district or state as the unit of analysis focuses attention on the district or state headquarters as the locus of political activity and thus on party organization and leadership as initiators. This results in a top-down view of political mobilization, in contrast to the bottom-up view from the village that would tend to root political action in village socio-economic structure. Second, examination of the district or state as a whole tends to obscure socio-economic heterogeneity and variations in political mobilization within the district or state. Clearly, such an approach would not help to pinpoint the deviant local agro-economic patterns that generally underlie agrarian radicalism.

The less common studies based on aggregate data analysis most frequently explore the relationship between electoral and socio-economic data across a number of districts (the district is almost always the unit of analysis because socio-economic data are not usually available at the electoral constituency level). These studies typically seek to determine the support base and electoral strategies of one or more parties by identifying the correlates of party performance (such as voter turnout, number of candidates, etc.) under varying electoral conditions. Until recently it has been unusual for such studies to clearly reveal party support bases or electoral strategies. In the first place, most of these analyses are carried out at the national, regional, or state level, and the degree of heterogeneity within such large areas tends to frustrate generalization.[12] In the second place, these studies share with the district case studies the assumption that the district is always a level at which the interaction of socio-economic structure and political mobilization is meaningful. This assumption may be tenable when analyzing the results of statewide or nationwide elections, but it does not hold up for other types of political participation, such as local elections, organizational activity, etc. In the third place, the district unit may also confound the analysis because geophysical, socio-economic, and political variability within the district is often as great as it is between districts.[13] In other words, the aggregation of these characteristics to the district level may well mask a great deal of vari-

---

[12] For a discussion of this problem, and one solution, see Francine Frankel, "Problems of Correlating Electoral and Ecological Variables: An Analysis of Voting Behavior and Agrarian Modernization in Uttar Pradesh," in *Studies in Electoral Politics in the Indian States*, ed. Myron Weiner and John O. Field (New Delhi: Manohar Book Service, 1974-1977), 3: 149-193.

[13] It must be remembered that the Indian district is a unit created for administrative convenience, and usually quite large (the average area of the twelve plains districts of Tamil Nadu State is 10,550 square kilometers).

ability and thus lessen explanatory power. Because of these limitations, the broad aggregate data analyses have not yet shed much additional light on the nature of relationships between socio-economic structure and political mobilization, especially for rural India.[14]

The primary objective of this study is to relate various ecological, agro-economic, and technological factors to the occurrence of agrarian radicalism. This requires an approach different from any of those just described, one that I term *comparative micro-ecological analysis*. Specifically, I plan to analyze in detail local-level agro-climatic conditions and agro-economic and social structure across a large number of local units and then to relate variations in these conditions to radical political mobilization.

The local (or micro) unit, in this case the village, is the most appropriate unit of analysis because it is at this level that conditions of terrain, soil, irrigation, etc., can be related most meaningfully to modes of productive organization and to agro-economic structure. The village is also the most appropriate unit for relating agrarian conditions to political cleavages because as both workplace and residence it is most likely to be the locus of conflict arising out of agrarian relations.

It is necessary to analyze a large number of villages in order to identify different patterns of interaction among the numerous dimensions of agro-ecology and agro-economic structure and to relate these to variations in political behavior. At the same time it is important to minimize the variation in relatively extraneous factors. I have therefore chosen to carry out the analysis within a single district that has a common administrative and political framework so that certain legal and institutional factors are controlled.

My analysis is based primarily on aggregate data on geophysical, demographic, and agro-economic conditions and on technological change and elections for 1,555 village panchayats in Thanjavur District. This data set is, to the best of my knowledge, unique in the study of modern Indian rural politics. Although the bulk of the analysis will be cross-sectional, some of the data are available across a limited time period, 1960 to 1972, and it will thus be possible to assess the effects of changes over time in some of the conditions under study.

[14] I will not attempt here to characterize the survey data studies, for the number of significant studies has been few and their objectives rather disparate. It is clear that such analyses could be useful for the study of the sources of agrarian radicalism, especially if the selection of survey locations were stratified with respect to ecological criteria.

Before describing in more detail the units and data I will analyze, it is important to be clear about the limitations of the kind of ecological analysis employed. The most notable limitation is the problem of inference known as the "ecological fallacy"[15] (ecological correlations at the level of territorial units cannot be taken as substitutes for individual correlations). Although most of the variables analyzed here are aggregate (derived from data on individuals, for example, the percentage of agricultural workers who are agricultural laborers) as opposed to global unit characteristics, the aggregate data analysis does not enable me to infer anything about the behavior of individuals within the units. Rather I am limited to inferences about variation at the unit level: for example, *villages* that have a high proportion of agricultural labor are also high in agrarian radicalism.[16]

However, it is my view that the limits on inference imposed by the "ecological fallacy" in this study are not as problematic as they might be in other circumstances. In the first place, several important variables are *global* characteristics (such as village topography, quality of irrigation) that may be expected to affect individual behavior. Second, the arguments under examination incorporate many "structural effects."[17] That is, the aggregated individual characteristics tell us something about the structural properties of the village that may have effects independent of individual characteristics. For instance, the relationship between the proportion of agricultural laborers in the village work force and agrarian radicalism is of interest not only because laborers form a key potentially radical group but also because at some point the proportion of agricultural laborers becomes a structural fact of the village that affects individuals' behavior (for instance, by creating a sense of socio-economic bipolarity in the village). There are many other such aggregate characteristics with potential structural effects of direct concern:

---

[15] W. S. Robinson, "Ecological Correlations and the Behavior of Individuals," *American Sociological Review* 15 (1950): 351-357. Robinson's famous paper has been followed by a great deal of discussion and debate on the issue, much of it summarized in Mattei Dogan and Stein Rokkan, eds., *Quantitative Ecological Analysis in the Social Sciences* (Cambridge, Mass.: The M.I.T. Press, 1969).

[16] For a discussion of various types of analyses and their relationship to the use of aggregate data, see Erik Allardt, "Aggregate Analysis: The Problem of Its Informative Value," in *Quantitative Ecological Analysis in the Social Sciences*, ed. Mattei Dogan and Stein Rokkan (Cambridge, Mass.: The M.I.T. Press, 1969), pp. 41-51.

[17] See Tapani Valkonen, "Individual and Structural Effects in Ecological Research," in *Quantitative Ecological Analysis in the Social Sciences*, ed. Mattei Dogan and Stein Rokkan (Cambridge, Mass.: The M.I.T. Press, 1969), pp. 53-68.

agrarian density, proportion of tenants, proportion of absentee landlords, etc. Further, as will be described in detail below, my measure of agrarian radicalism is a global characteristic, so that there is symmetry in the way the dependent and many key independent variables are operationalized.

Finally, while the main weight of analysis in this study rests on aggregate data, survey data will be used in a limited way to examine the sources of agrarian radicalism at the individual level in Thanjavur District. These data, which are analyzed in Chapter 7, allow me both to compare individual and aggregate correlates of agrarian radicalism, thus testing the validity of the aggregate analysis, and to probe the subjective dimensions of agrarian radicalism.

THE UNITS OF ANALYSIS

The main unit of analysis for this study is the statutory village panchayat. This is the lowest level unit at which data on land, population, agro-economic structure, and elections could be compiled.

The smallest unit of administration in Thanjavur District is the "revenue village," of which there were in 1971 about twenty-five hundred with an average area of about one thousand acres.[18] The system of revenue villages was, as the name implies, established by the British for the purpose of land revenue collection. While still the primary unit for that purpose (although the land tax is now a minor source of revenue for the state), the revenue village also remains an important unit for administration because it is at this level that records of land ownership and use are kept.

The relationship between the revenue village and the village panchayat is variable, but in Thanjavur District (see Table 2) the majority of the panychayats are coterminous with a single revenue village. Only in a very few cases is a revenue village split between two panchayats. This is important because the functioning of the revenue village, in particular the handling of land records, is often a factor in village conflicts.[19]

[18] Government of Madras, Director of Statistics, *A Statistical Atlas of the Thanjavur District: Revised and Brought Up To The Decennium Ending Fasli 1360 (1950-51)* (Madras, 1965), p. 30.

[19] For instance, in 1970 Communist leaders in Thanjavur complained that landlords were influencing the village *karnams* ("accountants") to falsify land records in

TABLE 2

Coherence between Revenue Villages and Village Panchayats, Circa 1965

	Number	%
Panchayats covering area of less than one revenue village	71	4.6
Panchayats coterminous with one revenue village	1006	65.4
Panchayats covering total area including more than one revenue village	462	30.0
Total	1539	100.0

SOURCE: Dharampal, *The Madras Panchayat System*, 2 vols. (New Delhi: Impex India, 1972), 2: 17.

The system of village panchayats was established in Thanjavur District in 1961. The creation of these units was the result of the Government of India's "*panchayat-i-raj*" (rule through panchayat) program. The official goal of the program was to promote local self-government and economic development by decentralizing power and administrative responsibility. It was also an effort on the part of the Congress party to strengthen its support at the village level.[20]

The village panchayat sits at the base of a three-tiered system of electoral councils that have varying degrees of direct and indirect control and influence over the allocation and distribution of development resources.[21] In Thanjavur District all adult residents of

order to frustrate government-ordered registration of tenants. See *Ulavu Chelvam* (Madras), May 1, 1970.

[20] One of the most important policy documents leading to the creation of this program is the so-called "Balwantrai Mehta Report." See Government of India, Planning Commission, *Report of the Team for the Study of Community Projects and National Extension Service* (New Delhi: Committee on Plan Projects, 1957). For a general study of community development and *panchayat-i-raj*, see Henry Maddick, *Panchayati Raj: A Study of Rural Local Government in India* (London: Longmans, Green, 1970). For a study of the panchayat system in Madras/Tamil Nadu State, see Dharampal, *The Madras Panchayat System*, 2 vols. (New Delhi: Impex India, 1972). For studies of panchayat politics, see M. V. Mathur and Iqbal Narain, eds., *Panchayati Raj, Planning, and Democracy* (Bombay: Asia Publishing House, 1969).

[21] The system of electoral councils varies from state to state. For a survey, see

each village and town panchayat area elect a panchayat council and president, normally every five years. During the period under study here, panchayat elections, which are the source of my indicator of agrarian radicalism, were held in 1961, 1965, and 1970.

In Thanjavur in 1961 the village panchayats were grouped into thirty-six panchayat unions. Each union included an average of forty-three panchayats (from a low of twenty-three to a high of sixty-five) and covered an area of about 150 square miles with an average population of about seventy-five thousand. The panchayat union is coterminous with the community development block, an administrative unit headed by a block development officer. The real political salience of the village panchayat derives from the fact that each panchayat president sits ex-officio on the panchayat union council, and the councils as a whole have a fair degree of authority over the allocation of the block development budget. In addition, individual members (the panchayat presidents) of course have access to official decision making and some patronage. Each union council in turn elects from among its members a chairman who sits ex-officio on one of two development councils in the district (one for the east and one for the west). The union chairmanship is a position of considerable influence and in Thanjavur has quite often been a steppingstone to candidacy for the state legislative assembly.

Although the village panchayat council and the panchayat president do not themselves have much power, the panchayats are directly tied into government and politics at successively higher levels and have become increasingly politicized. It is a widely accepted fact that the introduction of *panchayat-i-raj* succeeded in decentralizing the Indian political system to a very considerable degree. Making the village itself an electoral arena forced political parties to reach further down in their mobilizational efforts and certainly stimulated greater political participation at the village level. In fact, Rajni Kothari has argued that, as a result, political intermediaries and networks at the subdistrict level have begun to rival district- and state-level leaders for power and influence.[22] All this suggests that from the standpoint of political salience there is jus-

Government of India, Ministry of Community Development and Cooperation, *Report of the Committee on Panchayati Raj Elections* (New Delhi, 1965). For a summary statement of the relationship between panchayat politics and resource control, see Nicholson, *Panchayat Raj*, pp. 29-44.

[22] See Rajni Kothari, *Politics in India* (Boston: Little, Brown, 1970), pp. 132-138, and Robert L. Hardgrave, Jr., *India: Government and Politics in a Developing Nation*, 2d ed. (New York: Harcourt Brace Jovanovich, Inc., 1975), pp. 102-105.

tification for using the village panchayat as the unit of analysis in this study.

The average population of the 1,555 panchayats in Thanjavur District in 1961 was 1,844 persons. This average includes the population of "city" and town panchayats, which are defined as having the three following characteristics: 1) a population of at least 5,000, 2) a density of at least 1,000 persons per square mile, and 3) 75 percent of the male work force dependent on nonagricultural resources.[23] There were thirty city and town panchayats in 1961 (see Table 3). I decided that city and town panchayats should be included in this study because many of these panchayats have populations of less than 10,000 and are really large villages in terms of their functional character. Furthermore, I found that even some of the larger towns had significant proportions of agricultural workers in the work force.[24] However, in the course of the analysis I will examine the special effects, if any, of including the town and city panchayats in the analysis.

The number of panchayats in Thanjavur District increased from 1,555 in 1961 to 1,638 in 1970, an increase due largely to the break-

TABLE 3

Village and Town Panchayats in Thanjavur District

Year	Village Panchayats	Town / City Panchayats	Total Panchayats
1961	1525	30	1555
1970	1595	43	1638

[23] *Census of India, 1961*, vol. 9, *District Census Handbook, Thanjavur* (Madras: Superintendent of Census Operations, 1965), 1: 69 (hereafter India, *District Census Handbook, 1961*); and *Census of India, 1971*, ser. 19, *Tamil Nadu*, pt. X-B, *District Census Handbook: Village and Town Primary and Census Abstract, Thanjavur* (Madras: Director of Census Operations, 1972), p. 9 (hereafter India, *District Census Handbook, 1971*). The terminology of city and town is misleading. According to the 1961 census, "city panchayats" had populations of from 5,000 to 9,999 and "town panchayats" had populations of from 10,000 to 24,999. The terminology was modified in the 1971 census so that all panchayats with populations of from 5,000 to 24,999 are "towns."

[24] In the five largest nonmunicipal towns in Thanjavur District in 1971 all agricultural workers (cultivators and agricultural laborers) averaged 32.8 percent of the work force.

up of large panchayats formed in 1961.[25] This presented a problem for the analysis because in 79 of the divided panchayats the 1965 and 1970 election results could not be matched with the 1961 census data. I decided that using the 1961 panchayat data would, however, minimize the information loss because in several of the divided panchayats the 1965 and 1970 election results were the same across the new units and could therefore be applied to the parent panchayat. Therefore, all my analysis is based on the 1,555 village panchayats that existed in 1961.

THE DATA

The aggregate data on which this study is largely based were compiled from a great variety of sources. Some data were obtained directly from unpublished records of various government departments; the remainder were taken from the 1961 and 1971 census reports. Integrating all of these data sets (each of which was based on a different geographic unit) into a single unified data file required an extremely complex and lengthy process of matching, aggregation, and merger of units.[26] This process yielded a uniquely extensive set of data for a large number of units.

Measures of Independent Variables

GEOPHYSICAL CHARACTERISTICS

Data on terrain, soil quality, net area under cultivation, area under canal irrigation, cropping patterns, and land values were available from the 1961 and 1971 censuses (although not uniformly for each). Most of these factors did not change significantly over the 1961 to 1971 period and therefore were combined to describe a relatively constant geophysical ecology of village agriculture.[27]

[25] One town panchayat "dropped out" when it became a municipality after 1964.

[26] For instance, because the census tracts in 1961 and 1971 were not identical, I had first to prepare an elaborate computerized cross-index of 2,558 units listed by the two censuses. This enabled me to make the results of both compatible at the village panchayat level.

[27] For instance, data from other sources indicate that between 1960 and 1970 the net sown area increased by less than 8 percent and that the net irrigated area (mostly by canal) as a percentage of the net sown area decreased slightly, from 84.1 to 81.5 percent (due to the fact that almost all of the increase in net sown area was in unirrigated areas).

DEMOGRAPHIC CHARACTERISTICS

Data on general demographic characteristics, such as total population, overall density, and literacy, were taken from the 1961 and 1971 censuses.

AGRO-ECONOMIC STRUCTURE

Data describing village agro-economic structure were taken in part from the census. Most important were data on the size and composition of the agricultural work force in 1961 and 1971. Unfortunately there was a problem of comparability in these categories between the two censuses due to changes in the definitions of workers and cultivators.[28] The 1961 definitions were biased towards the classification of persons as workers (as opposed to nonworkers) and cultivators (as opposed to agricultural laborers). Therefore the proportions of workers and cultivators declined and the proportions of nonworkers and agricultural laborers increased under the stricter definitions imposed in the 1971 census. That these changes were largely due to definitional shifts is clearly indicated (see Tables 91 and 92 in the Appendix) by the fact that they were much greater for females, who were more likely to be misclassified in 1961. The effect is particularly marked in Thanjavur District where there is a high female participation rate in the agricultural labor force. A special study by the census commissioner has in fact shown that the definitional adjustments for males are marginal.[29] It is therefore possible to estimate changes in the composition of the agricultural work force over time by using the figures for males only. Where I am not concerned with changes over time, however, the more accurate 1971 data will be used.

Another important aspect of the agro-economic structure is tenancy. Data on the number of tenants and the area under tenancy at the village level were available from records produced as a result of 1969 legislation providing for the registration of tenancy rights

[28] *Census of India, 1971: Provisional Population Totals*, Paper 1 of 1971—Supplement (New Delhi: 1971), pp. 27-34 (hereafter *Census of India, 1971: Provisional Population Totals*).

[29] *Census of India, 1971: Report on Resurvey on Economic Questions—Some Results*, Paper 1 of 1974—miscellaneous Studies (New Delhi: Office of the Registar-General and Census Commissioner of India, 1974). See Table 92 in the Appendix for some results of this study. For an analysis of the implications of these changes, see V. S. Vyas, "Structural Change in Agriculture and the Small Farm Sector," *Economic and Political Weekly* 11 (January 10, 1976): 24-32.

in Thanjavur District.[30] This source is questionable because registration might have been manipulated by landlords through their influence over local officials. On examining the data, however, I became convinced for two reasons that they could be used in this study.

First, past studies have estimated the area under tenancy cultivation in Thanjavur District at between 25 and 50 percent of the net sown area.[31] According to the tenancy registration records completed as of December 1972, only 19.2 percent of the cultivated area was under tenancy. However, this figure is misleading because tenancy is not uniformly distributed throughout the district. The higher figures cited in other studies were based on areas of the district where tenancy is more extensive. In these areas the percentage area under tenancy according to the registration records ranges from about 20 percent to about 35 percent and averages close to 30 percent. The registration records do not therefore drastically underestimate the incidence of tenancy in the district. Second, and more important, the spatial *distribution* of tenancy in the district according to the registration records closely parallels that revealed by other sources (see Table 4). Since it is the *variation* in tenancy incidence from village to village rather than its absolute incidence for the district as a whole that is relevant to my analysis, there is ample justification for using the tenancy registration data.

[30] Government of Madras, *The Tamil Nadu Agricultural Lands Record of Tenancy Rights Act, 1969 (Act X of 1969), with Rule and Notifications* (Madras: C. Sitaraman & Co., 1970). Allegations about manipulation of the registration process appeared in the newspapers. See, for instance, *Indian Express* (Madras), May 23, 1973.

[31] In 1965 Wolf Ladejinsky estimated that half the cultivated acreage was under tenancy. See Ladejinsky, *A Study on Tenurial Conditions in Package Districts* (New Delhi: Government of India, Planning Commission, 1965). Andre Beteille, however, believes the Ladejinsky estimate was high, especially as there is reason to believe that the area under tenancy declined in the early 1960s. See Beteille, *Studies*, p. 151. The 1961 Census Household Sample (20 percent) Survey estimated the area under both pure tenancy and ownership-cum-tenancy at 55 percent (28 and 27 percent respectively). If half the area in the latter category is owned, then the actual area under tenancy cultivation would be 41.5 percent. See India, *District Census Handbook, 1961*, 1: 240. Another lower estimate was arrived at on the basis of a careful survey of about sixty villages in the district. According to this study, only 24.4 percent of cultivated area was under tenancy cultivation. See Badrinath, *A Report on the Implementation of the Tamilnadu Agricultural Lands Record of Tenancy Rights Act, 1969* (Madras, 1971), p. 31. Finally, the 1971 agricultural census found the area under pure tenancy was 12.3 percent of the net area and the area under ownership-cum-tenancy 12.5 percent, for a total of 24.8 percent. See the *World Agricultural Census, 1970-71 (Fasli 1380), Tamil Nadu*, vol. 2, *State, Regional, and District Tables* (Madras: Government of Tamil Nadu, 1974), pp. 133-134, for percentages computed from the data.

TABLE 4
Distribution of Tenancy in Thanjavur District, 1971-1972, by Taluk

Taluk	Tenancy Registration Records, 1971[a]		Sixty-Village Inquiry, 1971[b]		Agrarian Court Data, 1971-72[c]
	Number of Tenants as % of District Total (1)	Tenancy Area as % of Cultivated Area (2)	Number of Tenants as % of District Total (3)	Tenancy Area as % of Cultivated Area (4)	Number of Eviction Petitions Filed by Landlords as % of District Total (5)
Sirkali	11.0 (4)	34.8 (1)	17.8 (1)	41.3 (3)	4.7 (9)
Mayuram	17.7 (1)	29.6 (3)	11.5 (5)	37.6 (4)	14.7 (2)
Kumbakonam	15.5 (3)	33.0 (2)	13.8 (2)	45.9 (1)	25.3 (1)
Nannilam	15.7 (2)	24.0 (4)	8.3 (6)	41.2 (2)	10.3 (5)
Papanasam	9.5 (5)	22.7 (5)	6.7 (7)	19.8 (9)	11.1 (4)
Thanjavur	5.3 (9)	13.5 (8)	12.2 (3)	29.9 (6)	6.1 (8)
Orathanad	1.8 (10)	2.9 (11)	4.2 (9)	6.5 (12)	1.0 (10)
Mannargudi	6.7 (7)	17.3 (7)	12.0 (4)	30.7 (5)	11.7 (3)
Nagapattinam	7.2 (6)	22.0 (6)	5.5 (8)	24.9 (8)	7.4 (6)
Tiruthuraipoondi	6.6 (8)	10.5 (9)	3.5 (10)	11.4 (10)	6.4 (7)
Pattukottai	1.5 (12)	1.4 (12)	1.4 (12)	10.5 (11)	0.8 (11)
Arantangi	1.6 (11)	3.6 (10)	3.2 (11)	26.2 (7)	0.5 (12)
Total/Average	*	19.2	*	27.2	*

SOURCES: [a] Data collected from official records by author. [b] Badrinath, *A Report on the Implementation of the Tamilnadu Agricultural Lands Record of Tenancy Rights Act, 1969* (Madras, 1971). The data presented here were calculated from the raw data supplied in appendices to this report (pp. 80-260). My figure for the percentage area under tenancy for the whole district differs slightly from the figure quoted in the report. [c] Data collected by the author. The petitions mentioned here were filed in Thanjavur's revenue courts by landlords to evict tenants under various provisions of the Tamil Nadu Cultivating Tenants Protection Act of 1955 and the Tamil Nadu Public Trusts (Regulation of Agricultural Lands) Act of 1961.

NOTES: Rank-order correlations (Spearman's r')

between col. 1 and col. 3: r' = .650, signif. ≈ .01
between col. 2 and col. 4: r' = .825, signif. < .01
between col. 1 and col. 5: r' = .755, signif. < .01

Parenthetical column numbers denote rank.
* Does not add to 100 due to rounding.

The main weakness in my analysis of the agro-economic structure is the absence of any village-level data on size distribution of land holdings (both owned and operated). I will be able partially to compensate for this with land distribution data for larger units such as the taluk.[32] I also plan to use data from the taluk and block levels in other cases where they are not available at the panchayat level.

TECHNOLOGICAL CHANGE IN AGRICULTURE

No objective measure of change in agricultural technology at the village level was available. Therefore, I have had to rely on a "subjective" measure of change obtained by asking the chief agricultural extension officer and his staff in each of the thirty-six blocks to rank each of the village panchayats in their jurisdiction low, medium, or high on the combined basis of two criteria: the proportion of the cultivated paddy area under high-yielding varieties; and the extent to which cultivators of the village apply the recommended doses of chemical fertilizer to their crops. This "agricultural development rating" does not purport to measure actual changes in productivity per unit area.

GENERAL SOCIO-ECONOMIC DEVELOPMENT

Data indicating the level of socio-economic development in the village were available from the 1961 and 1971 censuses and included educational facilities, health facilities, drinking water facilities, communication facilities (travel, telecommunications), electrification, and agricultural infrastructural facilities (e.g., agricultural electrification, cooperative societies, banks, veterinary hospitals). These variables were combined into separate indices and an overall development index for both 1961 and 1971. Some initial problems in establishing comparability between the 1961 and 1971 measures were overcome.

The Dependent Variable:
Agrarian Radicalism and Communist Voting

The statistical measure of agrarian radicalism in this study is derived from village-level Communist voting. More specifically, it indicates whether or not a candidate affiliated with the undivided

[32] The twelve taluks in Thanjavur District are administrative units created by the British. They range in area from about 45 to about 1,300 square kilometers and in 1971 population from about 213,000 to about 440,000 persons.

(pre-1964) Communist Party of India, with the post-split Communist Party of India (CPI), or with the Communist Party of India (Marxist) (CPM) was elected to the presidency of the village panchayat in each of the three sets of panchayat elections, 1961, 1965, and 1970. This is certainly not an unassailable indicator of agrarian radicalism as defined in chapter 1, and as such it requires some explanation.

The Communist Party of India, founded in 1925, became a legal party in 1942.[33] At the time of independence it followed a line of loyal opposition to the Congress government. However, in the following four years, 1947 to 1951, the Party was torn by intense disagreement over three elements of strategy and tactics: 1) its attitude towards the Congress government, 2) its "class strategy" (whether the Party's thrust should be anticapitalist or anti-imperialist), and 3) whether violence was necessary. There were three "lines" on these questions. The "Ranadive line" identified the Nehru government as a bourgeois-capitalist government (it did not distinguish between progressive and reactionary sections of the Indian bourgeoisie) and called for a three-class anticapitalist strategy based on urban violence and armed insurrection in the countryside.[34] Discredited by the failure of the Telengana rebellion (1948-1951) the Ranadive line was succeeded by the "Andhra line," which depicted the Congress government as a colonial government still dominated by the big bourgeoisie. The Andhra line called for a neo-Maoist, anti-imperialist, and antifeudal strategy based on armed guerilla warfare and a united front of all classes except the big bourgeoisie. But the disastrous impact on the Party of futile attempts to organize guerilla warfare in the wake of the Telengana uprising led to the rapid succession, in the spring of 1951, of a third approach, the Joshi-Dange-Ghosh line. This line distinguished between progressive and reactionary sections of the Con-

[33] The following review is based on relevant sections in three recent studies of Indian communism that reach surprisingly similar conclusions on many aspects of their subject: Paul R. Brass and Marcus F. Franda, eds., *Radical Politics in South Asia* (Cambridge, Mass.: The M.I.T. Press, 1973), especially the introductory essay by Paul R. Brass, "Political Parties of the Radical Left in South Asian Politics," pp. 3-116; Biplab Das Gupta, *The Naxalite Movement*, Centre for the Study of Developing Societies, Monograph no. 1 (New Delhi: Allied Publishers, 1974); and Bhabani Sen Gupta, *Communism in Indian Politics* (New York: Columbia University Press, 1972).

[34] The three lines are named for their principal proponents within the Party: B. T. Ranadive; a group of Andhra Communists led by Rajeshwara Rao; and P. C. Joshi, S. A. Dange, and Ajoy Ghosh.

gress (the former led by Nehru) and called for a nonviolent anti-imperialist strategy that included the middle bourgeoisie.

In this early period, then, the Party was captured briefly by radical elements. However, with the ascendance of the Joshi-Dange-Ghosh line it entered a period in which an anti-imperialist strategy and nonviolent tactics were gradually adopted.[35] By the time of the Fifth Party Congress at Amritsar in 1958 the CPI had firmly established its commitment to the "peaceful, parliamentary path of Socialist transition." However, before and after 1958 there were differences within the Party over how parliamentary politics should be used. Although it began with the "Leninist approach" in which parliament is used to "break the constitution from within," the Party's electoral success in the 1952 national elections and later in the 1957 Kerala state elections together with pressure from Moscow caused it to elevate parliamentarism from tactics to a strategy that accepted the possibility of structural change through the parliamentary system. A related difference in attitudes towards the Congress government persisted. Some sections of the Party felt it was possible to ally with the progressive sections of Congress, while others felt the Party should try to dislodge Congress from power.[36] Although it was agreed upon to combine parliamentary with extraparliamentary but nonviolent mass action, adherents to the latter approach placed more importance on mass movements.

The 1964 split of the CPI into the CPI and CPM resulted from these disparities. The CPI took a differentiated view of the national bourgeosie and argued that a national democratic front that included progressive sections of the Congress was necessary. The CPM argued that the Indian revolution was at the agrarian stage and called for a people's democratic front excluding the entire national bourgeoisie. But on tactics the two parties remained fairly similar. The CPM continued the more skeptical view of the parliamentary process and placed more emphasis on mass movements, but in practice both parties combined parliamentary and extra-

[35] According to Brass, this was due to three events: 1) the failure of the Telengana rebellion, 2) growing concensus in the international Communist movement on an anti-imperialist strategy in which armed struggle was not universally prescribed, and 3) a series of shifts in international politics by which the Soviet Union came to accept Indian nonalignment and by which Indo-Soviet relations became cordial (Brass, "Political Parties," p. 37).

[36] Brass argues that these differences in fact derived from different strategies towards power in Indian politics, in turn related to whether or not the leaders in each camp had regional power bases (ibid., pp. 40-41).

parliamentary means. Although neither party ruled out violence, both were for the time being (the CPI somewhat hopefully) committed to peaceful means.

However, the key issues of the Communist relationship to the state and the use of violence were soon revived in a second period of intense ideological debate beginning in 1967. As the Telengana rebellion had precipitated the earlier debate, so the Naxalbari rebellion precipitated this one. A more radical element in the CPM split off, first forming the loosely knit Naxalite movement and then in 1969 the Communist Party of India (Marxist-Leninist), or CPI (M-L). The Naxalite strategy was antifeudal and called for agrarian revolution as the first task.[37] Although tactical differences emerged within the Naxalite movement early and increased as time went on, it clearly rejected parliamentarism and sought revolution through armed guerilla warfare. This phase of Indian communism ended effectively during 1970/1971 with the collapse of the Naxalite activities in Bengal and Andhra Pradesh and the arrest or killing of key Naxalite leaders.

From the previous discussion it becomes apparent that Indian communism has exhibited several tendencies throughout its history. All have shared a commitment to a transformation of the Indian social and economic system; what they have not shared is a vision of how that transformation can and should be achieved. There have been differences of strategy: How should Communists relate to the state and what is the correct alignment of classes? Tactics have diverged: Can the transformation be achieved gradually and peacefully or must there be violent revolution? And although it is clear that the less radical tendency embracing segments of the government and parliamentarism has been the dominant one, it is also clear that there is an enduring recessive tendency that rejects cooperation with the state and parliamentarism, advocating instead assault on state power through violence. During most of the post-1947 period, the influence of this recessive trait of Indian communism could only be dimly perceived. The fact that it did emerge dramatically in two widely separated periods, however, is grounds for using support for the Communist parties as a rough indicator of radicalism, especially since the periods of great-

---

[37] Although the Naxalities are often described as Maoists, Sen Gupta and Das Gupta both argue convincingly that, at least by the end, the movement was not truly Maoist (Sen Gupta, *Communism in Indian Politics*, pp. 347-353, and Das Gupta, *Naxalite Movement*, pp. 208-211).

est radicalism in Thanjavur have coincided with the most radical periods in Indian communism.

Similarly, justification for equating agrarian radicalism with communism in a political system where communism has drawn its strength primarily from urban areas is supported by the fact that the Communist parties in India have been the only parties that have made any significant effort in the modern period to mobilize elements of agrarian society in militant movements.[38] The first all-India peasant organization, the All-India Kisan Sabha, was founded in 1936 as a Congress party front but quickly came under Communist control. The Kisan Sabha and later groups, such as the labor organizations of the CPI and CPM, have been most active in those states, notably West Bengal and Kerala, and in those periods, notably the late 1960s, of greatest overall Communist strength.[39] The Communists have also been instrumental to all the major "peasant uprisings" in India in the modern period: Thanjavur and Telengana in 1946 to 1948 and Naxalbari and Srikakulam in 1968 to 1969. Following the 1964 split, the attention of both the CPI and the CPM shifted away from urban concerns and parliamentary tactics towards militant mobilization in rural areas.[40] Also, as noted in Chapter 1, the Communists have been active on the agrarian front in Thanjavur District since 1941, both through agrarian organizations (originally the Kisan Sabha and more recently the Agricultural Laborers' Union) and through leadership of strikes, agitations, and other forms of militant action.[41]

Finally, there is considerable precedent in earlier studies of India

[38] See Brass, "Political Parties," pp. 25, 54-50, 89-90; Sen Gupta, *Communism in Indian Politics*, pp. 291-293; and Das Gupta, *Naxalite Movement*, p. 20. Furthermore, the two most active periods in Indian communism have centered on radical agrarian movements.

[39] Hardgrave, *India: Government and Politics*, pp. 123-124. See also Kathleen Gough, "Indian Peasant Uprisings," *Economics and Political Weekly* 9 (Special number 1974): 1,391-1,412.

[40] The shift was certainly due in part to rivalry between the CPI and the CPM for control of the kisan and labor organizations (Sen Gupta, *Communism in Indian Politics*, pp. 292-295).

[41] The actual role the Communists have played will be examined in detail in Chapter 8 and Chapter 10. Communist activities during the different periods are described in several studies: Kathleen Gough, "Peasant Resistance and Revolt in South India," *Pacific Affairs* 41 (Winter 1968-1969): 526-544; K. C. Alexander, *Agrarian Tension in Thanjavur* (Hyderabad: National Institute of Community Development, 1975), pp. 34-46; and Kathleen Gough, "Harijans in Thanjavur," in *Imperialism and Revolution in South Asia*, ed. Kathleen Gough and Hari P. Sharma (New York and London: Monthly Review Press, 1973), pp. 222-245.

and other areas for arguing equivalence between agrarian communism, even where manifested only electorally, and agrarian radicalism.[42] Of course to do so builds into my measure of agrarian radicalism the contextual differences in national and regional political systems and in the roles the Communist parties play in them. I certainly am not arguing here that these are unimportant to an understanding of agrarian radicalism: on the contrary, a substantial component of the variance in the phenomenon of agrarian radicalism derives from these systemic political differences. Thus while an analysis of agrarian radicalism in Thanjavur must ultimately take into account the impact of external political events and forces, such as the character of Indian communism, the 1964 split, and the electoral fortunes of the Communist parties (see Chapter 10), the widespread and repeated identification of the Communists with radical agrarian movements, even where sporadic and limited in scope and goals, lends support to my choice of Communist strength as a measure of agrarian radicalism. Moreover, the variation in external political factors can be used to advantage in analyzing the "internal" sources of agrarian radicalism. For instance, the agro-economic support bases of the CPI and CPM in Thanjavur can be compared to determine whether they represent different types of agrarian radicalism.

Another question that might be asked about my measure of agrarian radicalism is whether the outcome of an electoral event is a valid indicator of radicalism. Whereas it would be preferable to have a direct measure of "radical" activity, either behavioral or attitudinal, such as the incidence of violent conflict between landlords and laborers or support for redistributive land reform measures, it is not feasible to employ such a quantitative measure (an "event score") due to the difficulty of obtaining the data and the relatively low overall incidence of such events (with the result that the variance is too low for statistical analysis).

However, the use of the electoral measure as a valid indicator of agrarian radicalism in Thanjavur can be demonstrated by comparing its distribution with crude indices of radical agrarian activity in Table 5. A comparison of column 1 with columns 2 to 4 shows

[42] For India, see Donald S. Zagoria, "The Ecology of Peasant Communism in India," *American Political Science Review* 65 (March 1971): 144-160. For Asia, see John Wilson Lewis, ed., *Peasant Rebellion and Communist Revolution in Asia* (Stanford, Ca.: Stanford University Press, 1974). For Europe, see Juan J. Linz, "Patterns of Land Tenure, Division of Labor, and Voting Behavior in Europe," *Comparative Politics* 8 (April 1976): 365-430.

that Communist panchayat strength is high in the same taluks where agitations (leading in some cases to arrests of thousands of persons) have taken place with greater frequency and intensity. Furthermore, it is possible to compare areas of Communist panchayat strength with the application of the Fair Wages Act of 1969 (see column 5). The Fair Wages Act was a direct and specific response to a period of intense and often violent radical agrarian activity during 1968 and 1969 in Thanjavur, including the Kilavenmani incident of December 1968 in which a landlord-laborer clash resulted in the deaths of forty-three people.[43] The table illustrates that the legislation applied to precisely those areas where Communist strength was greatest. Thus, the covariation of electoral success and radical activity within Thanjavur District provides an empirical justification for using the electoral indicator. I would add a theoretical argument: given Communist ideology, both electoral *and* agitational mobilization depend upon the emergence of a basis for solidarity that did not previously exist.

I have already defined the village panchayat as the unit of analysis for this study because politics at this level are related to intensely local factors such as agro-climatic conditions and agro-economic structure and because the panchayats are effectively tied into the wider political system. A comparison of Communist electoral strength at the panchayat and legislative assembly constituency levels in Table 5 further supports the latter argument. The taluk-by-taluk distributions of Communist strength are very similar.

Finally, the validity of the Communist electoral measure of agrarian radicalism is supported by the results of the survey data analysis presented in Chapter 7. First, as we shall see, the spatial distribution of individual Communist affiliation and of aggregate Communist electoral success in Thanjavur are closely correlated. Second, individual Communist affiliation and voting are highly correlated with other nonelectoral indicators of radicalism, such as attitudes towards agrarian issues, involvement in agrarian disputes, and membership in agricultural labor unions.

There is, however, one deficiency in my indicator of agrarian

---

[43] Following the Kilavenmani incident, the Government of Tamil Nadu set up a "one-man commission" to investigate the causes of agrarian unrest in Thanjavur and to advise the government on ways in which they could be eliminated. The main recommendation was the increase in wages for agricultural labor implemented by the Fair Wages Act of 1969. See Ganapathia Pillai, "Report of the Commission of Inquiry on the Agrarian Labour in Problems of East Thanjavur District," typewritten [1969].

TABLE 5

Communist Electoral Strength in Thanjavur District Panchayats Compared with Other Indicators of Agrarian Radicalism by Taluk

Taluk	Mean Communist Panchayat Electoral Strength, 1961-70[a] (1)	Arrests Reported in Agrarian Agitations				Taluks to Which Fair Wages Act of 1969 Applied (5)	Mean % of Vote Won by Communist Candidates in Legislative Assembly Elections, 1962, 1967, 1971[e] (6)
		January 1969[b] (2)	July 1969[c] (3)	August 1972[d] (4)			
Sirkali	0.244	Many (1000s)*	Yes (72)**	None***	Yes	24.0†
Mayuram	0.217	Some (100+)	Yes (64)	None	Yes	13.3
Kumbakonam	0.057	Few (100s)	Yes (37)	None	No	2.1
Nannilam	0.193	Many (5000)	Yes (122)	Many	Yes	21.5
Papanasam	0.130	None	Yes (8)	None	No	0.0
Thanjavur	0.022	None	None	None	No	0.6
Orathanad	0.038	None	None	None	No	0.0
Mannargudi	1.323	Very many (25,000)	Yes (268)	Some	Yes	32.6
Nagapattinam	0.774	Many (3,000)	Yes (185)	Many	Yes	37.0
Tiruthuraipoondi	0.762	Very many (25,000)	NA‡	Some	Yes	31.1
Pattukottai	0.166	None	Yes§	None	No	8.8
Arantangi	0.010	None	None	None	No	0.8

SOURCES: [a] Data collected by author.
[b] Data reported in CPI newsletter, *Ulavu Chelvam* (Madras), December 15, 1968.
[c] Data reported in newspaper, *Hindu* (Madras), July 17-18, 1969.
[d] Data reported in ibid., August 7, 10, 1972.

** Figures refer to arrests of "CPI volunteers."
*** Refers mostly to agitation organized by CPM.
† Mean of results for constituencies roughly coterminous with taluk boundaries.
‡ NA = data not available.

radicalism: it measures the *results* of voting, that is, whether or not the candidate elected was affiliated with the Communist parties,[44] and not the voting itself, that is, the percentage of votes won by the Communist candidate. It is thus a *zero-sum* measure of a graded reality. Much information (and variance) is lost. In the case of a Communist victory it is not possible to tell by what margin the candidate won; in the case of victory by a candidate of another party we don't know by how much the Communist candidate lost, or even if there was a Communist candidate. Although this weakness depresses the level of statistical explanation in the analysis, it does not prevent me from discerning the important relationships between the variables.

In constructing the actual indicator to be used in the statistical study, I have tried to introduce variability to compensate for this limitation. Thus, most of the analysis will employ measures of panchayat Communist electoral strength (for the CPI and CPM separately and together) that *combine* the results of all three panchayat elections.[45] For instance, a panchayat that never has had a Communist president would have a score of "0," while one that has always had a Communist president would have a score of "3." The problem with this approach is, of course, that analysis of changes over time is displaced. However, where possible and especially relevant I will also examine separately the variations in level and type of Communist strength over time.

The Survey Data

The survey, which brings together detailed data on cultivation and labor practices, organizational involvement, partisanship, voting, attitudes, family characteristics, and the agro-economic status of both cultivating and laboring households, was conducted during my fieldwork in Thanjavur District in 1972 and 1973. Designed primarily to explore relationships among the key variables in the analysis of agrarian radicalism at the individual level rather than

[44] No data on the 1960, 1965, and 1970 panchayat elections in Thanjavur were available in published form. I was given permission to copy the names and party affiliations of successful candidates for the roughly fifteen hundred panchayat presidencies from unpublished government records. These records contained no information about numbers and/or percentages of votes gained by candidate or party.

[45] Unfortunately after 1964 it was not always possible to know whether the panchayat president was affiliated with the CPI or the CPM. I have therefore chosen to rely mostly on a combined CPI-CPM measure, except when it is important to explore the implications of the difference between the two.

to estimate population parameters the survey employed both purposive and random sampling to yield data on 441 cultivating households and 311 laboring households.[46]

The first stage in the survey process was the division of Thanjavur District into five agro-economic zones defined by such basic agro-climatic and agro-economic factors as rainfall, soil type, irrigation, extent of double cropping, amount of tenancy, and percentage of agricultural laborers in the agricultural work force (see Chapter 5). These five zones formed the strata for the selection of twenty-six primarily agricultural village panchayats.[47] In each of these villages a full census of households was conducted to identify cultivating and laboring households and to provide data for the stratification of cultivating households according to tenurial status and holding size and of laboring households according to the type of labor performed and the degree of involvement in cultivation.[48] A disproportionate sample was then taken from these strata in order to assure representation of all strata and a large enough number to allow within-cell statistical analysis in the analytically most important cells.

[46] Cultivating households were defined as those receiving more than 50 percent of their income from cultivation. Agricultural laboring households received more than 50 percent of household income from labor in the fields or in other agricultural tasks. In most cases the head of the household was interviewed, but when that person was not available, the next most responsible adult was questioned. Although almost 500 cultivators and 350 laborers were originally surveyed, the results from two entire villages and from several individual respondents were found to be unreliable (in the case of the villages, because of a dishonest interviewer) and were thus discarded.

[47] Primarily agricultural panchayats were defined as those in which agricultural workers composed more than 50 percent of all resident workers. The number of villages selected in each zone was quasi-proportional to the number of agricultural workers by zone, subject to a minimum number of villages per zone (three) that would provide a zonal sample large enough to permit independent statistical analyses within each zone. The selection of villages within each zone was also stratified (disproportionately) according to agro-economic regions within the zone.

[48] Over nine thousand households were included in the census of twenty-six villages, of which about 80 percent were agricultural. For cultivating households there were five tenurial strata (purely owning, primarily owning, purely tenant, primarily tenant, and purely or primarily noncultivating owner) and four holding-size strata (0.00-2.49 acres, 2.50-4.99 acres, 5.00-9.99 acres, and 10.00+ acres). For laboring households there were four strata (purely laboring, laborer-cum-owner cultivator, laborer-cum-tenant cultivator, and attached farm laborer).

CHAPTER 4

Thanjavur District

THE AREA comprised by Thanjavur District in the state of Tamil Nadu is one of the most studied in India.[1] Scholars have been attracted by its economic, social, political, religious, and cultural importance, both historical and contemporary. The district's economic significance, past and present, derives from its agricultural productivity (it is widely known as the "granary of South India"), in particular from extensive wet paddy cultivation made possible by irrigation from the Kaveri (formerly Cauvery) River. Continuity and change in its complex social structure have invited close attention. The home of one of the great kingdoms of ancient and medieval South India, Thanjavur contributed disproportionately to the nationalist movement and post-Independence political change in that area. It has also been a religious center and consequently the cradle of South Indian high (Brahminical) culture, especially sculpture, music, and dance, which are historically associated with temple life. But perhaps the most intriguing aspect of Thanjavur is the complex interaction of all of these factors and how this interaction changes through time. This provides an opportunity to enrich the study of agrarian radicalism and makes the district an especially appropriate area in which to base my study.

BACKGROUND

Geography

Thanjavur District lies on the southeastern coast of India, its northern border about 150 miles south of Madras City and its

[1] Thanjavur was transliterated as Tanjore during the British raj and the early years of Independence. Tamil Nadu State was Madras Presidency during the raj and Madras State from Independence to 1967. Significant examples of studies of Thanjavur include Kathleen Gough, "Caste in a Tanjore Village," in *Aspects of Caste in South India, Ceylon, and Northwest Pakistan*, ed. E. R. Leach (Cambridge: Cambridge University Press, 1971), pp. 11-60; Andre Beteille, *Caste, Class and Power: Changing Patterns of Stratification in a Tanjore Village* (Berkeley, Ca.: University of California Press, 1965); K. C. Alexander, *Agrarian Tension in Thanjavur* (Hyderabad: National Institute of Community Development, 1975); and David Washbrook, "Political Change

southern border about 200 miles north of the southern tip of the subcontinent, Cape Comorin (see Figure 4). During the period of my study, it was bounded on the north by South Arcot District, on the west by Tiruchirapalli and Ramnathapuram districts, and on the east and south by the Bay of Bengal. The area of the district was about 3,600 square miles.

Generally speaking, Thanjavur is best described as a deltaic plain, though as we shall see there are important exceptions to this statement. The district encompasses the major part of the delta of the Kaveri River. The Kaveri originates in the mountains of Coorg (in Karnataka, formerly Mysore State) and flows down and across Tamil Nadu State, entering Thanjavur at its northwestern corner and dividing into several major and minor tributaries that reach the sea (see Figure 5). The irrigation potential of this river system was initially tapped centuries ago. The first major irrigation works, which regulated the entrance of Kaveri waters into the Thanjavur delta, were completed in the eleventh century and frequently modified and extended thereafter. The British made several major additions, notably the Cauvery-Mettur Project (CMP). The CMP included construction of a large dam on the river at Mettur in the Nilgiri hills to help assure a minimum water flow in the river (which ultimately depends on rainfall in the mountains during the Southwest Monsoon) and construction of the Grand Anicut Canal (GA Canal) to extend irrigation to about 300,000 acres in the western and southern areas of Thanjavur. In 1960/1961 the net irrigated area of the district was about 1.2 million acres, or about 80 percent of the net sown area. In almost all sections of the delta, which slopes gently towards the sea, irrigation is provided by the natural flow from river to channel and field to field. The soils, alluvial and clay, are excellent for wet paddy cultivation. In 1960/1961 the net area under paddy was also about 80 percent of the net sown area.

History

The recorded history of the Thanjavur areas goes back to the beginning of the Christian era when the Chola kingdom, the first dynasty of which we have authentic evidence, was established.[2] The Kaveri delta of Thanjavur formed the heart of this kingdom, en-

---

in a Stable Society: Tanjore District 1880 to 1920," in *South India: Political Institutions and Political Change, 1880-1940*, C. J. Baker and D. A. Washbrook (New Delhi: The Macmillan Co., 1975), pp. 20-68.

    [2] This capsule account is adapted from Gough, "Caste," p. 15.

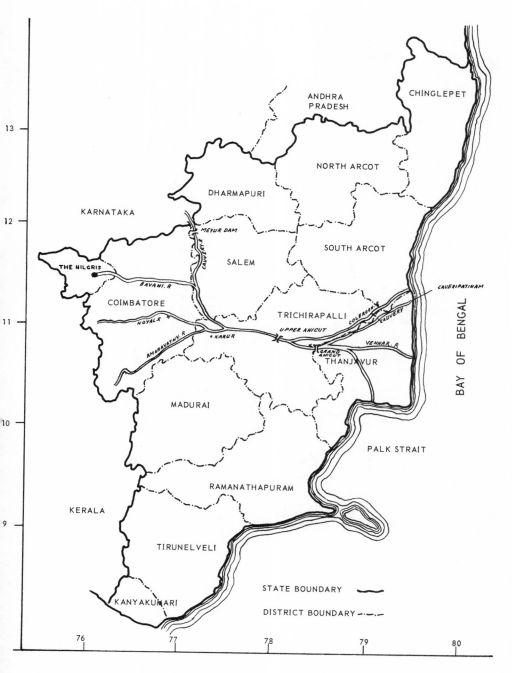

FIGURE 4. Tamil Nadu State with Districts and Thanjavur Delta River System, 1971

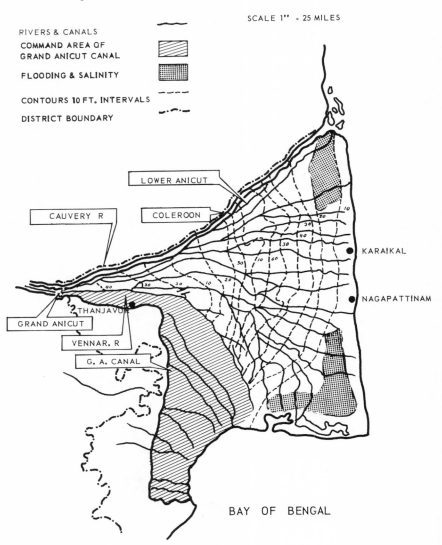

RIVERS & CANALS

COMMAND AREA OF
GRAND ANICUT CANAL

FLOODING & SALINITY

CONTOURS 10 FT. INTERVALS

DISTRICT BOUNDARY

SCALE 1" = 25 MILES

LOWER ANICUT

CAUVERY R

COLEROON

KARAIKAL

NAGAPATTINAM

THANJAVUR

GRAND ANICUT

VENNAR. R

G. A. CANAL

BAY OF BENGAL

FIGURE 5. River and Canal Irrigation in Thanjavur District, 1971

abling the Cholas to lay the foundation of an economic and social system based on irrigation, Brahmin-dominated village organization (the *agraharam*), and pervasive temples. The system survived intact until the advent of British rule, and its influence is still felt.[3] Although the Chola kingdom declined in the seventh century and became feudatory to other South Indian dynasties, it regained independence in the ninth century and reached its zenith in the tenth and eleventh centuries; during this period the first dam (the Grand Anicut) across the Kaveri and the famous temple of Bridhadeswara were constructed.

The Cholas declined again in the fourteenth century and became tributary to the Vijaynagar Empire. By the sixteenth century the dynasty had disappeared, and Thanjavur came under the rule of the Nayaks, Telugu governors appointed from Vijayanagar. The Nayak dynasty succumbed to the Maratha invaders in the late seventeenth century. Except for brief invasions by Muslim armies the Maratha dynasty ruled Thanjavur until its annexation by the British in 1799. The rule of the Nayak and Maratha dynasties partly accounts for the social and cultural diversity of the present district.

During the first half of the nineteenth century the British gradually formed a revenue district out of the Thanjavur area whose external boundaries were by 1860 about the same as they were at the time of this study. The British placed the district under overall charge of a "collector" and subdivided the district into taluks for revenue collection purposes. Both the district and the taluk continue to be important administrative units. Although his functions and power have been much curbed, the collector remains the chief executive officer of the district. A new administrative unit since Independence is the community development block or panchayat union.[4] In 1970 Thanjavur District had twelve taluks and thirty-six blocks (see Figure 6).

Population and Economy

In 1971 Thanjavur District had a total population of 3,840,732 persons. A densely populated area, Thanjavur had 395 persons per square kilometer in 1971, compared with 316 and 182 in Tamil Nadu and all India respectively (see Table 6). Its rural density is even more exceptional. The high densities probably account for

[3] Beteille, *Caste, Class and Power*, p. 13.
[4] See Chapter 3.

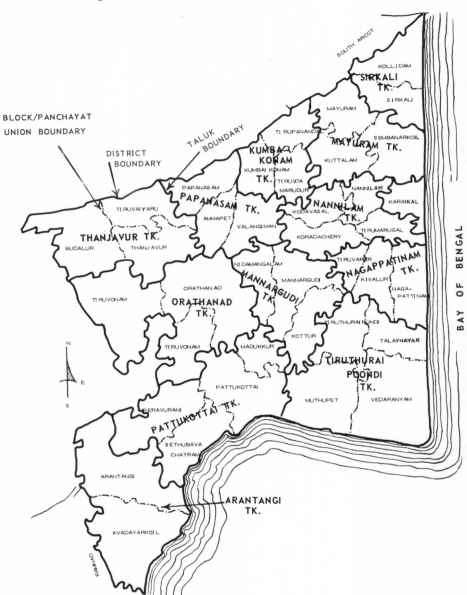

BLOCK/PANCHAYAT
UNION BOUNDARY

DISTRICT
BOUNDARY

TALUK
BOUNDARY

SOUTH ARCOT

KOLLIDAM

SIRKALI
TK.

SIRKALI

MAYURAM

TIRUPANANDAL

MAYURAM TK.

SEMBANARKOIL

KUMBA
KONAM
TK.

KUMBAI KONAM

KUTTALAM

TIRUVDA

PAPANASAM

MARUDUR

NANNILAM

KARAIKAL

PAPANASAM TK.

TIRUVAIYARU

NANNILAM
TK.

KODAVASAL

AMMAPET

VALANGIMAN

KORADACHERY

TIRUMARUGAL

THANJAVUR TK.

NIDAMANGALAM

TIRUVARUR

NAGAPPATTINAM
TK.

BUDALUR

THANJAVUR

MANNARGUDI

KIVALUR

NAGA-
PATTINAM

TIRUVONAM

ORATHANAD

MANNARGUDI
TK.

MANNARGUDI

ORATHANAD
TK.

TIRUTHURAI PUNDI

TIRUVONAM

MADUKKUR

KOTTUR

TALAYNAYAR

PATTUKOTTAI

TIRUTHURAI
POONDI
TK.

MUTHUPET

VEDARANYAM

PERAVURANI

PATTUKOTTAI TK.

SETHUBAVA
CHATRAM

ARANTANGI

ARANTANGI
TK.

AVADAYARKOIL

RAMNAD

BAY OF BENGAL

N
E
S

FIGURE 6. Thanjavur District Administrative Divisions, 1971

TABLE 6

General Demographic and Economic Characteristics of Thanjavur
District, Tamil Nadu, and All India, 1971

	Thanjavur District	Tamil Nadu	All India
Population density, 1971 (per sq. kilo.)			
Overall	395	316	182
Rural	276	198	—
Population growth, 1961-71	18.33	24.66	22.01
% of rural population, 1971	80.48	69.72	80.13
Workers as % of population, 1971	33.40	36.67	33.54
Rural workers as % of total workers, 1971	83.51	77.54	82.49
Agricultural workers as % of rural workers, 1971	81.75	76.37	80.86
Net sown area as % of total area	65	46	45
Net canal-irrigated area as % of net sown area	80	15	9
% of literates, 1971			
Overall	39.66	31.41	29.34
Rural	35.06	31.83	23.60

NOTE: 1971 figures unless otherwise noted.

the fact that Thanjavur's population grew at a slower rate during
1961 to 1971 than the population of Tamil Nadu or India.

According to 1961 figures, about 80 percent of Thanjavur's population lived in rural areas in about two thousand villages with an
average population of 1,361 each. However, as might be expected
from its economic function and political and cultural history, Thanjavur is not a hinterland. In 1971 20 percent of the population
lived in twenty-seven towns and five municipalities (formed in 1866),
including two, Thanjavur and Kumbakonam, with populations over
100,000. Extensive road and rail facilities link Thanjavur's rural
population with major urban areas such as Tiruchirappali, only
thirty-five miles to the west, and of course Madras City, an overnight
train journey to the north. The city of Nagapattinam on the eastern
coast is a port that has provided contact by sea with southeast Asia
for centuries. Furthermore, it is estimated that in 1970/1971 54.2

percent of Thanjavur District's net domestic product (at factor cost) was derived from nonagricultural activities.[5] In other words, in Thanjavur there is a juxtaposition of rural and urban, agricultural and nonagricultural life, and there are numerous longstanding linkages with the outside world.

However, the mainstream of life in Thanjavur remains resolutely rural and agricultural. Despite its exposure to urban life and modernizing influences over a long period the rural proportion of the district's population dropped only four percentage points in seventy years, from 84.3 percent in 1901 to 80.5 percent in 1971. Rural workers comprised 83 percent of all workers in 1971 and agricultural workers 82 percent of all rural workers. Net sown area was two-thirds of the total area, compared to less than half in Tamil Nadu and all India. One of fourteen districts in the state, Thanjavur normally produced more than 25 percent of its total paddy output.

Though predominantly rural and agricultural, Thanjavur's literacy rate for both the overall and rural population is considerably higher than that of Tamil Nadu and all India.

Finally, Thanjavur has continuing importance as a religious center. In 1971 it had only 9 percent of Tamil Nadu's population but 17 percent of the state's Hindu temples. Several of these temples are wealthy institutions that own thousands of acres of agricultural land and run schools and other facilities and thus still have considerable influence over the socio-economic life of the district.

This general overview of Thanjavur's geography, history, demography, and economy should alert us to the possible occurrence of agrarian radicalism in Thanjavur. The topography, the relatively plentiful irrigation, and the fertile soil have given rise to intensive cultivation that in turn has resulted in high population density and pressure on the land. In addition, its agricultural productivity, geography, and history early exposed the area to the market forces, urbanization, and education that are potentially disruptive to traditional agrarian relationships.

AGRARIAN SOCIETY

Agro-Economic Structure

At the time the British took direct control of Thanjavur there were three principal types of land rights in the area: *mirasi, inam,*

[5] Data made available to the author by the District Statistical Office, Thanjavur.

and *zamindari*. Although unusual elsewhere in South India, *mirasi*, or joint land rights, were prevalent in Thanjavur, particularly in the deltaic areas. Under this system, which seems to have arisen during the Chola period as a result of royal grants of undeveloped land to village communities, land was held and managed jointly by the several households of the dominant caste, usually Brahmins or high-caste non-Brahmins.[6] The village was jointly assessed and jointly paid land revenue to the government. At first the British maintained joint assessment, but gradually over the next seventy-five years responsibility for the payment of revenue devolved onto the individual households, undermining the system of joint rights.[7] The result was a de facto *ryotwari* system (long prevalent elsewhere in South India) under which individual households held, managed, and were assessed of revenue on land. There was no abrupt change, therefore, when the British formally and permanently converted Thanjavur to *ryotwari* settlement in the early 1890s.

The displacement of the *mirasi* system by *ryotwari*, though gradual, undoubtedly had some disruptive effect on the traditional agrarian system. By making revenue liability an individual responsibility, it may have lessened village solidarity and made the agricultural economy more responsive to market forces. However, as the *mirasi* system left considerable room for independent economic activity in the households and the changeover to *ryotwari* was gradual the disruption should not be exaggerated.[8]

One legacy of the *mirasi* system is the title *mirasdar*, still commonly used today in Thanjavur to describe someone who owns more than six and two-thirds acres (one *veli*) of irrigated paddy land. Though this is a substantial holding, the relatively low threshold for the honorific designation is a symptom of the high degree of pressure on the land in Thanjavur.

Inam ("gift") land was held by institutions and, more commonly, individuals (*inamdars*) in Thanjavur in perpetuity free of revenue assessment or assessed at concessional rates. The practice of granting *inam* lands, often whole villages, began and was most wide-

[6] Gough, "Caste," pp. 20-21.

[7] B. S. Baliga, *Tanjore District Handbook* (Madras: Government Press, 1975), pp. 351-363.

[8] Dharma Kumar, *Land and Caste in South India: Agricultural Labour in Madras Presidency in the Nineteenth Century* (Cambridge: Cambridge University Press, 1965), pp. 14-17. Washbrook seems to disagree with Kumar; he states that the imposition of *ryotwari* was largely responsible for giving Thanjavur its greater concentration of large landholdings (Washbrook, "Political Change," p. 22).

spread during the Maratha period. Grants were made to temples, mutts (Hindu monasteries), and charitable facilities to provide revenue for services and upkeep; allotments were given to individuals for personal service to the king or as payment to village servants. The British generally recognized the existence of *inam* lands and continued their exemption from land revenue in most cases.[9] The areas of *mirasi* and *inam* rights were largely exclusive, probably because at the time that *inam* grants were made the deltaic area of Thanjavur was largely settled. Thus in 1925 to 1926, 83 percent of the area under whole-village inams in the district were in the nondeltaic southwestern portion (the Pattukottai, Orthanad, and Arantangi taluks, and portions of Thanjavur and Mannargudi taluks).[10]

The third type of right, *zamindari*, was widespread in many parts of North India but minor in most of South India and certainly in Thanjavur. The *zamindari* system, which had evolved over many centuries from the time when the *zamin* was merely the government's revenue agent, granted a single individual or lineage proprietary rights over a large estate, often including several villages. In Thanjavur a few *zamindari* estates were created by the Nayak rajas through grants to local chieftains in return for military service.[11] They were located exclusively in the nondeltaic southwestern area of the district (Pattukottai, Orathanad, and Arantangi taluks).[12] In general, the British also recognized the existence of these estates and excluded them from *ryotwari* settlement, though not from land revenue.

Inamdari and *zamindari* lands in Thanjavur were cultivated by tenants under a variety of arrangements, most of them rather exploitative.[13] As elsewhere in India abolition of these increasingly criticized intermediaries was the first agrarian reform measure to be implemented in the years immediately following Independence. The Madras Estates Act of 1948 abolished all *zamindari* estates and whole-village *inams* in Thanjavur (minor *inams* were abolished by

[9] Baliga, *Tanjore Handbook*, pp. 370-372.

[10] K. N. Krishnaswami Ayyar, *Statistical Appendix, Together With A Supplement to The District Gazetter (1906) For Tanjore District*, ed. T. G. Rutherford (Madras: Govervnent Press, 1933), p. 21.

[11] Gough, "Caste," p. 20. See also G. Venkataramani, *Land Reform in Tamil Nadu* (Madras: Sangam Publishers for the Madras Institute of Development Studies, 1973), pp. 7-8.

[12] Ayyar, *Statistical Appendix*, pp. 21, 38-39.

[13] K. S. Sonachalam, *Land Reforms in Tamil Nadu: Evaluation of Implementation* (New Delhi: Oxford and IBH Publishing Co., 1970), p. 166.

an act in 1963).[14] The process of conversion into *ryotwari* lands was very drawn out (by 1956 only about 60 percent of the estate area had been converted), but by 1961 Thanjavur District was virtually a homogenous *ryotwari* area.[15] However, it is important to realize that many of the former *inamdars* and *zamindars* remained in possession of large areas of the former estates under a provision allowing for retention of lands under private cultivation.[16]

A brief word on how land rights are recorded under the *ryotwari* system is necessary to a later understanding of agrarian relations and reforms. The only thorough record of land rights is kept at the village level by the village accountant (*karnam*). The basic record (*adangal*) lists holdings by location and it is supposed to include the owner's name, the total extent under a given set of survey and subdivision numbers, the extent actually cultivated, and the name(s) of the cultivator(s) if different from the owner. Another account to be maintained by the *karnam* is the *Chitta*, which is supposed to list all lands owned in the village by a particular individual. The village records do not include lands owned by a resident outside the village. Deeds of ownership in the strict Western legal sense do not exist; rather, for each parcel of land owned singly or jointly a *patta* is issued stating the land revenue payable on that land and entitling the holder to sell or otherwise alienate the land. One individual may of course hold several *pattas* on different parcels of land. Designed to facilitate revenue collection rather than to keep track of the distribution of rights in land the land recording system has been a major obstacle to implementation of all types of agrarian reform in Thanjavur.[17] For instance, it lends itself to manipulation by the local landlords and the village *karnam*.

The historical evolution of Thanjavur's land system structure has yielded in the present an agro-economic structure with four widely noted characteristics: 1) a high degree of pressure on the land; 2) a relatively high degree of inequality in land ownership and control; 3) a high degree of tenancy; and 4) a large landless labor force. All these are theoretically related to agrarian radicalism.

[14] Sonachalam, *Land Reforms*, pp. 166-168.

[15] Government of Madras, Director of Statistics, *A Statistical Atlas of the Thanjavur District: Revised and Brought Up To The Decennium Ending Fasli 1360 (1950-51)* (Madras, 1965), p. 30.

[16] See Baliga, *Tanjore Handbook*, p. 377, and Sonachalam, *Land Reforms*, p. 167

[17] This problem has been widely noted, particularly with respect to tenancy reforms. See Government of India, Planning Commission, Socio-Economic Research Division, *Seminar on Land Reforms, Proceedings and Papers, 25th and 26th: February 1966* (New Delhi: undated), p. 18.

The pressure on the land is readily apparent. Not only does the district have a relatively high overall population density but also a high specific agrarian density when compared with Tamil Nadu and India as a whole (see Table 7).

Thanjavur has long had a reputation for extreme inequality in the distribution of land ownership.[18] Indeed, Dharma Kumar's study of landownership in the districts of Madras Presidency from 1853 to 1946 shows that Thanjavur had the sharpest inequalities over the entire period, although there was no increase in the degree of concentration over time.[19] She also concludes that her data probably underestimate the degree of inequality at any point in time.

TABLE 7

Pressure on Land in Thanjavur District, Tamil Nadu, and All India, 1971

	Thanjavur District	Tamil Nadu	All India
Per capita operated area (hectares)	0.18	0.19	0.30
Agrarian density (agricultural workers per 100 net sown acres)	65	60	35

SOURCES: For Thanjavur District and Tamil Nadu, see Tamil Nadu, Director of Agriculture, *World Agricultural Census, 1970-71 (Fasli 1380): Tamil Nadu*, 2 vols. (Madras, 1974), 1: 1, 22 (hereafter Tamil Nadu, *Agricultural Census*, and *Census of India, 1971*, ser. 19, *Tamil Nadu*, pt. X-B, *District Census Handbook: Village and Town Primary Census Abstract, Thanjavur*, 2 vols. (Madras: Director of Census Operations, 1972), 1: 3 (hereafter India, *District Census Handbook, 1971*); for all India, calculated from data in Government of India, Ministry of Agriculture and Irrigation, *All-India Report on Agricultural Census, 1970-71* by I. J. Naidu (New Delhi, 1975), p. 113 (hereafter *All-India Report*), and *Census of India, 1971: Provisional Population Totals*, Paper 1 of 1971—Supplement (New Delhi, 1971), p. 49 (hereafter *Census of India, 1971: Provisional Population Totals*).

[18] Kumar, *Land and Caste*, pp. 18-19.

[19] See Dharma Kumar, "Landownership and Inequality in Madras Presidency: 1853-54 to 1946-47," *The Indian Economic and Social History Review* 12 (July-September 1975): 229-261. Kumar's study utilizes the only available data for such an analysis, the distribution of *pattas* according to revenue assessment categories. It is very difficult to make reasonable inferences from these data about the distribution of ownership, but Kumar painstakingly categorizes and assesses the sources of error, thereby imparting more confidence to her final conclusions.

Various measures of land distribution for the 1961 to 1971 period compiled in Table 8 present a somewhat more qualified picture. The average holding size for the district is considerably lower than for Tamil Nadu or all India, but the summary measures of inequality of land distribution do not distinguish Thanjavur very clearly from the state and national patterns.[20] Looking at the two ends of the distribution, we find Thanjavur with a somewhat smaller percentage of large holdings and a somewhat larger percentage of so-called "dwarf" holdings. This may help to explain the similarity of the Gini coefficients. Taking into consideration the fact that a much greater proportion of Thanjavur's cultivated area is irrigated and that, therefore, a smaller area could be considered a "large holding" in Thanjavur, we can conclude that the distribution of holdings is in fact more unequal.

However, it is very possible that the degree of inequality of land ownership has been somewhat reduced in recent years. First, estate abolition did away with some of the largest holdings, but its effect was concentrated in the southwestern area where such estates were more common. Second, the Land Ceiling Act of 1961 placed a limitation of thirty standard areas (standardized according to quality of soil and irrigation in accordance with the revenue assessment categories) per undivided Hindu joint family.[21] Although the overall failure of ceiling legislation in India and in Tamil Nadu, due to both loopholes in the legislation and evasion of landlords, is an accepted fact,[22] this measure certainly squeezed the upper end of the distribution in Thanjavur. Table 9 shows a sharp decline in the percentage of wet area in Thanjavur under single *pattas* assessed at over Rs. 250.[23] It is possible but not probable that this decrease was entirely accounted for by *benami* ("bogus") transfers of land (to evade the land ceiling). Note for instance that the percentage area under *pattas* assessed at less than Rs. 10 doubled. It is unlikely that *benami* transfers alone account for this increase in small parcels. In addition, the impact of the land ceiling legislation on a limited

[20] All of these measures use available data on *operational* holdings that certainly underestimate the degree of inequality of *ownership*.

[21] Sonachalam, *Land Reforms*, pp. 63-87.

[22] See P. S. Appu, *Ceilings on Agricultural Holdings* (New Delhi: Ministry of Agriculture, 1972), and Venkataramani, *Land Reforms in Tamil Nadu*, pp. 36-38.

[23] I have used data on *pattas* for wet lands only because wet lands are predominant in the district. I have also confined myself to data for singly—rather than jointly—held *pattas* because the former cover about 75 percent of the wet area and because ownership by a single individual is a better indicator of concentration.

TABLE 8

Distribution of Land in Thanjavur District, Tamil Nadu, and All
India, 1961 and 1971

	Thanjavur District	Tamil Nadu	All India
Average size of operational holdings 1971 (hectares)[a]	1.23	1.50	2.30
Inequality of distribution (Gini coefficients for size distribution of operational holdings)			
1961[b]	.613	.618	NA
1971[c]	.691	.679	NA
Large holdings			
1961 (% of households cultivating more than 12.4 acres)[d]	5.1	6.0	NA
1971 (% of operational holdings over 12.4 acres)[e]	3.4	5.1	11.4
"Dwarf" holdings			
1961 (% of households cultivating less than 1.0 acre)[d]	15.8	14.8	NA
1971 (% of operational holdings under 1.24 acres)[e]	40.6	35.0	32.9

SOURCES: [a] Calculated from data in Tamil Nadu, *Agricultural Census*, 1: 1, 131, and *All-India Report*, p. 113.

[b] Calculated from data in *Census of India, 1961*, vol. 9, *District Census Handbook, Thanjavur*, 2 vols. (Madras: Superintendent of Census Operations, 1965), 1: 242 (hereafter India, *District Census Handbook, 1961*).

[c] Calculated from data in Tamil Nadu, *Agricultural Census*, 1: 181, 385.

[d] India, *District Census Handbook, 1961*, 1: 242.

[e] Tamil Nadu, *Agricultural Census*, 1: 181, 385, and *All-India Report*, p. 113.

NOTE: NA = data not available.

number of very large holdings in Thanjavur is also demonstrated
by the fact that as of 1967 one-third of the landowners affected
and one-third of the surplus declared in the state were in Thanjavur.[24] Overall, however, one cannot escape the conclusion that
the distribution of land ownership and control remains very une-

[24] Sonachalam, *Land Reforms*, p. 82.

TABLE 9

Distribution of Irrigated Area under Single Pattas of Various
Assessment in Thanjavur District, 1945-1970

	% of Wet Area under Single Pattas Assessed at (by rupee)				
	Under 10	10-50	50-250	over 250	
	Average Maximum and Minimum Holding Size (by acre)				
Year	under 1.25	1.25-6.3	6.3-31.5	over 31.5	Total Wet Area
1945-46	8.4%	25.9%	27.3%	38.0%	623,066
1955-56	9.7	30.7	30.8	28.8	591,265
1960-61	10.1	37.4	28.8	23.2	601,882
1965-66	14.4	40.3	29.3	16.1	651,015
1969-70	15.6	39.5	28.9	16.1	692,429
	Change, 1969-70/1945-46				
	+7.2	+13.6	+1.1	−21.9	

Sources: Computed from data in Government of Madras, *Report on the Settlement of the Land Revenue of the Districts in the Madras Province for Fasli 1355 (1945-46)* (Madras, 1947), pp. 45-53; ... *for Fasli 1365 (1955-56)* (Madras, 1957), pp. 45-53; ... *for Fasli 1370 (1960-61)* (Madras, 1963), pp. 46-57; in Government of Tamil Nadu, *Report on the Settlement of the Land Revenue in the Estates Taken Over and Not Taken Over Under the Act XXVI of 1948 in the Madras State for Fasli 1375 (1965-66)* (Madras, 1971), pp. 67-76; and in G. Venkataramani, *Land Reform in Tamil Nadu* (Madras: Sangam Publishers for the Madras Institute of Development Studies, 1973), pp. 81-100.

qual and that there is a very large proportion of holdings too small to be economically viable.

The significance of tenancy in the agro-economic structure of Thanjavur is less disputable, as can be seen in Table 10. Both the number of tenant-operated holdings and the area under pure tenancy cultivation are far in excess of the state and national averages. The actual incidence of tenancy in Thanjavur probably lies somewhere between the 1961 and 1971 figures.[25] In fact, districtwide

[25] The discrepancy between the 1961 and the 1971 figures is probably a result of over-reporting in 1961 and under-reporting in 1971. The 1961 data are from the census sample survey, in which self-reporting allowed many who were not actually tenants to claim that status. The 1971 data are from the agricultural census and are drawn from village land records, which certainly underestimated the amount of tenancy.

farm management studies in 1967/1968 and 1968/1969 concluded that about 22 percent of the operated area was under tenancy, and a study by the Tamil Nadu Agricultural College in the mid-1960s revealed that about 25 percent of operated holdings were under pure tenancy cultivation.[26] My own data and the results of a survey of sixty villages in the district show 19.2 and 27.2 percent of the area under tenancy respectively.[27] Thus, it seems safe to conclude that about one-fourth of the operational holdings and one-fifth to one-fourth of the operated area were under pure tenancy cultivation in the 1961 to 1971 period. The proportion of tenant-cum-owner cultivated holdings in Thanjavur is also higher than in Tamil Nadu and all India, but this figure is more difficult to interpret as it includes large owners "filling out" their holdings with leased acreage as well as the "dwarf" owner who leases in land to make a viable holding.

Traditionally there are two main types of tenancy in Thanjavur: *varam*, or sharecropping, and *kuttagai*, or lease tenancy for fixed payment in either cash or kind. Traditionally and perhaps as late as the 1940s *varam* was the most prevalent form.[28] According to the 1971 agricultural census (see Table 10) a much higher proportion of tenancy in Thanjavur is now on a fixed payment basis than in Tamil Nadu as a whole. The significance of this apparent change is a question I shall explore in greater detail in Chapter 8.

Finally, in turning to agricultural labor we find that although some historians have argued that the impact of British rule on peasant proprietorship created a large landless labor force in South India, Dharma Kumar has shown that in the pre-British period landless agricultural laborers were numerous in irrigated districts

[26] Government of India, Ministry of Agriculture and Irrigation, Directorate of Economics and Statistics, *Studies in the Economics of Farm Management in Thanjavur District (Tamil Nadu): Report for the Year 1967-68* by V. Shanmugasundaram (New Delhi: 1974), p. 43 (hereafter India, *Studies in the Economics of Farm Management in Thanjavur, 1967-68*); Government of India, Ministry of Agriculture and Irrigation, Directorate of Economics and Statistics, *Studies in the Economics of Farm Management in Thanjavur District (Tamil Nadu): Report for the Year 1968-69* by V. Shanmugasundaram (New Delhi: 1974), p. 34 (hereafter India, *Studies in the Economics of Farm Management in Thanjavur, 1968-69*); Coimbatore Agricultural College, Agricultural Economics and Rural Sociology Wing, "An Economic Appraisal of the Owner-Operated and Tenant-Operated Farms in Thanjavur District," mimeographed, undated, p. 2.

[27] See Chapter 3.

[28] K. G. Sivaswamy, *The Madras Ryotwari Tenant* (Madras: South Indian Federation of Agricultural Workers' Unions, 1948), pt. 1, pp. 63-65.

TABLE 10

Tenancy in Thanjavur District, Tamil Nadu, and All India, 1961 and 1971

	Thanjavur District	Tamil Nadu	All India
Pure tenancy holdings			
1961 (% of rural cultivating households)[a]	33.6	11.0	7.7
1971 (% of operational holdings)[b]	14.0	4.4	4.0
Pure tenancy area			
1961 (% of area under cultivation by pure tenant cultivating households)[c]	28.0	7.0	NA
1971 (area under pure tenancy holdings as % of total area)	12.3	3.1	2.4
Tenancy combined with ownership holdings			
1961 (% of rural cultivating households)[a]	19.1	NA	NA
1971 (% of operational holdings)[b]	7.4	3.4	3.9
Type of tenancy holdings (pure tenancy), 1971[d]			
% for fixed payment (cash or kind)	83.9	71.1	NA
% for share payment	12.3	28.3	NA

SOURCES: [a] Calculated from data in *India, District Census Handbook, 1961,* 1: 251-252.
[b] *Tamil Nadu, Agricultural Census,* 1: 186, 390, and *All-India Report,* p. 114.
[c] India, *District Census Handbook, 1961,* 1: 240.
[d] Calculated from Tamil Nadu, *Agricultural Census,* 1: 3-4, 133-134.

NOTE: NA = data not available.

such as Thanjavur and particularly in Thanjavur.[29] These were drawn largely from the lowest castes (the Harijan castes of today, namely Pallan and Paraiyan) and existed in a form of agrestic servitude. The large numbers of "attached" farm laborers (*pannaiyals*) in Thanjavur were a result of the greater demand for labor in irrigated paddy cultivation, the number of large holdings, and the unwillingness of Brahmin landowners to labor themselves.[30]

The current situation of agricultural labor in Thanjavur is clearly related to these historical facts. Although conditions of slavery died

[29] Kumar, *Land and Caste,* pp. 189-191.
[30] Ibid., pp. 42-45, 189-190.

out some time ago and the *pannaiyal* system has largely disappeared in the last twenty-five years, in 1971 agricultural labor (daily wage earners) still comprised 60 percent of the agricultural work force in Thanjavur (see Table 11), a much higher proportion than in Tamil Nadu or India as a whole. This can be explained in part by the many sections of the landowning community in Thanjavur that are unwilling to work in the fields (this unwillingness being no longer particular to Brahmins).[31] The data in Table 11 support this observation. A related fact is the low participation rate of females in the agricultural work force in Thanjavur, especially among cultivators.

Caste

In the preceding paragraphs I have mentioned the role of Brahmin landowners and Harijan laborers in the history of Thanjavur's agricultural economy. However, both historically and presently, the caste structure of Thanjavur District and its relationship to the agro-economic structure have been much more complex than these references would suggest.

Caste in Tamil Nadu is generally broken down into three main categories: Brahmin, non-Brahmin, and Adi-Dravida (or Harijan or Scheduled Caste). All of these categories are represented in the agrarian castes of Thanjavur, but unlike other districts where a single non-Brahmin caste is often dominant (as a combined function of numbers and economic status), Thanjavur District as a whole has no single dominant group.[32]

The only hard data available on representation of the various castes in Thanjavur's population are from the 1921 census. Table 12 illustrates the distribution of what were at that time and still largely are the wholly or primarily agricultural castes. I have also attempted to assign a modal agro-economic status to each of the groups, but it should be emphasized that especially in the non-Brahmin castes the economic status of caste members varies from area to area and even within a single village.

[31] Government of Tamil Nadu, Directorate of Agriculture, *Report of the Backward Classes Commission Tamil Nadu: 1970*, 2 vols. (Madras, 1975) 2: 167. Of the 441 cultivators surveyed in my research, less than half (44.2 percent) said they used family labor in their cultivation. Among the purely owning cultivators in the traditionally irrigated paddy growing areas of the district only about 15 percent said they use family labor in the fields.

[32] Ibid., pp. 162-163.

TABLE 11

Agricultural Labor in Thanjavur District, Tamil Nadu, and
All India, 1961 and 1971

	Thanjavur District	Tamil Nadu	All India
Agricultural laborers as % of agricultural workers, 1971[a]	59.2	48.5	37.5
Average number of family workers in household cultivation, 1961[b]	1.90	2.23	NA
Average number of hired workers in household cultivation, 1961[b]	2.72	1.84	NA
Female participation in agricultural work force, 1971 (females as % of each group)[a]			
Cultivators	7.2	14.1	12.4
Agricultural laborers	28.8	36.7	33.8
All agricultural workers	19.9	25.0	20.4

SOURCES: [a] For Thanjavur, calculated from data given in India, *District Census Handbook, 1971*, and for Tamil Nadu and all India, calculated from data in *Census of India, 1971: Provisional Population Totals*, pp. 66-69.
[b] India, *District Census Handbook, 1961*, 1: 242.

NOTE: NA = data not available.

Where numerical and relative economic superiority are combined with *geographic concentration* in a particular area of the district, a single caste may be dominant. In 1921 Brahmins were the dominant landowning group in certain areas of the district. Since then many Brahmins have left agriculture, the villages, and even the district, and at least their numerical presence has declined considerably.[33] Therefore the single most important landowning caste in

[33] Kathleen Gough, "Harijans in Thanjavur," in *Imperialism and Revolution in South Asia*, ed. Kathleen Gough and Hari P. Sharma (New York and London: Monthly Review Press, 1973), p. 230. See also Andre Beteille, *Castes, Old and New: Essays in Social Structure and Social Stratification* (Bombay: Asia Publishing House, 1969), pp. 171-173.

TABLE 12

Agricultural Castes in Thanjavur District, 1921, and
Their Relationship to Agro-Economic Structure

Caste Category	Caste and Caste Title	% of Population	Modal Agro-Economic Status
Brahmin	Brahmin	6.2	Landlords
Non-Brahmin	Vellalas (Padayachis)	9.9	Small landlords/ cultivators/ tenants
	Vanniars (Mudaliars, Pillais)	11.1	Landlords
	Kallars (Nattars)	9.2	Small landlords/ cultivators/ tenants
	Agamudayans	5.2	Cultivators/tenants
	Idayars (Konars)	3.4	Cultivators/tenants
	Ambalakarars (Servai)	2.6	Cultivators/tenants
	Odayars	1.7	Cultivators/tenants
Harijans/ Adi-Dravidas	Paraiyars	15.0	Agricultural labor
	Pallan	7.0	Agricultural labor
	Valayan	3.9	Agricultural labor
All agricultural castes		75.2	

SOURCE: India, *District Census Handbook, 1961*, 1: 16-17.

Thanjavur today is probably the Vellalas, though again they are much stronger in some areas than in others. The Kallars have become increasingly powerful as their economic status has improved over the last fifty years, and in sizable areas they are the dominant caste. The Vanniars and Agamudayans have also improved their economic position, and the former are dominant in some areas.

The main Scheduled Caste, the Paraiyars, was the largest single caste in 1921, and it has been estimated that today all the Scheduled Castes form an even greater share of the district's agricultural population.[34] They and the Brahmins are economically the most ho-

[34] *Backward Classes Commission Report*, pp. 162-163.

mogeneous groups in Thanjavur. As Dharma Kumar has argued, this suggests a strong relationship between social and economic status at the high and low ends of the structure.[35] The significance of this fact and of the looser relationship between social and economic status among the non-Brahmin castes for our understanding of agrarian radicalism in Thanjavur will be fully explored in Chapter 6.

AGRICULTURE

The Agricultural Process

As can be seen in Table 13, irrigated paddy cultivation is far and away the most important agricultural process in Thanjavur District. There are two main patterns of this type of cultivation: a single crop known as *samba* and a double crop sequence known as *kuruvai* and *thaladi*. In 1970/1971 the gross cropped area under irrigated paddy was about 1.675 million acres, of which about 46.8 percent was under the single crop, *samba*. The area under *kuruvai* and *thaladi* was 30.6 and 22.6 percent of the gross cropped area respectively. In other words, there was a 60:40 division of the net irrigated paddy area into single and double crop patterns.

The single crop is prevalent in areas of the district where water supply and control are relatively inferior, though it should be noted that the quality of water supply and control within many villages is so variable that both patterns may be found in a single village. Cultivation of the *samba* crop generally begins in August (after water is received in the canals) with preparation of the paddy nurseries. The seedlings are transplanted to the main fields four to five weeks later, a process that employs large numbers of female laborers. The duration of the *samba* crop is about 180 days. By late October and early November the level of water in the canals is considerably lower than at the outset of the season, and the *samba* crop depends heavily in its growth cycle on watering from the Northeast Monsoon that arrives in the district about that time and seldom fails. The crop is harvested in mid-January to mid-February, depending on the time of planting. Harvest is the most labor-intensive operation in the process, involving large numbers of male and female laborers to cut, carry, and thresh the paddy. In many areas, depending on the amount of residual moisture in the soil, a pulse crop is sown in the paddy field at the time of harvest.

[35] Kumar, *Land and Caste*, p. 190.

TABLE 13

Area under Principal Crops in Thanjavur District, 1971

Crop	% of Gross Cropped Irrigated Area	% of Gross Cropped Unirrigated Area
Paddy	95.20	15.76
Other foodgrains (mainly ragi and pulses)	0.99	36.76
Commercial crops		
Groundnut (peanut)	1.61	19.60
Coconut	0.08	10.77
Gingelly and other oil seeds	0.03	3.81
Sugarcane	0.55	0.03
Others	1.54	13.27
All crops	100.00	100.00

SOURCE: Tamil Nadu, *Agricultural Census*, 2: 389-400.

Double crop cultivation must begin somewhat earlier than single crop, and this is of course the main reason for its dependence on superior water supply, including earlier arrival of the freshes. The *kuruvai* nursery preparation begins in June, and transplantation takes place three to four weeks later. The duration of the *kuruvai* crop is about 120 days, and it is ready for harvest in mid- to late October. Whereas the Northeast Monsoon is essential to the success of the *samba* crop, it is a threat to the *kuruvai* crop because the heavy rains could damage the ripened grain if it is not harvested in time. The *thaladi* nursery is prepared in October, the seedlings transplanted in November, and the crop harvested in February or March.

A much inferior double crop pattern, the *Udu* or *Ottadan* system, is used in areas where water supply and control are more than adequate for a single crop but not sufficient for the normal double crop. *Kuruvai* and *samba* seeds are sown together as early as possible. All the plants are cut at the time of harvest, but the *samba* variety sprouts again and is harvested in February or March. In other areas where water supply during the *thaladi* season is marginal and the soil is sandy groundnut is often raised in lieu of *thaladi* paddy. It is also raised as a dry crop beginning in June in unirrigated areas.

Agricultural Development

Prior to 1960 there was little change in the traditional agricultural process in Thanjavur. Fluctuations in yield and total production of paddy were due almost entirely to variations in irrigation conditions (the timing and flow of river/canal water as determined by rainfall in the catchment areas of the Cauvery), weather conditions in the district, and net sown area. These factors, especially the first, continued to bear heavily on agricultural productivity, but in 1960 and 1961 changes in technology began to play an important role as well. Starting in that year, Thanjavur was a target of major agricultural development efforts conceived by the Government of India and implemented largely by the state government.

The first of these was the Intensive Agricultural District Programme (IADP), launched in 1960/1961.[36] The goal of the IADP was to increase farm-level productivity by making available and encouraging the cultivator to adopt a "package" of improved agricultural practices. Thanjavur was chosen as a site for the IADP precisely because of its relatively assured irrigation and good infrastructure. However, little positive change took place during the first five years of the program. Moderate increases in fertilizer consumption (see Table 14) were not translated into productivity gains for lack of a genuine yield-increasing technology and favorable cost-benefit ratios.[37]

The second phase in Thanjavur's recent development began in 1965/1966 with the introduction of an improved new paddy variety, ADT. 27. Developed by the local research station at Aduthurai, ADT. 27 was a short-duration variety suitable for *kuruvai* cultivation that could absorb somewhat larger doses of fertilizer and give significantly higher yields. In spite of very poor weather in 1965/1966 and 1966/1967 ADT. 27 caught on quickly with the result that the area under *kuruvai* cultivation almost doubled by 1967/1968 (see Table 14). Because ADT. 27's major effect was to enhance double cropping, little attention was paid during this period to the *samba* and *thaladi* crops or paddy agronomics with the result that overall paddy productivity did not improve.[38]

[36] See Government of India, Ministry of Food and Agriculture, *India's Food Crisis and Steps to Meet It: Report By the Agricultural Production Team* (New Delhi, 1959).

[37] Dorris D. Brown, *Agricultural Development in India's Districts* (Cambridge, Mass.: Harvard University Press, 1971), pp. 93-97. Brown found that the indices for change in output and yield from the 1956 to 1961 period to the 1961 to 1965 period were not significant in the case of Thanjavur.

[38] James Q. Harrison, "Agricultural Modernization and Income Distribution: An

TABLE 14

Agricultural Change in Thanjavur District, 1960-1972

	Nitrogenous Fertilizer Distribution[a] (tons of nutrient)	Area under Kuruvai as % of Gross Paddy Area[b]	Area under ADT. 27 and HYV as % of Gross Paddy Area[b]	Paddy Yields by Crop[c] (kg./acre)			
				Kuruvai	Samba	Thaladi	Combined
1960-61	3597	21.8	—	977	911	869	911
1961-62	4188	20.6	—	1007	1061	1025	1025
1962-63	5265	21.6	—	1049	917	844	917
1963-64	5804	18.7	—	977	904	856	892
1964-65	8380	18.2	—	1055	1076	984	1058
1965-66	12807	19.9	0.32	1042	897	735	907
1966-67	14825	17.4	12.89	835	926	758	840
1967-68	17867	36.2	31.21	1146	838	558	852
1968-69	18947	31.3	31.51	1175	1141	890	1067
1969-70	21005	30.4	27.51	1329	1068	810	1081
1970-71	23951	30.6	39.35	1156	1067	930	1050
1971-72	NA	30.5	NA	1302	1209	1129	1214

SOURCES: [a] Government of India, Ministry of Food, Agriculture, Community Development and Cooperation, Department of Agriculture, Expert Committee on Assessment and Evaluation, *Modernising Indian Agriculture: Fourth Report on the Intensive Agricultural District Programme (1960-68)*, vol. 2, *District Chapters* (New Delhi, undated), p. 35, and data provided by Intensive Agricultural District Programme (IADP) Office, Thanjavur.

[b] Computed from data provided by IADP Office, Thanjavur.

[c] Data provided by IADP Office, Thanjavur.

NOTE: NA = data not available.

The third phase of agricultural development efforts in Thanjavur began in 1968/1969 with the introduction of internationally developed high-yielding paddy varieties such as IR-8 and IR-5 (which were more responsive to fertilizer than ADT. 27) through the Government of India's High-Yielding Varieties Programme (HYVP). At the same time a program of adaptive research was initiated in the district to develop new varieties more suited to Thanjavur conditions. By 1970/1971 two or three such varieties had been identified. While the double crop area stabilized, these new efforts resulted in increased yields for all three paddy crops, and by 1971/1972 Thanjavur's combined paddy yield had increased about 33 percent over the 1960/1961 figures as compared with an all-India increase of about 12 percent over the same period. Also by 1970/1971 use of nitrogenous fertilizer per cropped acre had reached a level in Thanjavur roughly three times the all-India level.

Although it is now recognized that the scope of agricultural change in India during the late 1960s and early 1970s, the period of the so-called Green Revolution, was not as great as initially believed,[39] and although the magnitude of change in rice-growing areas was substantially less than that in wheat-growing areas,[40] it is clear that during the period 1960 to 1972 Thanjavur experienced significant changes in agricultural technology, primarily through the varietal innovation and particularly if these changes are viewed against the backdrop of a long-standing, traditional system.

THE POLITICAL CONTEXT OF AGRARIAN RADICALISM

In Chapter 3 I justified in some detail employing Communist panchayat-level electoral performance as an indicator of agrarian radicalism in Thanjavur. At this point I would like to put Communist electoral performance in the context of wider Communist electoral fortunes and the electoral performance of all parties in the district.

In Table 15 it is evident that although the Communist percentage of the vote in Thanjavur for the state legislative assembly has de-

---

Economic Analysis of the Impact of New Seed Varieties on the Crop Production of Large and Small Farms in India" (Ph.D. dissertation, Princeton University, 1972). See also Intensive Agricultural District Programme, Thanjavur, "A Note on Yield Trends of Paddy in Thanjavur District," typewritten, undated, p. 4.

[39] See Bandhudas Sen, *The Green Revolution in India: A Perspective* (New York: John Wiley & Sons, 1974).

[40] See Wolf Ladejinsky, "How Green is the Indian Green Revolution," *Economic and Political Weekly* 8 (December 29, 1973): A133-A144.

clined since 1952, it has remained high relative to Communist voting at the state and national levels throughout the period. This comparison is all the more striking when we consider that in Thanjavur Communist success has been won almost exclusively in rural areas whereas in most other areas of India Communist strength has been heavily urban.[41] Were we able to compare Communist electoral performance in Thanjavur with its performance in *rural* constituencies elsewhere in India, we would expect to find an even greater gap. Thus, although in absolute terms Communist electoral

TABLE 15

Communist Voting in Thanjavur District, Tamil Nadu, and All India, 1952-1971

	% of Valid Votes Polled in Legislative Assembly Elections				
	1951	1957	1962	1967	1971(-72)
Thanjavur District					
CPI	26.32	19.11	15.86	6.12	7.43
CPM	—	—	—	8.69	4.22
Total	26.32	19.11	15.86	14.81	14.65
Tamil Nadu					
CPI	12.96	7.40	7.72	1.80	2.32
CPM	—	—	—	4.07	1.65
Total	12.96	7.40	7.72	5.87	3.97
All India					
CPI	4.38	9.36	10.42	4.13	4.18*
CPM	—	—	—	4.60	4.62
Total	4.38	9.36	10.42	8.73	8.80

SOURCES: For Thanjavur and Tamil Nadu data, H. K. Ghazi, *Report on the Fifth General Elections in Tamil Nadu, 1971* (Madras: Government of Tamil Nadu, 1974), pp. 449, 472-473. For all-India data, Robert L. Hardgrave, Jr., *India: Government and Politics in a Developing Nation*, 2d ed. (New York: Harcourt Brace Jovanovich, 1975), pp. 182-183.

NOTES: CPI = Communist Party of India; CPM = Communist Party of India (Marxist)
* The all-India data are for 1972 when the "de-linked" legislative assembly elections were held in most states.

[41] Bhabani Sen Gupta, *Communism in Indian Politics* (New York: Columbia University Press, 1972), p. 291.

performance in Thanjavur is weak, its relative strength lends weight to my assertion that the phenomenon of agrarian radicalism in Thanjavur is significant and worthy of close study.

Another point that emerges from the data in Table 15 is the similarity of the patterns of Communist electoral performance over time in Thanjavur and in the state as a whole. This suggests a relationship between the fortunes of the state Party and developments in the district.[42] It should also be noted that although the Communist split is clearly reflected in the Thanjavur electoral data, as of 1971 it apparently had not weakened the underlying support base for Communist *parties*.

This brings me to a consideration of Communist electoral strength in relation to the strength of other political parties in Thanjavur over time. From the data in Table 16 the following conclusions can be drawn. First, the Congress party dominated electoral politics in Thanjavur through the 1962 general elections. The Communists were a force to be reckoned with in the 1952 elections, but after that they were unable to translate their popular vote into seats. Meanwhile the Dravida Munnetra Kazhagam (DMK) was gaining electoral strength, and by 1967 it was able to win the largest share of seats. In that same election the CPM undoubtedly benefiting from an electoral alliance with the DMK, suddenly emerged with three out of twenty-three assembly seats. The growing power of the DMK was demonstrated again in 1971 when their alliance with the CPI instead of the CPM kept the latter from winning any seats and enabled the former to win more seats than it had since 1952. The stability of the total Communist percentage of the vote after 1962 in contrast to the fluctuations in the share of seats won suggests that while nonlocal political factors determined the ability of the Communists to translate votes into parliamentary strength, local factors enabled them to maintain a core of popular support in the district.

The data on the results of panchayat elections in Thanjavur in Table 17 add to this impression. In spite of the proliferating tendencies in local-level politics reflected in the numerous parties represented and independents elected, and in spite of the shifting fortunes of the Congress and DMK (which parallel the general election results), the Communists maintained, even increased slightly,

[42] See Andre Beteille, *Studies in Agrarian Social Structure* (New Delhi: Oxford University Press, 1974), p. 170.

TABLE 16

Legislative Assembly Election Results in Thanjavur District, 1952-1971

Party	1952		1957		1962		1967		1971	
	No. of Seats	% of Vote	No. of Seats	% of Vote	No. of Seats	% of Vote	No. of Seats	% of Vote	No. of Seats	% of Vote
Communist Party of India	6	26.3	0	19.1	1	15.9	1	6.1	3	7.4
Communist Party of India (Marxist)	—	—	—	—	—	—	3	8.7	0	4.2
Dravida Munnetra Kazhagam (DMK)	—	—	0	11.9	4	26.8	9	33.3	17	44.3
Indian National Congress (R)	9	40.0	18	48.2	15	45.4	8	43.7	—	—
Indian National Congress (O)	—	—	—	—	—	—	—	—	1	37.8
Praja Socialist Party	—	—	1	2.0	—	—	1	2.3	1	2.7
Swatantra Party	—	—	—	—	0	3.5	—	—	—	—
Independents	4	33.6	1	18.8	0	8.4	1	5.9	1	3.6

SOURCE: H. K. Ghazi, *Report on the Fifth General Elections in Tamil Nadu, 1971* (Madras: Government of Tamil Nadu, 1974), pp. 472-473.

TABLE 17

Panchayat Election Results in Thanjavur District, 1960-1970

Party	% of Panchayat Presidencies Won by Candidates Affiliated with Parties		
	1960 (N = 1500)*	1965 (N = 1617)**	1970 (N = 1627)***
Communist Party of India	9.1	4.0	4.3
Communist Party of India (Marxist)	—†	1.9	3.1
Communist Party (unidentified)	—	4.5	5.4
Dravida Munnetra Kazhagam (DMK)	7.1	16.3	31.9
Indian National Congress	70.8	55.8	—
Indian National Congress (O)	—	—	28.3
Indian National Congress (R)	—	—	0.1
Praja Socialist Party	0.5	0.3	0.4
Swatantra Party	0.2	0.4	0.4
Dravida Kazhagam	2.6	2.9	1.9
Tamil Arasu Kazhagam	0.1	0.1	—
Muslim League	0.5	0.5	0.6
Republican Party	—	12.5	23.0

* The total number of panchayats in 1960 was 1,555; electoral data for 55 were not available.

** The total number of panchayats in 1965 was 1,622; electoral data for 5 were not available.

*** The total number of panchayats in 1970 was 1,637; electoral data for 10 were not available.

† All omissions due to fact that party either did not exist at the time of the election or did not run.

their share of the panchayat presidencies won over the period 1960 to 1970.

I would therefore suggest that the minor but persistent theme of Communist strength in the electoral politics of Thanjavur reflects an agrarian radicalism rooted in some enduring characteristics of

Thanjavur District. The theories of agrarian radicalism discussed in Chapter 2 offered many possible answers to the question of what those characteristics might be, and my overview in the preceding pages establishes a prima facie case for linking agrarian radicalism in Thanjavur to the impact of modernization, pressure on the land, proletarianization of the agro-economic structure, and technological change.

A preliminary statistical assessment of the relationship between many of these characteristics and agrarian radicalism as measured by Communist panchayat control is presented in Table 18. It can be seen that agrarian radicalism is not significantly correlated at the district level with my two crude indicators of modernization, overall development and literacy. And although it is positively correlated with the extent of cultivation and irrigation, there is no significant correlation with agrarian density and tenancy nor with agricultural development. In fact, only two factors stand out as

TABLE 18

Correlates of Communist Panchayat Control in Thanjavur District

Panchayat Characteristics	Communist Panchayat Control (N = 1490)
Overall development index, 1971	−.015
Literates as % of total population, 1971	.025
Cultivated area as % of total area, 1971	.103*
Irrigated area as % of cultivated area, 1971	.088*
Agrarian density, 1971 (agricultural workers per unit area)	.023
Area under "registered" tenancy as % of total cultivated area, 1971	.052
Agricultural laborers as % of total agricultural workers, 1971	.211*
Scheduled Castes as % of total population, 1971	.328*
Agricultural development rating, 1971	.007

NOTES: The variable "Communist Panchayat Control" is the same as the measure of agrarian radicalism described in Chapter 3. That is, each panchayat received a score of 0 to 3 according to whether a Communist won the presidency of the panchayat in none, one, two, or three of the elections held in 1960, 1965, and 1971.

* Significant at .001 level.

strong correlates of agrarian radicalism: the percentage of agricultural laborers in the agricultural work force and the percentage
of Scheduled Castes in the total population. Interpreting these
correlations requires a closer examination of the ecology and agro-
economic structure of Thanjavur District.

CHAPTER 5

Agrarian Variability in Thanjavur: The Agro-Economic Zones

THE SOCIO-ECONOMIC DIVERSITY of the Indian subcontinent is almost an article of faith among even the most casual observers of Indian society. In practice, however, the recognition of variability is often either not applied or not carried far enough in the efforts of social scientists to comprehend a given phenomenon. This may result from either the desire to generalize or, as mentioned in Chapter 3, from limitations in the method of study.

While some degree of generalization is the ultimate objective and methodological limitations are unavoidable in all social science research, it is especially important to attend to local variability in the study of agrarian questions. As Andre Beteille has observed, differences in agrarian relations are primarily adaptations to different ecological conditions, which in India are highly variable.[1] Different agro-climatic conditions (topography, soil, irrigation, rainfall, etc.) require different agricultural technologies, which in turn give rise to different agro-economic structures. This is particularly true in the case of paddy cultivation, which is agronomically locality-specific.[2]

Mattei Dogan has stressed the importance of these complex interrelationships in his analysis of agrarian communism in France and Italy:

> The granite soil votes for the Right and the chalky soil for the Left. . . . There is surely no direct causality in the rigorous sense of the word, but there is some correspondence between the nature of the soil, agrarian landscape, type of dwelling, distribution

[1] See Andre Beteille, *Studies in Agrarian Social Structure* (New Delhi: Oxford University Press, 1974), pp. 26, 144-145.

[2] See Bandhudas Sen, *The Green Revolution in India: A Perspective* (New York: John Wiley & Sons, 1974); also John W. Mellor, *The New Economics of Growth: A Strategy for India and the Developing World* (Ithaca: Cornell University Press, 1976), pp. 56-58.

of land ownership, degree of stratification of society, the stronger persistence of tradition, and political orientation.[3]

While I would agree with Dogan that there is no tight, mechanical linkage between ecological conditions, agro-economic structure, and agrarian relations,[4] I would argue that these relationships deserve considerable emphasis in the search for the sources of agrarian radicalism.

The importance of regional diversity in agro-ecology and agro-economic structure in relation to agrarian movements in South India has been noted by some scholars.[5] With the exception of Andre Beteille, however, outside observers of Thanjavur District have tended to see a homogeneous entity. For instance, in her study of *India's Green Revolution* Francine Frankel treats Thanjavur as a unit and concludes that because they co-occur, technological change in agriculture, deterioration in landlord-tenant relations, and agrarian unrest in the district are causally related.[6] Donald Zagoria's statistical study of the all-India district-level relationship between agro-economic variables and Communist voting also yields conclusions that are misleading if not wholly erroneous because the analysis does not take into account intradistrict variability.[7] As Beteille has pointed out, both studies unwittingly misrepresent synchronic internal diversity as evidence of diachronic change.[8]

This confusion is understandable if we recall from Chapter 4 the prominence and apparent association with agrarian radicalism at the district level of features such as high density, dwarf holdings and tenancy, and technological change and high literacy rates. But

[3] See Mattei Dogan, "Political Cleavage and Social Stratification in France and Italy," in *Party Systems and Voter Alignments: Cross-National Perspectives,* ed. Seymour M. Lipset and Stein Rokkan (New York: The Free Press, 1967), pp. 129-195.

[4] Here and throughout this study I will use the term ecological in the narrow geophysical sense, that is, to refer only to natural conditions affecting modes of agricultural production, such as soil, topography, irrigation, rainfall, and other climatic conditions.

[5] See Andre Beteille, "Agrarian Movements in India," mimeographed, undated, p. 4; also Robert L. Hardgrave, Jr., "The Kerala Communists: Contradictions of Power," in *Radical Politics in South Asia,* ed. Paul R. Brass and Marcus F. Franda (Cambridge, Mass.: The M.I.T. Press, 1973), pp. 138-139.

[6] Beteille, *Studies,* pp. 142-170; Francine R. Frankel, *India's Green Revolution: Economic Gains and Political Costs* (Princeton, N.J.: Princeton University Press, 1971), pp. 81-118.

[7] Donald S. Zagoria, "The Ecology of Peasant Communism in India," *The American Political Science Review* 65 (March 1971): 144-160.

[8] Beteille, *Studies,* p. 145.

correlations based on the local panchayat unit lead me to question most of these apparent associations and to focus instead on the role of agricultural labor and caste status. Analysis of intradistrict variability in agro-ecology and agro-economic structure will begin to help clarify the meaning of these findings.

My research has shown that Thanjavur District can be divided into five "agro-economic zones" based on covariant differences in agro-ecology and agro-economic structure. Before describing these zones, three interrelated points of caution are in order. First, the differences between the zones along any given dimension are sometimes sharp but more often a matter of gradation. Second, no single variable or even set of variables clearly differentiates all the zones from each other (although one set of variables may better distinguish one or two zones from the others). The zonal distinctions are best described in terms of typical patterns derived from the complex interaction of several ecological and agro-economic variables. Such multidimensional distinctions are difficult to grasp intuitively but are no less significant for our understanding of the sources of agrarian radicalism. Third, although the zonal distinctions are an effort to embrace diversity, one effect of using them is a degree of oversimplification of reality. The zones are in fact statistical creations; no clear zonal boundaries exist in reality. The zones "overlap" in reality, and "maverick" villages exist in every zone. Despite these limitations, the importance of the zonal distinctions is demonstrated by the contribution they make to an understanding of agrarian radicalism in Thanjavur.

ECOLOGICAL CONDITIONS

The configuration of the five agro-economic zones is described by the map in Figure 7 and by the data in Table 19. Zone 3 is the largest in terms of area and Zone 5 the smallest. Zones 1 through 3 have a disproportionate share of settlements and population compared to their share of the district area. This fact reflects the single most important basis of differentiation between the zones: differences in the availability and the quality of water supply through irrigation. The first level of difference is *whether or not there is any irrigation at all*. In this respect, Zone 5, the upland dry area in the extreme western and southwestern section of the district, is most clearly differentiated from the other four zones (see Table 20). Only 50 percent of the zone 5 cultivated area is irrigated, and two-

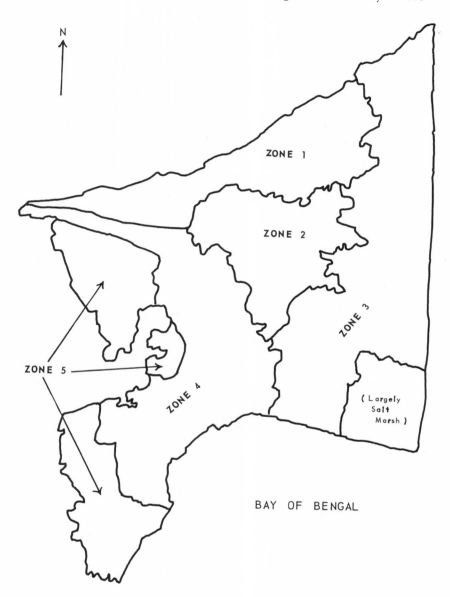

FIGURE 7. Agro-Economic Zones of Thanjavur District, 1971

TABLE 19

Agro-Economic Zones of Thanjavur District

Zone Number	Zone Name	Taluks Comprised	% of Total Area, 1971 (N = 1550)	% of Population, 1971 (N = 1555)	% of Cultivated Area, 1971 (N = 1555)	% of Panchayats, 1961 (N = 1498)
1	Old Delta-Cauvery	All of Kumbakonam; portions of Thanjavur, Papanasam, and Mayuram	17.9	25.8	20.3	25.4
2	Old Delta-Central	Portions of Nannilam, Papanasam, and Mannargudi	14.1	15.7	17.0	17.8
3	Old Delta-Coastal	All of Sirkali, Tiruthuraipoondi,* Nagapattinam; portions of Nannilam and Mannargudi	28.5	30.8	31.2	31.2
4	New Delta-CMP	All of Pattukottai; major portion of Orathanad; small portion of Arantangi and Thanjavur	20.2	18.3	19.2	14.7
5	Dry Area-Uplands	Major portion of Arantangi; small portions of Thanjavur and Orathanad	15.8	9.4	9.3	10.9

Notes: * Vedaranyam Block is excluded from this table because it is almost completely covered by salt marshes.
N = number of panchayats included in breakdown.

TABLE 20
Ecological Characteristics of the Agro-Economic Zones

Zone	Cultivated Area as % of Total Area, 1971	Irrigated Area as % of Cultivated Area, 1971	Canal Irrigated Area as % of Total Irrigated Area, 1971	Soil Quality Rating (mean), 1961	Average Overall Land Value, 1961 (Rs./acre)
1/Old Delta-Cauvery (N=390)	68.5	82.6	91.9	3.7	3151
2/Old Delta-Central (N=267)	73.4	87.5	87.4	3.3	2088
3/Old Delta-Coastal (N=468)	69.7	88.4	87.4	3.5	2208
4/New Delta-CMP (N=220)	60.1	73.4	75.6	2.1	1816
5/Dry Area-Uplands (N=163)	41.5	50.9	36.6	1.0	867
District Average (N=1498)	65.6	80.5	81.3	3.0	2221

SOURCE: Panchayat-level data set compiled by the author. Zonal figures are averages of figures for panchayats in that zone.

NOTE: N = number of panchayats in the zone.

thirds of this area is irrigated by rain-fed tanks rather than canals, with the consequence that a much lower proportion of the zone 5 total area is cultivated than in the other four zones.

The second level of difference is the *pervasiveness of canal irrigation* in those areas where this type of irrigation is the dominant source of water supply. Thus, Zone 4 is differentiated from Zones 1 through 3 by the somewhat lower proportion of canal irrigated area. Another distinguishing feature not observable in the statistics is relevant: the historical *continuity* of canal irrigation. Here again the "New Delta" (Zone 4), brought under canal irrigation only thirty to forty years ago by the Cauvery-Mettur Project, is contrasted with the "Old Delta" (Zones 1-3), which has been under canal irrigation for centuries.

A third level of difference, not directly observable in the data at hand, is the *quality and dependability of water delivery and management* under canal irrigation.[9] At this level some important differences emerge between Zones 1, 2, and 3, which otherwise appear very similar. Because it is nearer to the source the area of Zone 1 (Old Delta-Cauvery) receives water earlier and has better control over delivery to and drainage from the field. These are important factors affecting paddy cultivation, especially double crop paddy.[10]

On the other hand, the Zone 2 area and to an even greater extent the Zone 3 area, being farther from the source and relatively low-lying (especially the coastal area of Zone 3), suffer from proportionately later water delivery, poor irrigation, and poor drainage. The drainage problem is exacerbated in Zone 3 by heavy rainfall during the Northeast Monsoon and other coastal storms that often result in flooding and submersion of the paddy plants. The late arrival of water and drainage problems interact to make double cropping difficult and risky. The late water delays *kuruvai* planting, which in turn delays the harvest and exposes the ripened crop to damage from the Monsoon.[11] The liabilities of the low terrain in

[9] Ibid., p. 26.

[10] See Clyde Geoffrey Swenson, "The Effect of Increases in Rice Production on Employment and Income Distribution in Thanjavur District, South India" (Ph.D. dissertation, Michigan State University, 1973). See also Clifford Geertz, *Agricultural Involution: The Processes of Ecological Change in Indonesia* (Berkeley, Ca.: University of California Press, 1963), p. 31.

[11] A study of Kunnalur Village in Tiruthuraipoondi taluk of Thanjavur District discusses the depressing effect of "frequent flooding" on paddy yields during the Northeast Monsoon and other storms. See *Census of India, 1961*, vol. 9, *Madras*, pt. 6, *Village Survey Monographs, 11, Kunnalur* (Madras: Superintendent of Census Operations, 1964), pp. 2-3 (hereafter *Census of India, 1961: Village Monograph—Kun-*

Zones 2 and 3 may extend beyond the harvest. Transport from the village to market is also severely hampered by flooding so that cultivators in the area are forced to sell their grain after the bulk of *kuruvai* crop has reached the market and prices have dropped sharply.[12]

As can be seen in Table 20, soil quality in the zones tends to covary with irrigation. This is of course due to the deposit of alluvial soil in the deltaic areas. The soil in Zone 5 is almost exclusively red laterite, in Zone 4 a combination of red laterite and black soil, and in Zones 1 through 3 largely alluvial and clay. However, the soil in sizable areas of Zones 2 and 3 near the coast is sandy and saline and is poor by comparison with the soil of Zone 1.[13]

The zonal differences in water supply and soil quality entail differences in potential productivity and risk that are reflected in the average land values in each zone (see Table 20). Most interesting is the spread between land values in Zones 1 on the one hand and Zones 2 are 3 on the other. This demonstrates the importance of the differences in the *quality* of irrigation that are often overlooked and may have important agro-economic consequences.

Modes of Production and Agro-Economic Structures

The ecological variations just described give rise to zonal differences in mode of production and agro-economic structure. Both the gross and subtle distinctions in quantity and quality of water supply and soil quality are manifest in the cropping pattern variables in Table 21.[14] Overall cropping intensity is highest in Zone 1 and lowest in Zone 5 (it should be noted that Zone 4 does not trail far behind Zones 2 and 3). The greater pervasiveness and adaptation of canal irrigation in Zones 1 through 3 as opposed to Zone 4 is reflected in the lower percentage of net sown area to paddy in Zone 4. However, within the area sown to paddy in Zone 4 a greater percentage is double cropped than in Zone 3, illustrating the se-

---

nalur). This problem is also highlighted in Intensive Agricultural District Programme, Thanjavur, "Problems in Implementing Samba Conversion Programme in Thanjavur District," typewritten, undated, pp. 3-5.

[12] *Census of India, 1961: Village Monograph—Kunnalur*, p. 6.

[13] B. S. Baliga, *Tanjore District Handbook* (Madras: Government Press, 1957), p. 4.

[14] Data for these variables were not available at the village panchayat level. I have therefore used data for the taluks that are most representative of each zone and have followed the same procedure in several instances below.

TABLE 21

Cropping Patterns in the Agro-Economic Zones, 1970-1971,
by Representative Taluk

Zone	Taluk	Cropping Intensity (gross crop area/net sown area)	Net Area under Paddy as % of Net Sown Area	% of Area Double-Crop Paddy (paddy[II]/ gross area under paddy)
1/Old Delta-Cauvery	Kumbakonam	2.44	81.1	33.5
2/Old Delta-Central	Nannilam	1.31	92.8	18.7
3/Old Delta-Coastal	Nagapattinam	1.33	88.9	10.9
4/New Delta-CMP	Pattukottai	1.29	77.0	20.8
5/Dry Area-Uplands	Arantangi	1.13	76.6	13.9

SOURCE: Data provided by IADP Office, Thanjavur.

verity of constraints on double cropping in Zone 3.[15] Zone 1 also
has the highest incidence of double cropping in paddy.

The most obvious economic consequence of these ecological
variations is the size of population that can be supported by the
land, as shown by the population density data in column 1 of Table
22. A more precise measure is agrarian density, or the ratio of
agricultural workers to productive resources, that is, land (see column 4 of Table 22). As would be expected, Zone 1 has the highest
agrarian density and Zone 5 the lowest. It is interesting to note that
Zone 3 has a lower agrarian density than either Zones 2 or 4, again
demonstrating productivity constraints.[16] However, it is important
to realize that population density in the New Delta has approached
parity with that of the Old Delta only since and due to the introduction of canal irrigation in the 1930s, which greatly increased
the total area under cultivation and the area under paddy (as opposed to maize and millets).[17]

[15] The figures for double-cropping paddy in Zones 4 and 5 may be somewhat
exaggerated because in some areas of these zones "Paddy II" may be a first crop
rather than a second crop. "Paddy II" is strictly defined as paddy grown in the
second (rabi) season rather than the second paddy crop.

[16] The village of Kunnalur, which is very near the coast, has a population density
of 318 persons per square mile compared to 868 persons per square mile for the
district as a whole (Census of India, 1961: Village Monograph—Kunnalur, p. 31).

[17] Baliga, Tanjore Handbook, p. 124. Population growth in the New Delta area has
significantly exceeded the district average ever since 1941, although the differential

TABLE 22

Agro-Economic Structure: Work Force Composition by Zone, 1971

Zone	Population Density (per mi.^{2}) (1)	Cultivators Per 100 Cultivated Acres (2)	Agricultural Laborers Per 100 Cultivated Acres (3)	Agrarian Density (total agrarian workers per 100 cultivated acres) (4)	Cultivators as % of All Workers (5)	Female Cultivators as % of Total Female Workers (6)	Agricultural Laborers as % of Total Agricultural Workers (7)	Ratio of Agricultural Laborers to Cultivators (8)
1/Old Delta-Cauvery (N=390)	1245	26	50	75	27.4	13.5	65.3	2.71
2/Old Delta-Central (N=267)	906	24	47	71	27.8	13.2	66.9	3.61
3/Old Delta-Coastal (N=468)	973	17	41	58	23.1	10.8	71.1	3.86
4/New Delta-CMP (N=220)	941	38	33	70	49.4	23.0	41.9	1.42
5/Dry Area-Uplands (N=163)	500*	19	10	28	59.8	36.2	32.0	0.78
District average (N=1498)	1007	24	40	63	32.9	16.5	60.3	2.83

* The Zone 5 figure is approximate.

The impact of ecological variations in Thanjavur extends to *the way in which production is organized.* Broadly, there are three modes of production in the district: direct cultivation with family labor, direct cultivation with hired labor, and tenancy cultivation.[18] Of course within each of these broad categories there are important variations and the different modes can be combined on any given operational holding, so that reality is much more complex than these categories suggest.

A broad distinction is observable in the mode of production between Zones 4 and 5 on the one hand and Zones 1 through 3 on the other. Because canal irrigation and intensive paddy cultivation are very sparse and relatively recent in Zones 5 and 4 respectively, the prevailing mode of production is relatively direct and family-oriented: the land will not support, production does not require, or time has not allowed for the development of intermediaries or a large landless labor force. Thus in Zones 4 and 5 owner cultivation through family labor is the norm.[19] In those areas the "density" of cultivators (Table 22, column 2) is greater and agricultural laborers lower (column 3) than in Zones 1 through 3. Cultivators make up a large proportion of all workers (column 5) and laborers a smaller proportion of agricultural workers.[20] The sharp differential in the relative proportions and role of cultivators and agricultural laborers is summarized by the zonal figures for the ratio of laborers to cultivators (column 8). As would be expected these distinctions are sharper in the case of Zone 5.

---

has been decreasing (see Table 93 in the Appendix). See also K. S. Sonachalam, *Benefit-Cost Evaluation of Cauvery-Mettur Project* (New Delhi: Planning Commission, Research Programmes Committee, undated), pp. 31-33. For a thorough study of a village in this area, see T. S. Yeshwanth, *Re-Survey of a Tanjore Village: Madigai* (Madras: University of Madras, Agricultural Economics Research Centre, 1966).

[18] Beteille, *Studies*, pp. 151-155.

[19] Intensive Agricultural District Programme, Thanjavur, *Study on Tenancy Patterns in Thanjavur District, 1969-70* (Madras: Government of Tamil Nadu, undated), p. 10 (hereafter IADP, *Study on Tenancy Patterns in Thanjavur*).

[20] Examples are found in studies of three widely dispersed villages in Zone 4: Vilangulam in Pattukottai Block, where agricultural labor households are 19 percent of the total; Kadambangudi in Budalur Block, where they are 8.5 percent of the total; and Madigai in Thanjavur Block, where they are 43 percent of the total. See *Census of India, 1961*, vol. 9, *Madras*, pt. 6, *Village Survey Monographs, 25, Vilangulam* (Madras: Superintendent of Census Operations, 1966), p. 43 (hereafter *Census of India, 1961: Village Monograph—Vilangulam*); *Census of India, 1961*, vol. 9, *Madras*, pt. 6, *Village Survey Monographs, Kadambangudi* (Madras: Superintendent of Census Operations, 1965), pp. 38-39 (hereafter *Census of India, 1961: Village Monograph—Kadambangudi*); Yeshwanth, *Re-Survey*, p. 41.

An important aspect of family labor cultivation is the higher participation rates of females. Female cultivators are more numerous in Zones 4 and 5 than in Zones 1 through 3 (see Table 22, column 6). Also, female family workers are more active in cultivation in Zones 4 and 5 than in Zones 1 through 3 (see Table 23, column 2). Note that the high average number of hired laborers per cultivating household in Zone 5 (Table 23, column 4) would seem to contradict my earlier assertion of the relative unimportance of agricultural labor there. But the designation "hired labor" here does *not* take into account the fact that a much larger proportion of agricultural laborers in Zones 4 and 5 *also* work as cultivators (see Table 23, column 7).[21] This only serves to demonstrate further the relative lack of separation between supervision of cultivation and field labor (which defines family cultivation) in Zones 4 and 5.

Finally, tenancy is found by any measure (see Table 24) to be much lower in Zones 4 and 5 than in Zones 1 through 3.[22] Tenancy generally entails an even wider alienation of ownership from cultivation than does the employment of hired labor (which requires supervision by the owner). It is generally believed that tenancy cultivation is widely adopted in areas of low productivity in order to minimize risk to the owner. However, I would argue that this is true only if there is a floor to productivity which allows two parties minimal returns from cultivation even in the worst years (unless conditions permit extreme exploitation by the landlord). Tenancy is more likely to emerge as the predominant mode of production in relatively well-irrigated and fertile areas under increasing population pressure. Thus, the sparseness of irrigation in Zone 5 and the relatively recent introduction of irrigation in Zone 4 have not favored the emergence of tenancy cultivation.

Turning to the question of the distribution of land ownership, we find that Zones 4 and 5 are not so clearly differentiated from the other three as a group. The proportion of "dwarf" holdings

[21] This is the case, for example, in the village of Sengipatti, which lies in the dry portion of Thanjavur taluk. See Agricultural Economics Research Centre, Department of Economics, University of Madras, *Sengipatti: A Re-Survey of a Dry Village in the Fertile Thanjavur District* (Madras, 1969), p. 23.

[22] The figures for the zonal distribution of tenancy are corroborated by several studies based on surveys of one or more villages: IADP, *Study on Tenancy Patterns in Thanjavur*, p. 5; AERC, *Sengipatti: A Re-Survey*, pp. 30-31; *Census of India, 1961: Village Monograph—Vilangulam*, p. 43; *Census of India, 1961: Village Monograph—Kadambangudi*, pp. 43-46; India, *Studies in the Economics of Farm Management in Thanjavur, 1967-68*, p. 267; India, *Studies in the Economics of Farm Management in Thanjavur, 1968-69*, pp. 34-35.

TABLE 23

Agro-Economic Structure: Type of Labor by Zone for Representative Taluks, 1961

Zone	Taluk	Workers by Cultivator Household[a]						% of Agricultural Laborers Also Working as Cultivators[b] (7)
		Average Number of Family Workers			Average Number of Hired Workers (4)	Ratio of Hired to Family Workers (5)	% of Hired Workers Working on Holdings over 10 Acres (6)	
		Males (1)	Females (2)	Total (3)				
1/Old Delta-Cauvery	Kumbakonam	1.42	0.41	1.83	1.39	0.76	26.0	7.1
2/Old Delta-Central	Nannilam	1.30	0.46	0.76	2.36	1.34	40.3	1.4
3/Old Delta-Coastal	Nagapattinam	1.24	0.56	1.80	3.63	2.02	52.1	2.3
4/New Delta-CMP	Pattukottai	1.41	0.80	2.21	0.56	0.25	27.0	12.0
5/Dry Area-Uplands	Arantangi	1.43	0.92	2.35	2.91	1.23	24.7	18.4
District average		1.35	0.55	1.90	2.72	1.43	28.3	6.1

SOURCES: [a] Computed from data in India, *District Census Handbook, 1961*, 1: 256-270.
[b] Computed from data in *ibid.*, 1: 219-221.

TABLE 24

Agro-Economic Structure, 1971: Tenancy By Zone

Zone	Area under Registered Tenancy as % of Total Area	Registered Tenants as % of Total Cultivators	Registered Tenants as % of Total Agricultural Workers
1/Old Delta-Cauvery (n = 380)	26.2	81.1	22.0
2/Old Delta-Central (n = 267)	21.1	72.3	18.1
3/Old Delta-Coastal (n = 468)	20.9	83.2	18.1
4/New Delta-CMP (n = 220)	2.2	4.3	2.5
5/Dry Area-Uplands (n = 163)	1.4	4.3	2.4
District average (n = 1498)	17.4	60.5	15.1

(see Table 25, columns 1 and 2) is low in Zone 5 (such a small holding in a dry area would hardly be viable), while in Zone 4 they are almost 20 percent of the total holdings. In both Zone 4 and Zone 5, however, the percentages of large and very large holdings (over thirty acres) are relatively low, and the percentage of owner-operated medium-sized holdings (five to fifteen acres) is relatively high. In other words, the distribution of owner-operated holdings in Zone 4 and especially in Zone 5 tends to be bunched in the medium-sized categories, with fewer very small holdings than Zone 1 and fewer very large holdings than either Zone 2 or 3. Additional evidence of these variations in landholding patterns is found in the fact (Table 25, column 6) that in 1950/1951 Zones 2 and 3 taluks had the greatest percentage of very large *pattas* and Zones 4 and 5 the smallest.[23]

[23] In 1950/1951, ten years before the advent of land ceiling legislation, the *patta* distribution data were probably a fairly reliable measure of the incidence of large holdings. But in 1960/1961 and later the *patta* data almost surely underestimate the

TABLE 25

Agro-Economic Structure: Size Distribution of Holdings by Zone for Representative Taluks

Zone	Taluk	Size Distribution of Holdings,* 1961 [a]					1950-51 % Single and Joint Pattas for Holdings over 25 Acres[b] (6)
		"Dwarf" Holdings		"Medium"	Large	Very Large	
				% of Owner Cultivated Holdings, 5-15 Acres (3)	% of Owner and Owner/Tenant*** Cultivated Holdings		
		% of All Holdings** under One Acre (1)	% of Owner-Cultivated Holdings under One Acre (2)		15-30 Acres (4)	Over 30 Acres (5)	
1/Old Delta-Cauvery	Kumbakonam	19.2	24.1	10.8	2.4	0.43	1.03
2/Old Delta-Central	Nannilam	10.2	14.2	18.6	5.6	1.66	1.26
3/Old Delta-Coastal	Nagapattinam	14.5	19.1	14.8	4.7	3.24	3.73
4/New Delta-CMP	Pattukottai	18.2	19.8	17.1	1.9	0.43	0.22
5/Dry Area-Uplands	Arantangi	12.8	13.8	19.1	2.2	0.46	0.79
District average		16.0	18.6	16.4	2.9	0.92	2.66

SOURCES: [a] India, District Census Handbook, 1961, 1: 256-270, Table B-XI, Table B-XII; 1: 96-101, Table B-III, pt. B; 1: 219-221, Table B-VII, pt. A.

[b] Government of Madras, Director of Statistics, A Statistical Atlas of the Thanjavur District: Revised and Brought Up To The Decennium Ending Fasli 1360 (1950-51) (Madras, 1965), pp. 32-37.

NOTES: * Holdings = households engaged in cultivation.

** Includes households cultivating 1) owned land; 2) leased land; and 3) owned and leased land.

*** For measuring incidence of large and very large owned holdings because at this size they are likely to be primarily owned.

If all of these factors are considered together, we find in Zones
4 and 5 a mode of production and agro-economic structure that
resembles the classic definition of "peasant": direct cultivation primarily through family labor on small to medium-sized plots.[24] As
I pointed out in Chapter 2, there is some controversy over the role
of the "middle peasant" in radical agrarian movements. Wolf and
Alavi, for example, argue that the relative autonomy of the middle
peasantry inclines them toward such movements. I shall demonstrate shortly that at least in the Thanjavur context this is not the
case.

Just as the ecological variability within the Old Delta areas (Zones
1, 2, and 3) is narrower than that between the Old Delta on the
one hand and the New Delta/Dry Area on the other hand, so also
differences in agro-economic structure are narrower within the Old
Delta zones. But they are no less consequential. I already noted
that the densities of cultivators and agricultural laborers taken separately and the overall agrarian density decrease as we move from
Zone 1 to Zone 5, dropping off quite sharply in Zone 3 (see Table
22). Similarly, the percentage of cultivators and female cultivators
is slightly lower in Zone 3, all reflecting constraints on the gross
area and productivity of paddy.

But the lower man to land ratios are not the only consequence
of ecological variability between Zones 1, 2, and 3. The prevailing
mode of production also differs, particularly between Zone 1 on
the one hand and Zones 2 and 3 on the other. Along with higher
densities (and in part because of them) there has arisen in Zone 1
a complex, multitiered system involving elements of tenancy, hired
labor, and family labor, with tenancy and hired labor of almost
equal and family labor of much lesser importance. This pattern is
a function of the zone's high agronomic potential of irrigated paddy
cultivation under increasing population pressure, which results in
greater and greater subdivision and multiplication of rights (ownership *and* control) in land. (This is similar to the pattern of "agricultural involution" observed by Clifford Geertz in Sawah, Indonesia.)[25] A relatively stable floor of productivity per unit area,
built on the foundations of good water supply and control (even
in bad years) and fertile soil, has accommodated increasing population pressure, in this case through "vertical layering" (more in-

number of large *operated* holdings, as many large holdings were nominally broken
up into smaller holdings in order to evade the land ceilings.

[24] See Beteille, *Studies*, p. 24.
[25] Geertz, *Agricultural Involution*, esp. pp. 28-37.

termediaries) and "horizontal fragmentation" (smaller holdings, both owned and leased). In addition, to the extent that family labor is either not available (e.g., for social reasons) or insufficient, which is likely under intensive cultivation especially at the peak demand periods of transplanting and harvest, a landless or nearly landless labor force may also develop.

In contrast, the prevailing, though certainly not exclusive, mode of production in Zones 2 and 3 is hired labor obtained from a large predominantly landless labor force. Once again this is a function of ecological conditions. The relatively poor water supply and control and soils result not only in lower average productivity per unit area but also in greater year-to-year variability of returns, and thus higher risks. It is possible in these areas to lose the entire crop in a bad year. Higher risks require larger holdings and closer supervision of cultivation to ensure economic viability in normal years and to build a cushion against bad years. Larger holdings in turn require a larger landless labor force (available even at peak demand periods). If double cropping is attempted, even more labor is required to complete the harvest before the rains and to avoid damage to the crop. The desirability of close supervision of cultivation, even on large holdings, tends to reduce the incidence of tenancy.

These differences in productive organization give rise to agro-economic structural variations. The dominant agro-economic structure in Zone 1 is complex and multipolar, characterized by overlapping statuses and multiple groupings. The dominant agro-economic structure in Zones 2 and 3 is simple and bipopular, characterized by exclusive statuses and limited groupings.[26]

In Table 22 (column 7) it is apparent that agricultural laborers are a somewhat larger percentage of the agricultural work force in Zones 2 and 3 than in Zone 1. But more telling is a comparison of the *ratio* of agricultural laborers to cultivators, which is much higher in Zones 2 and 3, demonstrating that it is not simply the presence of a large agricultural labor force but its structural relationship to the rest of the agricultural work force that matters. This relationship is also evident in the higher ratio of hired workers to family workers in Zones 2 and 3 (Table 23, column 5). The *bipolar* tendency of the landowner-laborer relationship in Zones 2 and 3 is also evidenced by the following two facts: the higher percentage of large and very large holdings (Table 25, columns 4 and 5) in

[26] Beteille, *Studies*, p. 163.

Zones 2 and 3,[27] and the higher percentage of hired laborers working on holdings over ten acres (Table 23, column 6).

The multipolarity of agro-economic structure in Zone 1 is evident
in the greater number of small owner-cultivated holdings (Table
25, column 2), the larger area under tenancy cultivation, and the
greater number of tenants in the agricultural work force (Table
24).[28] While the difference in tenancy incidence between the zones
is not very sharp, an interesting distinction emerges if we take into
account the *size* of tenancy holdings. There is apparently some
tendency for tenant and owner/tenant-operated holdings to be smaller
in Zone 1 and larger in Zones 2 and 3 (see Table 26, columns 2-
3).

The agro-economic structure of Zone 1 is more complex not only
because it includes multiple agro-economic groupings but also because individual agro-economic status is more complex. A larger
proportion of agricultural laborers in Zone 1 also work as cultivators (Table 23, column 7). Also, a larger proportion of small
cultivators in Zone 1 are both owners and tenants than in Zones 2
or 3 (Table 26, column 1).

In summary, ecological variations between Zones 1, 2, and 3 have
given rise to different patterns of productive organization: in Zone
1 we find a combination of different modes, including many small
holdings cultivated through tenancy, hired labor, and family labor,
and medium and large holdings cultivated through tenancy and
hired labor; in Zones 2 and 3 all modes are present, but the dominant mode is medium and large holdings cultivated through hired
labor under owner supervision, with tenant holdings comparatively
large and therefore also cultivated largely through hired labor. As
a result, the agro-economic structure of Zone 1 is characterized by
the complexity of multiple significant groups and overlapping statuses. In contrast, the agro-economic structure of Zones 2 and 3 is
characterized by the relative bipolarity of two significant groups,
large owner-operators and landless labor, and by exclusive statuses.

The agro-economic structural differences between the five zones
are brought out graphically in Figure 8. Note the dominance of
middle groups in Zones 4 and 5, the dominance of the extreme
groups in Zones 2 and 3, and the relatively equal importance of

[27] See Ganapathia Pillai, "Report of the Commission of Inquiry on the Agrarian
Labour Problems of East Thanjavur District," typewritten, pp. 3, 6.
[28] The ratio of tenants to cultivators overestimates the incidence of tenancy in
Zones 2 and 3 because many of the poorer tenants are principally agricultural
laborers, and laborers are more numerous in those areas.

TABLE 26

Agro-Economic Structure: Tenurial Status of Holdings by Zone for Representative Taluks, 1961

Zone	Taluk	% of all Holdings under 2.4 Acres in Owner/Tenant Cultivation (1)	Size and Tenurial Status	
			% of Tenant and Owner/Tenant Cultivated Holdings over 10 Acres (2)	% of Tenant and Owner/Tenant Cultivated Holdings under 2.4 Acres (3)
1/Old Delta-Cauvery	Kumbakonam	9.5	7.1	48.5
2/Old Delta-Central	Nannilam	9.1	14.8	30.3
3/Old Delta-Coastal	Nagapattinam	5.7	15.6	38.5
4/New Delta-CMP	Pattukottai	10.5	5.6	53.7
5/Dry Area-Uplands	Araṇtangi	15.0	3.4	50.0
District average		9.5	8.6	46.1

SOURCE: India, *District Census handbook, 1961*, 1: 251-254, Table B-XI; 1: 256-270, Table B-XII; 1: 96-101, Table B-III, pt. B; 1: 219-221, Table B-VII, pt. A.

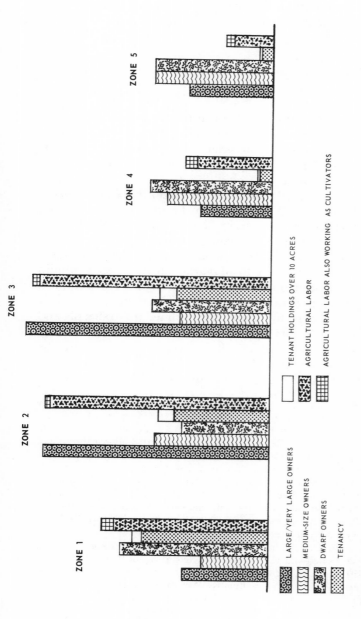

FIGURE 8. Agro-Economic Structure in the Five Zones

NOTES: The agro-economic categories used in this figure are defined as follows:

1. large/very large owners = percentage of owner- and owner/tenant-cultivated holdings over 15.0 acres
2. medium-size owners = percentage of owner- and owner/tenant-cultivated holdings over 5.0 and less than 15.0 acres
3. dwarf owners = percentage of owner-cultivated holdings over 1.0 and less than 5.0 acres
4. tenancy = "registered" tenants as percentage of all agricultural workers
5. agricultural labor = ratio of agricultural laborers to cultivators

For categories 2, 3, and 4 bar graphs are based on one unit for 1.0 percent. For category 1, one unit equals 0.2 percent and for category 5 one unit equals 0.1 percent. I have used variable units in order to highlight the structural relationship of the categories.

all groups, especially the lower groups, in Zone 1. In other words, "landlessness" is multidimensional in Zone 1 and comparatively unidimensional in Zones 2 and 3.

SOCIAL AND CULTURAL ORGANIZATION

Caste

Unfortunately we do not have statistical information on the spatial distribution of all castes in Thanjavur, even from 1921. Therefore this discussion must rely on accumulated evidence from various village studies for a rough profile of agricultural castes in the five agro-economic zones.

Several studies suggest that Brahmin landowners are concentrated in the Zone 1 area.[29] This is in accord with our understanding of the earliest settlement patterns in Thanjavur. Under the Cholas, Brahmin-controlled villages were concentrated in the natural delta area, along what is now the northern border of the district roughly from Thanjavur in the west to Mayuram in the east. Brahmin dominance has continued until quite recent times.[30] However, it is also generally agreed that over the last several decades the number of Brahmin landowners in this area has declined quite sharply and the number of non-Brahmin landowners increased, with the result that there are now many fewer villages where Brahmins are the dominant landowning caste. The Brahmin landowners remaining in the district are still concentrated in the Zone 1 area, however.[31]

[29] See Kathleen Gough, "The Social Structure of a Tanjore Village," in *Village India: Studies in the Little Community*, ed. McKim Marriott (1955; reprint ed., Chicago: University of Chicago Press, Phoenix Books, 1969), p. 94; Beteille, *Studies*, p. 150; K. C. Alexander, *Agrarian Tension in Thanjavur* (Hyderabad: National Institute of Community Development, 1975), pp. 10-11.

[30] See Kathleen Gough, "Caste in a Tanjore Village," in *Aspects of Caste in South India, Ceylon, and Northwest Pakistan*, ed. E. R. Leach (Cambridge: Cambridge University Press, 1971), p. 16. Beteille reports that at the turn of the century in the Zone 1 village of Sripuram very few non-Brahmins owned land. See Andre Beteille, *Caste, Class and Power: Changing Patterns of Stratification in a Tanjore Village* (Berkeley, Ca.: University of California Press, 1965), p. 193.

[31] Kathleen Gough, "Harijans in Thanjavur," in *Imperialism and Revolution in South Asia*, ed. Kathleen Gough and Hari P. Sharma (New York and London: Monthly Review Press, 1973), p. 226. See also Andre Beteille, *Castes, Old and New: Essays in Social Structure and Social Stratification* (Bombay: Asia Publishing House, 1969), pp. 177-178; Gough, "Social Structure," p. 101; Dagfinn Sivertsen, *When Caste Barriers Fall: A Study of Social and Economic Change in a South Indian Village* (Oslo: Universitets Forlaget, 1963), p. 45. According to Beteille, the non-Brahmins did not replace the

As non-Brahmins include many castes and are spread through-out the district it is more difficult to characterize their position and role. But it is worthwhile noting at this point that there seems to be a rough correlation between the time of settlement and the ritual rank of the dominant landowning caste in Thanjavur. I have noted that at least until recently Brahmins were the dominant landowners in the earliest settled area corresponding to Zone 1. In the next settled area, the central and coastal portions of the natural delta corresponding to Zones 2 and 3, high-caste non-Brahmins, partic-ularly Vellalas and Naidus (a Telegu caste that settled in Thanjavur under Nayak rule), were the traditional landowning castes, the latter especially in the Sirkali and Mayuram area, the former es-pecially in the Nagapattinam and Tiruthuraipoondi area. They are still the most important landowning castes in these areas (fewer of this group have left agriculture than have the Brahmins in Zone 1). As in Zone 1, but to a lesser extent, their control over the land has been increasingly rivaled over the last several decades by "mid-dle-caste" non-Brahmins, such as the Vanniars (especially in the Sirkali and Mayuram areas) and the Kallars, Agamudayans, and Odayars in the southern and western areas of Zones 2 and 3, who migrated to Thanjavur from other districts several generations ago and became tenants and small owners in the Zones 2 and 3 as well as Zone 1 area and have recently improved their economic status.[32] What distinguishes Zones 2 and 3 from Zone 1 in the past and present is the greater importance of non-Brahmin landowners in the former areas, except perhaps in Mannargudi.[33]

In Zones 4 and 5, the most recently settled, the "middle-caste" non-Brahmins, particularly the Kallars, have been and still are the dominant landowning group. There are very few Brahmin land-owners and relatively few Vellalas.[34] In Zone 1 the Kallars, Van-niars, and Agamudayans and other middle-caste non-Brahmins

Brahmins as large landowners but rather acquired land in small plots and became small owners and tenants (Beteille, *Caste, Class and Power*, pp. 193-194). A study of two villages near Kumbakonam in 1970/1971 found that Brahmins were still the dominant landowners (Swenson, "Effect of Increases in Rice Production," p. 23).

[32] Gough, "Caste," p. 17.

[33] Studies of two villages in these areas did find that Brahmins were not a signif-icant landowning group (Gough, "Harijans," p. 236; *Census of India, 1961: Village Monograph—Kunnalur*, pp. 11-13).

[34] The following village studies all document this point: *Census of India, 1961: Village Monograph—Vilangulam*, pp. 3-7; *Census of India, 1961: Village Monograph—Kadambangudi*, p. 23; Yeshwanth, *Re-Survey*, p. 21; AERC, *Sengipatti: A Re-Survey*, pp. 16-17.

may be (as one moves from village to village and area) medium-sized landowners, small landowners, tenants, and even in some cases agricultural laborers.[35] In Zones 2 and 3 they are more frequently medium-sized owners and owner-tenants but also small owners and tenants. In Zones 4 and 5 they are practically the exclusive landowning castes.

At the bottom of the ritual rank order of caste, the Harijans or Scheduled Castes, there is census data available that provides a clearer picture of their spatial distribution. In Table 27 it is evident (column 1) first that the percentage of Scheduled Castes in the total population is high in Zone 1, highest in Zones 2 and 3 and lowest in Zones 4 and 5. This distribution might have been inferred from our knowledge of the distribution of agricultural labor and the fact that the principal occupation of the Scheduled Castes in Thanjavur is agricultural labor. In fact, the correspondence between caste status and agricultural labor varies from zone to zone. Members of the Scheduled Castes are most likely to be laborers, and vice versa, in Zones 2 and 3. The correspondence is very low in Zone 5. In Zone 4 most of the Scheduled Caste workers are laborers, but most of the laborers are *not* Scheduled Caste.[36] The correspondence is high in Zone 1 but considerably lower than in Zones 2 and 3.

To summarize, there is a partial isomorphism between the caste structure and agro-economic structure of the zones. In Zones 4 and 5 the upper and lower ends of the ritual rank order are underrepresented, and there is a relatively low correspondence between caste and agro-economic status at the lower end. In Zones 2 and 3 land control is largely vested in the non-Brahmin castes (there are non-Brahmin tenants and small owners in these areas, but recall that as a group tenants and small owners are less important in the agro-economic structure), and agricultural labor is almost exclusively performed by Scheduled Caste workers. In Zone 1 land control, although Brahmin-dominated for centuries, is now

[35] See Gough, "Caste," p. 17.

[36] In the village of Kadambangudi in Budalur Block the Harijan population is small, and agricultural laborers are not drawn exclusively from any one caste (*Census of India, 1961: Village Monograph—Kadambangudi*, pp. 23, 38). In the village of Vilangulam in Pattukottai Block there is a large population of Pallars engaged in both cultivation and agricultural labor (*Census of India, 1961: Village Monograph—Villangulam*, p. 43). In the village of Madigai in Thanjavur Block most of the Parayars are agricultural laborers, but so are most members of a non-Brahmin caste, the Servaikarars (Yeshwanth, *Re-Survey*, pp. 25-30).

TABLE 27

Scheduled Castes by Agro-Economic Zone for Representative Taluks

| | | 1971 | 1961 | |
| | | % of Scheduled Caste Persons to Total Persons[a] (1) | % of Agricultural Laborers Who Are Scheduled Caste[b] (2) | % of Scheduled Caste Agricultural Workers Who Are Laborers[b] (3) |
Zone	Taluk			
1/Old Delta-Cauvery	Kumbakonam	29.7	63.8	73.4
2/Old Delta-Central	Nannilam	33.0	69.6	84.6
3/Old Delta-Coastal	Nagappattinam	38.1	82.3	86.8
4/New Delta-CMP	Pattukottai	12.2	27.2	60.4
5/Dry Area-Uplands	Arantangi	19.3	27.5	19.5
District average		29.2	62.0	74.1

SOURCES: [a] Zonal averages computed from panchayat-level data.
[b] India, *District Census Handbook, 1961*, 1: 335.

shared by Brahmins and non-Brahmins. However, there are still many non-Brahmin tenants in the Zone 1 area, and relatively fewer Harijans than in Zones 2 and 3, and fewer laborers.[37] In other words, the caste structure in Zones 4 and 5 is unimodal, in Zones 2 and 3 bimodal, and in Zone 1 multimodal, much the same as the agro-economic structure. Furthermore, in Zones 4 and 5 there is a relatively low correspondence between caste and agro-economic status, in Zones 2 and 3 there is a relatively high correspondence, and in Zone 1 a medium correspondence. The difference between parallel and cross-cutting agro-economic and social cleavages is crucial to an understanding of agrarian radicalism in Thanjavur,[38] and I shall consider it more closely in the next chapter.

Settlement

Settlement patterns also differ from zone to zone. The villages of Zone 1 are typically dense, closely spaced, and old in appearance (see Table 28). Many of the houses are made of stone or burnt brick; many villages are centered around ancient temples. Most villages are organized into separate but contiguous caste streets (the *agraharam* for Brahmins, the *cheri* for Harijans).[39] In contrast, the villages of Zones 2 and 3 are less densely settled and less closely spaced. There are fewer old dwellings. In Zone 1 it is possible to travel by road for miles without emerging into open country, but not so in Zones 2 and 3. Also, the caste streets of Zone 1 become in Zones 2 and 3 hamlets set quite far apart from the main village. Such residential segregation is often cited as a factor in the development of collective group consciousness.[40]

Villages in Zone 4 are even larger and less densely settled. There are few old stone or brick dwellings. Settlements are usually not organized into recognizable streets or caste units. Rather, the houses

---

[37] In three out of five Zone 1 villages surveyed by the Farm Management Study in 1967 and 1968 Brahmins and non-Brahmins shared landownership. In the other two, near Mayuram, landownership was shared by Vanniars and Odayars in one case and by Vellalas and Padayachis in the other (India, *Studies in the Economics of Farm Management in Thanjavur, 1967-68*, pp. 19-24; see also Beteille, *Caste, Class and Power*, p. 194).

[38] Kathleen Gough, "Indian Peasant Uprisings," *Economic and Political Weekly* 9 (Special number, 1974): 1,403.

[39] Beteille, *Caste, Class and Power*, p. 27; Gough, "Caste," p. 19; Sivertsen, *When Caste Barriers Fall*, pp. 24-27.

[40] *Census of India, 1961: Village Monograph—Kunnalur*, p. 45. On the role of residential patterns in group consciousness see Beteille, "Agrarian Movements," p. 18.

TABLE 28

Settlement and Temples by Agro-Economic Zone for Representative Taluks, 1961

Zone	Taluk	Persons Per Village (1)	Average Village Area (per mi.^{2}) (2)	% of Stone or Burnt Brick Dwellings (3)	Temples Per 10,000 Total Population (4)
1/Old Delta-Cauvery	Kumbakonam	1751	1.41	38.6	4.10
2/Old Delta-Central	Nannilam	1294	1.44	22.5	6.67
3/Old Delta-Coastal	Nagapattinam	1287	1.56	30.0	7.37
4/New Delta-CMP	Pattukottai	1321	2.07	11.4	2.03
5/Dry Area-Uplands	Arantangi	454	1.24	7.0	2.63
District average		1361	1.90	21.9	4.37

SOURCE: India, *District Census Handbook, 1961*, 1: 60, 70-71.

are usually grouped in a single circle or rectangle, in part because of the relative caste homogeneity of the area and in part because the original settlers, the Kallars, Agamudayans, and Ambalakarans, were at the time roving robber castes who needed a more secure type of settlement. Finally, in Zone 5 the settlement pattern is decentralized and sparse. There are many very small villages the size of a small hamlet in Zones 1, 2, or 3, each with only a few households. In Zone 4 and especially in Zone 5 one can travel relatively long distances without passing through a village. Also, in Zones 4 and 5 sizable areas of the open space between settlements may be dry and covered with scrub brush, whereas in Zones 2 and 3 and particularly in Zone 1 the space between settlements is completely under cultivation.

There is as clear a relationship between variations in settlement patterns and variations in agro-economic structure as there was between caste structure and agro-economic structure. The density and compactness of settlements in Zone 1 tend to reinforce the overlapping of agro-economic status, while the lower density and residential segregation in Zones 2 and 3 tend to reinforce the exclusivity of agro-economic status. The unitary village organization and the uniformity of dwelling construction in Zone 4 of course reflect the agro-economic and caste homogeneity of the area. Finally, the very low density and the fragmentation of settlement in Zone 5 reflect a very loose agro-economic structure based on extensive rather than intensive cultivation.

Temples

Greater cultural elaborateness is also generally associated with intensive cultivation in Thanjavur.[41] One of the most obvious examples of this fact is found in the distribution of temples. As mentioned in Chapter 4, temples have played a central role in the cultural life of the district. As would be expected, there is a much greater concentration of temples in Zones 1 through 3 than in Zones 4 and 5 (see Table 28). However, it is something of a surprise to find higher concentrations of temples in Zones 2 and 3 than in Zone 1. Although most older temples (pre-1750) are located in the Zone 1 area, out of 1,418 temples in existence in 1961, only 980 were built prior to 1750.[42] Since most temples were (and are) fi-

[41] Beteille, *Studies*, p. 150.
[42] India, *District Census Handbook, 1961*, 1: 61.

nancially dependent on income from agricultural lands, I would suggest that new temple construction took place largely in areas where agricultural land was available for grants toward construction or upkeep at the temple: after 1750 this was in the Zones 2 and 3 area. As we shall see later, the significance of this fact is economic and political as well as agricultural.

Literacy and Development

Although my principal concern in this chapter has been to discern patterns of variability in relatively enduring characteristics such as ecological conditions and agro-economic structure, the role played by literacy and developmental change in many explanations of agrarian radicalism directs me to look briefly, primarily for future reference, at their zonal distribution. Literacy is lower in Zones 4 and 5 than in Zones 1 through 3 (see Table 29). This is as expected, given what we already know about the areas. What is perhaps a bit surprising is the lack of any distinction between Zones 1, 2 and 3.

The index of overall development (based on a combination of physical facilities at the village level) is highest in Zone 1 and lowest in Zone 5, with very little difference between the three other zones. The only surprise here is the apparent lack of differentiation between the zones.

TABLE 29

Literacy and Development by Agro-Economic Zone, 1971

Zone	Literacy (literates as % of total population)	Overall Development (facilities) Index
1/Old Delta-Cauvery	36.7	7.14
2/Old Delta-Central	36.4	6.26
3/Old Delta-Coastal	37.4	6.55
4/New Delta-CMP	30.7	5.56
5/Dry Area-Uplands	28.1	5.25
District average	35.1	5.25

Source: Zonal averages computed from author's panchayat-level data.

One means of confirming and summarizing the preceding analysis of agrarian variability in Thanjavur District is a statistical technique known as *discriminant function analysis*. The technique determines mathematically which of a number of given variables best discriminates between specified groups. It does this by constructing one or more multivariate functions that separate the groups according to preselected criteria. More than one function is derived when the first function does not exhaust the discriminating power of the combined variance in the given variables. Each of the groups is assigned a mean discriminant score, or "centroid," for each of the functions derived. Thus, if two functions are found to discriminate significantly between the groups, the centroids may be plotted as coordinates on two axes, giving a two-dimensional graphical representation of the relationship between the groups. Finally, each case in the specified groups is assigned a score on each of the functions derived, which may then be used to "predict" in which group that unit should really be classified—in short, affording a measure of the actual homogeneity of the originally specified groups.

With the five agro-economic zones as the specified groups (the panchayats being the cases), and entering many of the variables used above, I have taken each of these analytical steps. The results are displayed in the tables and graph on the following pages. Four functions were derived (the maximum possible with five groups). However, the eigenvalues and relative percentages of discrimination (see Table 30) tell us that the first function contains most (27 percent) of the total discriminant power. The canonical correlation is a further measure of the discriminating power of each function; if squared it tells us how much of the variance in each discriminant function is "explained" by the groups. Function 1 evidently discriminates quite well between the groups (almost 64 percent of the variance in the function is explained by the groups). Wilks lambda is an inverse measure of the discriminating power remaining in the variables after each function is derived. After the first two functions were derived, relatively little variance remained. On the basis of all these statistics, and for the sake of clarity, I will focus my attention on the first two functions (which account for nearly 90 percent of the total discriminant power).

In Table 31 the function coefficients of each variable for each function can be examined (the size of the coefficient indicates the importance of that variable in the function). The first thing to notice is that no single variable dominates the first function. (This confirms one of the early points in the chapter: that the distinctions between

TABLE 30

Discriminant Function Analysis of Agro-Economic Zones
Relative Importance of Functions Derived

Function	Eigen-Value	Relative % of Discrimination	Canonical Correlation	Wilks Lambda	CHI Square
0*	—	—	—	0.1994	2310
1	1.7553	71.66	0.798	0.5495	858
2	0.4450	18.17	0.555	0.5495	330
3	0.1981	8.09	0.407	0.9514	71
4	0.0511	2.09	0.221	—	—

* Before any functions derived.

the zones are a result of the complex interaction of a number of factors.) In light of this, it should come as no surprise that the four strongest components of the function are soil quality, land value, cultivators as a percentage of total workers, and area under tenancy. We must bear in mind that the *interaction* between the variables governs in great part their contribution to a function derived so as to discriminate best among *all* the groups. But in order also to identify the single variable that best discriminates between all the groups (albeit poorly) I used the "stepwise" method of constructing the functions, selecting the most discriminating variable first: in this case Scheduled Caste as a percentage of total population. I will analyze the significance of this finding in the next chapter.

The discriminating power of ecological conditions is demonstrated by the high coefficient for land value in Function 2. Also relatively important are, as expected, percentage cultivated area, Scheduled Caste, and agricultural labor.

The plot of zonal centroids shows a very clear result (see Figure 9). Although the plot exaggerates the separation between the zones (as we shall see there is considerable overlap), the fact that Zones 1, 4, and 5 each occupy a separate quadrant, and Zones 2 and 3 the same quadrant, demonstrates graphically the basic distinctions I have described above. Also as could be expected, Function 1, the most discriminating, establishes the greatest distance between Zone 1, 2, and 3 on the one hand and Zones 4 and 5 on the other. Function 2 then picks up the lesser differentials between Zone 1

TABLE 31

Discriminant Function Analysis of Agro-Economic Zones
Standardized Function Coefficients

Variables	Coefficients	
	Function 1	Function 2
Canal irrigation, 1961	-0.0598	-0.1159
Soil quality, 1961	-0.1088	-0.0071
Land value, 1961	-0.0902	-0.4122
Cultivated area (as % of total), 1971	0.0401	0.1894
Agricultural workers (as % of total), 1971	0.0259	-0.0737
Cultivators (as % of total workers), 1971	0.0835	0.0158
Female cultivators (as % of female workers), 1971	0.0084	0.0422
Agricultural workers per irrigated acre, 1971	0.0143	-0.0013
Agricultural labor as % of agricultural workers, 1971	-0.0698	0.1858
Scheduled castes as % of total population, 1971	-0.0586	0.2001
Ratio of agricultural labor to Scheduled Caste population, 1971	0.0108	-0.0162
Tenants as % of cultivators, 1971	0.0518	-0.0403
Tenants as % of agricultural workers, 1971	-0.0469	0.0327
Area under tenancy as % of total cultivated area, 1971	-0.0761	-0.0083
Agricultural facilities, 1971	0.0176	-0.0988
Agricultural development rating, 1971	0.0147	-0.1194
Overall development rating, 1971	0.0045	0.0672

and Zones 2 and 3 and between Zone 4 and Zone 5 on many of the same variables—thus the relative greater contribution of percentage Scheduled Caste and agricultural labor to Function 2.

The comparison of the predicted with the actual zonal classification of panchayats in Table 32 recalls another introductory caveat to this chapter: that such a classification is necessarily rough (especially as the initial demarcation of the zones was based on "eyeball" comparison of block-level data for the key variables, and the zones could not be expected to correspond to these administrative divisions). As might be expected, the greatest percentage of correct classifications occur in the more distinctive Zones 4 and 5, the smallest percentage in Zones 2 and 3, which we have seen are very similar. If we were to collapse Zones 2 and 3, about 80 percent of

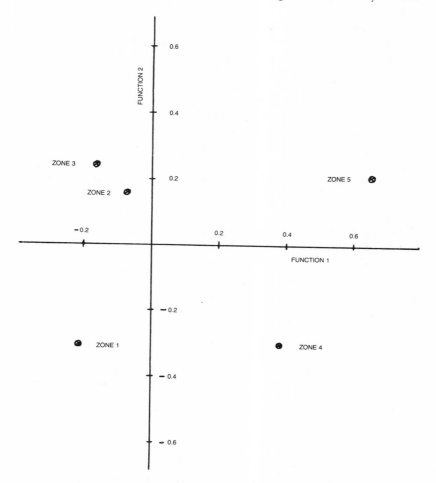

FIGURE 9. Discriminant Function Analysis: Plot of Zonal Centroids on Functions 1 and 2

the classifications would be correct in those zones as well.[43] In the case of Zone 1 the largest deviation is the classification of 20 percent of these panchayats into Zone 3. I suspect this is due to the inclusion in Zone 1 of panchayats in southern Mayuram taluk that rightfully

[43] Instead of collapsing these zones, which do have some distinctive features, I will treat them as a pair in subsequent chapters.

belong to Zone 3 because of inferior irrigation conditions (their identity could not be determined at the time of demarcating the zones).

Overall about 62 percent of the panchayats were correctly classified (see Table 33). It is instructive to compare this overall figure with the percentage obtained when different sets of variables are entered separately in the discriminant analysis. Variables measuring ecological conditions were most discriminating, with the agro-economic structural indicators a close second. This is as we might have predicted. Agrarian density and agricultural development were considerably less powerful discriminators. Although, as I have ar-

TABLE 32

Classification of Panchayats into Agro-Economic Zones
by Discriminant Function Analysis

Actual Zonal Membership	N	Predicted Zonal Membership				
		% of Panchayats Classified in Zone				
		(1)	(2)	(3)	(4)	(5)
1	372	62.9	12.6	20.4	3.5	0.5
2	264	6.8	45.8	33.7	11.4	2.3
3	461	11.9	21.5	59.4	3.9	3.3
4	201	2.5	5.0	2.5	80.1	10.0
5	147	4.1	2.0	2.7	20.4	70.7

TABLE 33

Correctness of Classification of Panchayats into
Agro-Economic Zones According to Type of
Discriminating Variables

Type of Variables	% of All Panchayats Correctly Classified
1 All variables	61.9
2 Ecological conditions	51.8
3 Agro-economic structure	48.3
4 Agrarian density	39.0
5 Agricultural development	32.7

gued, the ecological distinctions are most basic to the zonal patterns, other variables have an effect derived independently of any relationship they might bear to ecology: for example, caste and aspects of agro-economic structure that owe at least as much to historical as to ecological factors.

CHAPTER 6

Agrarian Structure and Agrarian Radicalism

THE EMPHASIS, sometimes unintended, in many studies of agrarian radicalism is on identifying the agrarian group or groups, stratum or strata, "responsible" for the emergence of agrarian radicalism. Thus, much discussion centers on the roles of middle peasants, poor peasants (variable defined), and landless labor. For instance, Wolf and Alavi emphasize the role of the "middle peasant," Scott, Stinchcombe, and Zagoria the tenant, and Paige the sharecropper or migratory laborer.

Arguments for the relative importance of these groups in radical agrarian movements turn on the question of their position in the agrarian property structure. Those favoring the middle peasant thesis argue that relative economic independence enables the middle peasant to challenge the landlord and/or urban interests with which he finds himself in conflict. Others would argue that precisely because the middle peasant is tied into the existing structure through land ownership he is less susceptible to radical political mobilization. On the other hand, while some argue that landless laborers are most amenable to radicalism because of the extremity of their position in agrarian society, others contend that their extreme economic dependence inhibits the development of radical movements among them. For this reason dwarf owners, whose low economic position is combined with a measure of independence, are sometimes identified as a leading element in agrarian radicalism, though the status ambiguity inherent in their position (frequently they must work as laborers to supplement their meager income from cultivation) might also be interpreted as a deterrent to radicalism. Finally, there are two variants of the argument linking tenancy with agrarian radicalism: one emphasizes landlessness per se (Zagoria) and another the effect of changes, real or perceived, in economic status (Scott).

While all of these hypotheses raise important considerations for understanding agrarian radicalism, the *positional approach* that they share is, I believe, inadequate. More informative is a structural-

relational approach, exemplified in Jeffery Paige's work, that in-
corporates consideration of economic position but focuses on the
nature of agro-economic and social relationships between the different groups. Perhaps because it encompasses greater variability,
the structural approach yields less easily to generalization. But it
does provide a fuller understanding of the sources of agrarian
radicalism.

For instance, in his study of agrarian communism in Western
Europe Juan Linz observed that:

> The correlation between the leftism of the farm workers and the
> property structure is not a direct one. It is more the type of farm
> enterprise and the organization of labor than the property struc-
> ture as such that seems to correlate with politics.[1]

In addition, the contribution of structural analysis is derived not
only from clarification of "what it means" to belong to a particular
agrarian group (by putting the group in a relational context) but
also from recognition of the historical roots of agrarian radicalism.
Both Dogan and Linz have noted the importance of historical considerations in the explanation of agrarian communism in Western
Europe, and they attribute this to the durability of agrarian structure (certainly because it is anchored in relatively unchanging ecological conditions).[2] We would similarly expect agrarian structure
in contemporary India to reflect historical adaptations to ecological
conditions: we have seen, for instance, the debt that Thanjavur's
present agrarian organization owes to the past.

I do not of course mean to deny the importance of agrarian
change in the development of agrarian radicalism. Almost by definition change of one sort or another is central to any explanation
of this phenomenon. Rather I wish to stress what is often overlooked: that the impact of change at any particular time and place
is shaped in part by local conditions that are the product of the
past. In the case of agrarian radicalism the nature of the interaction
between forces of change (such as the introduction of commercialized agriculture, agrarian reforms, or new technology) and local
conditions (such as the agro-technology or agro-economic struc-

---

[1] Juan J. Linz, "Patterns of Land Tenure, Division of Labor, and Voting Behavior
in Europe," *Comparative Politics* 8 (April 1976): 424.

[2] Mattei Dogan, "Political Cleavage and Social Stratification in France and Italy,"
in *Party Systems and Voter Alignments: Cross-National Perspectives*, ed. Seymour M. Lipset
and Stein Rokkan (New York: The Free Press, 1967), pp. 183-184; Linz, "Patterns
of Land Tenure," p. 386.

ture), mediated by other external factors (such as the political environment—nature of the regime, political parties), determines whether in fact agrarian radicalism emerges, and if so, how it develops.

With these general guidelines in mind I turn now to an investigation of the relationship between agrarian structure and agrarian radicalism in Thanjavur.

Agrarian radicalism, as measured by Communist panchayat control, is *not* evenly distributed among the five agro-economic zones of Thanjavur District. In fact, Table 34 indicates that it is heavily concentrated in Zone 2 and especially Zone 3, the Central and Coastal Old Delta areas, throughout the period 1960 to 1970. Well over 80 percent of the panchayats won by the Communists in the entire district in any of the three elections were in either of these two zones. And while it is true that the percentage of Communist

TABLE 34

Communist Panchayat Control, 1960-1970, by Agro-Economic Zone

Zone	% of Panchayats Won by Communist Party or Parties			Mean Communist Panchayat Control Score, 1960-70*
	1960	1965	1970	
1/Old Delta-Cauvery	2.3	2.9	3.2	0.09
	(341)	(378)	(378)	
2/Old Delta-Central	8.4	10.8	14.3	0.34
	(262)	(267)	(266)	
3/Old Delta-Coastal	20.5	22.6	28.2	0.71
	(468)	(468)	(465)	
4/New Delta-CMP	3.8	3.7	5.4	0.12
	(213)	(217)	(218)	
5/Dry Area-Uplands	0.6	0.6	1.2	0.03
	(161)	(162)	(162)	
District average	9.3	9.4	13.1	0.33
	(1445)	(1492)	(1489)	

NOTES: Figures in parentheses represent numbers of panchayats in which elections were held in each zone and year for which data were available.

* Each panchayat is scored 0-3 according to the number of elections in which a Communist won the panchayat presidency.

panchayats in Zones 1, 4, and 5 increased over this period, it increased even more sharply in Zones 2 and 3.

This same pattern is readily observable in data on Communist performance in the legislative assembly elections over the twenty-year period 1952 to 1971 (see Table 35). First, the Communists (whether CPI or CPM) contested more of the available seats in Zones 2 and 3 in almost every election than in any other zone. Second, when they contested a seat, the Communists almost always won a larger percentage of the vote in Zone 2 and 3 contests than in the other zones. The few exceptions were those occasions on which the average of several contests in Zone 2 or Zone 3 was lower than the figure for a single contest in another zone. Finally, out of ten rural seats won by the Communists between 1952 and 1971 nine were in Zone 2 or Zone 3.

The lack of a direct relationship between average percentage of the vote won and seats won is evident. This seems to be almost entirely a function of political factors: 1) poll strategy, such as whether or not a decision was made to concentrate electoral effort in a few constituencies, 2) a poll alliance, such as the alliance between the CPM and the DMK in 1967 and between the CPI and the DMK in 1971, and 3) the Communist split in 1964. In 1967, two years after the split, the average percentage of combined Communist vote in Zone 3 was highest for any election in any zone (45.83 percent), but the Communists did not win a single seat in that zone (the CPM won one seat in a constituency adjacent to the Zone 2 and 3 areas). This is a result of the fact that in four of the six races in Zone 3 the CPI and CPM ran against each other; together they had a majority of the vote in all four. In the other important race in Zone 3, Tiruthuraipoondi, the CPI ran alone and lost to the DMK. But in 1971 the CPI ran in that and two other constituencies with DMK support and won in all three. The CPM ran against the DMK in the five other constituencies of Zone 3, two in Zone 2 and two in Zone 1, and lost badly in all of them (it is noteworthy that their strongest showing was in Tiruvarur and Nagapattinam constitutencies in Zone 3). While these electoral outcomes reflect the political constraints on the development of agrarian radicalism in Thanjavur (which I will examine in more detail in Chapter 10), they do not detract from my assertion that agrarian radicalism has had for many years a geographically limited but sizable and consistent electoral base in Thanjavur, averaging about 25 percent of the vote in all contested races and about 25 percent in the constituencies of the Zone 2 and 3 areas.

TABLE 35

Communist Performance in Legislative Assembly Elections, 1952-1971, by Agro-Economic Zone

Year and Performance Characteristics	Zone 1	Zone 2	Zone 3*	Zone 4	Zone 5	District
1952 Number of rural seats contested**	1/4	3/4	5/5	1/2	0/1	10/16
Average % of vote won where contested	7.31	26.89	25.23	33.54	—	24.77
Number of seats won	0	1	4	0	—	5***
1957 Number of rural seats contested	3/6	3/3	5/5	1/2	0/2	12/18
Average % of vote won where contested	10.46	15.85	17.91	27.62	—	16.34
Number of seats won	0	0	0	0	—	0
1962 Number of rural seats contested	1/4	2/3	7/7	2/2	0/2	12/18
Average % of vote won where contested	11.16	24.13	29.72	16.34	—	25.01
Number of seats won	0	0	1	0	—	1
1967 Number of rural seats contested	2/5	0/3	6/8	1/3	0/2	9/21
Average % of vote won where contested	30.51	—	45.83	20.19	—	39.59
Number of seats won	1	—	0	0	—	1
1971 Number of rural seats contested	2/5	2/3	8/8	0/3	0/2	12/21
Average % of vote won where contested	6.41	10.80	32.50	—	—	24.53
Number of seats won	0	0	3	0	—	3

NOTES: "Communist performance" is measured by percentage of vote won by undivided CPI and, after the 1964 Communist split, by the combined vote for CPI and/or CPM. The legislative assembly constituencies are grouped according to zone as closely as possible. The match in 1967 and 1971 is very good. However, because the constituencies were larger, going back in time from 1962, there is considerable overlap of constituencies across zones in the earlier elections. This does not much alter the pattern except perhaps between Zones 1 and 2.

* Includes Vedaranyam Block, which is not included in my zonal analysis elsewhere. This tends to lower the average Communist vote in Zone 3 as the Communist percentage in the constituency that includes Vedaranyam is always lower than in the others.

** Rural seats = electorate more than 50 percent rural. This criterion excludes Kumbakonam and Thanjavur City constituencies in every election.

*** The zonal total of seats won does not add to 6 because in 1952 the Communists won a seat in Thanjavur constituency, which was primarily urban and therefore not included here. It should be noted that they also ran well in Kumbakonam constituency in 1952, securing 33.84 percent of the vote.

The pattern of Communist performance in the other zones during the 1952 to 1971 period varied considerably. The Communists never entered a race in Zone 5. In Zone 4 they found some early support that dwindled to nothing by 1971. In Zone 1 Communist performance, while clearly limited, appears somewhat changeable from election to election. This is probably due in part to the way the boundaries of constituencies were drawn at different times, but it may also reflect some underlying agro-economic changes. Finally, while the total number of seats contested by the Communists in the district did not change much over time, there seems to have been some narrowing of the geographic spread of the contests. This may also reflect a shift in agro-economic factors.

What accounts for the heavy concentration of agrarian radicalism (as measured by Communist panchayat control) in the Central and Coastal areas of the Old Delta in Thanjavur? The answer lies in the area's peculiar agro-economic and social structure: the bipolar arrangement of a large group of landless laborers at the bottom and a visible group of large landowners at the top, combined with sharp caste differentiation between these groups and the relative emptiness of the intervening agro-economic space. This explanation would be in accord with my earlier finding (see Chapter 4) that the two strongest correlates of agrarian radicalism in Thanjavur are agricultural labor and Scheduled Caste.

The existence of a large landless labor force in Zones 2 and 3 and in Zone 1 is, as I have mentioned earlier, a function of irrigated paddy cultivation. Irrigated paddy is highly labor-intensive, with labor being provided either from the family or through hire. Where family labor is the primary mode of cultivation, as in Zones 4 and 5, the large landless labor force does not exist. But in the Old Delta greater pressure on the land (due to the age of the system) and cultural restrictions on manual labor have led to the creation of such a force.

Furthermore, under irrigated paddy conditions the labor force tends to be impoverished. Because wet paddy areas are generally monocultural and the demand for labor is seasonal (but high at the peaks), employment is not adequate for a year-round labor force.[3] Of course this situation worsens under increasing population pressure. However, because of the "productivity floor" in wet paddy, economic deterioration takes place gradually rather than

[3] See John T. Purcal, *Rice Economy: Employment and Income in Malaysia* (Honolulu: University Press of Hawaii, 1972), pp. 125-129.

suddenly. Thus the integrity of the ecological system even under severe pressure inhibits abrupt agro-economic change and social disruption.[4]

To the extent that the ecology of irrigated paddy under population pressure tends to generate landlessness, of which landless labor is one form, Zagoria is correct in associating agrarian radicalism with these conditions. The relative absence of agro-economic differentiation in the agrarian structure of Thanjavur's New Delta and Dry Area is a direct result of ecological conditions and certainly the single most important reason for the absence of agrarian radicalism in these same areas. Economic inequality and social distance are minimal there compared to the Old Delta. The relatively "unimodal" agrarian structure lacks the "contradictions" that are generally thought to underlie radical agrarian movements. Of course there are cleavages and conflicts in the New Delta and Dry Areas, generally along caste and factional lines. But they lack the economic basis and confrontational form of cleavages and conflict in Zones 2 and 3.[5] Mobilization is "vertical" rather than "horizontal."

However, we must view such broad ecological differences as a "distant" rather than "proximate" source of agrarian radicalism. They are seldom, if ever, a "sufficient condition" for the emergence of agrarian radicalism. Thanjavur is a case in point. Although the entire Old Delta is under irrigated paddy cultivation and relatively high population pressure and has a large landless labor force, we find that agrarian radicalism does *not* occur throughout the area. Rather, within the Old Delta agrarian radicalism is associated with those areas *less well irrigated* and *less densely populated*—Zones 2 and 3. In other words, if we "unpack" the ecological argument and make distinctions according to the quality of irrigation we find that there is a curvilinear relationship between ecological conditions and agrarian radicalism (see Figure 10). This explains why, for instance,

---

[4] Clifford Geertz, *Agricultural Involution: The Processes of Ecological Change in Indonesia* (Berkeley, Ca.: University of California Press, 1963), pp. 32-36.

[5] In the village of Madigai in Thanjavur Block the salient cleavages are between lineages and hamlets. See T. S. Yeshwanth, *Re-Survey of a Tanjore Village: Madigai* (Madras: University of Madras, Agricultural Economics Research Centre, 1966), p. 16. In the village of Kadambangudi in Budalur Block conflicts between the various non-Brahmin castes predominate. See *Census of India, 1961: Village Monograph—Kadambangudi*, p. 114. In the village of Sengipatti in Thanjavur Block the important divisions are factional, with all factions led by notables of one dominant non-Brahmin caste, the Kallars. See Agricultural Economics Research Centre, Department of Economics, University of Madras, *Sengipatti: A Re-Survey of a Dry Village in the Fertile Thanjavur District* (Madras, 1969), p. 17.

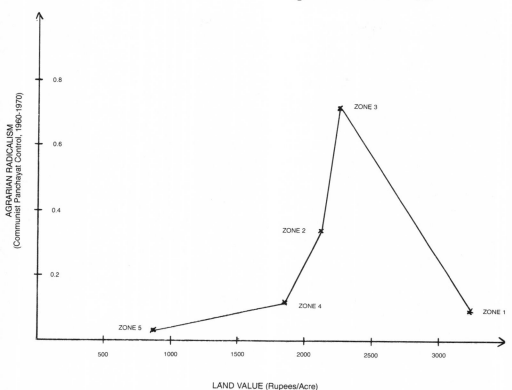

FIGURE 10. Plot of Land Value and Agrarian Radicalism by Agro-Economic Zone

at the district level there is no significant correlation between land value and agrarian radicalism, while within the combined Zones 1 through 3 there is a significant negative correlation.

The reason for this "reversal" in the relationship between eco-logical conditions and agrarian radicalism is the impact of "fine" ecological distinctions on the mode of production and on the agro-economic structure of each area. The less favorable conditions in Zones 2 and 3 have on the whole led to a larger and more impov-erished landless labor force than in Zone 1, larger because of the higher peak demand for labor on the more extensive holdings and more impoverished because of the lower cropping intensity and lower *average* demand for labor.

However, I must emphasize that it is not the magnitude of the labor force by itself that is critical. The differences between the zones along these dimensions are not great enough to account for the difference in agrarian radicalism. Much more important are the structural differences between the zones and the relational consequences of these differences.

First, the more polarized agro-economic structure of Zones 2 and 3 creates a *single sharp cleavage* between the two dominant groups, the large landowners and the landless laborers, out of which the perception of clearly opposing interests is more likely to arise. In contrast, the more complex agro-economic structure of Zone 1 is characterized by several cleavages, none of them as sharp as the landlord-laborer cleavage in Zones 2 and 3. Although the agro-economic structure in Zone 1 is "unequal" by almost any measure, the distance between groups is mediated by the *multi-dimensionality of landlessness*. Therefore no single "contradiction" stands out as a focal point for radical ideology or organization. In Zones 2 and 3, on the other hand, the "contradiction" between the laborer and landowner is highly visible.

Second, the greater economic homogeneity of agricultural labor in Zones 2 and 3 fosters the development of group consciousness and solidarity.[6] We have seen, for instance, that in Zone 1 more laborers also work as cultivators than they do in Zones 2 and 3. "Status overlap" among other semilandless groups in Zone 1, particularly tenants and small owners, is a deterrent to the development of radical ideology and organization because it disperses the conflict of interests. In Zones 2 and 3 the relative cohesiveness of and distance between two groups, labor and owners, tends to create a militant confrontation.[7]

Third, the greater concentration of agricultural labor *at the work place* in Zones 2 and 3 also facilitates the formation of group consciousness and organization. In Zones 2 and 3 more laborers work together on large holdings. In Zone 1 labor is spread out on more numerous small holdings.

A related contributing factor is the nature of labor involvement in the paddy production process. As I noted in Chapter 5, timely operations are crucial in irrigated paddy cultivation and especially in the relatively unfavorable ecological conditions of Zones 2 and 3.[8] The need for quick and efficient labor is heightened on large

[6] Andre Beteille, *Studies in Agrarian Social Structure* (New Delhi: Oxford University Press, 1974), pp. 164-167.

[7] Andre Beteille, "Agrarian Movements in India," mimeographed, undated, p. 16.

[8] C. Muthiah, "The Agricultural Labour Problem in Thanjavur and the New Agricultural Strategy," *Indian Journal of Agricultural Economics* 25 (July-September

holdings. Thus, labor in Zones 2 and 3 gains briefly a degree of bargaining power vis-à-vis the landlord that can be exploited, if the laborers are united, through the obvious means of a strike.[9] This incentive to solidarity is not so readily available in Zone 1 because the small landowner's scale of operations makes a strike less effective. In the Zone 2 and 3 areas large landowners have tried to counter this threat by importing outside labor at peak demand periods.[10] As we shall see in Chapter 10, the use of imported labor has been a key issue in the labor movement in Thanjavur for this very reason.

The relationship between small owners and tenants on the one hand and agricultural labor on the other demonstrates how the larger number of small owners and tenants in Zone 1 creates *cross-cutting cleavages* that inhibit the emergence of agrarian radicalism. Because in irrigated paddy cultivation all but the very smallest holdings require hired labor at peak periods, and labor costs are the single largest component of cultivation costs, small owners and tenants are likely to oppose one of the major demands of a radical labor movement, higher wages.[11] This makes an alliance between the "semilandless" and landless difficult to achieve. It also means that where small owners and tenants are numerous relative to labor resistance to the organization of agricultural labor will be greater.[12]

Eric Wolf and others have argued that a purely landless labor

1970): 15-23. Ganapathia Pillai, "Report of the Commission of Inquiry on the Agrarian Labour Problems of East Thanjavur District," typewritten [1969], p. 3.

[9] C. Muthiah, "Development of Landless Labourers: Role of Group Bargaining Power," paper presented to the Seminar on Weaker Sections held at the Indian Institute of Management at Ahmedabad, October 1972, typewritten, pp. 11-12.

[10] C. Muthiah, "Agricultural Labour Problem," p. 17.

[11] The resistance of small owners in Thanjavur to higher wages for labor has been noted by Ganapathia Pillai in his report on the labor problem in Thanjavur (Pillai, "Report on Agrarian Labour," p. 18). The resistance of tenants in one village to higher wages was noted in Dagfinn Sivertsen, *When Caste Barriers Fall: A Study of Social and Economic Change in a South Indian Village* (Oslo: Universitets Forlaget, 1963), p. 94.

[12] According to T. H. Marshall, "class conflict occurs when a common interest united adjacent levels in opposition to more distant levels." See Marshall, "The Nature of Class Conflict," in *Class, Status and Power: A Reader in Social Stratification*, ed. Reinhard Bendix and Seymour Martin Lipset (Glencoe, Ill.: The Free Press, 1953), p. 16. In writing this Marshall was of course thinking of industrial class conflict in which occupation rather than property underlies the operational definition of "levels." I would suggest that in agrarian class conflict property divisions are more important, and for this reason it is more difficult to unite "levels." Thus, agrarian class conflict is more likely where the lower class is least internally differentiated. See also Linz, "Patterns of Land Tenure," p. 413.

force is difficult to mobilize because of its extreme economic dependence, and therefore that laborers are more susceptible to radical mobilization when they own a minimal amount of land. But in the case of Thanjavur even a small amount of owned land tends to foster, in Barrington Moore's terms, "conservative" rather than "radical solidarity." Land ownership confers status and control over men as well as economic benefits.[13] This is especially true where land is as scarce as it is in Thanjavur. The result is that small owners and even tenants (who may hope to own the land eventually or whose terms of tenure give them considerable control over and use of the land) tend to identify their interests with those of other landowners, particularly in the Zone 1 area where land ownership and control are more attenuated than in Zones 2 and 3.[14] But Wolf was partly right. It is almost certainly true that landless agricultural labor is too economically dependent for sustained independent political action, but as others have noted, labor's economic dependence may be offset by political organization.[15] This is an important factor in agrarian radicalism in Thanjavur that will be discussed in detail in Chapter 10. Suffice it to say now that the Communists have been actively organizing in the Zone 2 and 3 area on and off since the early 1940s.

Juan Linz has compiled a list of key factors facilitating the radicalization of agricultural labor:

1) employment in large numbers on large farms in non-isolated work;
2) a minimum of internal occupational differentiation;
3) seasonal or permanent unemployment;
4) habitation in larger villages;
5) minimal independence derived either from ownership or tenancy or political organization.[16]

These are of course precisely the characteristics of agricultural labor in the agrarian structure of Zones 2 and 3, and they add up to a situation analogous to the classical Marxist vision of the class

[13] Barrington Moore, Jr., *Social Origins of Dictatorship and Democracy: Lord and Peasant in the Making of the Modern World* (Boston: Beacon Press, 1966), pp. 475-478. See also Walter C. Neale, "Land is to Rule," in *Land Control and Social Structure in Indian History*, ed. Robert Eric Frykenberg (Madison, Wis.: The University of Wisconsin Press, 1969), pp. 3-15.

[14] Linz points out that small owners are more conservative where land is more evenly distributed (Linz, "Patterns of Land Tenure," p. 393).

[15] Ibid., p. 420.

[16] Ibid.

structure under industrial capitalism.[17] There is irony in this analogy, for Marx's own analysis of "peasant society" led to the conclusion that the structure of peasant society ("homologous magnitudes") prevented peasants from forming a class.[18] But of course Marx's view of peasant society was undifferentiated in the extreme. If it is taken as a description of *one type* of agrarian structure, however, there is certainly more truth in it; for example, we have seen that the agrarian structure of Zones 4 and 5 resembles more closely the classical definition of peasant society (derived from European experience), and it is not conducive to agrarian radicalism.

The relationship between agrarian structure and agrarian radicalism in Thanjavur's Zones 2 and 3 lends support to Jeffery Paige's theory of rural class relations. The structural characteristics of these areas correspond closely to those of Paige's "decentralized sharecropping" system, which he finds is associated with revolutionary socialist movements. Under this system the noncultivating class derives its income largely from the land, the cultivating class largely from wages. The economic and social distance between the two classes is great. Both groups are economically and socially relatively homogeneous, the issues clearly and sharply defined. The result is a confrontation between a relatively well-organized and potentially radical lower class and an upper class reluctant to grant concessions. Paige also observes that this type of agrarian class structure resembles the industrial class structure that Marx believed would lead to revolution. However, it should be noted that the situation in Thanjavur, especially since the 1950s, differs from Paige's model in one important respect: the cultivating class in Zones 2 and 3 is now composed largely of laborers rather than sharecroppers. As I shall discuss in detail in Chapter 10, this distinction has important consequences for the degree and form of radical mobilization in Thanjavur.

Robert Hardgrave has found a similar relationship between agrarian structure and agrarian radicalism in Kerala.[19] He shows that both historically and currently Communist strength is greatest

[17] See Reinhard Bendix and Seymour Martin Lipset, "Karl Marx's Theory of Social Class," in *Class, Status and Power: A Reader in Social Stratification,* ed. Bendix and Lipset (Glencoe, Ill.: The Free Press, 1953), pp. 28-29.

[18] Karl Marx, *The Eighteenth Brumaire of Louis Bonaparte* (New York: International Publishers, 1963), pp. 123-125.

[19] Robert L. Hardgrave, Jr., "The Communist Parties of Kerala: An Electoral Profile," in *Studies in Electoral Politics in the Indian States,* vol. 4, *Party Systems and Cleavages,* ed. Myron Weiner and John Osgood Field (New Delhi: Manohar Book Service, 1975), pp. 201-206.

in those rural areas (Allepey, Palghat, and Cannanore districts) characterized by a clear "class-type" confrontation between a large landless labor force and a landowning upper class. Thus he finds that the higher the ratio of agricultural laborers to peasant cultivators the greater the support for the Communists. In these "factorylike conditions," writes Hardgrave, "communications and organizations are facilitated, making workers more immediately accessible to Communist mobilization."[20]

It is important to point out that the agro-economic structure of Zones 2 and 3 does not appear to be the result of the impact of "world capitalism" (either directly through the commercialization of agriculture or indirectly through generalized market forces) on what was once a typical peasant society. As noted in Chapter 4, Dharma Kumar has shown that the Thanjavur delta was cultivated primarily through a large landless labor force even at the advent of British rule and that there has been no significant change in the distribution of landownership in the area since the middle of the nineteenth century.[21] Rather this structure is the product of quite particular ecological conditions and historical factors.[22] The close relationship between agrarian radicalism and agro-economic structure should make us wary of generalizing about long-range causes. As Andre Beteille has written:

> A social fact like agrarian unrest has many causes and . . . the same cause produces different results at different places because it never acts in combination with the same factors everywhere.[23]

Up to this point my concern has been only with the agro-economic dimensions of the relationship between agrarian structure and agrarian radicalism in Thanjavur. Of perhaps equal impor-

[20] Robert L. Hardgrave, Jr., "The Kerala Communists: Contradictions of Power," in *Radical Politics in South Asia*, ed. Paul R. Brass and Marcus F. Franda (Cambridge, Mass.: The M.I.T. Press, 1973), p. 141.

[21] See Dharma Kumar, *Land and Caste in South India: Agricultural Labour in Madras Presidency in the Nineteenth Century* (Cambridge: Cambridge University Press, 1965), pp. 186-193, and Kumar, "Land Ownership and Inequality in Madras Presidency: 1853-54 to 1946-47," *The Indian Economic and Social History Review* 12 (July-September 1975): 229-261.

[22] However, as noted above, the Thanjavur situation does not appear to be unique. Both Robert L. Hardgrave and K. C. Alexander have found that agrarian radicalism in Kerala has grown out of a similar agrarian structure. See Hardgrave, "Communist Parties of Kerala," pp. 201-206, and Alexander, "Agrarian Unrest in Kuttanad, Kerala," *Behavioral Sciences and Community Development* 7 (1973): 15-16.

[23] Beteille, *Studies*, p. 169.

tance is the social dimension of caste, in particular the role of Harijans, as is suggested by the strong correlation between Scheduled Caste status and agrarian radicalism. First, we have seen in Chapter 4 that there are far fewer Harijans in Zones 4 and 5 than in Zones 1, 2, and 3 and that Harijans in the New Delta and Dry Area are occupationally more differentiated than in the Old Delta. The relatively compact and homogeneous caste structure of the New Delta and Dry Area reinforces the dampening effects of a unimodal agro-economic structure on the potential for agrarian radicalism.

The Old Delta zones are, on the other hand, generally characterized by greater social as well as agro-economic elaborateness and distance. There are more Brahmins and high-caste non-Brahmins and more Harijans. The isomorphism between caste and agro-economic structure is particularly striking if we compare Zone 1 with Zones 2 and 3. First, in present-day Thanjavur landownership and control in Zone 1 is divided between Brahmins and middle-caste non-Brahmins (especially Kallars and Vanniars), whereas in Zones 2 and 3 landownership and control is still dominated almost entirely by high-caste non-Brahmins. In the southern areas of Zones 2 and 3 middle-caste non-Brahmins (especially Kallars, Odayars, and Ambalkarans) now have a greater share of landownership and control than in the past. But the social distance between middle-caste and high-caste non-Brahmins is less than that between middle-caste non-Brahmins and Brahmins. In other words, landownership is more socially homogeneous in Zones 2 and 3 than in Zone 1.

Similarly, agricultural labor is more socially homogeneous in Zones 2 and 3 than in Zone 1. A larger percentage of agricultural laborers in Zone 2 and especially in Zone 3 are Harijans. Harijans are more numerous in Zones 2 and 3 and on the whole less occupationally differentiated than in Zone 1.

In summary, like the agro-economic structure, the caste structure of Zone 1 is characterized by greater complexity and that of Zones 2 and 3 by relative bipolarity. These differences are reinforced by residential patterns: greater proximity in Zone 1, greater segregation in Zones 2 and 3.[24]

The isomorphism of caste and agro-economic structure in the Old Delta contributes to the inhibiting effect of cross-cutting eco-

---

[24] To illustrate, an early observer of agrarian radicalism in Thanjavur notes that Thanjavur landlords tried to discourage residential concentration of laborers because it fostered a sense of corporate identity among them. See John Frederick Muehl, *Interview with India* (New York: The John Day Co., 1950), p. 278.

nomic cleavages on agrarian radicalism in Zone 1 and intensifies the confrontational character of the single, sharp economic cleavage in Zones 2 and 3.[25] The greater social homogeneity of both agricultural labor and landowners and the wider social gap between the two groups help to create a climate more receptive to radical ideology and organization. For instance, according to a Communist document, because "most of the workers belong to the Harijan community, a class hatred is created."[26] By contrast, in Zone 1 solidarity among either landowners or laborers is inhibited by greater social heterogeneity, and the perception of mutually opposing interests is blurred by intervening social complexity.

This analysis of the relationship between agrarian structure and agrarian radicalism has until now been based largely on interzonal comparisons. An examination of the correlates of agrarian radicalism *within* the Zone 2 and 3 areas (see Table 36) supports my interpretation. In both zones, taken separately and together, agrarian radicalism is positively and significantly correlated with the percentage of agricultural labor and the percentage of Scheduled Caste and negatively correlated with land value (not significant in Zone 2) and the percentage of tenancy. The correlation with the percentage of cultivated area fades in Zone 3 because in the extreme coastal areas the unfavorable irrigation conditions begin to limit the area under cultivation. The underlying import of the correlations with cultivated area and agricultural workers (lower in Zone 2 because the population there is so uniformly agricultural) is that radicalism *is* agrarian—based on agriculture. We also see that density per se is not a significant factor; the tendency to a negative relationship reflects the difference between the "typical" Zones 2 and 3 village and villages closer to the Zone 1 type.

The most striking aspect of this table is the relatively high correlation with the percentage of Scheduled Caste across the two zones. In fact, we find that if we control for Scheduled Caste, the correlation between agrarian radicalism and agricultural labor in

[25] Melvin Tumin has pointed to the importance of "non-class identities" in promoting class solidarity. See Tumin, *Social Stratification: The Forms and Functions of Inequality* (Englewood Cliffs, N.J.: Prentice-Hall, Inc., 1967), p. 54. Kathleen Gough has described how the Communists used the institution of Harijan caste assemblies to mobilize agricultural laborers in Thanjavur. See Gough, "Peasant Resistance and Revolt in South India," *Pacific Affairs* 41 (Winter 1968-1969): 526-544.

[26] Agricultural Workers' Association, "East Thanjavur District Agricultural Workers' Problems: A Memorandum Placed Before the Judge of the Enquiry Commission on Behalf of the Agricultural Workers' Association, Thanjavur, March 11, 1969," typewritten, undated, p. 6.

TABLE 36

Correlates of Agrarian Radicalism (Communist Panchayat Control)
for Zones 2 and 3

Variables	Zone 2 (N = 261)	Zone 3 (N = 465)	Zones 2 and 3 Combined (N = 726)
% of cultivated area, 1971	.188*	−.012	.033
% of agricultural workers, 1971	.083	.212*	.158*
Land value, 1961	−.049	−.176*	−.123*
Agrarian density, 1971	−.044	−.067	−.043
Agricultural labor as % of all agricultural workers, 1971	.257*	.129**	.186
Registered tenants as % of agricultural workers, 1971	−.074	−.119**	−.103**
% of cultivated area under tenancy, 1971	.014	−.066	−.043
% of Scheduled Caste in total population, 1971	.365*	.313*	.340*
Controlling for % of Scheduled Caste	(N = 258)	(N = 462)	(N = 723)
% of agricultural labor	.074	−.026	.013
% of registered tenants	−.136**	−.150*	−.146*

* Significant at .001 level or higher.
** Significant at .01 level or higher.

the separate and combined zones becomes insignificant, while the negative correlation with tenancy becomes slightly stronger. In order to explore the implications of this finding further we must look to the results of a regression analysis of agrarian radicalism in Zones 2 and 3 (see Table 37).

First, the regression results are disappointing in the sense that with all eligible variables entering the equation we are able to "explain" only about 20 percent of the variance (R^2) in agrarian radicalism. This is, I think, largely due to the weakness of the dependent variable to which I referred in Chapter 3: that is, whereas the independent variables are all finely scaled, the dependent variable, Communist panchayat control, is very crudely scaled. The variance in the dependent variable only very roughly approximates reality. I suspect that if there were available a more continuous measure of agrarian radicalism (such as panchayat voting) the results would be statistically more satisfying. However, the stability

TABLE 37

Results of Regression Analysis of Agrarian Radicalism (Communist Panchayat Control) for Zones 2 and 3

Zone	Variables Entered	Multiple R	R²	Δ R²	Beta
2/Old Delta-Central	*All*	.442	.196	—	—
	Only Five:				
	% of Scheduled Caste	.318	.101	.101	.242
	Land value	.378	.143	.042	−.143
	Agricultural development rating	.399	.159	.016	.104
	% of agricultural labor	.411	.169	.010	.128
	Soil quality	.424	.179	.010	−.118
3/Old Delta-Coastal	*All*	.457	.208	—	—
	Only Five:				
	% of Scheduled Caste	.318	.101	.101	.360
	Land value	.376	.141	.040	−.116
	Soil quality	.392	.154	.013	−.144
	% of tenants	.403	.162	.008	−.104
	Change in Scheduled Caste population, 1961-71	.413	.171	.009	−.096
2-3/Old Delta-Central/Coastal	*All*	.430	.185	—	—
	Only Five:				
	% of Scheduled Caste	.328	.108	.108	.335
	Land value	.377	.142	.035	−.127
	% of tenants	.391	.153	.011	−.093
	Soil quality	.402	.162	.009	−.113
	Isolation index	.408	.167	.005	.073

of the statistical results from level to level in my analysis is reason to have confidence in the orders of magnitude and direction of the relationships I have found. It is the pattern of these relationships that is my primary concern.

In order to examine the relative importance of those few variables that contribute most to the explanation of agrarian radicalism I restricted to five the number of variables that could enter the equation (note that in each case these five variables do in fact contribute most of the explained variance). In Zones 2 and 3, separately and combined, the percentage of Scheduled Caste is the most important factor (though somewhat less so in Zone 2): it contributes more than half of the explained variance and has the highest beta weight (the beta weight can be interpreted as the correlation between that variable and agrarian radicalism holding all others constant). Also uniformly important are land value and soil quality, in the direction expected. The absence of agricultural labor from the results of the combined zonal analysis confirms the results of the partial correlations in Table 36. Note however that agricultural labor *is* included in the five variables in Zone 2 and the percentage of tenancy is not. This suggests that there may be differences in the relationship of labor and tenancy to agrarian radicalism between and perhaps within these two zones.

I have heretofore argued that tenancy has not been a contributing factor to agrarian radicalism in Thanjavur. The general thrust of my argument has been that, where more widespread, as in Zone 1, tenancy adds to the complexity of the agro-economic structure, thereby blurring cleavage lines and reducing the polarity of interest conflict, which in turn reduces the potential for radicalization. More specifically, in contrast to those arguments that lump "poor peasants" and labor together I pointed out that because in irrigated paddy cultivation the interests of tenants and small owners tend to be opposed to those of labor a high incidence of tenancy and small ownership will actively inhibit the radical mobilization of labor. These arguments were of course supported by my finding that in Thanjavur agrarian radicalism is concentrated in those areas with an overall lower incidence of tenancy and small ownership and that there is a significant negative correlation between tenancy (unfortunately there is no panchayat-level measure of small ownership) and agrarian radicalism at both the district and zonal levels.

However, it is certainly possible to conceive of circumstances in which tenancy and small ownership would contribute to rather than inhibit the emergence of agrarian radicalism. First, as Linz has observed, radicalization is more likely to occur where tenants and small owners exist amidst a large, impoverished labor force and are themselves relatively underprivileged.[27] Second, tenants and small owners are more likely to ally themselves with agricultural labor where they themselves earn a substantial portion of their

[27] Linz, "Patterns of Land Tenure," pp. 390-391, 405, 409.

income from labor.[28] Third, tenants and small owners are more likely to ally themselves with labor where they share a social identity with labor.[29]

These conditions do exist in certain areas within Zones 2 and 3. We already know that throughout Zones 2 and 3 tenants and small owners co-exist with a large, impoverished labor force in the context of relatively greater concentration of landownership in the hands of large landlords. We also know that by virtue of their small holdings in an area of relatively poor irrigation and low productivity small tenants and small owners in Zones 2 and 3 are less well off than their counterparts in Zone 1.[30] In addition, because of their economic marginality small tenants and small owners in Zones 2 and 3 are more likely to supplement their income through labor on other farms, especially in those areas where their caste status does not bar them from manual labor in the fields.[31] Finally, in those same areas, of course, their caste identity tends to bind them with Harijan labor.

In Table 38 we see that in the Sirkali and Mannargudi taluks of Zones 2 and 3 Harijans are a relatively large percentage of the tenantry, and therefore we find as expected in Table 39 that agrarian radicalism is positively correlated with tenancy in those taluks. In view of the absence of any correlation between labor and radicalism it appears that in Sirkali tenancy was the principal source of agrarian radicalism (though, as we shall see in Chapter 8 the tenancy base is the reason for the relative weakness of radicalism in the Sirkali area) whereas in Mannargudi both labor and tenancy are strongly involved. In Nannilam and Nagapattinam, by contrast, Harijan tenants and small owners are few; therefore the negative relationship between tenancy and agrarian radicalism holds. Finally, in Tiruthuraipoondi we find that Harijan small owners are relatively numerous; thus there is no correlation between radicalism and tenancy but a relatively high correlation between radicalism and Scheduled Caste.

The last is an important point, for I am arguing that these variations in the relationship of tenants and small owners to agrarian

---

[28] Sivertsen found this was true in the Thanjavur village he studied in the late 1950s (Sivertsen, *When Caste Barriers Fall*, p. 94).

[29] Gough has noted the importance of caste differences in divisions between tenants and laborers in Thanjavur (Gough, "Peasant Resistance and Revolt," p. 540).

[30] See Badrinath, *A Report on the Implementation of the Tamilnadu Agricultural Lands Record of Tenancy Rights Act, 1969* (Madras, 1971), pp. 32-35.

[31] IADP, *Study on Tenancy Patterns in Thanjavur*, p. 32.

TABLE 38

Harijan Tenants and Small Owners by Zone and Taluk
(Aggregated Village Data)

Zone	Taluk	Harijan Tenants as % of All Tenants	Harijan Small Owner as % of All Small Owners	% of Harijan Households That Are		
				Labor	Tenant	Small Owners
1	Overall (15)	39.91	15.78	69.48	22.79	7.73
2 and 3	Overall (24)	29.68	20.26	77.43	13.00	9.57
	Sirkali (5)	43.19	25.42	61.73	26.45	11.82
	Nannilam (4)	7.24	4.38	92.29	5.85	1.86
	Nagapattinam (5)	26.40	7.44	84.81	11.23	3.96
	Mannargudi (5)	34.57	30.82	76.45	12.64	10.91
	Tiruthuraipoondi (5)	29.58	44.24	76.55	5.44	18.01

SOURCE: Calculated from data available in Badrinath, *A Report on the Implementation of the Tamilnadu Agricultural Lands Record of Tenancy Rights Act, 1969* (Madras, 1971), pp. 80-261. The data are aggregated village-level figures. The number of villages from which each zone and subzone average was computed is in parentheses.

NOTE: Small owner = owns one acre or less.

radicalism in the Zone 2 and 3 areas offer an explanation of the high correlation between Scheduled Caste and agrarian radicalism at the zonal level. There is no doubt that caste status per se is an important factor in the emergence of agrarian radicalism in Thanjavur because of the contribution it makes to group consciousness and solidarity, but it would be a mistake to infer from the statistical evidence that caste status (as opposed to economic status) is the dominant factor.[32] The high correlation between caste and radicalism reflects in part the independent effect of caste *but* also derives its strength from those instances where tenants and small owners join agricultural labor in support of agrarian radicalism. In other

[32] Hardgrave notes that in Palghat District, Kerala, the poor tenants and landless laborers who support the Communists are drawn primarily from the low-status Ezhava community. However, he rejects the interpretation that caste is the "social base" of communism in the area, noting that Ezhavas who have managed to move up economically do *not* favor the Communists. He thus concludes that Ezhava support "represents essentially a class orientation" (Hardgrave, "Communist Parties of Kerala," pp. 202-203). I am here making a very similar argument.

TABLE 39

Labor, Tenancy, and Caste Correlated with Agrarian Radicalism
for Different Taluks within Zones 2 and 3

| Taluks | Agrarian Radicalism Correlated with | | |
	Agricultural Labor	Tenancy	Scheduled Caste
Sirkali (N = 136)	.001	.149	.169
Nannilam (N = 176)	.148*	− .029	.237**
Nagapattinam (N = 124)	.197*	− .055	.230*
Mannargudi (N = 93)	.304*	.327**	.507**
Tiruthuraipoondi (N = 71)	.307*	.014	.379**

* Significant at .01 level or higher.
** Significant at .001 level or higher.

words, Harijan caste status is in part a surrogate measure for a type
of tenancy or small ownership that is likely to be allied with agricultural labor.

The correlations in Table 39 support this view. Note first that in
those areas where tenancy is negatively and labor positively related
to radicalism, i.e., Nannilam and Nagapattinam, the correlation
between caste and radicalism is not much higher than that between
labor and radicalism. In Mannargudi, though, where both labor
and tenancy are strongly correlated with radicalism, the correlation
between caste and radicalism is much higher than either of the
others. In Tiruthuraipoondi the higher caste correlation reflects
the role of small owners. But since we could logically expect that
small owners would be less inclined than tenants to ally themselves
with labor, we should not be surprised that the caste correlation
does not exceed the labor correlation by as much as in Mannargudi.
Finally, if caste status per se were the sole basis of radical solidarity,
we would expect to find a higher caste correlation in Sirkali (for

we know that Harijan laborers are numerous in Sirkali); but we do not.

Caste status functions in this way because there is a correlation between it and those economic characteristics of tenancy and small ownership that favor their alliance with agricultural labor—that is, economic weakness and involvement in agricultural labor. If caste solidarity per se were the main source of agrarian radicalism, we would not expect to find agrarian radicalism confined to the Zone 2 and 3 areas, for we know that Harijans are numerous in Zone 1 as well. Finally, my earlier assertion that tenants and small owners are more likely to be radicalized in the context of a polarized economic structure finds support in the fact that Harijan tenancy in Zone 1 has not resulted in tenant radicalism as it has in Mannargudi.

CHAPTER 7

Agricultural Labor and
Agrarian Radicalism

THE STRUCTURAL SOURCES of agrarian radicalism in Thanjavur District emerged quite clearly in the last chapter. Measured in the aggregate, radicalism is associated with a relatively bipolar structure in which a socially homogeneous, largely landless and impoverished labor force confronts a small and homogeneous group of large landowners. Thus, radicalism has its strongest base among Harijan agricultural laborers in Zones 2 and 3. Where tenancy and small landholdings are embedded in this structure, they also contribute to the development of radicalism.

The relationship between agrarian structure and radicalism can be more fully understood when the aggregate findings can be corroborated at the individual level. Such is the task of the present chapter, which draws on survey data collected from several hundred laboring and cultivating households in Thanjavur District. Because labor is so clearly central to the explanation of radicalism, I will focus attention on the characteristics of laborers, while also drawing on evidence from the survey of cultivators to describe relations between the laboring and landowning communities.

In addition, I will show that electoral support for the Communist parties—my principal measure of radicalism—is strongly correlated with other measures at the individual level, such as attitudes on agrarian issues and involvement in agrarian disputes. The same survey evidence will help to clarify the issues around which the mobilization of labor takes place. Finally, I will briefly examine the relationship between tenancy and agrarian radicalism at the individual level, drawing on both the laborer and the cultivator data.

AGRICULTURAL LABOR

I will begin by exploring the distribution of labor support for the Communist parties (CPI or CPM) in Thanjavur. All survey respondents were asked to indicate which political parties they support. Table 40 shows how many laborers, in comparison with the sampled cultivators, indicated that they support one or both of the Communist parties. It is clear that support for the Communists is much greater among laborers than among cultivators and is heavily concentrated in Zones 2 and 3 for both groups. As we shall see later in this chapter, cultivator support for the Communists comes largely from tenants and small owners in Zones 2 and 3, in accord with my earlier findings.

The only surprise in Table 40 is the relatively large proportion of laborers in Zone 5 indicating support for the Communists. This high figure, which was not at all reflected in the aggregate data, is partially a result of sampling techniques and partially a consequence of the nature of the Zone 5 agrarian structure. First, as explained in Chapter 3, the sampling techniques used for this survey were designed primarily to allow one to investigate relationships within different subsets ("cells") of the sample. Thus, certain groups were disproportionately sampled, and laborers in Zone 5 were among them. This may have caused laborers who support the Communist parties to be oversampled.[1] Second, the fact that significant individual labor support for the Communists in Zone 5 does not show up in Communist panchayat control or Communist voting in general elections (see Chapter 6) reflects the much smaller proportion of agricultural labor in the agricultural work force in that zone, 32

TABLE 40

Laborer and Cultivator Support for Communist Parties by Zone

Group	% Indicating Support in Each Zone					
	Zone 1	Zone 2	Zone 3	Zone 4	Zone 5	All Zones
Laborers	1.2 (84)	32.0 (72)	83.3 (60)	1.7 (58)	37.1 (35)	28.5 (309)
Cultivators	.9 (102)	9.1 (88)	28.7 (94)	5.1 (98)	5.1 (59)	10.0 (441)

NOTE: Figures in parentheses indicate the N of respondents for each zone and for the entire sample.

[1] If estimates of population parameters or districtwide statistical analysis were my primary purpose, it would be possible to overcome the disproportionate sampling by the weighting of different groups in the analysis.

percent as compared with 65 percent to 72 percent in Zones 1, 2, and 3. Thus, while the Communists may have acquired a significant following among laborers in Zone 5, this has not translated into the ability to contest or win elections. The nature of radicalism in Zone 5 will be further explored as I continue the survey data analysis.

The data on Communist party voting and party membership in Table 41 demonstrate further the concentration of agrarian radicalism in Zones 2 and 3. Note that the percentage of Zone 5 laborers voting Communist is much higher for the panchayat elections than for the general elections. This is a consequence of the radical base in the zone not being large enough (at least in 1970 to 1971) for the Communists to field a candidate in the general elections.

In pursuing the analysis of labor and agrarian radicalism in Thanjavur a single measure of Communist support will be employed that is more likely to reflect a stable pattern than does the voting data and that captures some variation in the level of support (see Table 42).[2] This new measure, "Communist Support," is a combination of several variables—the support and membership variables already described, and a third, "forced choice" variable based on whether respondents who did not initially indicate support

TABLE 41

Communist Voting and Party Membership Among Laborers by Zone

	% Voting Communist/Communist Members in Each Zone					
	Zone 1	Zone 2	Zone 3	Zone 4	Zone 5	All Zones
Voting (last election)						
Panchayat	1.8	33.4	91.2	10.7	21.7	27.2
General	2.5	18.5	66.3	7.8	4.3	20.5
Party members	—	15.2	21.6	—	8.6	8.7

[2] The variable "Communist Support" is, however, strongly correlated with a summary measure of voting for Communist parties in panchayat and general elections. Cross-tabulation of the two variables yields a Kendall's *tau* β of 0.7565 that is significant at the .0000 level.

TABLE 42

Communist Support (Summary Variable) Among Labor by Zone

Level of Communist Support	% in Each Category in Each Zone						
	Zone 1	Zone 2	Zone 3	Zone 4	Zone 5	All Zones %	(N)
No support	97.6	68.1	8.3	96.6	62.9	69.2	(213)
"Forced" support	1.2	0.0	8.3	1.7	0.0	2.3	(7)
Support	1.2	16.7	61.7	1.7	28.6	19.8	(61)
Party member	0.0	15.3	21.7	0.0	8.6	8.8	(27)
Total	100.0	*	100.0	100.0	*	*	
(N)	(83)	(72)	(60)	(58)	(35)		(308)

NOTES: Figures in parentheses indicate the N for each zone and for each category of support.
* Does not add to 100 due to rounding.

for a particular party said they would support the CPI or the CPM if they had to choose a party. However, the major breaking point in the variable is clearly between the categories of "Forced Support" and "Support."

Labor Type and Caste

Having shown that agrarian radicalism among individuals in Thanjavur is, as expected, concentrated among laborers in Zones 2 and 3, I can now explore the relationships between radicalism and the tenurial-labor status and caste of these laborers. My earlier analysis of the basis for agrarian radicalism leads to the expectation that it would be most widespread among purely landless Harijan laborers.

For my purposes the laborers have been divided into four groups: 1) purely landless, noncultivating laborers who work on a daily (casual) basis; 2) landless, noncultivating laborers who work on a long-term (seasonal or annual) contractual basis; 3) laborers who cultivate some rented land; and 4) laborers who own and cultivate some land.[3] Table 43 shows how each of these groups contributes

[3] Of 311 laborers surveyed, 135 cultivate some land (by definition no more than would yield income, together with nonagricultural income, amounting to 49.9 per-

to Communist support in the three zones where such support is significant. (The category of "Forced Support" is also eliminated from the analysis because it is insignificant—only seven cases.) In Zone 2 and especially in Zone 3 Communist support comes heavily from the casual landless laborers. In Zone 3 about 60 percent of both party supporters and members are from this group, *and* over 90 percent of all supporters and members are landless laborers (not shown in the table). The very high identification of this one group with the Communists provides a great deal of the solidarity needed for radical mobilization.

Part tenants and part owners are also a significant support group in both zones. For many of these individuals the marginality of their involvement in cultivation, their participation in a large, homogeneous labor force, and, as we shall see, their shared caste status all outweigh any "conservative" pull that their attachment to the land might exert. Again, this is particularly the case in Zone 3 where almost 90 percent of both labor-tenants and labor owners sampled provide some degree of support to the Communists.

The picture in Zone 2 is somewhat more complicated. First, no labor group in Zone 2 is as fully committed to the Communists as are all groups in Zone 3. About 65 percent of landless laborers, 73 percent of labor-tenants, and 83 percent of labor owners in that zone are not supporters. Second, attached laborers, whose prominence in Zone 2 is a vestige of the *pannaiyal* ("farm servant") system on the area's many large temple estates, are a significant fraction of Communist party members in the zone. All in all, the radical support base in Zone 2 is more heterogeneous and contingent than in Zone 3. This is of course reflected in the lower levels of Communist panchayat control in Zone 2.

Zone 5 presents a sharply different picture of radical support. Reflecting the much lesser role of pure landless labor in the agrarian structure of the zone, most Communist supporters come from the ranks of labor-tenants and labor-owners. They are also relatively isolated. Only 40 percent of the sampled labor-tenants and 40 percent of the labor-owners in the zone support the Commu-

---

cent of total household income). Of these 135, 58 cultivate all or mainly rented land, and 77 cultivate all or mainly owned land; 96 cultivate less than one acre, 29 cultivate one to two acres, and only 10 cultivate over two acres (8 of these as tenants). Of the 311 surveyed, only 36 respondents are attached laborers. Casual, landless laborers form the largest single group—145 respondents, or 45.0 percent of the total sample.

TABLE 43

Communist Support and Tenurial-Labor Status in Zones 2, 3, and 5

Zone	Tenurial-Labor Status	% of Respondents at Different Levels of Communist Support from Tenurial-Labor Status Groups		
		No Support	Support	Member
2/Old Delta-Central	Casual-landless	46.9	75.0	27.3
	Attached labor	16.3	—	54.5
	Labor-tenant	16.3	16.7	9.1
	Labor-owner	20.4	8.3	9.1
	Total	*	100.0	100.0
	(N)	(49)	(12)	(11)
3/Old Delta-Coastal	Casual-landless	25.0	59.5	61.5
	Attached labor	—	—	—
	Labor-tenant	25.0	13.5	7.7
	Labor-owner	50.0	27.0	30.8
	Total	100.0	100.0	100.0
	(N)	(4)	(37)	(13)
5/Dry Area	Casual-landless	9.1	30.0	—
	Attached labor	—	—	—
	Labor-tenant	27.3	20.0	66.7
	Labor-owner	63.6	50.0	33.3
	Total	100.0	100.0	100.0
	(N)	(22)	(10)	(3)

NOTES: Figures in parentheses indicate the N of respondents for each category of support in each zone.

* Does not add to 100 due to rounding.

nists. This situation helps to account for the political latency of radicalism in the zone.

Among the correlates of agrarian radicalism in the aggregate data analysis caste was even stronger than labor status. This appears to be the case at the individual level as well. In Table 44 Communist supporters in Zones 2, 3, and 5 are broken into three caste categories: Harijan (Scheduled Caste), Backward, and Forward (in

TABLE 44

Communist Support and Caste Status in Zones 2, 3, and 5

| Zone | Caste Category | % of Respondents at Different Levels of Communist Support from Various Caste Categories | | |
		No Support	Support	Member
2/Old Delta-Central	Harijan	49.0	72.7	100.0
	Backward	44.9	18.2	—
	Forward	6.1	9.1	—
	Total	100.0	100.0	100.0
	(N)	(49)	(11)	(11)
3/Old Delta-Coastal	Harijan	25.0	91.9	100.0
	Backward	—	—	—
	Forward	75.0	8.1	—
	Total	100.0	100.0	100.0
	(N)	(4)	(37)	(13)
5/Dry Area	Harijan	59.1	50.0	100.0
	Backward	36.4	50.0	—
	Forward	4.5	—	—
	Total	100.0	100.0	100.0
	(N)	(22)	(10)	(3)

NOTE: Figures in parentheses indicate the N of respondents for each category of support in each zone.

roughly ascending order of ritual status). In each zone one hundred percent of Communist party members are Harijans and in Zones 2 and 3 a large majority of supporters are Harijans. This confirms the importance of caste homogeneity as a factor in radical mobilization. The fact that 98 percent of the Harijans in Zone 3 are Communist supporters (not shown in Table 44) further underscores the point and may seem to suggest that caste per se is the major factor underlying Communist mobilization in Thanjavur. But this assertion is belied by the obvious fact that many Harijans in other parts of the district are not Communist supporters, including over 50 percent of Harijans in Zone 2, and additionally by the fact that 28 percent of Communist supporters in Zone 2 are non-Harijans. Caste status plays such a powerful role in radical mobilization because economic conflicts lie at the core of caste divisions. When these divisions are particularly sharp and visible, as in Zones 2 and 3, caste is a ready symbol, idiom, and cement for radical mobilization.

Non-Harijan caste members figure more importantly in Communist support in Zone 5 than in Zones 2 or 3. Overall, the combined caste distribution of Communist party supporters and members in Zone 5 differs little from the overall caste distribution for the zonal sample. This was also true for the labor-tenurial status distribution of Communist supporters and suggests again that radicalism is encapsulated within the zone's larger, nonsupportive agrarian context (more than 60 percent of both Harijan and Backward Caste members in the zone are not Communist supporters).

Meaning of Communist Support

Until now I have equated Communist party support with radicalism largely on the strength of the parties' association with radical ideological tendencies at the national level and with agrarian unrest in Thanjavur District. At this point I will use the survey data to probe both the specific content of individual labor support for the Communists and the relationship of the parties to other agrarian groups.

Table 45 compares the reasons given for party support by laborers supporting the Communists with those given by laborers supporting other parties. It is striking that much higher proportions of Communist supporters give reasons dealing either with general economic ideology or with specific agrarian policies (especially re wages) than do their counterparts. Clearly laborers in Thanjavur identify the Communist parties with the agro-economic issues that are at the heart of their conflict with landowners.

The other side of this conflict is how the landowners perceive the Communist parties. In Table 46 we see that of the large landowners (or *mirasdars*) who were asked which parties, if any, they particularly oppose, those in Zones 2 and 3 were most likely to express opposition to the Communist parties. This accords with my description of those zones as areas in which landowners and labor are in sharp confrontation. Out of all the Zone 2 and 3 cultivators who were opposed to the Communists, 56.7 percent specifically

TABLE 45

Reasons Given by Laborers for Party Support

	% Mentioning Reason	
Reason	Communist Party Supporters	Other Party Supporters
General ideology— "For poor, equality"	19.0	6.7
Party leadership/history— "Party of Independence, MGR"	0.0	10.4
Character of party— "Honest, good party"	3.6	7.4
Party identification— "It is my party"	2.4	12.6
Because others support it— village, street	16.7	23.0
Gives general assistance to us, people like us	7.1	12.6
For specific policies— agriculture	46.4	9.5
For specific policies— other	0.0	3.0
Unspecified—"I like it, I support it"	4.8	14.8
Total	100.0	100.0
(N)	(84)	(135)

NOTE: Figures in parentheses indicate the total N of party supporters.

mentioned Communist instigation of labor unrest and violence as reasons for their opposition.

The sharp landowner-laborer confrontation in Zones 2 and 3 is also evident in the patterns of membership in agrarian organizations. Membership in either the CPI or the CPM Agricultural Workers' Union[4] is heavily concentrated in those zones (see Table 47). These unions are closely affiliated with the parties, and thus membership is related to Communist support. Of union members in Zones 2 and 3, 84 and 92 percent respectively are either Party supporters or Party members. Similarily, membership in one prom-

[4] See Chapter 10 for a full description of the role of the unions.

TABLE 46

Opposition by *Mirasdars* to Communist Parties

	% Expressing Opposition to CPI and/or CPM					
Zone 1	Zone 2	Zone 3	Zone 4	Zone 5	All Zones	
18.8 (16)	43.8 (16)	50.0 (16)	33.3 (21)	7.7 (13)	30.5 (82)	

NOTES: The term *mirasdar* generally refers to a large landowner. Today the term specifically refers to someone owning more than about seven acres of irrigated paddy land. For the purpose of constructing this table I have chosen all respondents cultivating ten acres or more of owned or primarily owned land.

Figures in parentheses are the N of respondents for each zonal sample.

TABLE 47

Agricultural Workers' Union Membership by Zone

Whether Member	% Responding in Each Zone				
	Zone 1	Zone 2	Zone 3	Zone 4	Zone 5
No	98.8	73.6	38.3	100.0	100.0
Yes	1.2	26.4	61.7	—	—
Total (N)	100.0 (84)	100.0 (72)	100.0 (60)	100.0 (59)	100.0 (35)

NOTE: Figures in parentheses indicate the total N of respondents for each zone.

inent landowners' organization, the Thanjavur District Mirasdars' Association, is limited entirely to cultivator survey respondents living in either Zone 2 or Zone 3 (19 individuals in all out of 180). It is noteworthy that none of the Communist laborers in Zone 5 are union members, again suggesting that Communist support in that area is too limited and isolated to permit organized activity.

Attitudes

The analysis of agrarian radicalism so far presented has relied almost entirely on objective data. Survey data on the attitudes of Thanjavur laborers towards key agrarian issues afford an opportunity to examine the subjective dimension of radicalism. In particular, I will examine whether Communist laborers in Zone 2 and 3 hold more radical views on the issues.

The surveyed laborers were asked to agree or disagree with a series of opinion statements on specific agrarian issues (see Table 48).[5] Their responses to these statements were combined into an attitudinal scale with a low score of "0" and a high score of "4." The higher the score, the more radical the respondent's overall response. The distribution of labor attitude scale scores in Table 49 follows the pattern of other data. First, the scores are highest in Zones 2, 3, and 5. More importantly, the scores for Communist party supporters and members are sharply higher than the scores for nonsupporters. Indeed, among nonsupporters the variation across the zones almost disappears. Nor is the association between Communist support and more radical attitudes an artifact of the tenurial-labor status and caste composition of that support (see Table 50). Even among Harijan landless laborers the level of Com-

TABLE 48

Labor Opinion Statements

1. There should be a minimum wage for all agricultural laborers.
2. Tractors and other machinery put agricultural laborers out of work.
3. Use of tractors and other machinery should be controlled.
4. Cultivators can't afford to pay higher wages to agricultural laborers.
5. Cultivators shouldn't be allowed to use outside labor.
6. Agricultural laborers should have a union like other workers.
7. *Mirasdars* don't treat agricultural laborers with enough respect.
8. There is not enough work available for agricultural laborers to earn a decent living.
9. Agricultural laborers can get higher wages from *mirasdars* only when they stick together.
10. In times of family distress a laborer can always get help from the *mirasdar*.
11. Even if the wages are too low, the laborer has no choice but to work in the *mirasdars'* fields.
12. The *mirasdars* are too powerful to be challenged by the agricultural laborers.
13. In disputes with *mirasdars* all agricultural laborers must support each other.

[5] The actual possible responses were: strongly agree, agree, no opinion, disagree, strongly disagree.

TABLE 49

Labor Attitudes and Communist Support by Zone

Level of Communist Support	Scale Score for Respondents by Category and Zone					
	All Zones	Zone 1	Zone 2	Zone 3	Zone 4	Zone 5
No support	2.753 (211)	2.752	2.857	2.731	2.596	2.923
Support	3.047 (61)	2.539	3.077	3.089	2.615	2.946
Party member	3.114 (27)	—	2.986	3.160	—	3.385
Total (N)	2.849 (299)	2.743 (82)	2.914 (72)	3.086 (54)	2.601 (36)	2.969 (35)

NOTES: The category of forced support is omitted because of its very small size ($N = 7$).

The figures in parentheses are the total N of respondents for each zone and for each support category.

The entire table has an F value of 21.1682, significant at the .0000 level.

munist support has an independent effect on the scores—the higher the level of support, the higher the score.

However, among Communist supporters attitudinal differences across the zones persist—Zone 2 and Zone 3 supporters have higher scores—indicating again that the zonal context, in particular the agrarian structure, has an effect independent of Communist support. Zone 5 would seem to be an exception to this, as Communist supporters there have scores almost equal to those of Communist supporters in Zones 2 and 3, and Communist party members in Zone 5 have the highest average score of any group represented in Table 49. The persistent evidence of individual radical tendencies among laborers in Zone 5 suggests that they are responding to a structural situation analogous in some way to the bipolar opposition of landless labor and large landowners in Zones 2 and 3. The fact that Harijan labor-tenants have the most radical views among Zone 5 groups—as compared with Harijan landless laborers in Zone 3 (see Table 51)—suggests that tenancy relations might be the key to this structural context.

The more radical attitudes of laborers in Zones 2 and 3 are matched by the more conservative attitudes of large landowners,

TABLE 50

Attitude Scores for Harijan Landless Labor According to the Level of Communist Support in All Zones

Level of Communist Support	Scale Scores of Harijan Landless Laborers Only
No support	2.867
	(55)
Supporter	3.140
	(27)
Party member	3.175
	(11)

NOTE: Figures in parentheses indicate the total N of respondents in each category.

TABLE 51

Attitude Scores for Various Tenurial and Caste Categories of Laborers in Zones 3 and 5

Labor-Tenurial Type	Zone 3			Zone 5		
	Harijan	Backward	Forward	Harijan	Backward	Forward
Casual-landless	3.191	—	2.744	3.115	2.718	—
	(31)		(3)	(2)	(3)	
Labor-tenant	2.904	2.846	—	3.323	2.962	3.000
	(8)	(1)		(5)	(4)	(1)
Labor-owner	3.077	—	2.949	2.994	2.692	—
	(14)		(3)	(14)	(6)	

NOTE: Figures in parentheses indicate the N of respondents in each category.

again demonstrating the relative polarization in those areas. All cultivators surveyed were asked to respond to a number of opinion statements on various agrarian issues including six dealing specifically with labor-landowner relationships (see Table 52). Scored and scaled in the same manner as the labor responses these items yield a single attitudinal measure. In Table 53 we see the average scores

TABLE 52

Landowner Opinion Statements on Labor Issues

1. Cultivators can't afford to pay higher wages to agricultural laborers.
2. There should be a minimum wage for all agricultural laborers.
3. Tractors and other machinery put agricultural laborers out of work.
4. Use of tractors and other machinery should be controlled.
5. Cultivators shouldn't be allowed to use outside labor.
6. Agricultural laborers don't work sincerely these days.

TABLE 53

Attitude Scores on Labor Issues for Large Landowners by
Holding Size Category and Zone

Size Categories	Zone 1	Zone 2	Zone 3	Zone 4	Zone 5
10-20 acres	1.00	0.97	0.91	1.27	1.30
Over 20 acres	0.94	1.16	1.00	1.04	1.88
All Sizes	1.16	1.06	1.35	1.24	1.61

for large landowners (pure owners with holdings of ten acres or more) across the five zones. The lower the score, the more "conservative" the respondents' attitudes. In general, the landowners in Zones 2 and 3 stand out as being most opposed to labor interests. Note that this degree of opposition to labor is not shared by landowners in Zone 5. Some laborers, especially labor-tenants in that zone, may be as radicalized as their counterparts in Zones 2 and 3, but they do not appear to stand in as sharp confrontation with a broad group of landowners as their Zone 2 and 3 counterparts. This parallels my earlier finding that large landowners in Zone 5 do not single out the Communist party for opposition. Clearly agrarian radicalism in Zone 5 has not generated broad ideological and political conflict.

Disputes

The confrontation between landowners and laborers in Zones 2 and 3 that is so apparent in political affiliations and attitudes occasionally erupts in conflict or dispute. When disputes between landowners and laborers become bitter, frequent, widespread, and politically organized they constitute the most direct evidence of agrarian radicalism. It was precisely such episodes of landowner-laborer conflict in the late 1940s and again in the late 1960s that gave Thanjavur its reputation for radicalism. How these conflicts developed will be the subject of detailed examination in Chapter 10. At this point, analysis of the survey data allows me to explore whether landowner-laborer disputes in the late 1960s and early 1970s conform to the pattern revealed by my prior analysis of radicalism in Thanjavur.

Table 54 presents several measures of the reported occurrence of landowner-laborer disputes across the five zones. Clearly the frequency of such disputes is significantly higher in Zones 2 and 3 than elsewhere in the district, as might be expected. The fact that the reported occurrence of disputes in Zone 5 is relatively low again suggests that the radical potential in that area is not manifested in landowner-labor conflict.

The laborers and cultivators reporting landowner-laborer disputes were also asked to indicate what they thought the issues in those disputes were. The responses of those in Zones 1, 2, and 3 who reported the occurrence of one or more disputes are summarized in Table 55. About 75 percent of the reasons for the disputes cited by both laborers and cultivators center on the wage issue (this pattern does not vary significantly across the zones).

The centrality of the wage issue is perhaps a bit surprising given what we know about the sharpness and politicization of the landowner-laborer conflict in Zones 2 and 3. Normally we might expect that wage levels would be amenable to compromise by the parties and thus less likely to sustain such bitter conflict. But in the case of the Zone 2 and Zone 3 areas of Thanjavur District the wage issue lies at the core of the economic interests of each group. For a largely landless and highly impoverished labor force in an agro-economic setting where agricultural employment is available only a few months a year and other employment is hardly available at all the level of wages paid during the few months of employment is key to economic survival. For a landowning class facing relatively severe limits on total productivity and paying a larger share of production costs to labor wage levels are also key to survival. When the demand for labor is concentrated in a short space of time, as we know it is for paddy harvest in Thanjavur, labor has greater bargaining power to seek wage increases and landowners greater incentive to resist them.

TABLE 54

Reported Occurrence of Landowner-Laborer Disputes by Zone

Report and Dispute	% of Respondents in Each Zone Reporting Disputes				
	Zone 1	Zone 2	Zone 3	Zone 4	Zone 5
Laborers reporting one or more landowner-laborer disputes in village over last five years	11.9 (84)	15.3 (72)	25.0 (60)	0.0 (60)	8.6 (35)
Cultivators reporting disputes between landowners and laborers over last five years					
Few	4.9	15.9	8.7	—	—
Several	—	—	3.3	—	—
Many	1.0	—	—	—	—
Total	5.9 (102)	15.9 (88)	12.0 (92)	(98)	(59)
Cultivators reporting that disputes with labor are a somewhat or very important problem in their cultivation	1.0 (102)	26.2 (88)	21.3 (94)	2.0 (98)	— (59)

NOTE: Figures in parentheses indicate the total N of respondents for each zone for each measure.

The impact of this combination of low average demand and high peak demand for labor peculiar to the low-quality irrigated paddy system of east Thanjavur is evident in the responses of sampled laborers and landowners to questions about labor use and wage patterns. First, laborers were asked to cite the "greatest difficulties" they faced in their work (see Table 56). A distinct zonal pattern is evident. In Zones 1 and 4 conditions of work (hours, difficulty of field labor) are most frequently cited as the greatest problem. In Zone 5 wages are the only major concern. In Zones 2 and 3, however, the largest proportion of respondents say that availability of

TABLE 55

Key Issues in Landowner-Laborer Disputes Reported by Laborers
and Cultivators in Zones 1, 2, and 3

| Issue | % of Responses by Cultivators and Laborers in Each Category | |
	Laborer	Cultivator
Wages		
General	—	14.7
Labor requests higher wage	55.3	50.0
Landowner refuses to pay agreed or legally set wage	23.4	8.8
Outside labor use	6.4	20.6
Tractor use	2.1	—
Labor stops work	4.2	—
Other	8.5	5.9
Total	*	100.00
(N)	(47)	(34)

NOTES: Figures in parentheses are the total number of issues cited by each group.
This exceeds the number of respondents reporting disputes because some respondents cited more than one issue as central to the disputes.

* Does not add to 100 due to rounding.

work is their greatest problem. At the same time, if not forced to
single out the greatest difficulty 75 percent of laborers in Zones 2
and 3, as well as a very high proportion of respondents in other
zones, say that wage issues are "very important" to them. The
distinctiveness of the wage issue in Zones 2 and 3 lies in its linkage
with the problem of the very low availability of work throughout
the year.

The militancy of Zone 2 and 3 laborers on these issues was heightened in the late 1960s by their perception that the overall demand
for their labor was decreasing, in part as a result of the introduction
of the tractor for plowing and hauling operations (see Table 57).
While neither operation provides nearly as many man-days of em-

TABLE 56

Difficulties Faced by Agricultural Laborers in Their Work by Zone

	% of Respondents in Each Zone Mentioning Difficulty				
Difficulty	Zone 1	Zone 2	Zone 3	Zone 4	Zone 5
Wages	29.7	26.4	19.7	6.9	64.3
Availability of work	3.6	43.4	57.1	0.0	10.7
Conditions of work (hours, difficulty)	66.7	22.7	12.5	89.7	14.3
All other	0.0	7.5	10.7	3.4	10.7
Total	100.0	100.0	100.0	100.0	100.0
(N)	(54)	(53)	(56)	(29)	(28)

NOTE: Figures in parentheses indicate the total N of respondents for each zone.

ployment as harvesting, any reduction in total employment, however marginal, is seen as severely threatening.

This zonal pattern of laborer perceptions of the labor market is closely paralleled by the distribution of cultivator perceptions, demonstrating again how mutually opposing positions on the agro-economic issues provide the basis for political confrontation. As we can see in Table 58, cultivators in Zones 2 and 3 were more likely than their counterparts in other zones to see hired labor as both more necessary for their operations and more difficult to obtain (in the peak season). While all cultivators, not surprisingly, were paying higher wages, those in Zones 2 and 3 felt hardest hit by wage increases.

In order to probe more deeply the nature of wage disputes in Thanjavur the surveyed laborers were asked whether they or any members of their household were personally involved in any such disputes with landowners over the previous five years. Not surprisingly we find in Table 59 that the frequency of such involvement is higher in Zones 2 and 3 than elsewhere in the district. In fact, out of forty-two laborers mentioning involvement in one or more wage disputes, thirty-seven are in Zone 2 or Zone 3. Fully 45 percent of laborers in Zone 3 have been involved in one or two disputes.

176 — Agricultural Labor

TABLE 57

Laborer Perceptions of Employment by Zone

Laborer Perceptions	% of Respondents in Each Zone				
	Zone 1	Zone 2	Zone 3	Zone 4	Zone 5
Laborers who say they worked fewer days in 1972-73 than five years before	18.2 (66)	43.1 (65)	79.3 (58)	20.7 (58)	14.7 (34)
Laborers who "agree strongly" that:	(84)	(72)	(60)	(60)	(35)
Tractors put laborers out of work	14.5	34.7	59.3	1.8	17.1
Tractor use should be controlled by government	15.7	37.5	71.2	12.3	25.7

NOTE: Figures in parentheses indicate the total N of respondents for each zone for each perception.

We also find, as expected, that laborer involvement in wage disputes is closely correlated with ties to the Communist parties, especially in Zones 2 and 3. Table 60 shows that the great majority of those laborers are Communist party supporters or members, while in Zone 1 none are.

The wage disputes are connected in a wider pattern of politicized confrontation between labor and landowners, largely through the bond of Communist involvement. This is evident in the data presented in Table 61. All laborers who indicated that they had been involved in disputes were asked whether they sought help and, if so, from whom. Most of the disputants in Zones 2 and 3 did seek help, primarily from parties outside the village and from the Communist parties in particular. It is notable that none of the laborers in Zone 1 sought assistance. This was probably due either to the greater willingness of the landowner in Zone 1 to accept labor's demands without such pressure or to the inability of laborers in that zone to obtain assistance in the absence of the political organization provided by a party. In either case the implication is that wage disputes outside Zones 2 and 3 are less radicalized.

TABLE 58

Cultivator Perceptions of Labor Use, Availability, and Wage Levels by Zone

Cultivator Perceptions	% of Respondents in Each Zone				
	Zone 1	Zone 2	Zone 3	Zone 4	Zone 5
Cultivators who said they used more hired labor in 1972-73 than five years before	52.0 (102)	71.6 (88)	66.0 (94)	57.1 (98)	16.0 (50)
Cultivators who said they have difficulty getting labor	7.9 (101)	39.8 (88)	36.6 (93)	20.6 (97)	18.0 (50)
Cultivators who said they were paying higher wages in 1972-73 than five years before	65.7 (102)	97.7 (88)	98.9 (92)	91.8 (98)	75.5 (49)
Cultivators who said that wage increases are a "very important" problem in their cultivation	45.1 (102)	76.1 (88)	75.5 (94)	68.4 (98)	49.2 (59)

NOTE: Figures in parentheses indicate the total N of respondents for each zone for each perception.

The very fact that many Thanjavur laborers are able to tap a wider political network in seeking to resolve wage disputes has, in the prevailing political environment since the 1940s, tended more and more to result in outcomes favorable to labor. In Table 62 we see that most of the disputes cited by the surveyed laborers in Zones 2 and 3 ended in landowners agreeing to pay higher wages or to grant other concessions. This tendency in turn has helped to deflect much of the radical potential among Thanjavur labor into reformist channels. How and why this has happened will be explored in detail in Chapter 10.

TABLE 59

Laborer Involvement in Wage Disputes by Zone

Disputes in Which Laborer Household Was Involved Over Last Five Years	% of Respondents in Each Zone				
	Zone 1	Zone 2	Zone 3	Zone 4	Zone 5
None	94.0	86.1	54.2	100.0	100.0
One	6.0	11.1	37.3	—	—
Two	—	2.8	8.5	—	—
Total	100.0	100.0	100.0	100.0	100.0
(N)	(84)	(72)	(59)	(60)	(35)

NOTE: Figures in parentheses indicate the total N of respondents in each zone.

TABLE 60

Wage Dispute Involvement and Communist Support in Zones 1, 2, and 3

Level of Communist Support	% of Laborers Involved in Disputes in Each Zone at Different Levels of Communist Support		
	Zone 1	Zone 2	Zone 3
No support	100.0	30.0	—
"Forced support"	—	—	—
Support	—	40.0	74.1
Party member	—	30.0	25.9
Total	100.0	100.0	100.0
(N)	(5)	(10)	(27)

NOTE: Figures in parentheses indicate the total N of respondents in each zone.

TENANTS

I will now turn briefly to an examination of what the survey data reveal about the relationship between tenancy and agrarian radicalism in Thanjavur District. It will be recalled that at the conclusion of the last chapter I found evidence that this relationship may vary

TABLE 61

Assistance Sought by Laborers Involved in Wage Disputes in Zones 1, 2, and 3

Assistance Sought	% of Each Type of Assistance to the Total in Each Zone		
	Zone 1	Zone 2	Zone 3
None	100.0	35.7	14.8
Appointed officials (police, tahsildar, district collector)	—	7.1	11.1
Elected officials (panchayat president, panchayat union chairman)	—	7.1	3.7
Party leaders			
Unspecified	—	7.1	3.7
Communists	—	42.9	66.7
Total	100.0	*	100.0
(N)	(5)	(14)	(27)

NOTES: In the case of Zone 2 the number of types of assistance sought (14) exceeds the number of respondents involved in disputes (10) because each respondent could mention more than one type.

* Does not add to 100 due to rounding.

according to the precise nature of tenancy arrangements and the context in which they have developed and exist. Specifically I was able to suggest on the basis of the aggregate data analysis that tenants are more likely to be radicalized where they are economically marginal, where they live among and work with a large, impoverished labor force, and where they share a social identity with labor. These conditions are largely met in key areas of Zones 2 and 3, where in fact I found a positive relationship between tenancy and radicalism.

The analysis of the survey data on agricultural labor has already lent some additional support to this hypothesis, for it was discovered that in Zone 3, where the above conditions are most fully met, almost all of the labor-tenants are Communist supporters. A much smaller proportion of labor-tenants in Zone 2, where tenancy is a more mixed picture, supports the Communists. Somewhat of a

TABLE 62

Reported Outcomes of Wage Disputes in Zones 2 and 3 Combined

Outcome	% of Each Type of Outcome to the Total*
No settlement	4.4
Settlement (unspecified)	6.7
Landowner agrees to pay higher wages sought	73.3
Laborer accepts existing wage or wage lower than sought	15.5
Total	**
(N)	(45)

NOTES: * The total number of outcomes reported (45) exceeds the number of respondents reporting disputes because some respondents reported more than one dispute.
** Does not add to 100 due to rounding.

surprise, however, is the sizable proportion of labor-tenants in Zone 5 that supports the Communists and holds radical views.

It is appropriate at this point to suggest that this apparent anomaly in my findings is due largely to *inam* tenancy, a historical development peculiar to parts of Zone 5 as well as to Zones 2 and 3.[6] I will take a closer look at this institution in the next chapter, but it can be said here that *inam* tenancy created in the villages where it prevailed an agrarian structure analogous to the bipolar structure of Zone 3. This explanation would also account for the "encapsulation" of agrarian radicalism in Zone 5—that is, for the fact that it has not developed a wider base or become politically organized (no associational links or dispute involvement). It also explains the prominence of labor-tenants among Communist supporters in Zone 5.

The more difficult test of the relationship between tenancy and radicalism is in the data on *cultivator*-tenants who derive most, if not all, of their livelihood from tenancy cultivation rather than labor. In short, we would expect to find that tenants in Zones 2 and 3 are more likely than tenants in the other zones to support the Communists, to belong to the Communist Kisan Sabha ("Agriculturalists' Association"), to hold more radical views on tenancy

[6] See Chapter 4 for a description of *inam* tenancy.

TABLE 63

Tenants and Agrarian Radicalism across the Zones

Indicator of Radicalism	Tenurial Status	% of Pure Tenants* and Part Tenants** in Each Zone Who Give Response Indicated				
		Zone 1	Zone 2	Zone 3	Zone 4	Zone 5
Support for Communist parties	Pure tenant	5.0 (20)	23.1 (13)	75.0 (16)	30.0 (10)	0.0 (4)
	Part tenant	0.0 (18)	26.3 (19)	37.5 (16)	16.7 (6)	0.0 (7)
Kisan Sabha membership	Pure tenant	0.0 (20)	7.7 (13)	43.8 (16)	0.0 (10)	0.0 (4)
	Part tenant	0.0 (18)	10.5 (19)	18.8 (16)	0.0 (6)	0.0 (7)
Strongly agree tenants should not pay rent in bad years	Pure tenant	21.1 (19)	38.5 (13)	62.5 (16)	10.0 (10)	50.0 (4)
	Part tenant	0.0 (18)	25.0 (20)	46.2 (13)	0.0 (4)	20.0 (5)
Say disputes with landlords are very important problem	Pure tenant	15.0 (20)	38.5 (13)	31.3 (16)	0.0 (10)	0.0 (4)
	Part tenant	0.0 (18)	5.3 (19)	18.8 (16)	0.0 (6)	0.0 (7)

NOTES: Figures in parentheses indicate the total N of respondents for each category and zone on which the percentages are based.

* Pure tenants are respondents whose households cultivate only leased land.

** Part tenants are here respondents whose households cultivate mostly leased land (at least 50 percent) and some owned land.

issues, and to be involved in tenancy disputes. By and large the data in Table 63 are in accord with these expectations. Every measure shows a concentration of tenant radicalism in those areas of Thanjavur, Zones 2 and 3, where tenancy is embedded in an agrarian structure conducive to radicalism. Elsewhere in the district tenants show weak signs, at most, of radical behavior.

CHAPTER 8

Tenancy and Agrarian Radicalism

IN THE LITERATURE on agrarian radicalism the tenant plays a much larger role than the landless laborer. This is a consequence, I believe, of the basic model of change in peasant society that many Western scholars bring to the topic. The emphasis given by many studies (those of Wolf, Migdal, and Scott, for example) to the disruptive impact of capitalism on the "traditional lord-and-peasant" relationship focuses attention on the tenant's response to modernization as the key to understanding agrarian radicalism.

Yet the effort to define conditions under which the breakdown of traditional agrarian relations leads to radicalism faces many obstacles.[1] As Donald Zagoria has pointed out, "Clearly there are many intervening variables between the impact of commercialized agriculture and the vulnerability of agrarian societies to peasant unrest."[2] For instance, one must consider both the objective and subjective components of the landlord-tenant relationship. Scott argues that the tenant must perceive a threat to his "subsistence security." Wolf asks, is the dissatisfied tenant in a position to challenge the existing order, or is he too dependent? Moore's work suggests another consideration: How does the landlord-tenant relationship fit into the larger agrarian context? What is the character of other pre-existing social and economic relationships in the area? Finally, I would add another question: What is the response of external actors (the regime, political parties) to threats to or actual changes in the landlord-tenant relationship, and what is the effect of that response?

All of these considerations and more relate to an understanding of tenancy in Thanjavur. For, as has been demonstrated in Chapters

[1] Not all analyses of peasant politics share this emphasis on breakdown of traditional relationships. There is a considerable literature that views modern peasant politics in terms of highly adaptive "patron-client" relationships. For two well-known examples, see John Duncan Powell, "Peasant Society and Clientelist Politics," *American Political Science Review* 64 (June 1970): 411-425, and James C. Scott, "Patron-Client Politics and Political Change in Southeast Asia," *American Political Science Review* 66 (March 1972): 91-113.

[2] Donald S. Zagoria, "Peasants and Revolution," *Comparative Politics* 8 (April 1976): 325.

6 and 7, the relationship of tenancy to agrarian radicalism in Thanjavur at most contradicts the prevailing view or at least is highly contingent. The puzzle posed by my findings is illustrated by the following facts. A careful study of a Thanjavur village carried out in the late 1950s predicted that in the future agrarian conflict in the district would center on the abolition of tenancy.[3] But by the late 1960s, only a decade later, another close observer of the area had come to the conclusion that tenancy was no longer a radical issue in Thanjavur.[4] What could account for such contrasting assessments?

THE EVOLUTION OF TENANCY IN THANJAVUR

It is true that the landlord-tenant relationship in Thanjavur has been altered and strained, even to the breaking point, in the recent past. However, these pressures and changes have not all been in the same direction for three reasons: first, the forces of change have acted on varying types of tenancy;[5] second, the forces of change have operated in different social and agro-economic contexts; and third, external forces have conditioned the impact of change and the responses to it.

The evolution of tenancy in the Old Delta area of Thanjavur can be generally described as taking place in two phases. The first, probably beginning in the mid-nineteenth century and ending about 1945, saw a gradual transition in many areas from *pannai* cultivation (through *pannaiyals*, or attached labor) to tenancy cultivation (both *varam*, or sharecropping, and *kuttagai*, or fixed-rent). There were two forces behind this change: increasing pressure on the land, and market penetration of agriculture. The second phase, beginning in the late 1940s and continuing to the present, witnessed the almost total disappearance of both *varam* and *pannai* cultivation, both of which were replaced by *kuttagai* tenancy and/or cultivation

[3] Dagfinn Sivertsen, *When Caste Barriers Fall: A Study of Social and Economic Change in a South Indian Village* (Oslo: Universitets Forlaget, 1963), p. 12.

[4] Andre Beteille, "Agrarian Movements in India," mimeographed, undated, p. 17.

[5] As I have previously emphasized in the case of "landlessness," it is important to "unpack" the concept of tenancy, which refers only very generally to a position in the property structure and production process. The conditions of tenancy and the "rights" of the tenant vary widely and have great significance for the economic and political consequences of tenancy. For a discussion of this distinction, see Krishna Bharadwaj and P. K. Das, "Tenurial Conditions and Mode of Exploitation," *Economic and Political Weekly* 10 (June 21 and 28, 1975): A49-A55.

through hired casual (daily wage) labor. The main impetus to this change was the threat, and later the actual implementation, of tenancy reforms. The net effect of these changes was to polarize the institution of tenancy in Thanjavur: there was improvement in the status of tenants who were already relatively powerful vis-à-vis the landlord and deterioration in the status of tenants who were relatively powerless. For complex reasons I will now describe, improvement took place largely in the Zone 1 area and deterioration largely in the Zone 2 and 3 areas.

Early Phase: The End of the Pannai *System*

Although the *pannai* system of cultivation was widespread in Thanjavur prior to 1850, it was especially in vogue on the larger estates.[6] The *pannaiyals* were semiserfs, laborers bound to work on the lands of one landlord and usually paid primarily by the grant of a small parcel of land for their own cultivation. The *pannaiyal* system was a direct and close descendent of the system of agrestic servitude that Dharma Kumar found to be prevalent in Thanjavur well before the advent of British rule and the commercialization of agriculture. *Pannaiyals* were almost always drawn from the Scheduled Castes.

About 1850 the *pannaiyal* system began to yield to tenancy cultivation. First, increasing population pressure led to increasing fragmentation of landownership. Under these conditions the best way a landlord could ensure maximum returns with minimum risk was by leasing out his lands.[7] Second, on larger holdings increased returns due to expanding markets and higher prices for agricultural products allowed the landowner to abandon direct cultivation without any loss of income.[8] Third, the spread of education, urbanization, and new occupations gradually drew members of the rural landowning groups away from agriculture as an occupation, resulting in the growth of absentee landlordism.

The shift from *pannai* to tenancy cultivation probably began first in what is now the Zone 1 area, for it was under the greatest population pressure and affected earliest by market penetration.

[6] B. S. Baliga, *Tanjore District Handbook* (Madras: Government Press, 1957), pp. 19, 38-41, 378-379.

[7] V. V. Sayana, *The Agrarian Problems of Madras Province* (Madras: The Business Week Press, 1949), p. 192.

[8] K. B. Sivaswamy, *The Madras Ryotwari Tenant* (Madras: South Indian Federation of Agricultural Workers' Unions, 1948), pt. 1, p. 5.

Varam, or sharecropping tenancy, was probably prevalent at first as it afforded the landlord the greatest amount of control without responsibility over cultivation and the best ratio of returns to risk.[9] However, after the turn of the century and continuing through World War II *varam* increasingly gave way to *kuttagai* tenancy in the area. This was largely due to the rapid out-migration of Brahmin landowners, who because of their privileged social and economic status and traditional literacy were tapped early and heavily for service in the British administration.[10] As absentee rather than resident landlords they preferred *kuttagai* to *varam* tenancy because the former was more practical (though less remunerative). *Varam* required the landlord or his agent to be present at the harvest in order to oversee the division of the crop. Because many of the absentee landlords lived as far away as Madras and reliable agents were hard to find, the fixed payment of *kuttagai* was preferable. At first payment was usually required in kind, but later, as the links to the village became more and more attenuated, arrangements were often made for payment in cash.[11]

Tenants on the Brahmin lands were usually non-Brahmins, especially as absentee landlordism and *kuttagai* tenancy increased. There had been a large influx of non-Brahmins to the Zone 1 area during the nineteenth century. Some initially became *pannaiyals* and then *varam* tenants to Brahmin landowners. Although there are to this day non-Brahmin laborers in villages in Zone 1, by early in this century a few non-Brahmin families in many villages had significantly improved their status, usually by acquiring land.[12] As Brahmin landlords left the villages they often selected these non-Brahmins as tenants because their land could be offered as security and they had the resources to cultivate successfully.[13] Under the relatively favorable conditions of *kuttagai* tenancy many non-Brahmins were able further to improve their economic status.

The position of the non-Brahmin tenants vis-à-vis the Brahmin landlord was strengthened during 1920 to 1945 by the growing

[9] Ibid., p. 52.

[10] See Sivertsen, *When Caste Barriers Fall*, p. 16; also Marguerite Ross Barnett, "Cultural Nationalist Electoral Politics in Tamil Nadu," in *Studies in Electoral Politics in the Indian States*, vol. 4, *Party Systems and Cleavages*, ed. Myron Weiner and John Osgood Field (New Delhi: Manohar Book Service, 1975), p. 75.

[11] Sivertsen, *When Caste Barriers Fall*, p. 101.

[12] Indeed, two of the largest landowners in the area are non-Brahmin families, the Poondi Vandayars and the Kapistalam Moopanars, who acquired large amounts of land early in the twentieth century. Both are located in Papansam taluk.

[13] Sivertsen, *When Caste Barriers Fall*, pp. 46-47.

statewide political consciousness of non-Brahmins as a group.[14] Although the greatest strength of the non-Brahmin movement was in the towns, Brahmin control over many villages in the Zone 1 area was increasingly threatened.[15] The mounting challenge derived in part from the importance of the land as a source of control over men as well as income. As absentee landlords Brahmins lost some of their control over the economic benefits of the land and most of their control over its political benefits. The Brahmin families remaining in the villages were those least well-equipped to fend off the challenge. In the vacuum left by Brahmin absenteeism, and spurred by the economic independence gained through *kuttagai* and the political stimulus of the non-Brahmin movement, the non-Brahmin tenants became increasingly assertive vis-à-vis the Brahmin landlords, to the extent that many now felt they had a right to the land.[16] In some villages Harijans also benefited from these changes, becoming subtenants (sharecroppers) of the non-Brahmin tenants, but by and large up until the 1950s they remained *pannaiyals* of both Brahmin *mirasdars* and non-Brahmin tenants.[17]

The evolution of tenancy relations in the Zone 2 and 3 areas followed a somewhat different course. First, the shift from *pannai* to tenancy cultivation was less pervasive than in the Zone 1 area because pressure on the land and market penetration were less intense in the less productive Zone 2 and 3 areas. However, *varam* tenancy did emerge where productivity was lowest and most erratic, that is, in the extreme tail-end areas of Sirkali, Mannargudi, and Tiruthuraipoondi taluks because it enabled the landowner to minimize the risk of cultivating such lands. There was little to distinguish a *varam* tenant from a *pannaiyal*, save that the *varam* tenant

[14] On the rise of the non-Brahmin movement, see Eugene F. Irschick, *Politics and Social Conflict in South India: The Non-Brahman Movement and Tamil Separatism, 1916-1929* (Berkeley, Ca.: University of California Press, 1969). On the contemporary politics that are heir to this movement, see Marguerite Ross Barnett, *The Politics of Cultural Nationalism in South India* (Princeton, N.J.: Princeton University Press, 1976).

[15] Andre Beteille, *Castes, Old and New: Essays in Social Structure and Social Stratification* (Bombay: Asia Publishing House, 1969), pp. 171-173. See also Kathleen Gough, "Harijans in Thanjavur," in *Imperialism and Revolution in South Asia*, ed. Kathleen Gough and Hari P. Sharma (New York and London: Monthly Review Press, 1973), p. 230, and Christopher John Baker, *The Politics of South India, 1920-1937* (Cambridge: Cambridge University Press, 1976), p. 183.

[16] See Sivertsen, *When Caste Barriers Fall*, pp. 85-86, and Kathleen Gough, "The Social Structure of a Tanjore Village," in *Village India: Studies in the Little Community*, ed. McKim Marriott (1955; reprint ed., Chicago: University of Chicago Press, Phoenix Books, 1969), p. 46.

[17] Gough, "Harijans," p. 227.

bore the risks in a bad year because he paid the cultivation costs. *Varam* was "nothing but a device to pay a tenant no more than the wage of a *pannaiyal* . . . with the advantage (to the landlord) of reducing it in proportion to the yield." In these areas *varam* tenancy fell almost exclusively on the Harijans because their low economic and social status left them little alternative. Because the "position of the *varam* holder has all the disadvantages attaching to both a tenant and a laborer . . . ," it could "endure only on the basis of the existence of a class of ignorant and backward labour."[18] In sum, the transition to tenancy cultivation in Zones 2 and 3 was marked by continuity with the older system of cultivation through landless labor.

Varam tenancy in the coastal areas did not give way, as it did in the heart of the delta, to *kuttagai* tenancy. First, the chief advantage to the landlord of the *kuttagai* system, the convenience of a fixed rent, was meaningless where poor land meant the fixed amount could not be guaranteed. Second, the predominantly non-Brahmin landowners of Zones 2 and 3 left agriculture in far fewer numbers than did their Brahmin counterparts because they had long had a more direct involvement with cultivation and because fewer non-agricultural opportunities were open to them than to the Brahmins. Absenteeism probably increased in the Zone 2 and 3 areas, but not with the same effect as in Zone 1. The Zone 2 or 3 landlord frequently lived in a nearby town, appointed an agent or bailiff in the village to supervise cultivation operations, and supervised the harvest himself. He remained more directly involved with agricultural operations than did his Brahmin counterpart.

Although I have emphasized certain trends in the evolution of tenancy in Thanjavur, it is important to realize that throughout this early period it remained a highly complex and variable phenomenon. The term *tenancy* refers only to a very general model of property relations. The shape of the relationship is adaptive to local ecological, economic, and social conditions. For this reason it is difficult to generalize about the economic impact of tenancy or to predict its relationship to political behavior.

In addition, there is little readily available data to document this first phase in the evolution of tenancy in Thanjavur. However, in Table 64 I have compiled data from the 1951 census that helps to

[18] Sivaswamy, *Ryotwari Tenant*, p. 52. See also Gough, "Harijans," pp. 42-43, 68-69.

TABLE 64

Tenancy and Landlordism in Thanjavur District, 1951, by Zone and Taluk

Zone	Taluk	Rural Tenants as % of Total Rural Agricultural Workers (1)	Rural Noncultivating Owners/Rent Receivers as % of Total Rural Owners (2)	% All Noncultivating Owners/Rent Receivers Living in:		Ratio of Rural Tenants to Rural Noncultivating Owners/Rent Receivers	
				Towns (3)	Cities (4)	Rural (5)	All Areas (6)
1/Old Delta-Cauvery	Papanasam	26.03	24.35	10.94	—	3.58	3.18
	Kumbakonam	31.34	33.46	5.22	44.15	4.28	2.26
	Mayuram	32.70	34.02	20.87	—	4.30	3.44
2-3/Old Delta-Central/ Coastal	Sirkali	31.62	24.52	24.58	—	6.34	4.78
	Nannilam	19.35	34.92	4.89	—	1.86	2.16
	Nagapattinam	10.80	17.74	20.88	27.59	1.79	1.03
	Mannargudi	17.70	9.37	40.20	—	5.33	3.19
	Tiruthuraipoondi	15.87	5.02	29.69	—	6.64	4.67
4/New Delta-CMP	Pattukottai/ Orathanad	7.48	.192	18.51	—	5.46	4.45
5/Dry Area-Uplands	Arantangi	36.97	2.47	3.87	—	28.51	27.41

SOURCE: Calculated from data in Government of Madras, *1951 Census Handbook, Tanjore District* (Madras: Government Press, 1953), pp. 25-28, 31-32 (hereafter Madras, *1951 Census Handbook, Tanjore District*).

NOTE: Workers = "self-supporting persons"; tenants = cultivators of land wholly or primarily unowned; owners = cultivators of land wholly or primarily owned.

picture tenancy and landlordism in the different areas of the district at the end of this early period.

First note that *on average* tenants made up a smaller share of the agricultural work force in the Zone 2 and 3 areas than in Zone 1, and an even lower share in the Zone 4 area (see column 1). The high percentage of tenants in Zone 5 reflects the numerous *inam* and *zamindari* estates still present in that area in 1951. *Within* Zones 2 and 3 the tenancy rate varied considerably, but as might be expected from my previous findings it was highest in Sirkali and lowest in Nagapattinam.

The distribution of rural "landlordism" (noncultivating owners and rent receivers) corresponds generally to the distribution of tenancy and is highest on average in Zone 1 taluks (see column 2). Two facts are especially noteworthy here. First, the high percentage of non-cultivating owners and rent receivers in Nannilam and Nagapattinam relative to the percentage of tenants (reflected in the low "tenant-landlord" ratios in column 5) reveals two characteristics of those areas: larger leaseholds (recall from Chapter 6 that there were fewer Harijan tenants in these areas) and more large *pannai* holdings (run by noncultivating owners) than tenant-cultivated holdings (owned by rent receivers). Second, note that in Sirkali and Mannargudi the percentage of rural landlords is low relative to the percentage of tenants (as reflected in a high ratio in column 5). These facts suggest that tenancy was associated with agrarian radicalism in these areas in the late 1940s (and later, though to a lesser extent) because there existed a structural basis for radical mobilization: a high *ratio* of poor tenants to landlords analogous to the sharp laborer-landowner cleavage in other areas of Zones 2 and 3. (As mentioned previously, the very high ratio of tenants to landlords in Arantangi taluk is explained by the prevalence of whole-village *inam* and *zamindari* tenancy in that area.)

What about noncultivating owners and rent receivers not resident in the village? Unfortunately the data are not very helpful here because there is no way of knowing whether the urban-based landlords owned lands in the same or another part of the district. For instance, a large percentage of landlords in Kumbakonam taluk lived in Kumbakonam City, but many of these probably owned land in other taluks. However, the data do indicate that a large percentage of landlords in the high tenancy areas of Sirkali, Mannargudi, and Tiruthuraipoondi lived in the local towns.

In general, these data support my argument that the evolution of tenancy in large areas of Zones 2 and 3 through the 1940s paralleled the existing lines of agro-economic and social organization in those areas. The changes that occurred probably tended to widen the economic gap between landowners and the large Harijan population traditionally engaged in cultivation labor. In contrast, the evolution of tenancy in Zone 1 cut across the traditional agrarian structure and provided a means of upward mobility for the large number of non-Brahmin tenants and small owner-tenants.[19]

Late Phase: Tenancy Mobilization and Reform

Beginning in the mid-1940s and continuing into the early 1950s there were severe outbreaks of agrarian unrest in Thanjavur District. At the beginning of World War II the Communist Party of India began to organize the *varam* tenants through its peasant organization the All-India Kisan Sabha (Agriculturalists' Association).[20] The Party soon extended organizational activity to the *pannaiyals*. The organization of both sharecroppers and laborers was concentrated in the Mannargudi area. Although Party leaders later claimed that the choice of this area was "accidental,"[21] it is hard to resist the conclusion that it was related to the highly polarized agrarian structure of the area. At that time many of the large landowners in the Mannargudi area were still Brahmins, and cultivation was carried out by large numbers of primarily Harijan *pannaiyals* and *varamdars*, so that the economic and social cleavages were as wide as or wider than in any other area of the district.[22] Although as time went on the movement was increasingly dominated by laborers and their interests, it seems that the early efforts to organize the tenants, who included some middle-caste non-Brahmins, provided some impetus for the organization of labor. In other words, the early development of agrarian radicalism in Thanjavur was based in part on an alliance of "poor peasants" and laborers,

[19] One study of a village in Chingleput District (north of Thanjavur) has noted the absence of any marked change in the relationship between caste and economic status and ascribed this to the fact that there had not been any Brahmin landowners in the village whose departure could have "opened up" the system. See Joan P. Mencher, "A Tamil Village: Changing Social-Economic Structure in Madras State," in *Change and Continuity in India's Villages*, ed. K. Ishwaran (New York: Columbia University Press, 1970), pp. 210-211.

[20] K. C. Alexander, *Agrarian Tension in Thanjavur* (Hyderabad: National Institute of Community Development, 1975), p. 35.

[21] Ibid., p. 36.

[22] Beteille, *Castes, Old and New*, p. 166.

and crossed caste lines as well. This alliance was certainly facilitated by the very narrow gap between *pannaiyal* and *varamdar* status in the Zones 2 and 3.[23]

Steep price increases during World War II led to demands by laborers and tenants for increased wages and lower rents.[24] The concentration of the movement in the Mannargudi area is revealed by the fact that the first attempt at settling these disputes, the 1944 Kalappal and Mannargudi agreements, related only to villages in Mannargudi taluk. The terms of the agreements focused mainly on wage increases but included some concessions to tenants. However, these measures were not enough to alleviate the situation and between 1945 and 1948 the landlords reacted to tenant-labor unrest by evicting many tenants and boycotting local labor in favor of imported labor.[25] Tension grew until in 1948 the conflict produced a strike by laborers and tenants that, though still centered in the Mannargudi area, spread quite widely across what is now the Zone 2 and 3 areas.[26] This was settled by the Mayuram Agreement of October 1948, which gave the *pannaiyals* further wage increases. But many landlords continued to resist the organization and demands of the laborers and tenants, and violent clashes between the two sides continued into the early 1950s. The state government stationed armed special police in the district and detained many of the Communist organizers for long periods without trial.[27]

Ironically, the unrest was fanned by the government's more constructive efforts to deal with the situation. In the wake of a report by the All-India Congress Agrarian Reforms Committee, the Madras Government appointed a Land Revenue Reforms Committee (also known as the Subramaniam Committee) charged with examining the entire agrarian structure and recommending re-

[23] Alexander, *Agrarian Tension*, p. 35. See also Kathleen Gough, "Peasant Resistance and Revolt in South India," *Pacific Affairs* 41 (Winter 1968-1969): 533.

[24] Agricultural Workers' Association, "East Thanjavur District Agricultural Workers' Problems: A Memorandum Placed Before the Judge of the Enquiry Commission on Behalf of the Agricultural Workers' Association, Thanjavur, March 11, 1969," typewritten, undated, p. 10.

[25] Sivaswamy, *Ryotwari Tenant*, p. 27; Alexander, *Agrarian Tension*, p. 41.

[26] A Western observer who happened to visit the area during this strike described the area east of Thanjavur Town as a "Communist state." See John Frederick Muehl, *Interview with India* (New York: The John Day Co., 1950), pp. 284-285.

[27] Sivaswamy, *Ryotwari Tenant*, p. 81. See also Daniel Thorner, *The Agrarian Prospect in India: Five Lectures on Land Reform Delivered in 1955 at the Delhi School of Economics* (New Delhi: Delhi University Press, 1956), p. 37.

forms.[28] Seeing this and other straws in the wind, landlords throughout the district began to dismiss *pannaiyals* and to evict tenants out of fear of impending reforms legislation.[29] Many *pannaiyals* were reduced to the status of daily wage laborers. In the case of tenants resident landlords sometimes resumed personal cultivation of the land but more frequently merely changed the *varamdars* from year to year or even season to season in order to avoid their building up a claim to customary rights on the land.

In order to stop the dismissal of *pannaiyals* and to quell the resulting disturbances the Madras Government promulgated the Tanjore Pannaiyals Protection Ordinance in August 1952 and a few months later passed similar legislation. The ordinance and the act doubled the *pannaiyal*'s wages and gave him the right to twelve months notice and appeal before dismissal.[30] The act exempted from its purview landowners owning less than 6.66 acres of wet land in any village. Its effect, however, was counter to the government's intention, as landowners were not willing to pay the higher wages or to relinquish control over the labor force, and in fact increased their dismissals of *pannaiyals*, who were usually powerless to resist over any long period.[31] The effect was initially greatest in the Zone 2 and 3 areas for two reasons: *pannaiyals* were most numerous in those areas, and there were more large landlords than in Zone 1. This was the beginning of the virtual disappearance of the *pannaiyal* system throughout the district.[32] It was now more advantageous to the landowners to be able to draw from a pool of unattached wage laborers. Sivertsen reported that by the late 1950s even the largest landowners in a village near Kumbakonam scarcely kept more than one attached laborer. And by 1969 it was reported that *pannaiyals* were nonexistent on 95 percent of the holdings in Thanjavur.[33]

[28] Government of Madras, The Land Revenue Reforms Committee, *First Report* (Madras: Government Press, 1951).

[29] Sivaswamy, *Ryotwari Tenant*, p. 5; Sayana, *Agrarian Problems*, p. 276; Sivertsen, *When Caste Barriers Fall*, p. 17.

[30] K. S. Sonachalam, *Land Reforms in Tamil Nadu: Evaluation of Implementation* (New Delhi: Oxford and IBH Publishing Co., 1970), pp. 126-127.

[31] Alexander, *Agrarian Tension*, p. 42. In Kirippur Village in east Thanjavur (Zone 3) the *pannaiyals* initially forced the landowner to pay higher wages but later were reduced to the status of daily laborers (Gough, "Harijans," p. 240).

[32] Agricultural Workers' Association, "Memorandum," p. 12.

[33] Sivertsen, *When Caste Barriers Fall*, p. 78. See also Ganapathia Pillai, "Report of the Commission of Inquiry on the Agrarian Labour Problems of East Thanjavur District," typewritten [1969], pp. 29-30.

The tenancy reforms that followed in the mid-1950s had a similar effect, though not at all uniformly. The Madras Land Revenue Reforms Committee had recommended regulation of both rents and security of tenure. Thanjavur landlords of course opposed these recommendations and suggested, for instance, that the *varamdar* not be considered a tenant.[34] This suggestion was rejected by the committee, and in 1955 the Madras legislature passed the Madras Cultivating Tenants Protection Act and in 1956 the Madras Cultivating Tenants (Payment of Fair Rent) Act. The 1955 act was intended to prevent arbitrary eviction of tenants. It limited the reasons for which a landlord could evict a tenant and required that eviction be allowed only by petition to a specially constituted revenue court. It also gave the tenant the right to resumption of a leasehold from which he might have been evicted after December 1953 and allowed the landlord the right to resume personal cultivation up to a certain limited acreage according to the size of his existing holding.

The act of 1956 fixed the "fair rent" for various types of land; for instance, for wet land it was set at 40 percent of the normal gross produce or its value. The act also provided for proportional remission of rent to the tenant if the gross produce was reduced 25 percent or more below normal levels by adverse seasonal conditions. Both the tenant and the landlord were entitled to apply to a specially constituted rent court for fixation or remission of rent or settlement of other rent-related disputes. But of course such applications normally came from the tenant.[35]

While on paper these reforms appeared quite vigorous, in fact there were several loopholes that either resulted in eviction of the tenant or severely restricted his access to provisions of the act. First, and most important, both acts required that tenancies be verified by a written lease deed. Although a 1956 amendment specified that a register of all tenancies be prepared and maintained by the government (this clause was not to be implemented for many years), in 1955 very few tenants in Thanjavur District had written lease deeds and so passage of the 1955 act was followed by large-scale evictions outside the act. This requirement of course prevented many tenants from taking advantage of the provisions of both acts.[36] Second, tenants applying for restoration of a leasehold had

[34] Thorner, *Agrarian Prospect*, p. 40; Madras, Land Revenue Reforms Committee, *First Report*, p. 43.

[35] Sonachalam, *Land Reforms*, pp. 56-62.

[36] Ibid., pp. 36, 55.

to do so within thirty days of the commencement of the act. Considering that most tenants were poor and illiterate and the act poorly publicized, it was unlikely that many of them could take advantage of this provision.[37] Third, the provision allowing resumption of land for personal cultivation by the landlord was subject to much manipulation. By bribing the village *karnam*, the landlord could show that he fell within restrictions on size of landholding, evict the tenant, and turn the land over to another tenant. In this way the landlord could change tenants frequently.[38]

However, more important than any specific loophole in determining the impact of the legislation was the nature of the relationship between the landlord and the tenant. In Thanjavur as well as elsewhere tenancy reforms usually broke on the "rock of landlord power."[39] Where they did not, the tenants' position could well have improved. Thus several observers have noted the somewhat contradictory effects of these reforms: they strengthened the position of the upper stratum of tenants, sometimes to the point where they were able to acquire all or, more usually, part of the land, and they severely weakened the position of the lower stratum of tenants who now lost whatever security of tenure they may have had before or were converted into daily laborers. Indeed, some scholars have traced an observed decline in tenancy throughout India to the effect of tenancy reforms, while others are inclined to believe that the decline is largely apparent and that sharecropping tenancy has gone underground.[40]

[37] Gene Wunderlich, *Land Reforms in India* (Washington, D.C.: Agency for International Development, June 1970), p. 38.

[38] Wolf Ladejinsky, *A Study on Tenurial Conditions in Package Districts* (New Delhi: Government of India, Planning Commission, 1965), pp. 14-15. See also Daniel Thorner and Alice Thorner, *Land and Labour in India* (Bombay: Asia Publishing House, 1962), pp. 62-63.

[39] See A. M. Khusro, *The Economics of Land Reform and Farm Size in India*, Institute of Economic Growth Studies in Economic Growth, no. 14 (Madras: Macmillan, 1973), p. 13.

[40] See Hamza Alavi, "Peasants and Revolution," in *Imperialism and Revolution in South Asia*, ed. Kathleen Gough and Hari P. Sharma (New York and London: Monthly Review Press, 1973), pp. 330-331; P. C. Joshi, "Land Reforms in India and Pakistan," *Economic and Political Weekly* 5 (December 26, 1970): A145-A152; Gough, "Peasant Resistance and Revolt," p. 542; Dharm Narain and P. C. Joshi, "Magnitude of Agricultural Tenancy," *Economic and Political Weekly* 4 (September 27, 1969): A139-A142; Khusro, *Economics*, p. 22; S. K. Sanyal, "Has There Been a Decline in Agricultural Tenancy," *Economic and Political Weekly* 7 (May 6, 1972): 943-945; and Pranab Bardhan, "Trends in Land Relations: A Note," *Economic and Political Weekly* 5 (Annual number, 1970): 261-266.

In Thanjavur the opposite effects of the tenancy legislation were related to existing differences in the landlord-tenant relationship between Zone 1 on the one hand and Zones 2 and 3 on the other.[41] As I described previously, tenants in Zone 1 were on the whole in a stronger position vis-à-vis landlords. The absenteeism of the Brahmin landlords created a vacuum in the village economic and power structure that the non-Brahmin tenants had begun to fill. Many, though certainly not all, of these tenants were able to resist efforts by the Brahmin landlords to evict them. In some cases they even managed to defeat landlords in the revenue courts.[42] More often their relatively strong position enabled them to effect a compromise with the landlord. Where they were able to use the provisions of the Fair Rent Act to get their rent reduced that of course strengthened their economic position even further.[43]

In Zones 2 and 3 tenants were on the whole in a weaker position vis-à-vis the landlord. Many were Harijans. Most were *varam* tenants on terms hardly distinguishable from those of the *pannaiyal*. Many had been evicted and reduced to wage labor status at the time of the Pannaiyal Protection Act.[44] More were certainly evicted after the passage of the 1955 act. Some continued as *varam* tenants but with considerably less security. Others, certainly fewer, were able to resist eviction and, like their counterparts in Zone 1, were better off for it. But on the whole the tendency was for sharecropping to give way to owner-supervised cultivation with daily wage labor, further accentuating the polarization of the agrarian structure in Zones 2 and 3.[45]

[41] Andre Beteille, *Studies in Agrarian Social Structure* (New Delhi: Oxford University Press, 1974), p. 153.

[42] Sivertsen, *When Caste Barriers Fall*, p. 107. In a recent study of two villages in Kumbakonam taluk (Zone 1) Clyde Swenson found that in the village where most of the land was still owned by *resident* Brahmins, tenants had not been able to resist eviction; in the other village, where Brahmin landowners were absentee, the tenants had been able to resist eviction. See Clyde Geoffrey Swenson, "The Effect of Increases in Rice Production on Employment and Income Distribution in Thanjavur District, South India" (Ph.D. dissertation, Michigan State University, 1973), p. 30.

[43] Andre Beteille, *Caste, Class and Power: Changing Patterns of Stratification in a Tanjore Village* (Berkeley, Ca.: University of California Press, 1965), pp. 205-206. See also Sivertsen, *When Caste Barriers Fall*, pp. 101-102. Sivertsen observes that rent remission was granted more often by absentee landlords than by resident landlords (pp. 84-85).

[44] Agricultural Workers' Association, "Memorandum," p. 11.

[45] Newaj and Rudra have observed a similar pattern in parts of West Bengal. See Khoda Newaj and Ashok Ruda, "Agrarian Transformation in a District of West Bengal," *Economic and Political Weekly* 10 (March 29, 1975): A22-A23.

The proceedings of the Thanjavur revenue courts (set up by the 1955 act to settle disputes over tenure) lend indirect support to this interpretation of change and continuity in landlord-tenant relations in Thanjavur. Data collected for three early years (1958-1960) of revenue court proceedings are shown in Table 65.[46] The first fact to be noticed is that eviction petitions (column 1) far outnumbered all other types. Relatively few tenants filed petitions (columns 5 and 7) for restoration of leasehold or deposit (to forestall eviction for nonpayment of rent). Second, eviction and resumption petitions were filed against tenants in Zone 1 more frequently relative to their numbers than in Zones 2 and 3 (see also Table 66). The fact that landlords had to resort to court proceedings is, paradoxically, a reflection of the relatively strong position of the tenants in Zone 1. Third, if a tenant in any zone was able to persist in court action, he had a good chance of getting a favorable judgment—only 20 to 25 percent of the eviction petitions that came to a judgment were settled in favor of the landlord.[47]

Unfortunately, however, these data do not tell the whole story. There is good reason to believe that about 30 percent of all the evictions filed were "dismissed" not because of a judgment unfavorable to the landlord but rather because the petition was not pressed, usually a result of either the tenants' relenting to landlord pressure or a compromise of the dispute that triggered the eviction attempt.[48] In other words, in many instances bringing the dispute to court was probably an attempt by the landlord to harass the tenant.[49] But the fact that the landlord found this necessary was a clear sign of improvement in the tenant's status over the time when his economic dependence on the landlord alone was enough to force his compliance with the landlord's wishes. Finally, note in Table 66 the particularly low ratio of eviction petitions to tenants in Sirkali and Tiruthuraipoondi where Harijan "low-end" tenants were more numerous.

In summary, the tenancy reforms of the 1950s began the process

[46] These data are drawn from a 20 percent systematic sample of all petitions listed in the revenue court registers for the period.

[47] However, Sivertsen noted that in the late 1950s the attitude of the courts was "for the time being, unfavorable to the rentier" (Sivertsen, *When Caste Barriers Fall*, p. 87).

[48] Of all eviction petitions filed statewide up to July 1967 (of which about 50 percent were filed in Thanjavur), 27.8 percent were "not pursued or [were] withdrawn" (Sonachalam, *Land Reforms*, p. 43).

[49] The collector of Thanjavur suggested this was the case in a personal interview on April 12, 1973.

TABLE 65

Revenue Court Petitions and Judgments, 1958-1960, by Zone

Zone in Which Tenant Located	Filed by Landlord				Filed by Tenant			
	Eviction Petitions		Resumption Petitions		Restoration Petitions		Deposit Petitions	
	Filed (% of district total) (1)	Allowed (% of those filed) (2)	Filed (% of district total) (3)	Allowed (% of those filed) (4)	Filed (% of district total) (5)	Allowed (% of those filed) (6)	Filed (% of district total) (7)	Allowed (% of those filed) (8)
	N=687		N=140		N=87		N=137	
1/Old Delta-Cauvery	42.7	20.6	57.1	25.6	33.3	20.7	43.1	55.1
2/Old Delta-Central	20.2	23.6	25.0	35.7	26.4	17.4	25.5	54.3
3/Old Delta-Coastal	30.3	25.1	17.1	20.8	35.6	22.6	31.4	63.3
4/New Delta-CMP	1.5	37.9	0.7	0.0	1.0	0.0	0.0	—
5/Dry Area-Uplands	0.9	8.3	0.0	—	3.4	33.3	0.0	—
District total/average	*	22.7	*	27.1	*	20.7	100.0	57.4

NOTES: This table is based on a 20 percent sample of all revenue court petitions filed during the period.
* Does not add to 100 due to rounding.

TABLE 66

Tenancy Incidence and Eviction Attempts, 1958-1960,
by Zone and Taluk

Zone	Taluk	Tenants as % of District Total, 1951[a]	Eviction Petitions as % of District Total, 1958-60[b]	Number of Eviction Petitions Per 100 Tenants
1/Old Delta-Cauvery	Kumbakonam	13.6	25.0	6.3
2-3/Old Delta-Central/Coastal	Sirkali	8.4	6.4	2.6
	Nannilam	9.1	11.4	4.3
	Nagapattinam	3.6	5.2	5.0
	Mannargudi	8.0	11.0	4.7
	Tiruthuraipoondi	7.3	4.4	2.1

SOURCES: [a] Calculated from data in Madras, *1951 Census Handbook, Tanjore District*, pp. 31-32.
[b] Data collected by author from official revenue court records.

of "deradicalizing" tenancy in two ways. On the one hand, they helped the already better-placed tenants improve their status. Juan Linz has observed that in Italy as the status of tenants improved they began to stress their distinctiveness from labor and to dissociate themselves from the labor movement.[50] This is surely one factor behind the decline of tenancy as a radical issue in Thanjavur. On the other hand, where tenancy was potentially most radicalizing (i.e., where the status of tenants was already low), the reforms forced many tenants into the ranks of landless wage labor. This reduction in the magnitude of "low-end tenancy" reduced the salience of the tenancy factor in agrarian radicalism in Thanjavur. There is yet another consideration. For those tenants who did survive the spate of evictions during the 1950s, even for many low-end tenants, the scope, if not the ultimate overall efficacy, of the government-sponsored reforms must have held out hope that their position would improve in the future, perhaps even to the extent

[50] See Juan J. Linz, "Patterns of Land Tenure, Division of Labor, and Voting Behavior in Europe," *Comparative Politics* 8 (April 1976): 410.

of their someday owning land.[51] Such expectations of future gains in status helped to tie many tenants into the prevailing system at least temporarily, thus strengthening the forces of "conservative" as opposed to "radical solidarity." This is an interesting example of how subjective factors can displace objective factors in determining political behavior.[52]

But it would be a mistake to emphasize too heavily the impact of these early reforms. Conflict between landlords and tenants continued to be an important part of the agrarian scene, much of it expressed through the tenancy courts. Through June 1967 over 8,600 eviction petitions, or 53 percent of the statewide total, were filed in the Thanjavur revenue courts, and almost 3,200 rent fixation petitions, or 90 percent of the statewide total, were filed in the Thanjavur rent courts (see Table 67). Note that for the entire

TABLE 67

Tenancy Court Petitions and Judgments in Thanjavur District through June 1967

Court	Petition	Petitions Filed Up to July 1967		Petitions Allowed Up to July 1967	
		Number	% of State	Number	% of Filed
Revenue court (Act of 1955)	Eviction (L)	8641	52.6	1271	14.7
	Resumption (L)	420	25.9	28	6.7
	Restoration (T)	190	30.0	18	9.5
Rent court (Act of 1956)	Fixation (T)	3286	89.5	1615	49.2

SOURCE: K. S. Sonachalam, *Land Reforms in Tamil Nadu: Evaluation of Implementation* (New Delhi: Oxford and IBH Publishing Co., 1970), pp. 50-52, 61.

NOTE: (L) = filed by landlord; (T) = filed by tenant.

[51] My research supports this view. In my survey of cultivators and laborers around the district, when asked why they continued to cultivate when they were losing money on cultivation many tenants replied that they hoped to be given the land.

[52] Barrington Moore, Jr., *Social Origins of Dictatorship and Democracy: Lord and Peasant in the Making of the Modern World* (Boston: Beacon Press, 1966), p. 476. On the role of subjective factors in the tenant's perception of the legitimacy of his relationship with the landlord, see Linz, "Patterns of Land Tenure," p. 398.

period an even smaller percentage of the eviction petitions resulted in court-ordered eviction than during the early years and that almost 50 percent of the rent petitions resulted in fixation by the courts. The number of fixation petitions dropped sharply after the first year of implementation (see Table 68) but then remained on a plateau of 600 to 800 per year through 1969. The reason for the early peak is that once fixed, the rent amount was to stay in force for five years. Therefore those tenants who felt secure enough to petition the court for rent fixation did so early. Remission petitions (requiring the landlord to remit a portion of the rent when abnormal conditions reduced yields sharply) understandably peaked in the poor crop years 1966 to 1968. In fact, the poor yields in these years threatened the eviction of thousands of tenants for rent arrears. Facing an election in February 1967, the Congress Party government issued an ordinance in April 1966 and a few months later passed legislation preventing the eviction of tenants for nonpayment of rent. As a result, many tenants paid little or no rent,[53]

TABLE 68
Rent Court Petitions, Thanjavur District, 1957-1972

| | Rent Court Petitions (filed by tenant) | | |
Year	Fixation	Remission	Total
1957	2087	—	2087
1958	670	—	670
1959	748	—	748
1960	527	—	527
1961	NA	126	—
1962	428	133	561
1963	747	76	823
1964	689	433	1122
1965	648	70	718
1966	863	853	1716
1967	633	(684)*	1317
1968	819	911	1730
1969	632	149	781

NOTES: NA = data not available.
* The figure for 1967 is definitely low because part of the data was unavailable.

[53] One letter to the editor of the *Hindu* (Madras) on October 3, 1967, complained about such nonpayment.

and two years later the accumulation of arrears presented another potentially explosive situation to the year-old DMK government.

POLITICS, REFORM, AND DERADICALIZATION

During the period from 1952 to about 1967 Thanjavur's agrarian scene was quiet in comparison with the upheavals of the 1945 to 1952 period. There are several reasons for this.[54] Most importantly, the Communists had by choice and necessity virtually ceased organizational activity among both tenants and laborers in the district. Second, the first wave of agrarian reforms under the Congress government in the early and mid-1950s undoubtedly defused to some extent agrarian discontent. Third, there were no sharp economic jolts during this period that might have caused the persistent economic inequities to erupt in violence as did the price increases of World War II.

But by the mid-1960s the Communists had become active again, mostly as a result of Party policies framed with no specific reference to Thanjavur. By then the Communists' organizational efforts took account of the differences between tenants and labor. The CPI now had separate organizations for tenants and small owners on the one hand and landless laborers on the other: the Thanjavur Mavattam Vivasaya Sangham (Thanjavur District Agriculturalists' Association) for tenants and small owners and the Thanjavur Mavattam Vivasayi Thozhilalar Sangham (Thanjavur District Agricultural Workers' Association) for laborers.[55] The CPM also claimed the existence of an Agricultural Workers' Union in Thanjavur separate from the CPM-led Kisan Sabha,[56] although under whatever banner it was organized the CPM's support in Thanjavur always came much more heavily from landless laborers.

The CPI-led Agriculturalists' Association tried to capture the tenancy position. Thus, for instance, an association conference at Mannargudi in December 1967 called on the state government to renew the prohibition on evictions for rent arrears.[57] The DMK-led government responded to this appeal by issuing an ordinance

[54] I will return to this subject in more detail in Chapter 10.

[55] Note that the Communists, recognizing the power of Tamil regional and linguistic sentiment, now used Tamil terms in naming their organization.

[56] *Peasant and Labour* 2 (New Delhi: November 1973): 15. After the split both parties claimed leadership of the All-India Kisan Sabha. In fact, the CPM had control of the organization in most areas.

[57] *Ulavu Chelvam* (Madras), January 1, 1968, p. 11.

in April 1968 that allowed tenants to pay accumulated rent arrears in four equal annual installments and prohibited eviction unless the tenant defaulted on any of these payments. The Agriculturalists' Association complained that this measure was more helpful to landlords than tenants and in July 1968 organized a large agitation in Mannargudi to press the government for amendments before follow-up legislation was passed, though without success.[58]

At about the same time labor militancy was on the rise in Thanjavur District. In fact, from 1968 to 1972 the district was swept by a "second wave" of agrarian unrest that reached its highest point in late 1968 and early 1969. Although this second wave more than the first (1945 to 1952) drew its strength from landless labor and their grievances, it was, like the first wave, followed by a series of tenancy reform measures that further undermined the radical potential of tenancy in Thanjavur. These measures were again not without loopholes, but it is obvious that the DMK government was making a concerted attempt to capture the allegiance of a large portion of the tenantry in Thanjavur. There is considerable evidence that it was quite successful.

The first and most important measure was the Tamil Nadu Agricultural Lands Record of Tenancy Rights Act of 1969 that sought to implement the long-ignored provision in the 1956 act for an official record of tenancies. The absence of such a record had of course prevented most tenants (who had oral leases) from taking advantage of the earlier reforms. It was widely considered the key to meaningful tenancy reform.[59] Precisely because of its potential impact, the DMK government treated the issue rather gingerly. It began by appointing a select committee of the Tamil Nadu legislature to tour the districts and hear testimony from representatives of both landlords and tenants.[60] In the course of the committee's deliberations several key issues emerged: 1) How would the record be prepared? for example, How would it be publicized? How would evidence be taken? 2) How would appeals be processed? and 3) How would intermediaries and subtenants be treated?

The first issue grew out of the belief among the Communists and others that the purpose of the act would be defeated if preparation

---

[58] Ibid., May 1, 1968, p. 16; August 1, 1968, p. 14; September 1, 1968, p. 2.

[59] Khusro, *Economics*, p. 32; Ladejinsky, *Study on Tenurial Conditions*, pp. 16-17.

[60] Government of Madras, *The Madras Agricultural Lands Record of Tenancy Rights Bill, 1968 (L.A. Bill No. 18 of 1968): Report and Proceedings of the Select Committee of the Tamil Nadu Legislative Assembly* (Madras, 1969). (Hereafter Madras, *Tenancy Rights Bill Select Committee Report.*)

of the record were a strictly official process open to manipulation by the landlords. Thus, the Communists demanded that the intention to prepare a record be widely publicized in the villages, that the recording officer take evidence in public, and that oral statements from two witnesses be sufficient to establish a tenancy in the absence of either a written lease deed or an entry in the village records.[61] Landlords, on the other hand, wanted evidence taken in private (not "on the basis of any political party") and insisted that the recording officer should be a high-ranking official (to which they would have easier access). In addition, landlords wanted the civil courts to have appellate authority because that would enable them to delay final preparation of the record almost indefinitely through litigation.[62]

The issue of intermediaries and subtenants is a particularly revealing one. In the acts of 1955 and 1956 a tenant was defined as someone who "personally cultivates" the land through his own or his family members' labor; intermediaries were legally excluded from protection of the two reform measures. However, the draft legislation for the Record of Rights Act gave legal status to the intermediary and subtenant. Since the act also stipulated that tenant status before the revenue and rent courts would be defined by entries in the Record of Rights, the Communists were concerned that unless the 1955 act were amended to recognize a subtenant, the Record of Rights would in fact result in many subtenants being evicted.[63] The landlords, however, were reluctant to have intermediaries and subtenants recognized because it would give legal protection to an arrangement over which they felt they had less control.

I noted earlier in this chapter that a pattern of non-Brahmin tenants subletting their lands to Harijans emerged in the late 1940s. In testimony before the select committee all parties seemed to agree that subleasing had become quite common in the district. Therefore, it seems that recognition of intermediaries was included by the DMK specifically for the benefit of their non-Brahmin constituency among the tenantry. The Communists, of course, were concerned about their constituency, the Harijan subtenants. And it is, I believe, not coincidental that the witness who spoke for the landlords on the issue was a Brahmin. Thus, the issue reveals the con-

---

[61] Ibid., pp. 22, 34-36. Also reported by *Ulavu Chelvam*, October 15, 1968, p. 5.
[62] Madras, *Tenancy Rights Bill Select Committee Report*, pp. 26-27, 41-42, 46.
[63] Ibid., p. 20.

tinuing political salience of caste differences among tenants. In any case, as finally enacted the measure did recognize the intermediary and subtenant, and the 1955 and 1956 acts were amended to recognize the subtenant.

The importance of the other issues surrounding the record of rights proposal lay in the extent to which governmental initiative and procedure would be used to overcome the local economic and political power of the landlord. And whereas the final provisions of the legislation did in fact incorporate several of the suggestions made by the Communists, there was one key omission: the initiative for making entries in the Record of Rights was left to the individual tenant; it was necessary for him to write the record officer stating his claim within one month after publication of the intention to prepare a record for the village. As in the earlier reforms this procedure clearly disadvantaged the very poor and illiterate Harijan tenant. Furthermore, the record officer did rely heavily on the *karnam*'s records in the actual preparation of the record.[64] Thus, although the Agriculturalists' Association did attempt to help get tenants registered, it was not surprising that the Communists criticized implementation of the act. The DMK government amended the act in August 1972 to give the record officer authority to conduct inquiries *suo moto*, but a year later both the Communists and the DMK were still unhappy with the results of the legislation.[65] These deficiencies notwithstanding, this first major reform measure under DMK rule indicated the Party's growing seriousness about addressing the tenancy issue.

Several other measures followed. In 1970 the number of rent courts in Thanjavur District was expanded from two to five, making them more accessible to tenants in the Sirkali, Mannargudi, and Tiruthuraipoondi areas. Then, in 1971 and 1972 the arrears issue arose once more, with many tenants apparently facing eviction because they had not made the payments mandated by the 1968 legislation.[66] In April 1972 the DMK introduced and quickly passed, in the face of considerable protest from Thanjavur landowners,

---

[64] See Badrinath, *A Report on the Implementation of the Tamilnadu Agricultural Lands Record of Tenancy Rights Act, 1969* (Madras, 1971), p. 75. See also report in *Ulavu Chelvam*, October 15, 1968, p. 5.

[65] Hindu, August 25, 1972; *Indian Express* (Madras), April 30, 1973; May 23, 1973.

[66] Kamaraj Nadar, former president of the All-India Congress Committee and then leader of the Tamil Nadu Congress (0), gave a speech in March 1972 in which he asserted that twenty-five thousand tenants throughout the state were about to be evicted for nonpayment of arrears. See the *Hindu*, March 17, 1972.

legislation wiping off all arrears due as of June 30, 1971. This measure was certainly far-reaching in its effects, as reflected in the fact that the Communist legislative assembly members from Mannargudi and Tiruthuraipoondi constituencies actively supported the legislation. One letter to the editor protesting the measure cited it as evidence that the DMK was actively vying for tenant support in Thanjavur.[67]

One reason for widespread tenant resistance to payment of arrears was the expectation that perhaps before too long the land might become theirs.[68] And in fact one year later the DMK government introduced and the assembly passed legislation giving tenants the right to purchase the land they were cultivating. Known as the Tamil Nadu Cultivating Tenants (Right to Purchase Landowners' Rights) Act, 1973, it gave the tenant (defined as one who personally cultivates the land) the right to purchase all or part of the land provided that the resultant operational holding would not exceed five standard acres.[69] However, prior to the tenant's right to purchase the landowner had the right to resume for personal cultivation up to half the area leased to the tenant subject to the same maximum operational holding size. The act also exempted the lands of religious, charitable, and educational institutions up to a maximum of ten standard acres. If the landlord and the tenant could not agree on a purchase price, the act mandated a price equivalent to twelve times the fair rent (40 percent of normal gross produce in the case of wet land) payable in twelve equal annual installments, or 75 percent of that amount if the tenant paid the total in one lump sum. Though certainly not free of loopholes, the measure was considered radical by many and generated a storm of criticism from many landowning quarters.[70] Even the general council of the DMK was disturbed by the move.[71] Whereas DMK leaders stated that the legislation was proof of their commitment to the goal of making the "genuine tiller of the soil an owner of

[67] Ibid., April 4, 1972; April 3, 1972.

[68] Interview with the head clerk, rent court, Thanjavur, on November 11, 1972. He explained this was also the reason that rent fixation petitions had fallen off sharply after 1970.

[69] *Hindu*, March 30, 1973; April 4, 1973. For definition of a standard acre, see Sonachalam, *Land Reforms*, p. 173. The concept was introduced in land ceiling legislation in order to standardize units of land area for irrigation and soil quality. For instance, three dry acres are equivalent to one standard acre.

[70] *Hindu*, April 8, 11, 15, 18, 20, 1973.

[71] Ibid., June 18, 1973.

the soil,"[72] numerous critics argued that many of those recorded as cultivating tenants were in fact only intermediaries and that therefore the legislation would transfer ownership of land to a new group who were no more tillers than the existing owners.[73]

In spite of objections to the substance of the right-to-purchase legislation, only one party, the conservative Swatantra, actively opposed it. The other parties, including the CPI and CPM (the CPI had broken its alliance with the DMK in March 1972), were caught in a bind. On the one hand, they recognized that the law could be "used to liquidate gradually the rural support they now enjoy."[74] On the other hand, they could not oppose a measure so clearly in accord with their own positions. In fact, the bold DMK move created a deep rift between state CPI leaders and Thanjavur leaders A. K. Subbiah and Manali Kandaswamy, the legislative assembly members (MLAs) from Mannargudi and Tiruthuripoondi constituencies (in Zone 3) respectively. Both Subbiah and Kandaswamy actively supported enactment of the right-to-purchase legislation, and shortly thereafter DMK leaders publicly spoke of Kandaswamy's appreciation for the Party's reforms.[75] About the same time state CPI leaders strongly criticized the Right to Purchase Act on several grounds, concluding that it could only help the big landowners.[76] A few weeks later the rift became a clean break when Subbiah and Kandaswamy both resigned from the CPI on the grounds that the state Party leaders "blindly opposed" the "progressive measures" taken by the DMK.[77] Although Subbiah and Kandaswamy quickly formed a new party, the Tamil Nadu Communist Party, it was clear that they had allied themselves with the DMK.[78]

Although the defection of Subbiah and Kandaswamy was not entirely due to DMK initiatives in the area of tenancy reforms,[79] the fact that these two men represented areas of the district where agrarian radicalism had long found support among *both* tenants and labor suggests that the DMK measures helped greatly to deflect

[72] Ibid., May 2, 1973.
[73] Ibid., May 22, 1973; *Indian Express*, May 7, 1973.
[74] *Hindu*, April 8, 1973.
[75] Ibid., April 15, 1973.
[76] *Ulavu Chelvam*, April 15, 1973.
[77] *Hindu*, July 5, 1973; *Indian Express*, July 6, 1973.
[78] *Indian Express*, July 7, 11, 1973.
[79] I will deal with the other factors, such as CPI policies, the labor situation, factionalism, etc., in Chapter 10.

whatever radical thrust the tenancy issue might have once had in Thanjavur, even among the "low-end" tenants of the Mannargudi and Tiruthuraipoondi taluks. Actually, as I have argued above, the "deradicalization" of tenancy in Thanjavur had much older roots, dating back to changes in the agrarian structure of Thanjavur during the late nineteenth and early twentieth centuries and continuing with the first phase of tenancy reforms under the Congress government in the 1950s. All of these developments contributed to a cumulative dissociation of tenants as a group and tenancy rights as an issue from the radical agrarian potential in Thanjavur.

I do not, however, intend to imply that tenant grievances had been completely eliminated in Thanjavur by 1973. Certainly the absolute and relative economic status of most tenants in Thanjavur was still very low. Many tenants were still largely dependent on the economic and political power of the landlords, in some ways more so than in the traditional relationship. But two fundamental changes blocked the emergence of tenancy as a challenge to the legitimacy of the agrarian structure: the "bifurcation" of tenants into "high-end" and "low-end" sectors, based on subtle but important distinctions in the terms and conditions of tenancy, in caste status, and in the political climate, all of which contributed to important differences in the quality of the landlord-tenant relationship; and substantial improvements in status for some tenants, marginal improvements for others, and the hope of improvement for still others, all the result of incremental changes in the content and climate of landlord-tenant relations brought about by tenancy reforms.

The growing weakness of tenancy as a radical issue in the late 1960s is revealed in the activities of the CPI-led Agriculturalists' Association. First, judging from published reports and personal interviews with association leaders, it seems that the association's activities were largely confined, as might be expected, to the Mannargudi-Tiruthuraipoondi area. For instance, in September 1970 the association held an intensive series of organizational meetings; five out of the eight meetings were held in Mannargudi and Tiruthuraipoondi taluks, with one in Nannilam, one in Sirkali, and one in Kumbakonam.[80] Second, although every reported meeting of the association dealt with tenancy rights, each also gave considerable attention to "nonstructural" concerns, such as paddy prices and procurement.[81] At a district-level meeting of the association

[80] *Ulavu Chelvam*, October 6, 1970, p. 5.
[81] Ibid., December 15, 1968; January 1, 1969; February 1, 1970.

held in January 1973 paddy price and procurement and fertilizer distribution were the sole concerns.[82] In other words, although the association dealt almost exclusively with poor tenants, the fact that it was forced to deal with issues embraced by all cultivating groups was an indication of how even these tenants were tied into a larger agrarian system.

"Low-End" Tenancy and Radicalism: Inams and Temples

One exception to this pattern of tenancy deradicalization was the institution of *inam* tenancy, the vestiges of which continued to produce tenant-landlord confrontations reminiscent of agrarian unrest in Thanjavur during the later 1940s. For instance, in May 1969 there was a violent clash between tenants and the former *inamdar* in Adaikalathevan Village in Pattukottai taluk and another in December 1970 between tenants and the former *inamdar* in Pakiri-tyhaikal Village in Sirkali taluk.[83] As suggested in the previous chapter, the structural legacy of the *inam* system was probably also responsible for the development of a limited radical base among labor-tenants and labor-owners in Zone 5, where most of the *inam* villages in the district had been located.

In some of the former *inam* villages the opposition of a largely landless group to a single large landowner survived *inam* abolition (completed only in the early 1960s) as a result of the former *inamdars'* evasion of abolition measures. In these villages the former *inam* tenants were reduced to the status of daily wage laborers or, more likely, earned their livelihood through a combination of daily wage labor and cultivation of small plots of leased or owned land acquired through *inam* abolition (the marginal cultivation in Zone 5 makes subsistence on daily wage labor alone very difficult). This structure, closely analogous to the polarization of landless labor and large owners in non*inam* areas of Zones 2 and 3, almost certainly explains the support for the Communist parties and the radical attitudes found among laborers in Zone 5. It is in fact a variant of the low-end tenant radicalism I have described for Zones 2 and 3, with the structural framework provided by the *inam* legacy. That the Zone 5 radical base has developed among both Harijans and non-Harijans (see Chapter 7) demonstrates the radicalizing

[82] Ibid., February 1, 1973.

[83] Ibid., May 15, 1969, p. 18; January 1, 1971, p. 11. See Chapter 4 for a description of the *inam* system and its abolition.

effect of a polarized agro-economic structure in spite of caste differences (the tenants involved in the clashes in former *inam* villages mentioned above were all non-Harijans).

The Communists, in particular the CPI, made limited efforts to organize laborers and tenants on former *inam* estates. In June 1969, for instance, the CPI held a conference of "agriculturalists" of *inam* villages.[84] They also sought amendment of the *inam* abolition legislation to make tenants owners of the land.[85] However, the relative segregation of radicalism in former *inam* pockets, together with other constraints on political organization imposed by the overall agrarian structure of Zone 5, severely limited the development of a broad and solid radical base. This supports my finding in the survey data analysis that individual radical identification and attitudes among laborers in Zone 5 had not been translated into agrarian organization or greater leverage vis-à-vis landowning elites. The radical potential in that area is likely to remain limited as long as its present productive, demographic, and economic patterns persist.

Of much wider significance is another special feature of tenancy in Thanjavur District, the large amount of land owned by "public trusts," including temples, *mutts*, and related endowments (created by donations of land for the stated purpose of providing income for religious, charitable, and educational activities usually connected with the temples or *mutts*). In 1961 the major institutions in Thanjavur (those assessable under the Hindu Religious and Charitable Endowments [HRCE] Act of 1959) amounted to about 1500 temples, 27 *mutts*, and 165 specific endowments.[86] The largest institutions included three *mutts* (or *adheenams*) at Dharmapuram and Tiruvaduthurai in Mayuram taluk and at Tirupanandal in Kumbakonam taluk that control about 70,000, 40,000, and 30,000 acres respectively of mostly wet land belonging to numerous temples located in different taluks.[87] The affairs of most other temples in the district are administered by the government under the HRCE Act. Their landholdings range from a few acres to about 11,000

[84] *Ulavu Chelvam*, June 1, 1969.
[85] Ibid., June 1, 1968, p. 15; February 1, 1970, p. 11; April 15, 1971.
[86] Government of Madras, Hindu Religious and Charitable Endowments (Administration) Department, *Administration Report for the Year from 1st April 1960 to 31st March 1961* (Madras, 1962), p. 49 (hereafter Madras, *HRCE Report*).
[87] *Ulavu Chelvam*, August 1, 1970, p. 3. See also S. S. Iyer, "A Case Study of Thanjavur District: Anatomy of Agrarian Unrest," *People's Action* 5 (New Delhi: May 1971): 25.

acres in the case of the Vedaranyam Temple in Tiruthuraipoondi taluk. Estimates of the total amount of agricultural land owned by these institutions have ranged from 200,000 to 500,000 acres, though I suspect the lower figure is much closer to the truth.[88] In any case, it is clear that these lands are a major factor in Thanjavur's agrarian system.

The impact of public trust lands is greatest in the Zone 2 and 3 areas where they are concentrated. Although the list of temple holdings in Table 69 is not exhaustive, I believe it is roughly representative of the distribution by taluk. About 65 percent of the temple lands are located in the taluks of Zones 2 and 3; also the average area owned by temples in those taluks is generally higher, particularly in Sirkali, Nagapattinam, and Tiruthuraipoondi taluks. The public trust lands are cultivated almost exclusively through tenancy. There are, however, important variations in the nature of the tenancy arrangements.

One common pattern, observed as long ago as the early 1950s, is for the temple to lease large chunks of land to single individuals, usually non-Brahmins owning some land themselves who would then either sublet the land to small tenants or cultivate it with hired labor.[89] This could be very profitable. The temple authorities' greatest concern was to assure some income with a minimum of involvement on their part, so that they were willing to accept relatively low fixed rents.[90] The big tenants could then demand higher rents from the subtenants or cultivate the land with cheap hired labor. This pattern was especially common in areas of Zones 2 and 3 where temple holdings were larger, the poor Harijan tenants had few alternatives, and labor was abundant. This is why we found in Chapter 5 that a relatively large percentage of tenants in Zones 2

[88] Iyer, "Case Study," p. 25. See also the *Hindu*, April 11, 1970. Of seventy-two temples in Tamil Nadu with annual incomes of Rs. 50,000, thirty-four are located in Thanjavur District. See Richard Kennedy, "Status and Control of Temples in Tamil Nadu," *The Indian Economic and Social History Review* 11 (June-September 1974): 284.

[89] Madras, Land Revenue Reforms Committee, *First Report*, pp. 63-64.

[90] Shortly after the passage of the HRCE Act, one purpose of which was the financial management of temples, it was found that temple lands were being let at low rates through collusion between temple authorities and the lessees. The new HRCE Administration Department had therefore instituted auctions of lease to get better terms for the temples. But it appears that the department was soon co-opted by local power structures in the form of area committees composed primarily of powerful landlords who were sent up to oversee temple affairs (Madras, *HRCE Report*, pp. 20, 33-34). See also IADP, *Study on Tenancy Patterns in Thanjavur*, p. 36.

TABLE 69

Temple Lands and Tenant Cooperative Farming Societies, 1961, by Taluk

Taluk	Temples Owning Lands[a]				Tenant Cooperative Farming Societies[b]		
	Number of Temples	Total Extent[c] (acres)	% of District Total	Average Area Per Temple (acres)	Total Number	% of District Total	Average Area Per Society[d] (acres)
Thanjavur	14	1586	2.3	132	0	—	—
Papanasam	11	700	1.0	78	3	4.5	173
Kumbakonam	48	12000	17.6	293	9	13.4	98
Mayuram	27	7514	11.0	398	12	17.9	106
Sirkali	14	11731	17.2	902	6	9.0	78
Nannilam	23	5317	7.8	266	8	11.9	302
Nagapattinam	13	8531	12.5	776	13	19.4	194
Mannargudi	15	3877	5.7	298	6	9.0	73
Tiruthuraipoondi	8	15467	22.6	1740	10	14.9	131
Orathanad	3	449	0.7	225	0	—	—
Pattukottai	9	859	1.3	143	0	—	—
Arantangi	3	300	0.4	150	0	—	—
District total/average	188	68331	*	435	67	100.0	136

Sources: [a] Compiled from information available in *Census of India, 1961*, vol. 4, pt. XI-D, *Temples of Tamil Nadu*, vol. 7 (i), *Thanjavur* (Madras: Superintendent of Census Operations, 1971).
[b] Compiled from data available in Government of Madras, Hindu Religious and Charitable Endowments (Administration) Department, *Administration Report for the Year from 1st April 1960 to 31st March 1961* (Madras, 1962).
[c] The figures on area owned are for 158 of the 188 temples owning land; data was not available for the other 30.
[d] The average area per society is based on 64 societies for which data was available.

Note: * Does not add to 100 due to rounding.

and 3 were cultivating more than ten acres. Although legislation passed in 1961 (extending to tenants of public trust lands the same protection as did the 1955 act to tenants of individual landlords) restricted the size of a tenancy holding to five standard acres, the practice continued into the 1960s with the big tenants executing bogus leases to evade the law. This also enabled the temples to circumvent restrictive provisions of the act.[91]

Big landlords often acted as agents for temple authorities in the leasing of lands. They also colluded with temple authorities to evade provisions of the 1961 Tamil Nadu Land Ceiling Act. Because religious institutions were exempted from the ceilings, these landlords, especially those in Zones 2 and 3 who were most vulnerable to the ceilings, would either nominally donate lands to the temples or set up bogus endowments but then continue to cultivate the land as "tenants" paying little or no rent.[92] It helped that these landlords were often trustees of the temple or temples involved. It is therefore not surprising that the Communists advocated removal of all ceiling exemptions for religious institutions.[93] In 1972 the DMK government introduced a bill that would have removed or limited the exemption from land ceilings allowed to religious institutions, but after an investigation and report by a select committee the resulting legislation instead *extended* the scope of these exemptions.[94] Evidently the DMK discovered this measure would cut too deeply into the support it had been building since 1967 through control over temple administration.[95]

As part of an effort to promote cooperative farming throughout India in the late 1950s tenant cooperative farming societies were

[91] Pillai, "Report on Agrarian Labour," pp. 41-42. See also Iyer, "Case Study," p. 25.

[92] Testimony by G. Veeraiyan, district secretary for the CPM's Kisan Sabha, before a select committee of the Tamil Nadu legislative assembly, Government of Tamil Nadu, *The Tamil Nadu Land Ceiling (Amendment) Bill, 1972: Report and Proceedings of the Select Committee of the Tamil Nadu Legislative Assembly* (Madras, 1972), pp. 141-142. See also report in *Ulvau Chelvam*, September 15, 1972, and Sonachalam, *Land Reforms*, pp. 64-65. As of December 1972, 64 percent of the land notified as surplus in Thanjavur District was in either Zone 2 or Zone 3. However, the absolute amount was very small—about 1,813 acres (data provided by the Authorised Office, Thanjavur.

[93] *Ulavu Chelvam*, January 1, 1968, p. 11; May 15, 1972, p. 8. See also Mythili Shivaraman, "Thanjavur: Rumblings of Class Struggle in Tamil Nadu," in *Imperialism and Revolution in South Asia*, ed. Kathleen Gough and Hari P. Sharma (New York and London: Monthly Review Press, 1973), pp. 246-264.

[94] *Hindu*, April 7, 1972; August 18, 1972.

[95] Kennedy, "Status and Control of Temples," pp. 284-287.

established on temple lands in various parts of Thanjavur. These societies were also seen by HRCE administrators as a way of breaking the system of *benami* ("bogus") leases by big landlords.[96] About seventy-five were founded in the ten years between 1959 and 1969. The available data (see Table 69) indicate, as expected, that most were located in Zones 2 and 3. The temple authorities and big landowners of course opposed the societies and worked in collusion with cooperative officials to undermine them by making it difficult for them to function and by reporting that they were not functioning well. The landowners and temple authorities were successful, and by the late 1960s most of the societies had been closed.[97]

In summary, the dominant patterns of temple tenancy paralleled and reinforced the overall bipolar character of the agrarian structure in Zones 2 and 3: the temple authorities, big landowners, and big tenants were all allied against small tenants and landless laborers.[98] Data on eviction petitions filed under the provisions of the Public Trust Act of 1961 during 1971 and 1972 demonstrate this relationship (see Table 70). Note that the ratio of eviction petitions allowed to petitions dismissed is higher in Zone 2 than in Zone 1, and higher in Zone 3 than in Zone 2. Evictions were more likely where big landlords and disguised big tenants controlled temple lands cultivated by low-end cultivating tenants.

However, another pattern emerged where the low-end tenant stood in a direct relationship with temple authorities. For instance, in the village of Kunnalur in Tiruthuraipoondi taluk virtually all of the land was owned by the Vedaranyam Temple and cultivated by predominantly Harijan tenants.[99] There was no local big landlord standing between the tenants and the temple authorities. Partly for this reason and partly because the tenants put up a solid front (in spite of the fact that 25 percent of them were not Harijans) they were in a strong position vis-à-vis the temple authorities. Although 60 percent of them were heavily in arrears, the temple was not able to evict any of them. The tenants in this village were not better off economically than their counterparts in other villages, but they were not dependent on a local landlord. Because of the

---

[96] Sonachalam, *Land Reforms*, pp. 38-40. See also Madras, *HRCE Report*, p. 20.

[97] See *Ulvau Chelvam*, July 1, 1968, pp. 7-8; IADP, *Study on Tenancy Patterns in Thanjavur*, p. 38; Iyer, "Case Study," p. 25.

[98] Iyer, "Case Study," p. 25. Joan Mencher has observed the same pattern in Chingleput District. See Joan P. Mencher, "Problems in Analysing Rural Class Structure," *Economic and Political Weekly* 9 (August 31, 1974): 1,502.

[99] *Census of India, 1961, Village Monograph—Kunnalur*.

TABLE 70

Eviction Petitions Filed against Tenants of Public Trust Lands, 1971-1972, by Zone

Zone in which Tenant is Located	Eviction Petitions Filed under 1961 Act				Eviction Petitions Filed under 1968 Act			
	Filed (% of district total)	Action (% of total filed)			Filed (% of district total)	Action (% of total filed)		
		Allowed	Dismissed	Pending		Allowed	Dismissed	Pending
	N = 472				N = 320			
1/Old Delta-Cauvery	27.3	17.9	25.4	56.7	44.4	11.1	31.8	57.1
2/Old Delta-Central	17.6	30.5	30.2	39.3	15.6	17.0	24.0	59.0
3/Old Delta-Coastal	50.8	30.1	16.5	53.4	37.5	26.6	11.6	61.7
4/New Delta-CMP	3.6	50.1	14.5	35.3	1.9	58.3	8.3	33.3
5/Dry Areas-Uplands	0.6	66.7	33.3	0.0	0.6	12.5	0.0	87.5
District average	*	27.8	21.4	50.8	100.0	18.7	21.4	58.9

* Does not add to 100 due to rounding.

distance and noninvolvement of the temple authorities the agrarian structure in this village lacked the element of confrontation prevalent in many parts of Zones 2 and 3, and thus was less radicalizing (in fact, Kunnalur had never had a Communist president). In other words, temple tenancy relations are more apt to be radicalizing where the involvement of local landowners creates a situation resembling the polar opposition of a large individual landlord and a large group of poor tenants.

To illustrate further, we can compare the relationship of tenancy to agrarian radicalism in Mannargudi and Tiruthuraipoondi taluks. In 1971 the two taluks had almost equal tenancy rates (9.45 and 9.07 percent respectively). In the same year they also had comparable proportions of Harijan tenants (34.6 and 29.6 percent respectively). But the correlation between tenancy and agrarian radicalism in Mannargudi was .327 and in Tiruthuraipoondi .014! Furthermore, although the data indicate Mannargudi had much less area under temple tenancy than Tiruthuraipoondi (see Table 69), in 1971 and 1972 there were more temple land eviction petitions in Mannargudi than in Tiruthuraipoondi (17.1 percent of the district total and 14.7 percent of the district total respectively).

What might account for the more conflictive character of temple tenancy in Mannargudi? I would suggest that it was the local presence and greater involvement of large landlords in Mannargudi's agrarian structure which tended to generate a "class-type confrontation" even in the case of temple tenancy. One must reach back to the 1951 census data to provide some evidence (Table 71). At that time the percentage of noncultivating owners/rent receivers in

TABLE 71

Landlordism in Mannargudi and Tiruthuraipoondi Taluks, 1951

| | Noncultivating Owners/ Rent Receivers as % of Total Owners | |
	Rural	Total
Mannargudi	9.37	15.67
Tiruthuraipoondi	5.02	7.15

SOURCES: Calculated from data in Madras, *1951 Census Handbook, Tanjore District*, pp. 27-28.

Mannargudi was twice that in Tiruthuraipoondi. The difference is small but significant. (By comparison, for instance, the percentage of large and very large holdings in Zones 2 and 3 is only about two-and-a-half times that in Zone 1.)

For the numerous and complex reasons advanced in this chapter, the role of tenancy in agrarian radicalism in Thanjavur has been limited and declining. Although it certainly contributed to the agrarian unrest of 1945 to 1952 and continued to be a source of agrarian radicalism in selected areas of the district, the role of tenancy has been strongly conditioned by its *structural context* (i.e., low-end tenancy in areas with a bipolar agro-economic structure). This illustrates the importance of "unpacking" the concept of tenancy and moving beyond the positional approach in order to understand the role of various agrarian groups in agrarian radicalism, a method that I have adopted in this study. By exploring the historical background and agrarian context of tenancy in Thanjavur we are able to see why tenancy is a positive factor in agrarian radicalism in some areas, a negative factor in others, and a neutral factor in still others.

The overall impact of variations in tenancy over time and space on agrarian radicalism in Thanjavur is apparent in Table 72 and Figure 11. In Table 72 we find that agrarian radicalism has been declining in those panchayats where tenancy is a more important

TABLE 72

Tenancy and Trends in Agrarian Radicalism in Thanjavur District, 1960-1970

Agrarian Radicalism	Tenancy, 1972	
Whether Communist Control of Panchayat over 1960-70 is:	Tenants as % of Agricultural Workers	Area under Tenancy as % of Total Area
Declining	18.2	24.1
Gaining	13.6	16.8
Always strong	13.5	17.9

NOTE: "Declining" = CPI/CPM candidate won panchayat presidency in 1960 only, 1965 only, or 1960 and 1965 only; "Gaining" = won 1965 and 1970 or 1970 only; "Always strong" = won all three years.

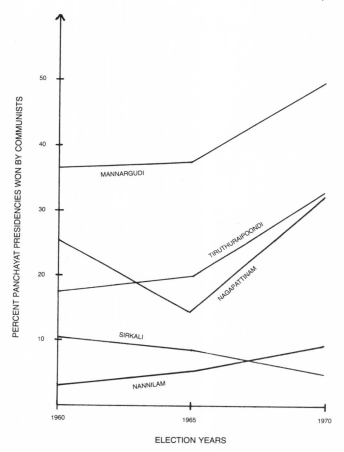

FIGURE 11. Trends in Agrarian Radicalism Over Time (1960-1970) for Taluks of Zones 2 and 3

factor and gaining where it is less important. In Figure 11 we see that there is only one area, Sirkali, in Zones 2 and 3 where agrarian radicalism has lost strength over the period 1960 to 1970. If we recall (see Table 39) that Sirkali is the only area in which agrarian radicalism is correlated *only* with tenancy, the declining radical potential of tenancy is nicely demonstrated.

The increase in agrarian radicalism from 1960 to 1970 in all the other areas is a function of its success among labor. The higher level of radicalism at all times in Mannargudi is a result of the combination of labor and tenancy factors; Mannargudi is the one area in which tenancy was recently still positively related to radicalism. The source of agrarian radicalism in the other areas has been almost exclusively labor, a strong source in Tiruthuraipoondi and Nagapattinam, and a weak source in Nannilam.

CHAPTER 9

Technological Change and
Agrarian Radicalism

IN THE 1970s the study of agricultural change in developing societies gave heightened attention to the impact of technological
change on the *distribution* of agricultural wealth and income.[1] The
shift in emphasis from growth to equity considerations resulted,
ironically enough, from a dramatic breakthrough, real and apparent, in agricultural growth in the late 1960s and early 1970s.[2] During this period several Asian countries achieved significant gains
in foodgrain productivity, especially in wheat, through the introduction of new, more fertilizer-responsive varieties developed by
international research institutes.[3]

At first these innovations were thought to revolutionize agricultural production in these countries and so were collectively labeled
the "Green Revolution." But as economists and other social scientists began to look more closely at the changes, concern grew
that the new technology was not equally available to all sizes and
types of cultivators. Where some degree of mechanization of agriculture either accompanied or closely followed the varietal innovations, there was also concern that agricultural labor would be
adversely affected by a decline in employment.[4] These concerns

[1] For example, see Keith Griffin, *The Political Economy of Agrarian Change: An Essay
on the Green Revolution* (Cambridge, Mass: Harvard University Press, 1974), and Carl
H. Gotsch, "Technical Change and Distribution of Income in Rural Areas," *American
Journal of Agricultural Economics* 26 (May 1972): 326-341.

[2] I say shift in emphasis because, as Ilchman and Uphoff have pointed out, all
growth strategies have implicit equity considerations. In other words, there is a
distributional formula for every production model. See Warren F. Ilchman and
Norman T. Uphoff, "Beyond the Economics of Labor-Intensive Development: Politics and Administration," paper presented to the Seminar on Administrative Requirements for Labor-Intensive Development Organized by the Development
Administration Panel on the Southeast Asian Development Advisory Group, Sin-
gapore, July 23-27, 1973.

[3] See Lester R. Brown, *Seeds of Change: The Green Revolution and Development in the
1970s* (New York: Praeger, 1970).

[4] An influential study of the Indian case is found in V. S. Vyas et al., "New
Agricultural Strategy and Small Farmers: A Case Study in Gujarat," *Economic and*

gave rise to a more general fear that the so-called Green Revolution would result in increasing economic disparities in the agricultural sector, which might in turn lead to social dislocation and heightened agrarian tensions. To the extent that these changing socio-economic alignments and increased tensions became politicized, the potential for violent agrarian conflict was greater.[5] Thus talk of the "Green Revolution" led to talk of a "Red Revolution."[6] Academic interest in these relationships was heightened by the coincidence of increased attention to the distributional and socio-political consequences of technological change in agriculture with the focus on the role of peasants in revolution stimulated particularly by the Chinese and Vietnamese experiences.

Not too long after the label Green Revolution was applied scholars began to realize that it might well be a misnomer. It became increasingly clear that truly revolutionary change, in the sense of sudden, quantum leaps in productivity, was limited to certain crops and regions and therefore proved to be the exception rather than the rule. Along with this realization developed a more cautious interpretation of the relationship between technological change, economic disparities, social disruption, and agrarian conflict. It was pointed out that with few exceptions the new technology per se was not responsible for its unequal benefits. Rather whatever disparity-increasing effects there might be could be largely attributed to existing inequalities in the agro-economic structure.[7]

Political Weekly 4 (March 29, 1969): A49-A53. For general approaches to this problem, see Robert d'A. Shaw, *Jobs and Agricultural Development*, Overseas Development Council Monograph no. 3 (Washington, D.C.: Overseas Development Council, 1970); Uma J. Lele, "Jobs, Poverty, and the 'Green Revolution'," *International Affairs* 48 (January 1972): 20-32; and Montague Yudelman et al., *Technological Change in Agriculture and Employment in Developing Countries*, Development Centre Studies, Employment Series, no. 4 (Paris: Development Centre of the Organisation for Economic Cooperation and Development, 1971). Two early studies of the Indian scene included Pranab Bardhan, " 'Green Revolution' and Agricultural Labourers," *Economic and Political Weekly* 5 (July 1970): 1,239-1,246, and Martin H. Billings and Arjan Singh, "Labour and the Green Revolution: The Experience in Punjab," *Economic and Political Weekly* 4 (December 1969): A221-A224.

[5] See Lester R. Brown, "The Social Impact of the Green Revolution," *International Conciliation*, no. 581 (January 1971), pp. 5-61, and Clifton R. Wharton, Jr., "The Green Revolution: Cornucopia or Pandora's Box?" *Foreign Affairs* 47 (April 1969): 464-476.

[6] See editorial in the *New York Times*, December 28, 1968.

[7] See Wolf Ladejinsky, "How Green is the Indian Green Revolution," *Economic and Political Weekly* 8 (December 29, 1973): A133-A144; Martin E. Abel, "Agriculture in India in the 1970s," *Economic and Political Weekly* 5 (March 28, 1970): A5-A24;

Thus, as briefly noted in Chapter 2, there are two main variants to the technological explanation of agrarian radicalism. On the one hand, it is argued that technological change by its very nature creates economic divisions in agrarian society that cut across traditional relationships. Where the traditional pattern is the relatively egalitarian one of subsistence-oriented peasant households, the new technology makes agrarian society vulnerable to economic imperatives (profit, market-orientation) that result in the creation of new economic divisions as resources become increasingly concentrated in the hands of those who respond most rapidly and effectively to the new technology. Where the traditional pattern is already hierarchically ordered in the manner of lord and peasant, the new technology alters incentives and the relative status of agrarian groups, thus undermining the vertical integration of agrarian society and creating new horizontal cleavages. More specific conclusions concerning the impact of technological change on the agrarian socioeconomic system require close consideration of the *nature* of the new technology: To what extent does it actually alter the means of production and the relationship of various agrarian groups to the means of production?

On the other hand, it is argued that the effects of technological change are not inherent in the technology but result rather from differential access to use of new technology inherent in the existing socio-economic divisions of agrarian society. For instance, the varietal-fertilizer innovation is not capital-intensive in the strict sense, but the large landowner may be more able to adopt it than the small owner or tenant because he has more assured access to inputs and markets and more risk-bearing capacity (generally speaking, he has greater control over the environment of production). In this view, whether or not new technology is disruptive of the existing agrarian economic and social order depends on how the structure and relations of production affect access to the means of production.

In reality, of course, it is hard to separate these two arguments or to give primacy to one or the other. But in taking note of this analytical distinction I mean to highlight two considerations: 1) that the *content and context* of technological change are variable, and 2) that they interact. It is only by taking account of the interaction of

---

Bandhudas Sen, *The Green Revolution in India: A Perspective* (New York: John Wiley & Sons, 1974): and Wolf Ladejinsky, "Green Revolution in Bihar. The Kosi Area: A Field Trip," *Economic and Political Weekly* 4 (September 27, 1969): A147-A162.

the two variables, both in themselves quite complex, that we can come to an accurate determination of the economic impact of technological changes. Even if it can be determined that in a given situation technological change does result in increasing economic disparities, does that automatically lead to a "realignment" of the agrarian structure (e.g., from vertical to horizontal cleavages) and then to political mobilization of the new groupings? Not necessarily, of course. First, it depends on exactly what the agrarian structure was originally like. If there are several groups in the agrarian structure, it depends on which groups gain and which lose *relative* to each other. Is there an overall tendency to polarization of the agrarian structure, or is it only groups at the upper and/or lower ends of the structure that move up and down? Second, several factors intervene in the relationship between agro-economic change and agrarian radicalism such as individual perception of the direction and degree of change and the organization and leadership of affected groups.

I have previously argued that certain features of agrarian structure in Thanjavur are conducive to agrarian radicalism. In this chapter I will examine the interaction of technological change and agrarian structure in Thanjavur to see whether and how technological change has contributed to the development of agrarian radicalism in the period 1960 to 1972.

TECHNOLOGICAL CHANGE IN THANJAVUR

We have seen in Chapter 4 that there is practically a zero correlation (.007) between agricultural development and agrarian radicalism across all panchayats in the district. There are several reasons for this. The first and most general is the *limited extent* of agricultural change in Thanjavur during the period under examination. Although Thanjavur was selected as a pilot area for the Intensive Agricultural District Programme (IADP) and High-Yielding Varieties Programme (HYVP) because of its relatively assured irrigation and good infrastructure, it did *not* experience the sort of dramatic breakthrough in agricultural productivity described by the term Green Revolution. Increases in per acre productivity in Thanjavur pale by comparison with those of wheat-growing areas in North India where the Green Revolution got its name: rice yields in Thanjavur increased 33 percent between 1960/1961 and 1971/1972; wheat yields in Ludhiana District in Punjab increased 86 percent between 1961/1962 and 1967/1968. Even prior to the introduction of the high-yielding varieties (which were responsible for the great burst in productivity in wheat areas), Thanjavur's performance was not outstanding compared to that of other IADP pilot districts.[8] If the *rate* of change is crucial to the hypothesis linking agricultural change to disruptive economic change and agrarian unrest, then we should not expect to find agricultural change a factor in agrarian radicalism in Thanjavur. As Barrington Moore says, "The timing of changes in the life of the peasantry, including the number of people simultaneously affected, are crucial factors in their own right. . . . Economic deterioration by slow degrees can become accepted by its victims as part of the normal situation."[9]

There were three principal reasons for the limited degree of agricultural change in Thanjavur. First, and most important, were the constraints inherent in the technology itself.[10] During the early years, 1960 to 1965, Thanjavur lacked a significant yield-increasing technology, specifically, more fertilizer-responsive paddy varieties to give greater effect to the gradual improvement in cultural practices that was taking place.[11] The introduction of ADT. 27 did raise *kuruvai* yields, but its main impact was to increase the double cropped area.[12] The more significant yield-increasing varieties were introduced only in 1968 and 1969 and did not spread very rapidly.

The conversion to double cropping and the spread of high-yield-

[8] Government of India, Ministry of Food, Agriculture, Community Development and Cooperation, Expert Committee on Assessment and Evaluation, *Modernising Indian Agriculture: Fourth Report on the Intensive Agricultural District Programme (1960-1968)*, vol. 2, *District Chapters* (New Delhi, undated), p. 258. See also Dorris D. Brown, *Agricultural Development in India's Districts* (Cambridge, Mass.: Harvard University Press, 1971), p. 36.

[9] Barrington Moore, Jr., *Social Origins of Dictatorship and Democracy: Lord and Peasant in the Making of the Modern World* (Boston: Beacon Press, 1966), p. 474.

[10] See Chapter 4. On the limitations of new rice technology, see George Rosen, *Peasant Society in a Changing Economy: Comparative Development in Southeast Asia and India* (Urbana, Ill.: University of Illinois Press, 1975), p. 191.

[11] Intensive Agricultural District Programme, Thanjavur, "Study of Awareness and Acceptance of the Package of Practices Recommended under the Intensive Agricultural District Programme, 1963-64," Operational Research Study no. 2, typewritten, undated, p. 1. See also Intensive Agricultural District Programme, Thanjavur, "A Note on Yield Trends of Paddy in Thanjavur District," typewritten, undated, p. 4.

[12] See James Q. Harrison, "Agricultural Modernization and Income Distribution: An Economic Analysis of the Impact of New Seed Varieties on the Crop Production of Large and Small Farms in India" (Ph.D. dissertation, Princeton University, 1972), p. 122.

ing varieties were limited by the second set of constraints—ecological factors, in particular the quality of water supply and control. In 1967 the IADP hoped to convert 65 percent of the *samba* lands into *kuruvai* but achieved a conversion of only 8.9 percent. *Kuruvai* cultivation, even with the shorter duration ADT. 27, required earlier water supply and better drainage than *samba* cultivation. Since the cost of *kuruvai* cultivation was also higher, cultivating *kuruvai* on land with inferior water supply and control entailed greater risks.[13] Although water supply and control is superior in Zone 1, much of that area was already under double cropping. The spread of the later varietal innovations was contained by irrigation difficulties, too, and also by the sheer ecological variability of Thanjavur. The agronomic specificity of the high-yielding varieties meant that no one, not even three or four varieties, could attain their yield potential (and thus return the higher cultivation costs incurred) under all conditions. Adaptation of the new varieties to varying conditions through hybridization was possible but would require years of painstaking research.

Finally, the adoption of available new technology in Thanjavur was inhibited by relative prices and market conditions determined largely by external factors. Most significantly, the use of fertilizer was kept down by the high increase in fertilizer prices relative to the increase in paddy prices.[14] From 1960/1961 to 1970/1971 the price (current) of nitrogenous fertilizers increased by about 65 percent. Over approximately the same period the price for paddy obtainable by most cultivators rose by only about 26 percent. The price of paddy was held down by government regulation of the paddy markets, and as the main supplier of paddy to the urban areas of the state, Thanjavur was particularly hard hit. Thanjavur farmers were required to sell a portion of their crop to the government at fixed prices that were far below what the open market would bring. During the years 1964/1965 to 1968/1969, for instance, the state government procured on average about 50 percent of the total *kuruvai* and *samba* production.[15] Procurement was en-

[13] Intensive Agricultural District Programme, Thanjavur, "Quick Study on the Causes for Not Converting The Entire Proposed Samba Lands into Double Crop Lands During 1967-68," typewritten, undated, p. 7. See also, IADP, "Study of Awareness," pp. 9, 33.

[14] Brown, *Agricultural Development*, pp. 92-93, and IADP, "A Note on Yield Trends," p. 1. See also, Intensive Agricultural District Programme, Thanjavur, "Note on Fertilizer Use in Thanjavur District," typewritten, undated, p. 6.

[15] Data provided by the Intensive Agricultural District Programme Office, Thanjavur.

forced by the tight regulation of paddy movement out of the district. Thus, the economic incentives for Thanjavur farmers to adopt a riskier and more expensive technology were rather weak.

All these factors helped to hold down the pace and magnitude of agricultural change in Thanjavur, inspite of large development programs (some might say because of them) over the period from 1960 to 1972. Overall agricultural change in Thanjavur could best be described as incremental. This is not the sort of change process that might be expected to disrupt the agrarian social order and fan the embers of agrarian radicalism.[16]

TECHNOLOGICAL CHANGE IN THE AGRO-ECONOMIC ZONES

Given the role of ecological conditions in limiting the adoption of new technology we might expect to find Thanjavur's five agro-economic zones at different levels of agricultural development. In fact, it is apparent from Table 73 that the zones have undergone different degrees of technological change and that these differences are generally what would be expected. Zone 5 has the lowest agricultural development rating; Zone 3 also has a low rating. What is perhaps a little surprising is the performance in Zones 2 and 4.

TABLE 73

Agricultural Development in the Agro-Economic Zones

Zone	Agricultural Development Rating	
	Mean	Standard Deviation
1/Old Delta-Cauvery	2.26	1.08
2/Old Delta-Central	2.28	0.96
3/Old Delta-Coastal	1.89	0.76
4/New Delta-CMP	2.38	0.89
5/Dry Area-Uplands	1.79	1.17
District average	2.12	0.98

NOTE: $F = 19.7$; significant at .01 level.

[16] K. C. Alexander's most significant finding in his own study of Thanjavur District is that the impact of technological change bears little relationship to radical ideology. See Alexander, *Agrarian Tension in Thanjavur* (Hyderabad: National Institute of Community Development, 1975), pp. 93-112.

Zone 4 (New Delta) has the highest rating of all the zones, and Zone 2 has a rating comparable to that of Zone 1.

The superior performance of the New Delta may be explained as follows. In the past the somewhat inferior irrigation and soil of the New Delta have limited its productive possibilities in relation to those of the Old Delta. But the technology that became available in the 1960s, in particular the short-duration variety ADT. 27, enabled New Delta cultivators to overcome these marginal deficiencies. As can be seen in Table 74, the *kuruvai* acreage increased very sharply in the New Delta between 1962/1963 and 1969/1970.[17] Furthermore, the nature of the agro-economic structure of the New Delta is favorable to the adoption of new technology, particularly the low incidence of tenancy and the high degree of family involvement in cultivation. Because he does not own the land, the tenant generally lacks the incentive and access to resources that facilitate technological innovation. The high-yielding paddy varieties are most productive when they are cultivated intensively and carefully at every stage of growth. This kind of attention is greatest when family labor input is high. Finally, since the varietal-fertilizer

TABLE 74

Double Cropping in the Agro-Economic Zones[a]

| Zone | Kuruvai as % of Net Area Sown to Paddy | | % Change in Kuruvai Area, 1969-70/1962-63 |
	1962-63	1969-70	
1/Old Delta-Cauvery	42.7	60.0	31.8
2/Old Delta-Central	18.6	42.4	143.6
3/Old Delta-Coastal	22.5	36.9	60.8
4/New Delta-CMP	17.9	49.1	97.9
5/Dry Area-Uplands	13.1*	5.7	−22.5**

SOURCE: Calculated from data provided by IADP Office, Thanjavur.

NOTES: [a] Zonal figures computed by aggregating block-level data. Three blocks, Budalur, Thanjavur, and Thiruvonam, are omitted because they overlap two or more zones. Vedaranyam also omitted because it is not included in previous zonal analyses.

* Arantangi data are for 1963-64.
** Decline in Zone 5 kuruvai due to poor weather in 1969-70.

[17] These years are used in making the comparison because both were years of good weather. Also, by 1969/1970 the area under *kuruvai* paddy had stabilized.

technology introduced in Thanjavur was not especially capital-intensive, the small and medium-sized cultivators of the New Delta generally had adequate resources for adoption of the technology.[18]

There is a general point to be made here about the relationship between technological change and agro-economic structure. Thanjavur District was chosen as a pilot area for technological change primarily on the basis of its relatively assured irrigation. But, ironically, the long-standing availability of canal irrigation had given rise to an agro-economic structure in the Old Delta that was less receptive to technological change because of its attenuated man to land relationship. It is the *combination* of relatively good irrigation and a closer, more direct relationship between the cultivator and the land in the New Delta that, in my view, favored rapid agricultural change. The point is not that the New Delta was inherently more productive (it still faced ecological constraints) but that both its geophysical *and* human resources were receptive to change.[19]

The better than expected performance in Zone 2, Old Delta-Central, was also due to the fact that its ecological deficiences were not totally inhibiting to technological change. The Central region of the Old Delta suffers from poor water supply and control relative to Zone 1 but not from the severe problems of Zone 3. Thus, the single most important element of agricultural change, the conversion to double cropping, was possible in Zone 2 precisely because the shorter duration of ADT. 27 freed many cultivators from the constraints of marginal water supply and control (see Table 74). In Zone 3 (Old Delta-Coastal), on the other hand, conversion to double cropping was much more limited by late water supply and particularly by drainage problems.[20]

The percentage increase in double cropping was smallest in Zone 1, of course, because so much of this area was already double cropped. After the conversion period it still had the highest percentage area under *kuruvai*. But notice that Zones 2 and 4 had by then outstripped Zone 3 in terms of area under *kuruvai*. It should

[18] Several studies have found that in general productivity per unit of land is higher on small holdings. This fact is in turn attributed to larger labor inputs by the small owner and his family. See Ashok Rudra, "Marginalist Explanation for More Intense Labour Input in Smaller Farms," *Economic and Political Weekly* 8 (June 22, 1973): 989-994.

[19] It is interesting in this context to note that one careful study of the Green Revolution in India found that "benefits are biased neither against the small farmer, nor in favour of the large farmer, but in favor of the medium size farmer" (Sen, *Green Revolution*, p. 104).

[20] IADP, "Quick Study," p. 9.

TABLE 75

Regional Pattern of Crop Inputs in Thanjavur District
(in rupees)

| Region | Total Value of Material Inputs Per Acre, 1969-70[a] (1) | Value of Labor Input Per Acre, 1969-70[a] | | Utilization of Capital for All Crops per Acre, 1965-68[b] (4) | Total Cost of Cultivation | | |
| | | Kuruvai (2) | Samba (3) | | All Crops Per Hectare, 1967-68[c] (5) | Paddy Per Acre, 1969-70[a] | |
						Kuruvai (6)	Samba (7)
Old Delta	81.17	171	166	74.51	978	279	261
Coastal Area	82.81	182	179	65.41	707	265	242
New Delta	87.68	186	181	122.95	1207	286	272
District average	NA	180	175	NA	959	279	255

SOURCES: [a] Intensive Agricultural District Programme, Thanjavur, *Study on Tenancy Patterns in Thanjavur District, 1969-70* (Madras: Government of Tamil Nadu, undated), pp. 12-17. Hereafter IADP, *Study on Tenancy Patterns in Thanjavur*.
[b] Coimbatore Agricultural College, Agricultural Economics and Rural Sociology Wing, "An Economic Appraisal of the Owner-Operated and Tenant-Operated Farms in Thanjavur District," mimeographed, undated.
[c] Government of India, Ministry of Agriculture and Irrigation, Directorate of Economics and Statistics, *Studies in the Economics of Farm Management in Thanjavur District (Tamil Nadu): Report for the Year 1967-68; Report for the Year 1968-69* by V. Shanmugasundaram (New Delhi, 1974). Hereafter India, *Studies in the Economics of Farm Management in Thanjavur*.

NOTES: Old Delta = Zones 1 and 2; Coastal Area = Zone 3; New Delta = Zone 4. NA = data not available.

be noted that the zonal differentials in double cropping correspond closely to the zonal differences in my measure of agricultural development (which is based on area under new varieties and fertilizer), a further reason for confidence in this measure.

Several other studies have found similar regional patterns of agricultural practices and productivity in Thanjavur. In Table 75 we find that on several measures of crop inputs the New Delta (Zone 4) ranks highest, the Old Delta (roughly Zones 1 and 2) next highest, and the Coastal Areas (roughly Zone 3) lowest. And in Table 76 we see that the New Delta usually ranks highest and the Coastal Areas usually lowest in terms of productivity per unit area.

It would seem from these findings that there is a near *inverse* relationship between technological change and agrarian radicalism in Thanjavur, for agrarian radicalism during the same period was heavily concentrated in the one area, Zone 3, that by all indications was least affected by new technology.[21] That is because within the

TABLE 76

Regional Pattern of Productivity in Thanjavur District

| | Yields of Paddy (kgs./acre) | | | Value of Output |
| | 1965-68[a] | 1969-70[b] | | for All Crops (Rs./hectare) |
Region	All Seasons (1)	Kuruvai (2)	Samba (3)	1967-68[c] (4)
Old Delta	939	1168	1017	995
Coastal Area	574*	1140	1026	707
New Delta	975	1215	1171	1062
District average	939	1175	1071	936

SOURCES: [a] Coimbatore Agricultural College, Agricultural Economics and Rural Sociology Wing, "An Economic Appraisal of the Owner-Operated and Tenant-Operated Farms in Thanjavur District," mimeographed, updated.

[b] IADP, *Study on Tenancy Patterns in Thanjavur*, pp. 12-17.

[c] India, *Studies in the Economics of Farm Management in Thanjavur (1967-68)*, p. 92.

NOTES: Old Delta = Zones 1 and 2; Coastal Area = Zone 3; New Delta = Zone 4.

* This figure is particularly low because it includes broadcast paddy in the extreme coastal areas.

[21] A negative correlation between the agricultural development rating and Com-

TABLE 77

Agrarian Radicalism Correlated with Agricultural Development
Rating, 1971, for Zones 1, 2, and 3

Zone	N*	Correlation between Agrarian Radicalism and Agricultural Development
1/Old Delta-Cauvery	326	.017
2/Old Delta-Central	257	.173**
3/Old Delta-Coastal	452	.094

* The N is the number of village panchayats included in the analysis for each zone. Town and city panchayats are excluded from this analysis.
** Significant at .01 level or higher.

deltaic boundaries of the district technological change is constrained by the same ecological conditions that are conducive to
agrarian radicalism through their agro-economic structural effects.
The situation in Zone 2 perhaps represents an exception to this
generalization as it is the zone with the second highest incidence
of agrarian radicalism and the second highest agricultural development rating. In fact, Zone 2 is the only zone in which there is a
significant correlation (although not a high one) between agricultural development and agrarian radicalism (see Table 77). It should
also be recalled that in my regression analysis of agrarian radicalism
agricultural development showed up among the five "best" explanatory variables only in Zone 2.[22] There is some evidence, then,
that recent technological change has played some role in agrarian
radicalism in this area. The reason for this will become apparent
in an examination of the impact of technological change on important agro-economic groups in Thanjavur.

TECHNOLOGICAL CHANGE AND SMALL FARMERS

The central question in the debate over the economic and political
consequences of the Green Revolution has been whether the "small

munist panchayat control in the combined Zones 1-4 might be expected. However,
because radicalism and agricultural development are very weak in Zone 5, the
correlation for the district as a whole tends to zero.
[22] See Chapter 4.

farmer" (variously defined) has been able to participate in and reap the benefits of technological change. There are various approaches to the question, according to one's view of the problems faced by the small farmer. One view is that the barrier to small farmer participation is inherent in the technology. If the technology is highly capital-intensive, as in the case of mechanization, the small farmer is excluded entirely for lack of investible capital. If the technology entails increasing returns to scale, that is, if it is more efficient (gives more output per unit of input) on larger holdings, the small farmer may not be barred from entry, but eventually, assuming an open market situation, he would be forced out because the larger farmer can undercut him in the market. In either event there would be a long-range tendency for the small farmer to be forced off the land.

Most observers agree that the problem of the small farmer is not one of scale, at least in the strict physical sense. The varietal-fertilizer technology is *not* directly capital-intensive, though ancillary technologies, such as ground water irrigation, may be.[23] The investment required is divisible rather than "lumpy." Therefore it should be neutral to scale.

In actuality, considerable evidence has accumulated that Indian agriculture is generally characterized by decreasing returns to scale; small farmers get higher yields per unit area because, it is thought, small farms are on average 1) more completely irrigated, or 2) more intensively cultivated (the labor input per unit area is higher). Others have challenged this conclusion on the grounds that the analysis of returns to scale measured in terms of acreage and yields is misleading, precisely because it subsumes considerations of factor quality. They argue that if scale is measured in terms of farm business income, returns to scale are either constant or increasing.[24] Three studies have found, for instance, that the distribution of

[23] See Ralph W. Cummings, Jr., and S. K. Ray, "1968-1969 Food-grain Production: Relative Contribution of Weather and New Technology," *Economic and Political Weekly* 4 (September 27, 1969): A163-A174.

[24] On the first interpretation, see S. K. Sanyal, "Size of Holding and Some Factors Related to Production," *Economic and Political Weekly* 4 (August 16, 1969): 1,345-1,347; Bandhudas Sen, "Opportunities in the Green Revolution," *Economic and Political Weekly* 4 (August 16, 1969): 1,345-1,347; and Sen, "Opportunities in the Green Revolution," *Economic and Political Weekly* 5 (March 28, 1970): A33-A40. For the second view, see G. R. Saini, "Farm Size, Productivity, and Returns to Scale," *Economic and Political Weekly* 4 (June 28, 1969): A119-A122, and A. G. Majumdar, *Distribution of Agricultural Income Arising from Crop Production in India 1960-61 and 1970-71* (New Delhi: Economic and Scientific Research Foundation, 1973).

farm business income may become increasingly unequal while the distribution of land remains unchanged. However, they do not tell us whether the increase in inequality is due to increasing returns to scale.[25]

Another view is that the barrier to small farmer participation is environmental. First, because of his relative economic and political weakness the small farmer lacks entirely or has limited access to the inputs he requires. Access to credit is most frequently mentioned as a problem. Thus, while many studies agree that the small farmer who is able to participate in the new technology does as well as the larger farmer (indicating at least constant returns to scale), they also agree that fewer small farmers participate.[26] Second, the small farmer may be disadvantaged in the market. Because he usually cannot afford to store grain for long periods he is forced to enter the market at a time when prices are at the lowest point.

Against this background we can examine how small farmers have fared in Thanjavur. The general consensus of several studies seems to be, quite well. First, there is agreement that the small farmer has participated in the various technological changes that have taken place. Farms of under three acres had a higher rate of conversion to double cropping than most other size groups. Harrison found that small farmers (under 3.8 acres) used new techniques and inputs as much per unit operated area as did medium and large farmers.[27] Data from the *Farm Management Study for 1968-69*

[25] Pranab Bardhan, "Inequality of Farm Incomes: Study of Four Districts," *Economic and Political Weekly* 9 (February 1974): 301-307; G. R. Saini, "Green Revolution and the Distribution of Farm Incomes," *Economic and Political Weekly* 11 (March 27, 1976): A17-A21; P. N. Junankar, "Green Revolution and Inequality," *Economic and Political Weekly* 10 (March 29, 1975): A15-A18.

[26] See Norman K. Nicholson, *Panchayat Raj, Rural Development and the Political Economy of Village India*, South Asia Occasional Papers and Theses, no. 2 (Ithaca: Cornell University Rural Development Committee and South Asia Program, 1973), p. 21; C. H. Hanumantha Rao, "Farm Size and Credit Policy," *Economic and Political Weekly* 5 (December 26, 1970): A157-A162; B. K. Chowdhury, "Disparity of Income in the Context of HYV," *Economic and Political Weekly* 5 (September 26, 1970): 90-96; Waheeduddin Khan and R. N. Tripathy, *Intensive Agriculture and Modern Inputs. Prospects of Small Farmers: A Study in West Godavari District* (Hyderabad: National Institute of Community Development, 1972); G. Ojha, "Small Farmers and HYV Programme," *Economic and Political Weekly* 5 (April 4, 1970): 603-605.

[27] IADP, "Quick Study," p. 8, and Harrison, "Agricultural Modernization and Income Distribution," pp. 2-3. See also James Q. Harrison "Small Farmer Participation in Agricultural Modernization: Report on a Survey of Two IADP Districts

also indicate that the small farmer was not lagging far behind in the use of improved practices or fertilizer (see Table 78). We also know that small farmers adopted high-yielding varieties readily: in 1969 holdings under five acres accounted for 39 percent of the cultivated area but 42 percent of the area under high-yielding varieties (still largely ADT. 27 at that point).[28]

The picture of small farm productivity and returns in Thanjavur is a bit confused, but it does not indicate that the small farmer was falling seriously behind the larger farmer economically. In Table 78 we see that paddy yield and net income (for *kuruvai*-ADT. 27) are lower in the under 1.16 hectares size group than in most others,

TABLE 78

New Technology Usage and Productivity by Farm Size in Thanjavur District, 1968-69

| Size of Holding (hectares) | Use of Improved Practices | | Kuruvai Paddy (ADT. 27) | | |
	% of Holdings	% of Crop Area Per Holding	Nitrogenous Fertilizer Applied Per Hectare (kgs.)	Yield Per Hectare (quintals)	Net Income Per Hectare (Rs.)
0-1.16	90.9	53.5	39.6	29.4	907
1.17-2.02	86.1	44.7	45.5	30.8	926
2.03-3.05	97.1	54.8	40.4	29.9	956
3.06-5.71	96.2	57.2	42.2	29.6	803
Over 5.71	100.0	65.1	31.8	31.6	976
All sizes	93.3	57.8	38.8	30.4	915

Source: India, *Studies in the Economics of Farm Management in Thanjavur (1968-69)*, pp. 46, 141-42, 146.

(West Godavari and Thanjavur)," mimeographed, staff document, The Ford Foundation, New Delhi, December 1970, pp. 42-45.

[28] C. Muthiah, "The Green Revolution—Participation by Small Versus Large Farmers," *Indian Journal of Agricultural Economics* 26 (January-March 1971): 57-58. See also Agricultural Economics Research Centre (AERC), Department of Economics, University of Madras, "Study of High Yielding Varieties Programme in Thanjavur District, Tamil Nadu: Kharif 1968-69," typewritten (Madras, 1969), pp. 47-48.

but not by a large margin.[29] Harrison actually found that small farmers get higher paddy yields than other groups. Other studies have found no clear pattern of significantly lower or higher yields on small farms at any point in time.[30] In his study of two Kumbakonam villages Swenson found, for instance, that the increase in paddy yields on small farms (under 2.5 acres) over a five-year-period equaled the average increase for all size groups. He also found that while the distribution of income from paddy production was highly skewed at both points in time, it did not become significantly more so.[31]

Three factors account for the small farmer's relatively high rate of participation in and benefit from technological change in Thanjavur. First, as already noted the technology introduced in Thanjavur was by and large not capital-intensive: no large investments were required (with one possible exception that I will return to in a moment). Second, the Thanjavur small farmer had better access to necessary inputs than small farmers in other areas. The intensive agricultural development programs in Thanjavur, beginning with the IADP in 1960 and followed by the HYVP, made agricultural credit, seeds, fertilizer, pesticides, technical advice, et cetera, much more widely available than otherwise would have been the case. Furthermore, from the beginning there was an effort to reach as many farmers as possible. While the system was by no means perfect, and larger farmers certainly had an advantage through the economic and political influence they were able to wield (particularly in the cooperative credit societies), there was nonetheless a considerable percolation of agricultural resources in Thanjavur.[32]

[29] The holding size classes in Table 54 include leased-in area.

[30] Harrison, "Agricultural Modernization and Income Distribution," p. 118. The following studies found no meaningful relationship between farm size and yield: AERC, "High Yielding Varieties Programme," p. 66; Intensive Agricultural District Programme, Thanjavur, "Study on Low Consumption of Phosphatic and Potassic Fertilizers," typewritten, undated, p. 14. Another study found that yields on small farms are equal to those on large farms: Intensive Agricultural District Programme, Thanjavur, "Farm Management Study of 114 Farms, 1962-63," typewritten, undated, p. 22.

[31] Clyde Geoffrey Swenson, "The Effect of Increases in Rice Production on Employment and Income in Thanjavur District, South India" (Ph.D. dissertation, Michigan State University, 1973), p. 88.

[32] A study in the village of Madigai in Thanjavur District found that the cooperative society was a tool of village politics. See T. S. Yeshwanth, *Re-Survey of a Tanjore Village: Madigai* (Madras: University of Madras, Agricultural Economics Research Centre, 1966), p. 21. Other studies have found that larger farmers in

Finally, because of the pervasiveness and quality of irrigation in Thanjavur, most small farmers had relatively secure access to water.

There is one exception to the absence of a capital requirement for technological change in Thanjavur. Ironically, it concerns water. I have noted several times the importance of early water supply for double cropping, particularly when ADT. 27 is planted. If the planting takes place too late, the *kuruvai* harvest is delayed into the onset of the Northeast Monsoon, possibly causing the grain to germinate and thereby almost complete loss of the crop. An earlier harvest also means less difficulty in getting labor and market access at a more favorable time.[33] Therefore, as double cropping became more feasible with the shorter duration varieties, the installation of wells and pumpsets for early irrigation became very desirable. For that reason the Tamil Nadu Government introduced a program to make the equipment and finance available on relatively liberal terms for installation of two different types of ground water irrigation, filterpoint wells and tubewells. The former were intended for use in areas with a high water table, the latter for areas with a low water table. Tubewells are accordingly much more difficult and costly to acquire and install.

Before the introduction of the filterpoint pumpset only large farmers could afford to install a well. The availability of the relatively inexpensive filterpoint and liberal credit from the government gave many medium and some small farmers in the Zone 1 area, where the water table is high enough for the filterpoint (see Table 79), access to ground water for early nurseries.[34] Since small holdings are numerous in the Zone 1 area this was an important

Thanjavur get a greater share of their credit from the cooperatives than small farmers. See, for example, AERC, "High Yielding Varieties Programme," p. 62, and K. C. Alexander, "Economic Status and Source of Agricultural Credit of Farmers in East Thanjavur," *Community Development and Panchayati Raj Digest* 5 (July 1973): 20-23.

[33] Swenson, "Increases in Rice Production," p. 81. See also M. R. Haswell, *Economics of Development in Village India* (London: Routledge and Kegan Paul, 1967), pp. 27-28. The timing of the harvest is particularly important in the case of the *kuruvai* crop because all but the largest farmers want to sell the entire crop to pay expenses for the upcoming Deepavali festival. See V. K. Gupta et al., *Studies on Modernization in Paddy Rice Systems* (Ahmedabad: Indian Institute of Management, 1969), p. 35.

[34] C. Muthiah, "Problems and Progress in Farm Mechanization in South India," paper submitted for the Seminar on Farm Mechanization in Southeast Asia, mimeographed, November 27-December 2, 1972, p. 5. Of the 2,913 filter-points in Zone 3, 80 percent are in the area of Sirkali and the adjoining Sembanarkoil Block, both of which adjoin Zone 1.

TABLE 79

Filterpoint and Tubewells Installed, 1965-1972, by Zone

Zone	Filterpoints		Tubewells	
	Numbers	%	Numbers	%
1/Old Delta-Cauvery	6132	61.6	681	37.3
2/Old Delta-Central	899	9.0	540	29.6
3/Old Delta Coastal	2913	29.3	348	19.1
4/New Delta-CMP	4	0.1	218	11.9
5/Dry Areas-Uplands	0	0.0	40	2.2
District total	9948	100.0	1827	*

SOURCE: Data provided by district agricultural engineer, Thanjavur.

NOTE: * Does not add to 100 due to rounding.

step in preventing the exclusion of a large and potentially powerful group of cultivators from the process of technological change in Thanjavur. Filterpoints are sparse outside Zone 1 because the water table is too low.

Tubewells are more evenly spread across the zones with almost 50 percent of the total concentrated in Zones 2 and 3 where more numerous large farmers could afford to install them (see Table 79). Because tubewells become more expensive and less reliable as the water table gets lower, *and* because drainage is also a serious problem in Zone 3, fewer landowners in Zone 3 installed tubewells than in Zone 2.

Thus, even in the case of this relatively capital-intensive component of technological change the interaction of the technology with varying zonal ecological conditions had agro-economic consequences parallel to the effects of the varietal-fertilizer technology. In Zone 1 the impact of capital-intensive technology on small farms was softened by favorable ecological conditions. In Zone 3 adverse ecological conditions limited the access of most farms to this technology. In Zone 2, however, the high installation rate of expensive tubewells relative to the inexpensive filterpoints suggests that the opportunities for and benefits from technological change may have been more skewed. This helps us to understand how Zone 2 landowners overcame water supply constraints to expand their double cropping so dramatically. As we shall see later, this in itself is an important factor in the relationship of technological change to agrarian radicalism.

TECHNOLOGICAL CHANGE AND TENANCY

The disabilities of the tenant with respect to technological change are understandably greater than those of the small farmer. First, if the tenant owns no land at all it is much more difficult for him to raise capital or to get credit for production expenses because he has no collateral. Second, because he does not own the land he has little incentive to make permanent improvements on it, such as installing wells or leveling, that may be necessary to gain the greatest advantage from even noncapital-intensive technology. Third, if the new technology results in greatly increased productivity, many landlords will want either to raise rents or to resume personal cultivation.[35] However, if the small tenant owns a bit of land, if the new technology is not capital-intensive, if he is able to get production credit, if the land he operates is relatively well-irrigated, and if he remains in possession of the land paying a fixed rent that increases not at all or at a rate slower than productivity he will probably be able to utilize and to gain from the new technology. Note that all of these conditions are more likely to be satisfied in Zone 1 than in Zones 2 or 3.

Virtually all studies of tenancy and technological change in Thanjavur report that tenants lag behind owner and owner-tenant cultivators in the use of new technology. In 1968 to 1969 fewer tenants used improved varieties and fertilizer and, more importantly, those that did used them on a much smaller proportion of their cropped area (see Table 80). Fewer tenants converted *samba* lands to *kuruvai* after the introduction of ADT. 27,[36] and only 7 percent of the early cultivators of IR-8 were tenants (Table 80, column 3). It should come as no surprise to find that tenants are not daring or early innovators. More important is the recognition that they are limited in the amount they can invest in production expenses, not to mention capital improvements. The greatest impact is on that staple of agricultural change, chemical fertilizer. While many tenants in Thanjavur used some chemical fertilizer, very few were able to apply anything approaching the recommended dosage (see the fertilizer expense data in Table 80, column 4). The tenant's hired

[35] Ladejinsky, "How Green is the Green Revolution," p. A137.
[36] The figures are 4.3 percent of tenants as opposed to 12.8 percent of owners (IADP, "Quick Study," p. 4).

TABLE 80
Use of New Technology by Tenurial Status in Thanjavur District

| | Use of Improved Practices, 1968-69[a] | | % Cultivators of IR-8 in 1969-70[b] | Cultivation Expenses Per Hectare, 1968-69[a] | | |
	% of Holdings (1)	% of Crop Area (2)	(3)	Ferti- lizer (Rs.) (4)	Hired Labor (Rs.) (5)	Total (Rs.) (6)
Owner	96.2	61.9	67	95	269	1168
Owner-cum-tenant	93.2	54.4	26	82	295	1076
Tenant	85.2	39.4	7	48	193	804
All types	93.3	57.8	NA	87	270	1095

SOURCES: [a] India, *Studies in the Economics of Farm Management in Thanjavur (1968-69)*, pp. 46, 97.
[b] Intensive Agricultural District Programme, Thanjavur, "Study on the Cost of Cultivation of IR8 Paddy," typewritten, undated, p. 11.

NOTE: NA = data not available.

labor input and total production expenses were also lower than those of the owner and owner-tenant.[37] On average, then, the Thanjavur tenant finds it difficult to meet the operating expenses necessary for maximum benefit from the varietal-fertilizer technology.

There are two reasons for this. First, where rent is a fixed amount (as is now the case, whether in cash or kind, throughout Thanjavur), the tenant is more reluctant to risk high expenditures. If the crop is wholly or partly lost due to poor weather, his loss is amplified by the fact that he still has to pay rent to the landlord, unless of course he is able to get rent relief through the courts.[38] It follows that

[37] Several studies over a period of years have noted these tendencies: Dagfinn Siversten, *When Caste Barriers Fall: A Study of Social and Economic Change in a South Indian Village* (Oslo: Universitets Forlaget, 1963), p. 80; IADP, "Farm Management Study," p. 18; IADP, *Study on Tenancy Patterns in Thanjavur*, pp. 16-17, 34. Total cultivation costs include rent paid or, in the case of owners, rental value of the land. The tenant's lower hired labor input is not offset by a proportionately higher family labor input.
[38] The losses incurred in such an event are greater in the case of the high-yielding

tenants in Zone 1 would face a lesser risk than tenants in Zones 2 and 3 because of the superior ecological conditions and stronger position of the tenant vis-à-vis the landlord. One study of tenancy in Thanjavur did in fact find that tenants in the coastal areas spend less on fertilizer than tenants in the rest of the Old Delta.[39]

Even if tenants are willing to assume the risks inherent in the adoption of new technology, they are likely to have difficulty raising the necessary financial resources. Loans from government-financed cooperative credit societies offered the only opportunity for tenants to buy into the new technology, but even that outlet had its limitations. Cooperative loans on personal surety (the only type available to the pure tenant during the period of this study) were limited to a maximum total of Rs. 1,000 (as opposed to Rs. 5,000 for the owner) or the amount necessary to cultivate the five acres allowed to tenants, whichever was less.[40] Towards the end of the 1960s the cooperative societies did make a special effort to make credit available to tenants, probably with some positive effect. In 1970 and 1971, 24 percent of all loans disbursed went to tenants (see Table 81, column 1), but this figure probably overstates the participation of tenants, as many medium and large owner-operators did not participate in the cooperative loan program.

There is some suggestion in Table 81 that tenants in Zone 1 were more successful at getting cooperative credit than tenants in Zones 2 and 3. A comparison of the percentage of tenants among borrowers by zone with the zonal distribution of tenancy (they are roughly parallel but the proportion of tenants among borrowers is high relative to the proportion of tenants among cultivators in Zones 1, 4, and 5) indicates that tenants in Zones 2 and 3 were somewhat less successful in getting cooperative credit. But the statistical evidence is too weak to draw a firm conclusion. What is clear, however, is that whether or not the tenant had a written lease deed does not seem to have affected the number or amount of loans made to tenants. The higher loan amounts in Zones 2 and 3 prob-

varieties (HYV), such as IR-8, not only because of higher production expenses but also because the HYV are not adapted to local climatic conditions and thus fail more completely under adverse conditions. In other words, the "productivity floor" of the HYV is lower than that of traditional varieties, or may not exist at all.

[39] IADP, *Study on Tenancy Patterns in Thanjavur*, pp. 12-13. Another study finds that whereas half the cultivators in Zone 1 who converted *samba* lands to *kuruvai* in 1967/1968 were tenants, none of the cultivators converting in the coastal area were tenants (IADP, "Quick Study," p. 7).

[40] AERC, "High Yielding Varieties Programme," p. 29.

TABLE 81

Cooperative Credit Disbursed to Tenants, 1970-1971, by Zone

	Short-term Production Loans				
	Number of Loans Disbursed to Tenants as % of Total Loans	Number of Loans Disbursed to Tenants with Oral Lease as % Loans to Tenants	Average Loan Amount Disbursed Per Tenant (Rs.)		
			All	Written Lease	Oral Lease
Zone	(1)	(2)	(3)	(4)	(5)
1/Old Delta-Cauvery	35.2	36.8	526	492	584
2/Old Delta-Central	24.8	58.0	621	686	573
3/Old Delta-Coastal	26.0	32.7	657	622	731
4/New Delta-CMP	19.9	75.0	645	645	645
5/Dry Area-Uplands	20.1	75.1	424	426	423
District average	24.1	54.5	587	584	589

SOURCES: Compiled from block-level data provided by Thanjavur and Kumbakonam Cooperative Central banks, Thanjavur District.

NOTE: Zonal figures in this table do not include data for Thanjavur, Budalur, or Thiruvonam blocks, which overlap two or more zones. District figures are based on all blocks except Vedaranyam.

ably reflect the higher average holding size (even among tenants) in those areas. The credit participation of the relatively few tenants in Zones 4 and 5 is perhaps the most striking fact in Table 81. Unfortunately, the data do not tell us how tenants actually used the credit they received. All cooperative loans included a mandatory "kind" portion, mostly fertilizer. As tenants were particularly unlikely to apply the full recommended fertilizer dosage and were most in need of cash for nonproductive purposes there is some reason to believe that cooperative credit did not contribute very much to increasing productivity on tenant holdings.[41]

The tenant's limited access to and use of new technology—in particular, the fertilizer required to realize the yield potential of the new varieties—is reflected in lower per acre productivity and returns. Although tenants have probably always gotten lower yields

[41] One study found that tenants in particular were selling most of the fertilizer component on the black market (Haswell, *Economics of Development*, p. 30).

(because owners tend to lease out poorer quality lands and tenants have always had less control over the production environment), there is some evidence that on the whole tenants in Thanjavur have fallen further behind owner-operators. A study of tenant's participation in the IADP in 1962 and 1963 when technological change was marginal found that paddy yields did not differ significantly by tenurial status.[42] However, according to three studies conducted in the mid-to-late-1960s, paddy yields were significantly lower on tenant-operated holdings (see Table 82). Furthermore, the net return (after rent payment) per unit area of paddy was much lower for tenants—about half that of owner-cultivators. It is not surprising that many tenants were tempted to withhold all or part of their rent payments.

However, all tenants were not similarly affected. The tenant who was already cultivating or was able to switch to a double crop and who paid a stable fixed rent was more likely to benefit from technological change.[43] From what we already know of tenancy conditions in the district we can infer therefore that tenants in Zone 1 were more likely to benefit than tenants in Zones 2 and 3. For instance, Swenson found that between 1965/1966 and 1970/1971 the average yield on tenant-operated holding in two Zone 1 (Kumbakonam taluk) villages increased as much as the average yield on owner-operated holdings. Over the same period the average net return per acre on tenant-operated holdings also increased substantially, but less than on owner-operated holdings (45 versus 58 percent). (The discrepancy between changes in yield and change in net return is due to two factors: lower market prices obtained by tenants and the effect of variation in rental payments.) Swenson

[42] IADP, "Farm Management Study," p. 2.

[43] See IADP, *Study on Tenancy Patterns in Thanjavur*, p. 24. However, if fixed rents are continually increased, as Ladejinsky argued was the case in Thanjavur, the tenant has little incentive to try to produce more. See Wolf Ladejinsky, *A Study on Tenurial Conditions in Package Districts* (New Delhi: Government of India, Planning Commission, 1965), p. 14. N. D. Abdul Hameed argues however that rents have *not* increased for most Thanjavur tenants. See Hameed, "Tenancy and Technological Progress in Thanjavur District Agriculture," in *Agricultural Development of India: A Study of the Intensive Agricultural District Programme*, ed. V. Shanmugasundaram (Madras: University of Madras, 1972), pp. 272-273. In fact, much depends on the nature of the relationship between the landlord and the tenant. For instance, the tenant is more likely to be able to resist rent increases where the landlord is far removed from control over the land. For more on the relationship of technological change and forms of rent, see Krishna Bharadwaj and P. K. Das, "Tenurial Conditions and Mode of Exploitation: A Study of Some Villages in Orissa," *Economic and Political Weekly* 5 (February 1975): 235-239.

TABLE 82
Productivity and Net Return by Tenurial Status in Thanjavur District

| | Paddy Yields (kgs./acre) | | | | Value of Output Per Hectare (Rs.), 1968-69[c] (5) | Net Return to Paddy Civilization Per Unit Area | | | |
| | 1965-68[a] | 1969-70[b] | | | | 1965-68[a] | 1967-68[c] | 1969-70[b] | |
	All Seasons (1)	Kuruvai (2)	Samba (3)	Thaladi (4)		All Seasons (6)	Kuruvai ADT.27 (7)	Kuruvai/ Thaladi (8)	Samba (9)
						(Rs./acre)	(Rs./hectare)	(Rs./acre)	(Rs./acre)
Owner	1010	1295	1098	975	1366	170	598	580	326
Owner-tenant	915	1187	1060	867	1252	151	414*	540	304
Tenant	861	1075	1018	790	1004	147	259*	272*	157*
Average	936	1175	1071	814	1300	158	521	NA	NA

SOURCES: [a] Coimbatore Agricultural College, Agricultural Economics and Rural Sociology Wing, "An Economic Appraisal of the Owner-Operated and Tenant-Operated Farms in Thanjavur District," mimeographed, undated, p. 15.
[b] IADP, Study on Tenancy Patterns in Thanjavur, pp. 19, 21.
[c] India, Studies in the Economics of Farm Management in Thanjavur (1967-68, 1968-69), pp. 344, 107 respectively.

NOTE: * Net of rent owed to landlord.
NA = data not available.

reports that the fixed rent quantity stayed the same over this period: thus, as a result of increased *kuruvai* yield tenants cultivating double crop lands paid out a smaller proportion of their crop as rent in 1970/1971 (39 percent) than in 1965/1966 (47 percent). But tenants cultivating *samba* paid the same proportion of the crop as rent in 1970/1971 as in 1965/1966 and suffered either an absolute loss or relative decline in net return per acre.[44] Obviously the latter situation was more characteristic of tenants in Zone 2 and especially in Zone 3 where double cropping possibilities were more limited and tenants were by and large in a weaker position vis-à-vis landlords. This view is supported by the pattern of correlations in Table 83. In Zone 1 there is a tendency for tenancy to be uncorrelated or positively correlated (not significantly) with agricultural development, while in Zones 2 and 3 there is a consistent tendency to a negative correlation.

In summary, if there was any tendency towards increasing income disparities between cultivating groups as a result of technological change in Thanjavur it was among tenants. This tendency was not inherent in the technology but rather resulted from the existing tenurial differentials in incentives and opportunities for adoption of technological innovations. These incentives and opportunities were directly affected by variations in tenancy rights and the landlord-tenant relationship. As a result, technological change in Zone 1 probably contributed to the upward mobility of tenants

TABLE 83

Tenancy and Agricultural Development in Zones 1, 2 and 3

	Correlation between Agricultural Development Rating and	
Zone	% of Tenants in Agricultural Work Force	% of Cultivated Area under Tenancy
1/Old Delta-Cauvery	.008	.083
2/Old Delta-Central	−.118	−.046
3/Old Delta-Coastal	−.084	−.040
2-3/Old Delta-Central/ Coastal	−.096	−.039

[44] Swenson, "Increases in Rice Production," pp. 66, 88, 90-97.

and thus to further deradicalization of the tenancy issue in that area. In Zones 2 and 3 on the other hand "low-end tenants" undoubtedly found it more difficult to participate in the new technology, and many probably suffered some decline in income relative to the owner-operators. This may have exacerbated tensions in the landlord-tenant relationship and contributed to support for the Communists among tenants, although there is no direct evidence to this effect. In fact, the published statements of the CPI-led Agriculturalists' Association contain no explicit reference to this issue and give little attention to the problem of tenant participation in technological change.[45] It would seem that the diffuse and variable impact of technological change on the landlord-tenant relationship was overshadowed by the prior basic issue of tenancy rights, which, as we have seen in Chapter 8, was effectively exploited, even preempted, by the DMK. We can conclude, therefore, that technological change did not contribute directly or significantly to the relationship between tenancy and agrarian radicalism in Thanjavur during the 1960 to 1972 period.

TECHNOLOGICAL CHANGE AND AGRICULTURAL LABOR

The effect of technological change on the development of agrarian radicalism in Thanjavur has been greatest in its impact on the relationship between landowners and laborers, although not in the direction usually expected. By *increasing*, rather than lessening, the demand for labor, technological change exacerbated the tensions in the landowner-labor relationship, especially in those areas of the district (Zones 2 and 3) where the availability of hired labor was critical to successful implementation of the varietal-fertilizer technology and the landlord-laborer relationship was already marked by conflict. In this way technological change helped to spark Thanjavur's "second wave" of agrarian unrest in the late 1960s.

It has already been noted on several occasions that irrigated paddy cultivation is a labor-intensive process. The introduction of the varietal-fertilizer technology only heightened the labor requirements. More labor was required for more thorough ploughing, line planting, more intensive weeding, application of fertilizers, and, of course, harvest and threshing of the larger crop. For instance, ADT.

[45] A meeting of the association in Sirkali taluk on January 8, 1970, demanded pumpset loans for tenants, and a district-level association conference in January 1973 demanded that fertilizer be distributed to cultivators through public committees rather than through the cooperatives (a demand stemming from landlord control over the crops). See *Ulavu Chelvam* (Madras), February 1, 1970, p. 10.

27 required a 26 percent greater labor input than traditional *ku-ruvai* varieties, and IR-8 a 40 percent greater labor input than ADT. 27. With the exception of ploughing none of the increased demand could be efficiently offset by mechanization because suitable mechanized techniques were not available at lower or comparable costs. But by far the greatest increase in the demand for labor resulted from the conversion to double cropping, which as we have seen was the single most important component of agricultural change in Thanjavur prior to 1969. Double crop paddy required 60 percent more labor than *samba* during the October to November period alone primarily for *kuruvai* harvest but also for *thaladi* nursery and field preparation.[46]

The labor requirement increased more sharply in Zones 2 and 3 than in Zone 1, primarily because the increase in double cropping was greater in Zones 2 and 3.[47] The effect of the increase was felt more acutely in these zones because of the less favorable ecological conditions and the bimodal agrarian structure. First, later *kuruvai* planting and the vital need to harvest the crop before the onset of the monsoon meant that the increased demand was concentrated in a particularly short space of time. Second, the large number of extensive holdings relying exclusively on hired daily labor meant that the demand for labor was very "lumpy"—each of these farms required a large number of laborers at the same time. The result was an acute shortage of labor during this critical period.[48] In contrast, not only was the increase in the demand for labor less in Zone 1 but the impact of the increase was also cushioned by the flexibility inherent in the ecological conditions and agrarian structure of the zone.

Thus, the effect of technological change on agricultural labor was to strengthen its bargaining position, again especially in Zones 2 and 3, where, as we have seen, the agrarian structure also fostered labor militancy and organization.[49] Agricultural laborers were en-

[46] C. Muthiah, "The Agricultural Labour Problem in Thanjavur and the New Agricultural Strategy," *Indian Journal of Agricultural Economics* 25 (July-September 1970): 15-23.

[47] For instance, Swenson reports that labor use in paddy cultivation in two "typical" Kumbakonam (Zone 1) villages increased by 7 percent between 1965 and 1966 and 1970 and 1971 as compared with an estimated increase of about 15 percent for the entire district (Swenson, "Increases in Rice Production," p. 73).

[48] Muthiah, "Agricultural Labour Problem," p. 16, and Ganapathia Pillai, "Report of the Commission of Inquiry on the Agrarian Labour Problems of East Thanjavur District," typewritten [1969], p. 6.

[49] See Andre Beteille, *Studies in Agrarian Social Structure* (New Delhi: Oxford University Press, 1974), pp. 163-164.

couraged to demand higher wages (especially at harvest) from land-lords who were vulnerable because they wished to augment their incomes through double cropping and high-yielding varieties. For this reason, as I will detail in Chapter 10, agricultural wages were the dominant issue of radical agrarian politics in Thanjavur during the late 1960s. Precisely because harvest wages were such a large share of their overall costs, the landlords were apt to resist strongly any wage increases.[50] It was in this way, not by displacing labor, that technological change in Thanjavur immediately aggravated tensions in landlord-labor relationships.

Even so, this might not have been of much consequence for the development of agrarian radicalism were it not for the fact that the same factors which created the pressure of increased labor demand had also fostered a confrontational relationship between landlords and agricultural labor. This illustrates the importance of considering the effects of technological change in the ecological and agro-economic context.

In the Thanjavur case agrarian radicalism among agricultural labor in the Zone 2 and 3 areas predated significant technological change by many years. This radicalism had lain dormant since the early 1950s for lack of leadership, organization, and the burning issue that could ignite it. The resumption of Communist organizational activity among Thanjavur's agricultural laborers in the mid-1960s provided a degree of renewed organization and leadership. The impact of technological change on the demand for labor revived the wage issue and simultaneously enhanced the ability of agricultural labor to challenge the landlords. Organization was crucial to exploitation of the wage issue because the only way labor could enforce its demands was to strike, which, as shall be seen in Chapter 10, was precisely what happened. The conflict escalated when landowners sought to import outside labor in hopes of breaking the labor organization and the strike and thus avoiding higher wages.[51]

[50] Harvesting and threshing together represent about 44 percent of the labor input for IR-8 paddy. Intensive Agricultural District Programme, Thanjavur, "Study on the Cost of Cultivation of IR8 Paddy," typewritten, undated, p. 9. Overall labor costs were about 29 percent of total per acre cultivation expenses for ADT. 27 in 1967/1968 and 1968/1969 (India, *Studies in the Economics of Farm Management, 1967-68* and *1968-69*, pp. 324-325 and 135-136).

[51] East Thanjavur District Agricultural Workers' Association, "Memorandum Before the Judge of the Enquiry Commission of the East Thanjavur District Agricultural Workers' Problems, Thanjavur, March 11, 1969," typewritten, p. 10.

It was such a chain of events that led to the infamous Kilavenmani incident of December 1968 in which local laborers clashed with outside laborers and were later attacked by *goondas* ("toughs") hired by the local landlord (resulting in the deaths of forty-two persons, mostly wives and children of the local laborers). Although this incident was immediately interpreted as a portent of widespread agrarian unrest brought on by the socio-economic dislocations of technological change, my analysis shows that in fact the contribution of technological change to agrarian unrest in Thanjavur was different.

A principal reason for this was of course the specific, limited character of technological change in Thanjavur. In the case of agricultural labor the key limitation was the absence of a significant labor-displacing component. People speak loosely of the impact of "mechanization" on human labor, but that concept must be unpacked to understand the actual process. For instance, in Thanjavur mechanized ground water retrieval served to increase the demand for labor by helping to make double cropping feasible. The case of tractors is a bit more complicated.

We find in fact that there was a sizable increase in the number of tractors in agricultural use in Thanjavur during the 1960s and early 1970s. At the end of 1962 there were only about 170 tractors in use in the district, but between 1963 and 1972 about 925 tractors were newly registered in Thanjavur, the bulk of the increase coming after 1968, for a total of about 1,100. This is still a small number considering the area under cultivation, but it takes on added significance when we consider the geographic distribution of new tractors (see Table 84). Over 50 percent were registered to owners in the taluks comprising Zones 2 and 3. This suggests the possibility that opposition to tractorization helped fuel the radical labor movement in those areas during the late 1960s.

Although the survey data indicated that many laborers in Zones 2 and 3 opposed the use of tractors because they displaced labor, there were several reasons why tractors did not become a central issue in Thanjavur's labor movement. First, the impact of tractors on the demand for labor was mixed. Tractors could not be used in the critical *kuruvai* harvest-thresh operations. They were used for *thaladi* ploughing during the same period, but this use had relatively little impact on the demand for labor. In fact, ploughing is the only major field operation that could be performed by the kind of tractors that were available in Thanjavur at the time. The tractor's principal function in paddy cultivation was the transport

TABLE 84

Tractors in Thanjavur District, 1963-1972, by Taluk

Location of Tractor Registrant (by taluk and principal zone)	New Tractor Registrations, 1963-72		
	Number	% of District Total	Number Per 1000 Gross Paddy Acres, 1970-71
Sirkali (3)	67	7.2	.69
Mayuram (1)	132	14.2	.85
Kumbakonam (1)	80	8.6	.65
Nannilam (2)	120	13.0	.73
Papanasam (1)	47	5.1	.36
Tanjore (1)	65	7.0	.49
Orathanad (4)	11	1.2	.10
Mannargudi (2)	99	10.7	.60
Nagapattinam (3)	135	14.6	1.18
Tiruthuraipoondi (3)	102	11.0	.67
Pattukottai (4)	45	4.9	.26
Arantangi (5)	25	2.7	.28
District total/average	928	*	.58

SOURCE: Compiled from official records of Motor Vehicle Registration Office, Thanjavur.

NOTE: * Does not add to 100 due to rounding.

of grain and straw, which had limited labor-displacing effect. In fact, some have argued that the net effect of increased tractor use on labor was positive because it facilitated double cropping.[52]

Second, the agricultural labor movement in Thanjavur either chose not to exploit the tractor issue or failed to do so. In a 1969 memorandum to a governmental commission cn the agricultural labor problems in Thanjavur, the CPI-led Agricultural Workers' Association discounted the effect of tractors.[53] Later that same year, however, the CPM organized an antitractor agitation. The CPM's principal support base was in the Nagapattinam area, and the ratio

[52] Muthiah, "Agricultural Labour Problem," pp. 4, 10. Swenson notes that tractors were a factor in double cropping even in the Kumbakonam area (Swenson, "Increases in Rice Production," p. 230).

[53] East Thanjavur District Agricultural Workers' Association, "Memorandum," p. 12.

of tractors to gross paddy area was by far the highest in Nagapattinam taluk (see Table 84), so it may well be that laborers and organizers in that area perceived at least a potential threat to employment opportunities. Perhaps more important to the CPM organizers was a desire to widen the goals of the labor movement. In any case, the agitation was not a success. The CPI refused to support it, and even the CPM leadership was divided over it. The DMK government reacted strongly and deployed extra police divisions in the eastern taluks to contain it. But this effort was probably unnecessary. On the first day of the agitation only nineteen CPM workers were arrested in a single village near Nagapattinam, and the whole effort fizzled shortly thereafter, largely because there was little real conviction that tractors were a threat to agricultural labor in Thanjavur.[54] In fact, if we control for cropped area we find relatively little difference in the number of tractors in the Old Delta taluks (see Table 84). The Nagapattinam exception can be explained by the extraordinarily high proportion of very large holdings in that taluk.

Thus, it can be safely concluded that the only significant effect of technological change on agricultural labor in Thanjavur was to increase the demand for labor, principally through the expansion of the total cropped area.

However, an explanation is still needed for the relationship between agricultural development and agrarian radicalism in Zone 2, the only part of the district where these two phenomena were significantly correlated. We should recall first that agrarian radicalism has been weaker in Zone 2 than in Zone 3. This is because most of the factors identified as contributing to agrarian radicalism in Thanjavur are somewhat weaker in Zone 2, and the movement found its first solid base in Zone 3. However, between 1960 and 1970 agrarian radicalism gained ground more rapidly in Zone 2 than in Zone 3 (though still remaining behind Zone 3): the percentage of panchayats controlled by the Communists increased by 70.2 percent in Zone 2 compared to 37.6 percent in Zone 3. I would argue that this radical gain in Zone 2 was in good part attributable to the impact of technological change. At this point we should further recall that by far the greatest increase in double cropping took place in Zone 2. Prior to this development the propensity of many agricultural laborers in Zone 2 to be attracted by Communist

[54] *The Hindu* (Madras), June 22, 1969, and July 12, 24, 1969. See also Muthiah, "Problems and Progress," p. 3.

appeals was marginal compared to that of agricultural laborers in Zone 3. But it was enough so that when the sharp increase in the demand for labor took place, thus enhancing the position of labor vis-à-vis landlords, many more were drawn to the Communist side. This situation must have encouraged some laborers to break away from the local landlord. This then could explain the unique relationship of agricultural development to agrarian radicalism in Zone 2.

In summary, on examining closely technological change in Thanjavur District during the 1960 to 1972 period we find that, limited in degree and shaped by the ecological and agro-economic environment, it contributed only tangentially to the development of agrarian radicalism. It certainly did not result in a significant alteration of the agro-economic structure in any part of the district. In fact, I have found that the very factors that underlay agrarian radicalism tended to impede technological change. However, where technological change did combine with these factors it acted as the catalyst for a heightening of agrarian tensions, which then resulted in a resurgence of agrarian unrest in Thanjavur most characterized by conflict between landlords and laborers over wages.

It is appropriate, therefore, to turn now to a fuller explanation of the mobilization of agrarian radicalism in Thanjavur, particularly during the 1960 to 1972 period, and to the purely political factors that shaped it.

CHAPTER 10

The Mobilization of Agrarian Radicalism

IN THE LAST SEVERAL CHAPTERS I have attempted to isolate and describe the geophysical, agro-economic, and technological factors that have been conducive to the emergence of agrarian radicalism in Thanjavur District. I have argued that certain agro-economic structural conditions arising out of the adaptation of paddy production to gross and subtle distinctions in soil, water, and climatic conditions, combined with parallel social structural characteristics, are associated with agrarian radicalism. More precisely, these conditions both form the "objective situation" and foster the "subjective awareness" necessary to the development of a radical orientation. In particular, the polarized agrarian structure that characterizes many villages in Zones 2 and 3 of Thanjavur tends to create sharply defined class interests and heightened class consciousness conducive to radical mobilization.

However, as the choice of terms belies, I am not taking a determinist view of the relationship between these largely objective conditions and agrarian radicalism in Thanjavur. The identification of class interests, the development of class consciousness, and the translation of the class situation into radical orientation and action are highly influenced by others factors, notably internal and external political forces. Therefore, in this chapter, I turn my attention to an examination of the mobilization of agrarian radicalism in Thanjavur and the factors that have shaped its strength and direction. The two main themes in this chapter are 1) that radical agrarian mobilization in Thanjavur has been initiated and guided "from the top down" by political parties, specifically and almost exclusively the Communist parties, and 2) that there has been a strong reformist trend in the evolution of agrarian radicalism in Thanjavur. I will show how the strategies and fortunes of the Communist parties and their relationship to other parties at the district, state, and national levels have both made possible and limited the emergence and mobilization of agrarian radicalism. This analysis of the dynamics of Indian communism and the Indian party system will help to explain why, in spite of the close correspondence between the agrarian structure in Thanjavur's Zones 2 and 3 and

Paige's predicted structural basis of agrarian revolution, the movement in Thanjavur has developed in a progressively reformist direction.

AGRARIAN ORGANIZATION IN THANJAVUR

Thanjavur is one of the few areas of India in which conflicting agrarian interests have been organized over a long period of time.[1] Although the strength and composition of agrarian organizations in Thanjavur, principally landowner and laborer organizations, have varied over space and time, there is no doubt that they have been a significant element in the mobilization of agrarian radicalism. In general laborer organizations have tended to offset the laborers' economic dependency and enabled them to confront the landlord,[2] while landowner organizations, although usually less effective than laborer organizations, have contributed to the militancy of the landowner-laborer conflict and so also deserve some attention. Both types of organizations were strongest in the Zone 2 and 3 areas where, as we have seen, the two groups were more economically and socially homogeneous and widely separated, a further bit of evidence in support of my argument linking agrarian structure to agrarian radicalism.[3] However, especially in the case of the laborer organizations, the parameters of organizational activity were set by the political parties on which they were almost wholly dependent.

Labor Organizations

From their beginnings in the 1940s efforts to organize agricultural labor in Thanjavur have been closely associated with the Communist parties. As noted briefly in Chapter 8, the CPI began its organizational efforts among non-Brahmin *varamdars* (sharecroppers) in the Mannargudi area in the late 1930s. At that time the policy of the CPI's All-India Kisan Sabha (AIKS—then the only

[1] Another is Alleppey District in southern Kerala, where, as in Thanjavur, landowners and laborers have been in militant confrontation since World War II. See K. C. Alexander, "Emerging Farmer-Labour Relations in Kuttanad," *Economic and Political Weekly* 8 (August 25, 1973): 1,551-1,560.

[2] Linz points out that the economic weakness of labor may be offset by political organization. See Juan Linz, "Patterns of Land Tenure, Division of Labor, and Voting Behavior in Europe," *Comparative Politics* 8 (April 1976): 420.

[3] In another area of Tamil Nadu, Chingleput District, Joan Mencher finds the absence of landowner and laborer organization is due to the lack of a sharp cleavage between the two groups. See Mencher, "Problems in Analyzing Rural Class Systems," *Economic and Political Weekly* 9 (August 31, 1974): 1,502.

national agrarian organization) was to concentrate on broad peasant demands, such as security of tenure, debt relief, and cheap
credit. Furthermore, the local leadership reportedly did not want
the organization to be exclusively identified with predominantly
Harijan laborers, which they believed might prevent non-Brahmins
from joining.[4] However, the AIKS leaders soon extended their
efforts to laborers, organizing the first labor union at Mannargudi
in 1939. Of course, as noted in Chapter 8, at that time there was
little economic distinction between the *varamdar* and the *pannaiyal*
(attached laborer) in areas such as Mannargudi, so that it must not
have been too difficult to fashion an appeal to both groups. Nevertheless, the Communist decision to broaden their efforts at this
early stage suggests that they recognized the greater radical potential of agricultural labor in Thanjavur.

These early Communist efforts were clearly quite successful. In
1944 a meeting held in Mannargudi was attended by five thousand
kisans. A Western observer of the 1948 strike noted that Communist
organization was very extensive and was struck by the fact that the
terms *kisan* and Communist seemed to be used interchangeably.[5]
According to another account, the Communists

> formed well-knit and unified organizations of the kisans under
> the guidance of proper leaders in every taluk, in every firka, in
> every village and even in every *miras*. . . . They instigated the
> kisans to make extravagant demands upon the mirasdars in re-
> gard to *varum*, bonus, wages, etc. . . . [and] the mirasdars found
> themselves utterly helpless, while the Government found them-
> selves faced with a grave situation.[6]

[4] See K. C. Alexander, *Agrarian Tension in Thanjavur* (Hyderabad: National In-
stitute of Community Development, 1975), p. 35. The Communists were probably
also anxious to open some identification with the growing and non-Brahmin-based
Tamil regionalist movement. See also Andre Beteille, "Agrarian Movements in
India," mimeographed, undated, p. 5. There was apparently some discussion at the
national level of setting up a separate organization for agricultural labor, but the
AIKS leaders were deterred by three considerations: they were guided by the COM-
INTERN's "popular front line," they took the "Menshevik view" that a bourgeois-
democratic revolution must precede peasant revolution, and they felt that peasants
were too strongly dominated by landlords to be an independent political force. See
Hamza Alavi, "Peasants and Revolution," in *Imperialism and Revolution in South Asia*,
ed. Kathleen Gough and Hari P. Sharma (New York and London: Monthly Review
Press, 1973), p. 39.

[5] John Frederick Muehl, *Interview with India* (New York: The John Day Co., 1950),
pp. 272-285.

[6] B. S. Baliga, *Tanjore District Handbook* (Madras: Government Press, 1957), p. 120.

These accounts probably overstate the early impact of Communist organization. For instance, Gough reports that sharecroppers and laborers in the one Nagapattinam village who struck for higher shares and wages in 1948 were soon forced back to work.[7] But the Communists were successful enough to evoke a severe response from the landlords and the government. Tensions remained high, and clashes between landlords, tenants, and laborers continued into the early 1950s. But these early organizational efforts were eventually stalled by the landlords' repressive measures, the Congress government's response to tenant-laborer demands, and, perhaps most importantly, the CPI's own policy shift in the early 1950s (more on this later). The AIKS was declared illegal in the mid-1950s, and as the organization's leaders went underground so did the movement, demonstrating its dependence on the organizational initiative of the Communists.[8]

Communist activity reappeared in Thanjavur in the mid-1960s, reached a peak in the late 1960s, and faded again in the mid-1970s. The resurgence of activity in the mid-sixties was due largely to the 1964 split. The CPM's more militant tactical line focused greater attention on the role of the poor peasantry in revolutionary strategy; the outbreak of peasant rebellion at Naxalbari in 1967 and the formation of the CPI (Marxist-Leninist) in 1969 reinforced this tendency. Competition with the CPM for control of the agrarian organizations and the loyalty of the rural poor forced the CPI to increase the level and militancy of its agrarian activities.[9]

The CPI's renewed organizational effort did not, however, take exactly the same form it had in the 1940s. It was now marked by the creation of a separate organization for agricultural laborers, the Thanjavur Mavattam Vivasayi Thozhilalar Sangham (Thanjavur District Agricultural Workers' Association). The new labor organization played the leading role in the heightened activity of the late 1960s and early 1970s.[10] This was due in part to the CPI's quest for a more militant agrarian line. In Thanjavur it was also a

[7] Kathleen Gough, "Harijans in Thanjavur," in *Imperialism and Revolution in South Asia*, ed. Kathleen Gough and Hari P. Sharma (New York and London: Monthly Review Press, 1973), p. 239.

[8] Hari P. Sharma, "The Green Revolution in India: A Prelude to a Red One?" in *Imperialism and Revolution in South Asia*, ed. Kathleen Gough and Hari P. Sharma (New York and London: Monthly Review Press, 1973), p. 95.

[9] Bhabani Sen Gupta, *Communism in Indian Politics* (New York: Columbia University Press, 1972), pp. 292-293, 320.

[10] Interview with Manali C. Kandaswamy, M.L.A., Madras, July 12, 1973.

response to changed circumstances, particularly the partial de-radicalization of tenancy that had occurred since the 1940s. According to the secretary of the CPI Workers' Association, the interests and demands of tenants and small owners were too disparate to be accommodated in a single organization.[11]

Perhaps because it had been able to take control of the All-India Kisan Sabha in other important areas following the split, the CPM's initial organizational efforts in Thanjavur were carried out under the Kisan Sabha banner. But the CPM focused its efforts on landless labor even more than did the CPI and by 1972 also opted for a separate agricultural workers' union.[12]

Both the CPI and CPM labor organizations were strong only in the eastern taluks of Thanjavur that comprise Zones 2 and 3; indeed, they barely existed in the other zones. According to its secretary, the CPI-led Union had 100,000 members in 1973, most of whom were from Zones 2 and 3. The secretary of the CPM-led Union told me that it had 60,000 members in 1973, of whom 45,000 were located in Zones 2 and 3.[13] Both membership figures were undoubtedly much exaggerated, and whatever their total strength it was probably even more concentrated in the eastern taluks than the leaders were willing to admit. Both leaders said that the unions were stronger in Zones 2 and 3 for two reasons: the larger number of big landowners and the greater caste homogeneity (Harijan) of labor in those areas.

[11] Interview with P. Ramalingam, secretary, Thanjavur Mavattam Vivasayi Thozhilalar Sangham (Thanjavur District Agricultural Workers' Association), Kottur, June 20, 1973. Bhabani Sen Gupta suggests that competition between the CPI and the CPM may have forced local CPI organizations to adopt a sharper posture than national strategy would suggest (Sen Gupta, *Communism*, p. 320). In fact, the emergence of a separate labor organization in Thanjavur predated the appearance of the CPI's national labor group, the Bharatiya Khet Mazdoor Union (Indian Agricultural Labor Union), which met for the first time in 1968.

[12] Interview with G. Veeraiyan, secretary, CPM Agricultural Workers' Union, Tiruvarur, June 22, 1973. See also Beteille, "Agrarian Movements," p. 6.

[13] Interviews with P. Ramalingam, CPI, Kottur, June 20, 1973, and with G. Veeraiyan, CPM, Tiruvarur, June 22, 1973. According to the CPM's national agrarian affairs newsletter, *Peasant and Labour*, the membership of the CPM's All-India Kisan Sabha in Tamil Nadu in 1974 was 75,829. This figure definitely included laborers in Thanjavur. See *Peasant and Labour* 3 (November-December): 2. Manali Kandaswamy, one of the original leaders of the Thanjavur labor movement and later a CPI MLA, told me in 1973 that the combined membership of the CPI's Agriculturalists' Association and Labor Association was at one time 100,000 but had declined to 30,000 to 40,000 by 1973, of whom he estimated 10,000 were in the Agriculturalists' Association (interview at Madras, July 12, 1973).

However, CPI and CPM organizational strength were not distributed evenly within the combined Zone 2 and 3 areas. According to several sources, by 1972 the CPI organization was strongest in the Mannargudi and Tiruthuraipoondi taluks, and the CPM organization was strongest in the Nagapattinam and Nannilam taluks.[14] These observations correlate closely with the data in Table

TABLE 85

Relative Strength of CPI and CPM Panchayat Control in Four Taluks of Zones 2 and 3, 1965 and 1970

		Communist Panchayat Control*			
	Total Number of Panchayats	Total Number Won by CPI or CPM	% of Total Won by Either CPI or CPM		
Taluk/Year	(1)	(2)	N	CPI (3)	CPM (4)
Nannilam					
1965	178	12	9	77.8	22.2
1970	177	17	17	58.8	41.2
Nagapattinam					
1965	125	25	7	0.0	100.0
1970	124	40	14	14.3	85.7
Mannargudi					
1965	95	53	52	92.5	7.5
1970	95	58	43	86.0	14.0
Tiruthuraipoondi					
1965	72	26	11	45.5	54.5
1970	71	33	23	82.6	17.4

* Unfortunately the data do not always allow us to determine whether the winning candidate was affiliated with the CPI or CPM. In Nagapattinam and Tiruthuraipoondi taluks in both years, and in Mannargudi in 1970, a large percentage of the Communist presidents were identified as "Communist" only. The figures in column 2 include these panchayats. But the percentages in column 3 and 4 are based on the panchayats (N) for which the winning candidates's affiliation was clearly indicated either CPI or CPM.

[14] P. Ramalingam, the CPI Labor Union secretary, told me in 1973 that the union had members in 100 percent of the villages in Mannargudi taluk and 90 percent of the villages in Tiruthuraipoondi taluk (interview at Kottur, June 20, 1973). Of eleven meetings held by the CPI Union in July 1969, seven were in Mannargudi or Tiruthuraipoondi taluks; only one was in Nagapattinam taluk. *Ulavu Chelvam*

85 on the distribution by taluk of Communist panchayat control in 1965 and 1970. In 1965, immediately after the split, the CPI was heavily predominant in Mannargudi taluk and the CPM in Nagapattinam taluk. This pattern did not change appreciably by 1970. Mannargudi was thus the "hard core" of CPI strength and Nagapattinam the "hard core" of CPM strength.

The distribution of strength in the other two taluks was more fluid. In the first few years after the split the two parties were competing for control in several areas.[15] The CPI held on to most of the Communist strength in Nannilam immediately after the split, but the CPM had made heavy inroads in that area by 1970. In Tiruthuraipoondi the division was about even in 1965, but by 1970 the CPI was much stronger. This close correlation between the reported organizational strength and CPI/CPM panchayat control reflects the dependence of the agrarian organizations on the parties.

Both organizations claimed to limit membership to persons who were predominantly laborers, although there may have been subtle distinctions in the criteria they applied to this limitation. When I asked the CPI Union leader whether any of the members owned land, he replied that even someone owning only an acre of land becomes "a mirasdar" and therefore only the "landless are laborers." However, later in the interview he indicated that some members owned lands "subject to the land ceiling limit of 15 acres."[16] He also revealed that many laborers who were also tenants belonged to the association. The CPM Union leader was more categorical about the restriction to "wage-earners," and the CPM had the reputation of appealing to landless laborers almost exclusively.[17]

The apparent distinction in the agro-economic status of CPI and CPM organizational membership is consistent with the geographic

---

(Madras), July 15, 1969, p. 5. See also Alexander, *Agrarian Tension*, p. 38. Corroborating accounts appear in the *Hindu* (Madras), June 19, 1969; July 12, 1969; and April 1, 1973.

[15] The CPI's agrarian newsletter, *Ulavu Chelvam*, reported in 1968 that laborers in villages in Mannargudi and Sirkali taluks had returned to the CPI Union after having left it to join the CPM group because they did not like the "way in which the Marxist party approach the public, and lead the members and create chaos and confusion" (*Ulavu Chelvam*, November 11, 1968, p. 7).

[16] Interview with P. Ramalingam, Kottur, June 20, 1973. In December 1969, shortly after the Kilavenmani incident, the CPI called for unity of all laborers, tenants, and small landowners in opposing the *mirasdars* (*Ulavu Chelvam*, January 1, 1969, p. 2).

[17] Interview with G. Veeraiyan, Tiruvarur, June 22, 1973.

division of party strength. Laborers and big landowners are proportionately more numerous in Nagapattinam. "Low-end" (Harijan) tenants are more numerous in Mannargudi.[18] And we have seen in Chapter 6 that Communist panchayat control is correlated with tenancy in Mannargudi subzone but not in Nagapattinam subzone. The labor survey data also provide evidence of the distinction. Eighty-six percent of the CPM supporters in Zones 2 and 3 were landless laborers, compared to only 58 percent of CPI supporters in these zones. The other CPI supporters came from the ranks of labor-tenants and labor-owners. Furthermore, the difference between the CPI and CPM organizational appeals is consonant with differences in the agrarian class approach of the two parties. The Marxists saw the landless agricultural worker as the principal revolutionary ally of the industrial proletariat, while the CPI emphasized "the basic unity of the interests of the great mass of peasants with those of agricultural workers as a class."[19] In sum, while it is clear that both parties adapted their organizational strategies to the agro-economic realities of Thanjavur, giving more emphasis to labor than party strategy or practice elsewhere would indicate, it is also clear that their strategic differences were reflected in the Thanjavur organizations.

It should not be inferred from this discussion of membership that the CPI and CPM labor unions functioned fully as mass membership organizations. Rather, the organizations were run by small groups of leaders who were also party functionaries. Both organizations claimed to have elaborate committee structures paralleling the district administrative structure, with a district committee at the top, regional committees at the taluk or block levels, and village committees in those areas where they were strong. In fact, such an elaborate structure existed on paper only.[20] The unions generally operated out of party offices: the CPI in Thanjavur, Sirkali, and Mannargudi; the CPM in Tiruvarur (in Nagapattinam taluk). Although the regional committees were supposed to organize meet-

[18] In 1971 laborers comprised 67.6 percent and 77.8 percent of the agricultural work force in Mannargudi and Nagapattinam taluks respectively. In 1961 owner and owner/tenant households cultivating 30.0 acres or more were 0.7 and 3.24 percent of all owner and owner/tenant households in Mannargudi and Nagapattinam respectively.

[19] Sen Gupta, *Communism*, p. 318. I will examine these differences in greater detail below.

[20] Interview with Manali C. Kandaswamy, Madras, July 12, 1973. See also Alexander, *Agrarian Tension*, p. 36.

ings and study classes on a regular basis, the only noticeable activity at this level took place during "crisis periods" when the party leaders traveled widely in the district to "explain" the situation to members.[21] It is true that in villages where each party had substantial support the organizations had a "representative," probably the village party leader. But this reflected much more a political presence than an organizational capability.[22]

The political presence may have been translated into organizational capability at critical times, however. During those periods of CPI- or CPM-led "struggles"for higher wages in Thanjavur, the unions were active locally in organizing strikes and agitations to press the wage demands. But this happened on the initiative of party leaders and generally only where the party was strong. There is little evidence that the unions built over a wide area village-level mechanisms activated and controlled by local laborers to develop common demands and to organize united resistance to landlords. On the other hand, it is certainly true that the organizational efforts of the Communists led to a growth in political consciousness among laborers in Zones 2 and 3, which made it more likely that they would be able to unite against the landowner. CPI and CPM leaders told me in 1973 that it was much easier to organize than it had been ten or twenty years ago because laborers were politically more conscious.[23] However, this was, more accurately, a result of politicization rather than of organizational mobilization.

Although I will examine in more detail the issues of the Thanjavur labor movement in the next section, I should mention here that the labor organizations have been almost exclusively concerned with two related issues, wages and the employment by landlords of outside labor. As mentioned in Chapter 8, during the 1940s, the movement (under the Kisan Sabha banner) addressed some tenancy issues. At that time, and especially during the late 1960s, the main issue was wages. When I asked the CPI and CPM Union leaders how they appealed to laborers, they all replied that they told laborers they could get higher wages if they organized. The

[21] For instance, the meetings of the CPI Union referred to above were organized at the high point of the 1968/1969 wage disputes.

[22] A common sight in Thanjavur at that time was a cluster of bamboo poles in the center of a village flying the flags of various parties. The flags of the CPI and CPM were noticeably more numerous in the Zone 2 and 3 areas.

[23] Interviews with P. Ramalingam, Kottur, June 20, 1973; G. Veeraiyan, Tiruvarur, June 22, 1973; Manali Kandaswamy, Madras, July 12, 1973; and K. R. Gnanasambandan, a CPM leader and ex-M.P., Nagapattinam, June 22, 1973.

issue of outside labor was ancillary to the wage issue; it was by employing outside labor that landowners tried to avoid paying higher wages. As a result of the wage settlement first reached in 1969 and then revised in 1972 even the wage issue had lost much of its force by 1973. The secretary of the CPI Union told me in 1973 that its main aims were 1) that laborers should be provided (by the government) with land for cultivation and house sites, and 2) that the government should provide employment for laborers in the off-season.[24] The CPM Union secretary said the main achievement of his organization, aside from higher wages, was that laborers were now free to walk anywhere in the village.[25] It is thus evident that the goals of the labor organizations have not generally been radical: they have focused on the distribution of income from agriculture rather than the redistribution of the means of agricultural production, land. As I will argue more fully later in this chapter, this moderation was due primarily to the policies of the political parties on which the organizations were so dependent and to the nature of the party system.

Factors other than their own considerable success in raising the wage levels contributed to a decline in the activity of the Communist labor organizations after 1972. First, the impetus given by the Communist split and the Naxalite movement to agrarian organizational activity was beginning to wear off. As a result, intense debate over the right "class approach" to the peasantry surfaced again. At the national level there was a reaction against the increased role of agricultural labor in the peasant movement and renewed emphasis within the CPI on "the necessity of developing a broad and diversified mass peasant movement, encompasing the vast masses in the countryside. . . ." It was argued that the Kisan Sabha should give problems facing the landowning peasantry, such as prices, inputs, and credit, attention equal to land reforms.[26] Similarly, within the

[24] Interviews with P. Ramalingam, Kottur, June 20, 1973; and G. Veeraiyan, Tiruvarur, June 22, 1973.

[25] This is a reference to the fact that traditionally Harijans have not been allowed to enter the streets of caste Hindus, especially of Brahmins (interview with G. Veeraiyan, Tiruvarur, June 22, 1973).

[26] The National Council of the CPI reported in 1973 that both its All-India Kisan Sabha and Bharatiya Khet Mazdoor Union were "virtually hibernating in a state of stagnation" after the spurt of the late 1960s and early 1970s. See *Resolutions and Reports Adopted by the National Council of the Communist Party of India, New Delhi, 15 September 1973* (New Delhi: Communist Party of India, 1973), pp. 65-67. At the same time the weakness of the CPI's peasant organizations was noted in several issues of its newsletter, *Peasant and Labour,* leading to a call for uniting the CPI and

CPM Kisan Sabha there was debate about bringing "middle peasants" into the movement. In Tamil Nadu the 1974 State Kisan Sabha Conference recommended that, while agricultural labor was basic to the movement, attempts should be made to develop strength among "toiling peasants." Second, although the 1964 Communist split was initially responsible for quickening the pace of agrarian organizational activity, in the longer run it weakened the organization of agricultural labor in Thanjavur.[27] The competition between the CPI and CPM organizations made them less effective and in some areas undermined the solidarity that had been achieved earlier.[28] Finally, after the breakup of the CPI-DMK alliance in March 1972 the DMK began trying to organize its own labor organization in Thanjavur and met with some success even in the strongholds of the CPI and the CPM because laborers hoped that association with the then ruling party would bring them some benefits.[29] By 1975 it was apparent that the DMK's entrance on the Thanjavur labor scene had weakened the CPI and CPM unions.[30]

In his own study of Thanjavur, K. C. Alexander contrasts the moderate goals and weak organization of the Thanjavur labor movement with the more radical aims and stronger organization of the labor movement in Kuttanad, Kerala.[31] He suggests that the difference may be due to lower levels of literacy among laborers and the greater socio-economic gap between laborers and organ-

---

CPM Kisan Sabhas. See *Peasant and Labour* 2 (January 1973): 13-14; 2 (February 1973): 2; 2 (October 1973): 15.

[27] "Report on the 17th. State Conference of the Tamil Nadu Kisan Sabha," in *Peasant and Labour* 3 (January-February 1974): 12. At a national conference later in 1974, the Tamil Nadu representative argued that agricultural labor and poor peasants must be organized first. "Report on 22nd. Session of the All-India Kisan Sabha at Sihar, Rajasthan, April 11-14, 1974," in *Peasant and Labour* 3 (May-June 1974): 7-9. See also S. S. Iyer, "A Case Study of Thanjavur District: Anatomy of Agrarian Unrest," *People's Action* 5 (New Delhi: May 1971): 24.

[28] According to one leader I spoke with, "the labourers are attached to various parties and each one of them claims his party as the best." Interview with G. Narayanaswami Naidu, ex-Congress M.L.A., Mayuram, June 4, 1973.

[29] In 1973 I visited one village in Nagapattinam taluk, Puduputhur, where there had been protracted conflict between the resident big landlord and the laborers, who had all been CPM supporters. At the time I visited, the laborers had been refused work by the landlord for over a year. They had just joined the DMK's Vivasayi Thozhilalar Sangham (Agricultural Workers' Association) in the hope that their affiliation with the ruling party would force the landlord, who was a Congress supporter, to relent.

[30] *Hindu*, April 8, 1975.

[31] Alexander, *Agrarian Tension*, p. 37.

ization leaders in Thanjavur. I would argue that one much more important reason for the contrast lies in the different state political environments. Since 1957 the Communist parties have been a major, though unstable, force in Kerala state politics.[32] The Communists were perhaps a major force in Tamil Nadu politics for only a brief period following their strong showing in the 1952 elections. Their statewide political weakness has surely limited Communist mobilization in Thanjavur. In addition, the CPM's alliance with the DMK in 1967 and the CPI's alliance with the DMK between early 1971 and March 1972 obliged them to moderate their tactics. Later, strong competition from the DMK undercut their established organizational networks. And while the agrarian structures of Thanjavur and Kuttanad are very similar, accounting for the fact that both have nurtured a radical agrarian potential,[33] in Thanjavur external political forces have set more reformist limits on the mobilization of that potential.

Landowner Organizations

Landowner organization has always been weaker and more fragmented than labor organization in Thanjavur. One reason for this weakness is divisions among Thanjavur landowners along caste and size-of-holding lines. Thus, we find the strongest organizations in those parts of the district where landownership is socially and economically most homogeneous—in the areas of Zones 2 and 3 (but especially in the Nagapattinam subzone), although even here the organizations have suffered from disunity. From time to time the landowners' organizations have tried to create at least an image of representing both large and small landowners but without success. Landowner organizations have thus attracted little support from the major political parties seeking to widen their rural support bases and consequently have been on the political defensive.

Landowner organizations have been so weak in Thanjavur that it is difficult to trace their history, and so fragmented that, while many organizations have emerged in name, it is difficult to distinguish the real from the paper ones. According to Alexander, one

[32] See Robert L. Hardgrave, Jr., "The Communist Parties of Kerala: An Electoral Profile," in *Studies in Electoral Politics in the Indian States*, vol. 4; *Systems and Cleavages*, ed. Myron Weiner and John Osgood Field (New Delhi: Manohar Book Service, 1975), pp. 167-209.

[33] Alexander, "Emerging Farmer-Labour Relations," pp. 1,551-1,553, and Hardgrave, "Communist Parties of Kerala," pp. 203-204.

organization, the Thanjavur District Landowning Farmers' Association, headquartered in Kumbakonam, has been in existence since the 1920s but was active only in the 1930s and 1950s and, more recently, in organizing legal action against land reform legislation.[34] However, my own research revealed only one instance of activity by this association in the 1960 to 1972 period. Several other organizations emerged briefly in the early 1950s in reaction to the agrarian conflicts of the late 1940s and to the reforms or threat of reforms that followed them. For instance, four local landowner associations gave evidence before the Land Revenue Reforms Committee in Thanjavur in 1950.[35] A group called the Tanjore District Mirasdars' Conference met in November 1953 and expressed its opposition to the land ceilings legislation then under consideration by the state government and again in April 1955 to oppose all the recommendations of the Ramamurthi Committee on land reforms.[36] Another organization, the Thanjavur Paddy Producers' Association, appeared briefly in the 1960s. Its main concern was to get the state government to increase the paddy procurement price. It was dominated by Brahmins from the Kumbakonam and Papanasam areas and died out in 1968 or 1969.[37]

By and large, then, the landowner organizations whose names have appeared from time to time have sprung up in response to a particular problem and disappeared just as quickly. Many seem to have been specific to a locale and even a caste group. One example is reported by Sivertsen in his study of a village ("TM") near Kumbakonam in the late 1950s.[38] Several large Brahmin estate owners cultivating their land with hired labor formed an association in 1957 to fight laborers' demands for higher wages. Because the estate owners wished to enlist the support of small landowners in the village they called it the "Little Landlords' Association." But the smaller landowners, most of whom rented out their land, recognized their interests would not be served and were anxious to stay out of the conflict. Moreover, the association was weakened by

[34] Alexander, *Agrarian Tension*, p. 39.
[35] Government of Madras, The Land Revenue Reforms Committee, *First Report* (Madras: Government Press, 1951), pp. 162-164.
[36] See Daniel Thorner, *The Agrarian Prospect in India: Five Lectures on Land Reform Delivered in 1955 at the Delhi School of Economics* (New Delhi: Delhi University Press, 1956), pp. 37-39.
[37] Interview with K. S. Sivavadivel Odayar, president, East Thanjavur District Mirasdars' Association, Tiruvarur, June 22, 1973.
[38] Dagfinn Sivertsen, *When Caste Barriers Fall: A Study of Social and Economic Change in a South India Village* (Oslo: Universitets Forlaget, 1963), pp. 91-92, 131-133.

conflict between two subcastes within the Brahmin community. This example illustrates two points I have made: first, that caste and holding size can have a divisive effect, and second, that even though the village is in the Zone 1 area the agro-economic structure in which this effort took place is similar to the Zones 2 and 3 where very large owners cultivate with hired labor. However, as my earlier analysis would have predicted, the efforts were thwarted in part by the cross-cutting effect of tenancy relations.

One organization, the Thanjavur District Mirasdars' Association, was prominent for some time. It is not known exactly when it began, but at some point in the mid-to-late 1960s it split into the West and East Thanjavur District Mirasdars' Associations.[39] The East Thanjavur Association was by far the more active of the two in the years that followed. The split was due to conflict between the predominantly Brahmin landowners of the Zone 1 area and the predominantly non-Brahmin landowners of the Zone 2 and 3 areas. The inactivity of the West Thanjavur Association reflects the constraints embodied in the agrarian structure of Zone 1 and described in Chapter 6. Because of the past out-migration of Brahmins large landowners cultivating with hired labor were relatively few in Zone 1. In the 1960s Brahmin landowners continued to sell their land and to leave agriculture at a faster rate than their non-Brahmin counterparts in the Zone 2 and 3 areas.[40] The resulting weakness of the landowning group together with the complex cleavages among other cultivating groups made it difficult to organize effectively in the Zone 1 area.

The East Thanjavur District Mirasdars' Association (sometimes referred to in press accounts as *the* Thanjavur District Mirasdars' Association) was headquartered in Tiruvarur, in Nagapattinam taluk (Zone 3). According to the man who had been its president from its inception, K. S. Sivavadivel Odayar, the organization had a membership of fifteen thousand in 1973, mostly from the eastern taluks. However, very few of this number were active members. The main objectives of the association were to solve the problems of labor relations and to obtain increases in procurement prices of paddy. In fact, the association was quite active in the conflicts over

[39] The president of the East Thanjavur District Mirasdars' Association told me that the split occurred in 1968 or 1969 (interview with K. S. Sivavadivel Odayar, Tiruvarur, June 22, 1973). Press reports of association activities did not always make it clear in the later years that the more active East Thanjavur Association was not the earlier districtwide one. See also Alexander, *Agrarian Tension*, p. 39.

[40] Interview with K. S. Sivavadivel Odayar, Tiruvarur, June 22, 1973.

agricultural wages in the late 1960s and early 1970s, frequently holding conferences to publicize the position of landowners, meeting with officials and political leaders to argue the landowners' interests, and representing landowners in the negotiations that produced the various wage settlements. Although the association did not organize direct action against the laborers, to the extent that it articulated a common landowner position it certainly contributed to the sense of confrontation that characterized this period.

However, when I met with the association's president in 1973, he seemed a discouraged and disgusted man. He reported that the membership of the association was declining and that the remaining members did not take interest in it. He gave several reasons for this. First, he said, many *mirasdars*, especially Brahmins and non-Brahmins with education, were selling their lands and leaving agriculture because they sensed that "general conditions are against their interests." Second, those who remained on the land either had or were developing nonagricultural sources of income to which they were paying more and more attention. Third, he described most landowners as unwilling to act jointly except at critical times. Rather than try openly to prevent or resist policies and legislation unfavorable to them, most landowners preferred to escape their impact through loopholes.

Furthermore, he complained that even the landowners of East Thanjavur could not unify because of caste, economic, and political differences.[41] Although the Brahmin/non-Brahmin cleavage was less salient for the East Thanjavur Association because of the relatively low number of Brahmin landowners in the region,[42] caste differences among the non-Brahmin landowners were also a problem.[43] And, of course, Brahmin/non-Brahmin differences continued to interfere with cooperation between landowners in the east and west. For instance, in March 1970 representatives of the East Thanjavur District Mirasdars' Association and the Tanjore District Landowning Agriculturalists' Association (based in Kumbakonam)

[41] A newspaper report in 1973 concluded that in Thanjavur landowners did not have an association "worth mentioning" because of their lack of unity (*Hindu*, April 1, 1973).

[42] Of seventy-two major contributors to the association in 1968/1969, only seven were Brahmins. See East Thanjavur District Mirasdars' Association, "Statement and Accounts, November 1, 1968 to January 1, 1970," mimeographed, pp. 13-16.

[43] A Congress leader of Sirkali also reported to me that the *mirasdars'* association that had once existed in the area had been "ruined by caste feeling." Interview with P. Ethiraj, Sirkali, June 6, 1973.

agreed to convene jointly a conference to protest passage of the 1969 Land Ceiling Reduction Act and to form a trust committee to challenge the law in the courts.[44] However, the conference and the subsequent meeting with the state chief minister were disrupted by disputes between the Brahmin and non-Brahmin leaders of the two associations. Cooperation broke down to the point where the two groups could not agree on which auditors should check on charges and countercharges of financial mismanagement.

Recognizing the political vulnerability of organizations devoted to the interests of relatively few large landowners, these associations tried from the beginning to include or give the appearance of including small landowners. They chose terms for their names that would encompass the small owner, such as "agriculturalist" or "farmer." A new association formed in Nagapattinam in 1973 was called the Thanjavur District Vivasayigal Sangam (Agriculturalists' Association), but its president was a very large landowner from Nagapattinam who had just been acquitted of murder charges stemming from the Kilavenmani incident.[45] One pamphlet of the East Thanjavur Association included a statement entitled, "Who is A Mirasdar?" which argued that the term applies to anyone who cultivates land, regardless of size of holding or tenurial status.[46] Although Communist leaders reported their fear that these efforts by big landowners would "confuse the small owners and tenants and make it difficult to organize them,"[47] it is clear that the landowner organizations were not successful in broadening their base.

This fact is the root of the landowners' political difficulties, for from Independence onwards, and increasingly so, no major party was willing to espouse openly the large landowners' cause when to do so would bring them few votes and risk losing many. As one landowner said bitterly, "The majority of political parties, including the party at the helm of affairs . . . aim at introducing agricultural legislation to win cheap popularity at the expense of others." As a result, as early as 1953 the Tanjore District Mirasdars' Conference called for organization of a conservative party to fight land reforms. In 1957 a group of Kumbakonam landlords attempted to organize a new party, the "Welfare Party," to take up their causes, and for

[44] Tamil Nadu Ceiling Reduction Objection, State Conference, Thanjavur, "Statement of Income and Expenditure," pamphlet, undated, p. 107.

[45] *Hindu*, May 8, 1973.

[46] East Thanjavur District Mirasdars' Association, "Statement and Accounts," back cover.

[47] Interview with M. Kathamuthu, M.P., January 12, 1973.

a brief period in the 1960s the conservative Swatantra party had a following among Thanjavur landlords, especially Brahmins.[48] But no party could survive on this narrow base. Even the Congress (0) party, which Thanjavur landlords decided to support in 1971 because of the DMK's newly formed alliance with the CPI, told the landowners to adjust to changing times and come to terms with the demands of labor.[49] In such a situation it was not surprising to find many landowners going their own way politically, seeking political affiliations based on local factors.

In summary, the dependence of the Thanjavur labor organizations on political parties imposed limits on the organizations' ideology and programs, but it was also the key to their achieving limited goals. Conversely, the lack of strong linkages between the landowners' organizations and the political parties was an important reason for their weakness.

THE MOBILIZATION OF LABOR IN THANJAVUR: ISSUES, TACTICS, AND OUTCOMES

There have been two periods of intense activity in the Thanjavur labor movement, 1944 to 1952 and 1967 to 1972. The pattern of events, issues, tactics, and outcomes have been remarkably similar in the two periods. In both cases labor unrest has followed in the wake of rapidly rising prices. The erosion of real wages by inflation, coming after periods of relative wage and price stability, led to demands for higher wages. These demands were organized and articulated by the Communist parties. The first response of the landowners was to refuse any increases. Communist-led strikes and agitations followed, often resulting in violence. The threat to public order forced the state government to intervene in search of a settlement. A series of agreements giving labor small wage increases followed. Either because landowners tried to avoid paying the higher wages (often by employing outside labor) or because labor demanded further increases the conflict continued, leading to a "peak episode" (the 1948 strike and the 1968 Kilavenmani incident) that

[48] Thorner, *Agrarian Prospect*, p. 41; Sivertsen, *When Caste Barriers Fall*, p. 16. The Swatantra won 3.5 percent of the district vote in the 1962 general elections. Swatantra candidates won panchayat presidencies in three panchayats in 1960, six panchayats in 1965, and seven panchayats in 1970. See also Andre Beteille, *Caste, Class and Power: Changing Patterns of Stratification in a Tanjore Village* (Berkeley, Ca.: University of California Press, 1965), pp. 175-177.

[49] *Hindu*, February 24, 1971, and September 30, 1972.

brought the state government into the act even more forcefully. Commissions were appointed to study the situation. Their recommendations resulted, sooner or later, in legislation that mandated substantially higher wages for labor, although the actual impact of the legislation was not the same in both periods. Two other factors were common in the decline of the movement: a change in economic conditions and a change in external political forces.

While there were many similarities between the two periods, there were also important differences. First, as mentioned in Chapter 8, tenants were more active in the movement in the 1940s than in the 1960s, for three reasons. In the former period, in areas of low-end tenancy there was little to distinguish the sharecropper from the then predominant *pannaiyal*. The highly exploitative sharecropping arrangements, also intensified by inflation, made the *varamdar* the natural ally of the *pannaiyal* (as both received most of their income from a share in the crop). In the 1960s sharecropping had been almost completely replaced by fixed-rent tenancy and attached labor by daily wage labor. Second, because of the latter change, the focus of the early period was the attached laborer and the focus of the later period was the daily laborer. Third, in the early period many landowners ultimately evaded the legislated wage increase by dismissing their *pannaiyals* in advance, but this escape was not open to them in the 1960s. Ironically, the landowners' action in the early period laid the groundwork for the unrest of the later period by creating a large and more alienated labor force. Further, technological changes played a larger, though still minor, role in the movement of the 1960s. The increase in double cropping in the mid-1960s strengthened the laborers' bargaining position. A few years later the modest but significant increases in paddy yields made possible by the advent of high-yielding varieties helped the landowners absorb wage increases and thus softened the conflict.

The Early Period: 1944-1952

As elsewhere in India, the Depression created acute economic distress in Thanjavur. Severely reduced prices for agricultural products resulted in growing indebtedness. For this reason it was during the 1930s that many of the old rural landowning elite left agriculture to take up new occupations in the towns. While elsewhere in the Madras Presidency these economic conditions led to rural agitations, Thanjavur was quiet.[50] Although the impact of the Depression was undoubtedly deeply felt by tenants and laborers in the district, there is no evidence of protest. This can be attributed to the fact that, once the Depression had set in, the 1930s were characterized by relative stability of prices, albeit at low levels, and in Thanjavur agrarian discontent has been associated with rapid economic swings rather than with prolonged depression.

Following the outbreak of World War II, prices began to rise rapidly in Thanjavur. In Figure 12 I have graphed an index of average annual prices in the district for inferior rice, which dominates the diet of rural people and thus the rural price index, over the period 1931/1932 to 1950/1951.[51] The correlation between the rise in prices and the beginning of unrest in the 1940s is apparent. By 1942/1943 prices were rising very rapidly, and it was during this period that the first strikes and agitations by Communist-led laborers occurred. Of course the stage had already been set by developments in the 1930s. First, the social upheaval created by the Depression, in particular the attenuation of landlord-tenant and landowner-laborer relations resulting from the economic squeeze and growing absenteeism, undoubtedly disturbed the equilibrium of the Thanjavur agrarian system, with the result that many of the traditional constraints on social protest must have been weakened. Second, as I have just described, the Communists had begun organizing sharecroppers and laborers in Thanjavur in the late 1930s. They became more active in mid-1942 when, following the British legalization of their own party and the ban on the Congress, they sought to win rural support away from the Congress. Their activity was concentrated in the Mannargudi area, where in 1944 they were able to assemble five thousand tenants and laborers in a conference that demanded increased wages and reduced rents.[52]

The first wage settlements were reached that year (see tables 86 and 87). The Kalappal and Mannargudi Agreements gave substantial regular daily and harvest wage increases to *pannaiyals*, stipulated how wages were to be paid, and prohibited punishments such as forcing laborers to drink cow dung mixed with water. But there was no means of enforcing these agreements, and in many areas the landlords refused to pay the new rates. Prices leveled off

[50] See Christopher John Baker, *The Politics of South India, 1920-1937* (Cambridge: Cambridge University Press, 1967), pp. 174-184, 200-211.

[51] Unfortunately, comparable systematic data for wages and paddy production during this period were not available to me.

[52] Baliga, *Tanjore Handbook*, p. 118.

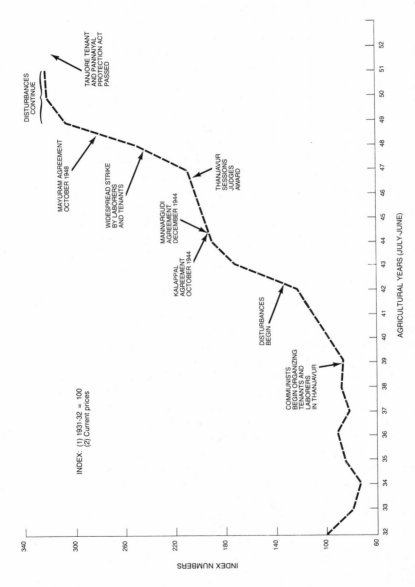

FIGURE 12. Index of Average Annual Price of Rice (Second Sort), 1931/1932 to 1950/1951, Correlated with Labor Unrest and Wage Settlements in Thanjavur District

SOURCE: Price index data from Government of Madras, Director of Statistics, *A Statistical Atlas of the Thanjavur District: Revised and Brought Up To The Decennium Ending Fasli 1360 (1950-51)* (Madras, 1965), p. 47.

TABLE 86

History of Thanjavur District Wage Settlements, 1944-1952

Year	Settlement	Provisions	
		Wages	Other
1944	Kalappal Agreement	Increase in both regular and harvest wages for pannaiyals	Prohibits harassment of laborers Allows tenants to harvest own field
1944	Mannargudi Agreement	Increase in both regular and harvest wages for pannaiyals	Harvest wage to be measured with "stamped" (certified) measures Landlord has to give receipt after measurement
1946	Thanjavur Sessions Judge's Award	Increase in regular wages only	
1948	Mayuram Agreement	Increase in regular wages only	Specifies how and when harvest wage is to be paid Other "concessions" such as residential plots
1952	Tanjore Tenants and Pannaiyal Protection Act	Increase in regular wages only	Regulates other conditions of employment Restricts right of landowner to dismiss pannaiyal Sets up conciliation machinery

TABLE 87

Wage Rates Fixed by Wage Settlements, 1944-1952

| Year | Settlement | Regular Daily Wage | | Harvest Wage* | |
		Amount (in paddy)	Increase (%)	Amount (in paddy)	Increase (%)
		(Madras measures per day)		(marakkals per kalam)	
1944	Kalappal Agreement	1.00	—	1.75	—
1944	Mannargudi Agreement	1.50	50.1	2.0	14.3
1946	Thanjavur Sessions Judge's Award	1.75	16.7	**	—
1948	Mayuram Agreement	2.00	14.3	2.0	0.0
1952	Pannaiyal Protection Act	4.00	100.0	**	—

NOTES: Wage rates apply to males only.

* Includes *kalavadi* or share of harvest traditionally due to farm and other village servants.

** Settlement did not apply.

briefly in 1944 to 1946, but the expulsion of Communists from the Congress party in 1945 gave the movement a new political impetus, and wage agitations continued. The government appointed the Thanjavur sessions and district judge to arbitrate the wage dispute. For the first time labor representatives were invited to participate in discussions in the judge's chambers, and the judge awarded the laborers a modest increase in daily wage rates. But once again the settlement was overtaken by economic and political events. The entire state was plagued by a series of bad harvests beginning in 1946/1947, and prices took another sharp upward turn in 1947 and 1948.

At about the same time Communist party strategy, influenced by the outbreak and early successes of the Telengana rebellion, became more radical (with the ascendence of the "Ranadive line"). In Thanjavur landlord-laborer clashes became more frequent and violent. Many local instances of violence resulted from landlords trying to break the movement by importing outside labor. In response to the widespread disorder the Madras Government passed a special act (the Madras Maintenance of Public Order Act of 1947) providing for preventive detention, imposition of collective fines, censorship, control of all meetings, and processions and requisition of property. The act was amplified and renewed in 1948 and again in 1949. Special armed police were stationed in Thanjavur. Police firings and mass arrests were common. All of this culminated in a strike so extensive that one witness described eastern Thanjavur as a "Communist state." In the village of Kirippur in Nagapattinam taluk, for instance, the *varamdars* and *pannaiyals* struck, demanding 50 percent of the crop and a doubling of wages respectively.[53]

The response of the state government to the deteriorating situation in Thanjavur was twofold. On the one hand, it continued to use force in dealing with the strikes and agitations. On the other hand, it re-opened negotiations on the wage demands, which resulted in the Mayuram Agreement of October 1948 that gave the laborers another modest increase in daily wage rates. Once again, however, no means of enforcement was provided, many landowners continued to resist paying the higher wages, and sporadic outbreaks of violence continued.[54] The situation was aggravated further by the reaction of landowners to the state government's decision

[53] Several studies provide accounts of these events: see *ibid.*, pp. 120-122; Thorner, *Agrarian Prospect*, p. 37; Alexander, *Agrarian Tension*, pp. 40-42; and Muehl, *Interview with India*, p. 284.

[54] Gough, "Harijans," p. 239.

in May 1950 to create the Land Revenue Reforms Committee to study and make policy recommendations on a wide range of agrarian issues, including "the conditions of cultivating tenants and laborers."[55] Sensing the possibility of legal regulation of the *pannaiyal* system, many landowners began dismissing their *pannaiyals*, which led to even more disturbances. As a result, in 1952 the Madras legislative assembly passed the Tanjore Tenants and Pannaiyal Protection Act. It was intended to regulate the wages and conditions of employment of *pannaiyals*, but the result was to hasten the demise of the *pannaiyal* system. Ironically, landowners used technicalities of the act to pay unacceptably low wages, thus forcing out those who had not previously been dismissed.[56]

Although the dismantling of the *pannaiyal* system surely contributed to the decline of the Thanjavur labor movement after 1952, other factors were probably more important. First, it was clear that the government was ready to use force to contain the movements. Second, economic conditions improved considerably. Prices declined after 1950 (between 1950/1951 and 1955/1956 the rural price index for Thanjavur dropped 17 points), while wages continued to increase (the index of average annual field labor wages in Thanjavur rose from 100 in 1950/1951 to 172 in 1955/1956). Third, with the discrediting of both the Ranadive and Andhra lines and the advent of the Joshi-Dange-Ghosh line in 1951, the CPI's strategy on the agrarian front changed sharply. The party was no longer committed to agrarian revolution but increasingly to the nonviolent, parliamentary path. At the state level the CPI ran very well in the 1952 elections, becoming the largest opposition party in the Madras legislative assembly. Given the CPI's exclusive role in the Thanjavur labor movement these changes in the Party's ideology and position at the national and state levels had a moderating influence on the Thanjavur movement's goals and tactics.

The late 1940s witnessed a genuine radicalism in the mobilization of labor in Thanjavur. The frequency and scale of violence certainly suggest that the leaders and laborers were prepared to use violent means to achieve their ends. However, it is also quite clear that the goals of the movement never became completely radical. As far as can be determined from the available evidence, the aim of the movement never shifted from the reform of wages to the radical

[55] Government of Madras, The Land Revenue Reforms Committee, *First Report*, pp. 151-153.
[56] Alexander, *Agrarian Tension*, p. 42.

restructuring of land relations. There may have been some brief thought of challenging state power in the 1948 strike, but it passed quickly, especially in the face of tough repressive measures.

The movement's reformist aims were in part a reflection of the agrarian structure of Thanjavur. First, the economic dependency of the *pannaiyals* on the landlord still outweighed whatever independence their political organization could give them. Second, the relationship of the marginal *varamdar* and *pannaiyal* to the land was historically too tenuous to suggest readily that they might have a claim to ownership. This would have required a much greater change in consciousness than was likely to have occurred in this short period. Thus, while they may have been prepared to use violent means to gain what they perceived as their rightful share in the product of the land, they were not ready for an assault on the land system itself. The small owner and the more substantial sharecropper or fixed-rent tenant who might have asserted a claim on the land were not participants in the movement for the reasons discussed in Chapter 6 and Chapter 8. Finally, I suspect but cannot prove that the movement's local leaders, most of whom were natives of Thanjavur, never fully subscribed to the tenets of the Ranadive or Andhra lines. In this respect the Communist party is like others in the Indian system: adjustments to the diversity inherent in India's geography and social institutions usually outweigh ideology.[57]

The Later Period: 1967-1973

The years 1955/1956 to 1965/1966 were a time of relative quiet on the Thanjavur agrarian scene. This may be attributed to several factors. In the first place, economic conditions in the district were relatively stable during most of the period. Between 1955/1956 and 1961/1962 paddy production, rural prices, and farm wages rose steadily but gradually (see Figure 13). While wages rose at a slightly lower rate than prices, there were no sudden, wild swings in the price-wage relationships. Furthermore, increases in production stayed ahead of prices and wages. But beginning in 1962/1963 Thanjavur experienced increasingly sharp fluctuations in all three variables and their interrelationship. In 1964/1965 prices, wages, and production all increased sharply, but the following year production and wages dropped precipitously while prices continued their steep

[57] Paul R. Brass, "Political Parties of the Radical Left in South Asian Politics," in *Radical Politics in South Asia*, ed. Paul R. Brass and Marcus F. Franda (Cambridge, Mass.: The M.I.T. Press, 1973), p. 7. See also Sen Gupta, *Communism*, pp. 307, 438.

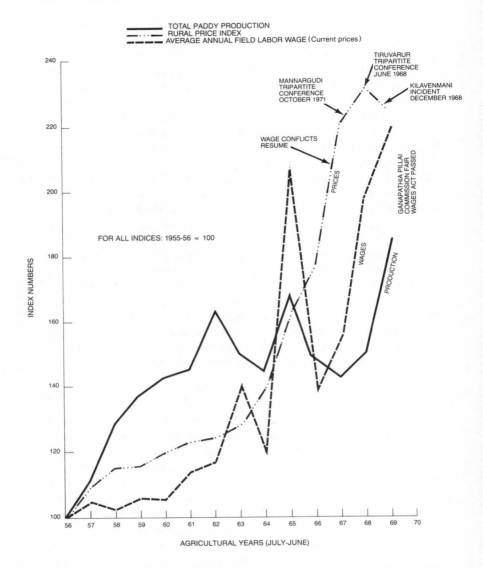

FIGURE 13. Indices of Wages, Prices, and Paddy Production, 1955/1956 to 1968/
1969, Correlated with Labor Unrest and Wage Settlements in Thanjavur District

SOURCE: Indices constructed from data available in Government of Madras, Director of Statistics, *Season and Crop Report for the Year 1955-56 (Fasli 1365)* (Madras,
1958), and in subsequent annual issues of the same publication.

upward climb, creating for the first time since the 1940s a sudden, wide lag of wages behind prices. Wages turned upward again in 1966/1967, but the gap between wages and prices remained substantial, as paddy production continued to suffer from poor weather conditions.

Widespread, organized demands for wage increases did not, however, develop until 1966/1967. The mobilization of labor discontent lagged behind disruptive economic changes for political reasons. First, internal Communist party developments deprived the movement of strong leadership. Beginning in 1959, worsening Sino-Indian relations led to the arrest of many "left Communists" accused by the central government of having pro-Peking inclinations. Those leaders not arrested before were jailed at the outbreak of the 1962 Border War, and most remained in jail until the mid-1960s. One effect of these developments was that the "rightists" gained control of the CPI, and "parliamentarism" became the dominant strategy in Party affairs.[58] Further, the Thanjavur movement was deprived of active leadership when many labor leaders went underground during this period.[59]

After the 1964 split, which took place after leftist leaders emerged from jail to find the rightists in almost complete control of the Party apparatus, it took some time for the two parties to sort out strategic, tactical, and organizational questions. Although the economic slump of 1965 to 1967 and the 1965 war with Pakistan led the two parties to try to work together, increasingly they competed for support, especially in the strongholds of the undivided CPI. As a result, the CPI shifted its tactical position somewhat to the left while the CPM shifted its position somewhat to the right. As the 1967 elections approached, both parties saw a chance to use the deteriorating economic conditions to dislodge the Congress. In Tamil Nadu the CPM forged an electoral alliance with the DMK and won eleven seats in the legislative assembly, including three from Thanjavur, to the CPI's one (also in Thanjavur). Thus, by 1967 the CPI's control over the Communist political base in Thanjavur was severely challenged by the CPM. In rejecting parliamentarism and seeking a more militant tactical line, the CPM had focused on the mobilization of the rural poor. Thus, it is not surprising that their early gains

[58] For a discussion of the impact of the Sino-Indian dispute on Indian communism, see Sen Gupta, *Communism*, pp. 48-65.

[59] C. Muthiah, "Development of Landless Labourers: Role of Group Bargaining Power," paper presented to the Seminar on Weaker Sections held at the Indian Institute of Management at Ahmedabad, October 1972, mimeographed, p. 11.

would be made in an area like Thanjavur, especially at a time when economic conditions were again straining agrarian relationships in the district. The CPI was, of course, obliged to fight back.[60]

By 1967 the political rivalry between the CPI and the CPM provided renewed militant leadership for economically hard-pressed laborers in Thanjavur. For the first time since 1952 conflicts broke out between landowners and laborers over demands for increased wages, and there were several wage agitations in 1967 led by the CPI or CPM.[61] As in the earlier period they were concentrated in the Zone 2 and 3 areas of the district. These disturbances led to a "tripartite" conference of labor and landowner representatives with the district collector at Mannargudi on October 8, 1967. The parties at this conference agreed to increase the existing harvest wage rates (then varying between 3.25 and 5.6 litres of paddy per *kalam* of about 45 litres) by about half a litre, up to a maximum of 5.6 litres (see tables 88 and 89). However, as in the case of the early agreements of the 1940s there was no way to enforce these wage rates, and the agreement specifically allowed landowners to use outside labor "provided the local labor is utilized." It was impossible to prove that all local labor was not utilized, and so many landowners evaded paying the higher rates by importing outside labor.

Demands for higher wages were renewed before the beginning of the 1968/1969 season, resulting in another tripartite conference at Thanjavur on June 8, 1968. This agreement specified a single rate for regular daily wages (all nonharvest work) that was higher than the existing rate in some areas of the district.[62] But wage disputes and agitations continued as landowners refused to pay or the competing CPI and CPM sought to press their demands harder.[63] The CPI organized a large demonstration in support of implementation of the Tiruvarur Agreement at Tiruthuraipoondi on July 16, 1968. As the *kuruvai* harvest began, the situation grew more tense. At a meeting on October 20 the Thanjavur District Landowners' Association called for police protection during the

[60] Sen Gupta, *Communism*, pp. 84, 88-89, 292.

[61] Alexander, *Agrarian Tension*, p. 43.

[62] According to a document prepared by the CPI-led Agricultural Workers' Association, the daily wage rates for nonharvest work in 1967/1968 ranged from Rs. 2.50 to Rs. 3.00. See Agricultural Workers' Association, "East Thanjavur District Agricultural Workers' Problems: A Memorandum Placed Before the Judge of the Enquiry Commission on Behalf of the Agricultural Workers' Association, Thanjavur, March 11, 1969," typewritten, undated, p. 53.

[63] Alexander, *Agrarian Tension*, p. 43.

TABLE 88

History of Thanjavur District Wage Settlements, 1967-1973

Year	Settlement	Provisions	
		Wages	Other
1967	Mannargudi Tripartite Conference	Increase in harvest wages only subject to maximum	Outside labor may be employed provided local labor is not available. Disputes to be referred to tahsildar.
1968	Tiruvarur Tripartite Conference	Increase in regular wages only	Landlords need not employ "lazy" laborers. Outside labor may be employed provided local labor is not available.
1969	Thanjavur Tripartite Conference	Increase in harvest wages only	Outside labor may be employed provided local labor is not available.
			Disputes to be referred to "conciliation committee" consisting of tahsildar, two representatives of landlords, and two of laborers.
1969	Ganpathia Pillai Commission recommendations as implemented in Fair Wages Act	Increase in regular and harvest wages Mode of computing harvest wages fixed Wages to be paid in kind wherever possible	Outside labor may be employed as long as local labor is not available. "Conciliation offices" established by government to settle disputes.
1972	Thanjavur Tripartite Conference	Increase in regular wages only Wages to be paid in kind wherever possible	
1973	Thanjavur Tripartite Conference	Increase in regular wages only	

TABLE 89

Wage Rates Fixed by Wage Settlements, 1967-1973

Year	Settlement	Regular Daily Wage				Harvest Wage	
		Paddy	Cash	Total (cash equiv-alent)	Increase*	Amount (in paddy)	Increase* (minimum-maximum)
		(litres)	(Rs.)	(Rs.)	(%)	(litres/Kalam)	(%)
1967	Mannargudi Tripartite Conference	**	**	**	**	3.7-5.6	0.0-14.6
1968	Tiruvarur Tripartite Conference	6.0	1.00	2.64***	**	**	**
1969	Thanjavur Tripartite Conference	**	**	**	**	4.2-5.6	0.0-11.9
1969	Fair Wage Act	6.0	1.25	4.25	61.0	6.0	7.1-42.9
1972	Thanjavur Tripartite Conference	6.0	1.50	5.20	22.4	6.0	0.0
1973	Thanjavur Tripartite Conference	6.0	1.75	5.75	10.6	6.0	0.0

NOTES: Wage rates apply to males only.

* Increase over previous settlement or, where known, prior existing wage rates.

** Settlement did not apply.

*** For 1968, calculated with retail paddy price data; for other years, cash equivalent is stipulated in agreements.

harvest. The CPI newsletter, *Ulavu Chelvam*, reported that land-lords were trying to resist wage increases and break the movement by using imported labor, calling in the police, hiring their own *goondas* to attack the laborers, and exploiting caste and political divisions. It reported that "many murders have taken place" and accused the landowners of trying to drive a wedge between the DMK and the CPM by blaming the murder of a CPM party worker on the DMK.[64]

An "all-party conference" was held at Mannargudi on November 21. Representatives of the CPI, CPM, DMK, and DK tried to thrash out a common position on the wage question. They resolved 1) to request the collector to convene another tripartite conference, 2) to have party representatives meet at the taluk level to settle problems, and 3) to have two more all-party conferences at Nagapat-tinam and Nannilam. In spite of these efforts to create a united front on the labor issue interparty differences did emerge. For instance, the DMK proposed and the CPI Union rejected the suggestion that wages fixed at the proposed tripartite conference be in force for five years.[65] Still, it is noteworthy that even at this early stage the DMK, the ruling party in the state, was cooperating with the Communists.

On December 16, 1968, the CPI's Agricultural Workers' Association organized a districtwide agitation to press the wage demands. According to CPI sources, over 25,000 marched in Mannargudi and in Tiruthuraipoondi, 5,000 in Nannilam, 3,000 in Nagapattinam, "thousands" in Sirkali, and "hundreds" in Mayuram and Kumbakonam.[66] But the confrontation between landowners and laborers continued in an increasingly charged atmosphere. Two weeks later the Kilavenmani incident took place, dramatizing and drawing great attention to the situation in Thanjavur and thereby forcing the state government to take several more forceful steps.[67]

First, the state government announced very shortly afterwards that it would appoint a one-man Commission of Enquiry to look into the problems of agricultural labor in East Thanjavur (Zones 2 and 3) and to recommend legislative and other action. S. Gana-

[64] *Ulavu Chelvam*, November 1, 1968, p. 4, and November 15, 1968, pp. 2-4, 13.

[65] Ibid., December 1, 1968, p. 5, and January 1, 1969, p. 12.

[66] Ibid., p. 10. Note that these attendance figures correlate closely with the distribution of CPI strength reported in Table 85.

[67] For instance, see Ashok Thapar's article, "Warning from Tanjore," *Times of India*, January 20, 1969.

pathia Pillai, a retired judge of the Madras high court, was appointed to the commission. Second, the collector of Thanjavur called for a tripartite conference to be held on January 16, 1969. At first the landowners' representatives refused to attend, but later they changed their minds. At the conference groups of labor leaders, landowners' representatives and the legislative assembly members (M.L.A.'s) of all parties met separately with the collector, who then announced a small increase in harvest wages. The agreement stipulated that these new rates would be in effect for three years or until the government acted on the recommendations of the newly appointed Commission of Enquiry. As in earlier agreements it was specified that imported labor could be used provided local labor had employment. As in the past this provision was the source of continuing conflict. Only a month after the conference the Communists were already reporting that landlords were refusing to pay the new rates, bringing in outside labor, and, when the local laborers protested, accusing them of refusing to abide by the agreement.[68]

The Ganapathia Pillai Commission began its work quickly, collecting information on the Thanjavur situation and soliciting statements from interested parties. The CPI Agricultural Workers' Association submitted a long memorandum to the commission on March 11, 1969, recommending a wide range of reforms, including:

1. Substantial increases in both regular daily and harvest wages sufficient to give the average labor household a monthly income of Rs. 125;
2. Measurement of the harvest wage before deduction of the *kalavadi*, or traditional share for farm and village servants;
3. Use of the litre rather than the *marakkal* to measure out the harvest wage because the latter requires that the grain be heaped at the top and thus facilitates cheating;
4. Payment of all wages in paddy, except where cash is specified;
5. Establishment of uniform wage rates throughout East Thanjavur;
6. Establishment of a tripartite wage board to review wage rates periodically and to make adjustments for increases in the cost of living;
7. Establishment of a tripartite conciliation board to settle disputes on wages and other labor issues;

[68] *Ulavu Chelvam* February 1, 1969, p. 25, and February 15, 1969, p. 10.

8. Employment of local labor as a general rule;
9. Recognition of the right of agricultural laborers to strike and bargain collectively;
10. Institution of a six-hour work day;
11. Recognition of the labor unions and representation for them in various consultative boards of government;
12. No police "interference" in disputes between laborers and landowners;
13. Amendment of land ceiling and temple land regulation acts in order to make more land available for cultivation by tenants and laborers;
14. First preference be given to laborers in distribution of surplus land;
15. Ownership of laborers' housesites (which usually belong to the landlord) to be conferred on laborers.[69]

The Ganapathia Pillai Commission submitted its report to the state government in May 1969.[70] On the central issue of wages its recommendations went far toward the Communist position. The commission concluded that although wages in Thanjavur had risen more than in other districts since 1959, the number of days of full employment in East Thanjavur was so low (150 to 190) that most laborers did not earn a living wage for the full year. It also concluded that landowners were capable of paying the higher rates and therefore recommended fixation of varying rates for the non-harvest operations and of a uniform rate of six local measures (about 5.7 litres) per *kalam* for harvest. The commission agreed with the CPI position on the deduction of *kalavadi* and use of the litre measure (it recommended that enforcement of this provision be transferred from the labor department to the panchayat unions). However, the commission did not recommend that payment of wages in kind be mandatory, nor that landowners be barred from employing outside labor unless doing so resulted in a threat to law and order, nor that police intervention in labor disputes be curtailed. But it did recommend that "Labor Courts" be established in various parts of East Thanjavur to help settle disputes. This provided the crucial element of enforcement missing in the various tripartite agreements. Finally, it recommended that a committee review the wage rates every three years.

[69] Agricultural Workers Association, "Memorandum," passim.
[70] Ganapathia Pillai, "Report of the Commission of Inquiry on the Agrarian Labour Problems of East Thanjavur District," typewritten [1969].

In June 1969 the CPI's Workers' Association moved to try to force the state government to implement the recommendations of the commission immediately by issuing an ordinance.[71] On the other side, the East Thanjavur Mirasdars' Association passed a resolution on July 15 refusing to accept the recommendations of the commission.[72] Another two-day demonstration in support of the commission's recommendations was organized by the CPI on July 16 and 17. Over two thousand volunteers were arrested on the two days, most of them in Mannargudi, the CPI's stronghold.[73]

On August 1 the governor of Tamil Nadu promulgated an ordinance implementing, with a few changes, the wage-related recommendations of the commission for the six eastern taluks of Thanjavur. A uniform regular daily wage of Rs. 4.25 or 6 litres of paddy and Rs. 1.25 was prescribed for all kinds of cultivation work.[74] For harvest the wage would be six litres (rather than six measures, which is less) of paddy for every 45 litres harvested, before any deduction for *kalavadi*. The ordinance also established conciliation offices in Mayuram, Nagapattinam, and Mannargudi, to which a laborer or landowner could apply for settlement of a wage dispute. The provisions of the ordinance were passed into law later in the year by the Tamil Nadu Agricultural Labourers' Fair Wages Act of 1969, which made them effective through August 3, 1972.

The overall Communist reaction to the ordinance was generally favourable, although the CPM's was noticeably less so, and even the CPI had some problem with it. The latter would have preferred that it mandate payment of wages in kind and employment of local labor, but it did tell its followers to return to work. The *mirasdars* were of course unhappy. Their principal complaints were that the ordinance did not guarantee to them the right to use imported labor and did not fix the working hours. They also preferred to pay the wages in cash.[75]

But in spite of these complaints the Fair Wages settlement gained rapid and widespread acceptance among both landowners and la-

[71] *Ulavu Chelvam*, July 1, 1969, p. 8.

[72] *Hindu*, July 16 and 18, 1969.

[73] Ibid., July 17 and 18, 1969. The CPI newsletter, *Ulavu Chelvam*, reported later that 4,090 persons had been arrested between July 16 and July 21 (*Ulavu Chelvam*, August 1, 1969, p. 3).

[74] *Hindu*, August 2, 1969.

[75] Ibid., August 8 and 11, 1969. Landowners preferred to pay cash because they wanted to maintain their stock of paddy in order to take advantage of market fluctuations (*Ulavu Chelvam*, January 1, 1969, p. 12).

borers in East Thanjavur. For the next three years (the life of the
original act) there were only isolated instances of conflict over wages
in Thanjavur. The fact that the act did not regulate the use of
outside labor did not, as it had in the past, lead to widespread
evasion by landowners because it was clear to them that payment
of the new wages was politically inescapable. In fact, the conciliation
machinery set up by the act was hardly used at all. The only office
that received a significant number of complaints was the one in
Nagapattinam, and even there the numbers were small: seventy-
six in 1969, twenty-two in 1970, and thirty-five in 1971.[76] In fact,
by 1970 or 1971 wages in some areas were higher than the rates
fixed by the Fair Wages Act.[77] This was possible because of the
economic cushion created by the sizable increases in productivity
in those years.

The sudden deceleration of the Thanjavur labor movement after
the Fair Wages settlement demonstrates clearly the limited goals of
the movement, as does the failure of nonwage-related agitations in
1969 and 1970. In July 1969, while the CPI was focusing on the
wage issue, the CPM attempted to carry out an "antitractor" agitation in Thanjavur. As described in Chapter 9, it was a dismal
failure because it encountered stiff resistance from the state government, little support among laborers, and divided opinion in the
CPM's own ranks. In 1970, as part of a symbolic national effort
the CPI organized a "land grab" movement in Thanjavur. Large
farms in seven villages around the district were to be "occupied"
by the CPI volunteers. But in the week before the "grab" was to
take place the DMK arrested thousands of CPI leaders and workers
statewide, most of them in Thanjavur. Not surprisingly, the movement fizzled out completely.[78] Although the preemptive arrests
were a factor in preventing the Communists from making even a
symbolic point, it was also clear that the movement had no popular
support in the district.

The CPI played the major leadership role in the 1968/1969 wage
agitations, spurred on by the CPM's successes in the 1967 elections.
The CPM's activity was limited by two factors: its continuing alliance
with the DMK, and its organizational weakness at the local level in
Thanjavur. However, by 1972, when the Fair Wages Act was due

[76] Data collected by the author from the conciliation offices. The Mayuram office
received two complaints in 1969 and fourteen in 1970.
[77] Interview with K. R. Krishnaswami, conciliation officer, Mannargudi, December
13, 1972.
[78] *Hindu*, August 9-11, 1970, and August 17, 1970.

to expire, these roles had been reversed. The CPI had made an alliance with the DMK for the 1971 general elections. That alliance was broken in March 1972, but during this period a close relationship developed between the DMK and the two most important CPI leaders in Thanjavur, Manali Kandaswamy and A. K. Subbiah. The resulting rift between the state CPI leaders and the Thanjavur leaders, which led to the latter's resignation from the Party in 1973, surely constrained the Party's activity in the district.[79] In addition, although the CPM was still not as strongly entrenched in the district as the CPI, it had established itself more firmly at the local level, especially in the Nagapattinam area.

As early as April 1972 the Thanjavur District Mirasdars' Association went on record opposing revision of farm wages when the Fair Wages settlement expired on August 3. In July both the CPI and the CPM came out for higher wages, but now it was the CPM that announced plans for a strike if the new demands were not met. Soon the pattern of events began to resemble the 1968/1969 pattern. Extra police were stationed in the district to protect farm work. On August 1 an ordinance extended the life of the act for another three years but without any revision of the wage rates. By now Thanjavur landowners were divided over how to respond. At an August 1 meeting of the Mirasdars' Association some members said they were already paying higher wages while others did not want to pay more and suggested that cultivation of the *kuruvai* crop should be abandoned as a way of thwarting the laborers. Starting August 2, the CPM-led Union organized a series of strikes and work stoppages, mostly in Nagapattinam and Nannilam taluks, which resulted in the arrest of over eight hundred laborers by August 10. On August 8 the Mirasdars' Association requested a tripartite conference to resolve the issue. The conference was held in Thanjavur on August 13, and the participants agreed that the regular daily wage rate would be raised from a cash equivalent of Rs. 4.25 to Rs. 5.20. A few clashes between Marxist laborers and landowners occurred in the Nagapattinam area in late August and September 1972, apparently to force compliance with the new rates, but on the whole the transition to the new rates went smoothly.[80]

In 1973 the CPM was even more isolated in its fight over the wage issue. The Thanjavur CPI leaders Kandaswamy and Subbiah

[79] See Chapter 8.

[80] This account is based on press reports appearing in the *Hindu* and the *Indian Express* (Madras) from April through September 1972.

had resigned from the Party and formed the Tamil Nadu Communist Party, in a tacit alliance with the DMK. Furthermore, by now the DMK had developed a following of its own among Thanjavur laborers. Thus, when another tripartite conference was held on July 1, 1973, the CPI and DMK labor groups agreed to a small increase in the daily wage that the CPM rejected.[81] Once again there were a few clashes between landowners or police and laborers loyal to the CPM in Nagapattinam, but the CPM's effort to widen the conflict had died out by September, marking the end of this active period in the history of the Thanjavur labor movement.[82] On February 23, 1976, the *Times of India* reported that in Thanjavur "disputes relating to wages and other matters between landholders and agricultural labor, which were frequent in the past, are no longer there and farm operations are going smoothly."

How do we account for the agrarian calm that had descended on Thanjavur within four years after the militant and violent confrontations of 1968 and 1969? The explanation is similar in many ways to that offered for the decline of the movement in the early period. First, there was substantial improvement in economic conditions in Thanjavur in the early 1970s. The increases in paddy production in 1968/1969 and 1971/1972 and increases in the paddy procurement price made the absorption of wage increases relatively painless for the landowners. And at least until late 1971 general prices were not rising as sharply as they had in the mid- and late-1960s. Second, once again there had been changes in the strategies and fortunes of the Communist parties at both the national and state levels that bore on the Thanjavur situation. In particular, the demise of the Naxalite movement led to a reassessment of strategy and tactics within the Communist camp. Both the CPI and the CPM began in 1973/1974 to question the agrarian strategy and tactics they had adopted in the 1960s, such as the emphasis on labor and the more militant tactical line. Third, the competition between CPI and the CPM for control of the Communist political base in Thanjavur had weakened their control of the labor movement and made it easier for other parties to win labor support.

This brings to the fourth and perhaps most important consideration, the role the DMK played in Thanjavur. It should be noted, as it was in the section on organization, that the electoral alliances first between the DMK and the CPM and later between the DMK

---

[81] *Hindu*, July 2, 1973. See also *Peasant and Labour* 2 (August 1973): 17.

[82] *Hindu*, July 17, 20, 23, 1973, and August 15, 1973.

and the CPI acted to contain the movement. More importantly, while it did not act as openly or as forcefully as it did in the tenancy area, the DMK played an increasingly direct and active role in the Thanjavur labor situation, most effectively in the support of wage increases. Furthermore, other DMK policies brought it support in the labor community. Most popular was the *kudiyiruppu* program.

As mentioned briefly above, most laborers and many small tenants, especially in the Zone 2 and 3 areas, lived in houses situated on wastelands belonging to local landowners. This gave the landowners an important weapon for intimidating laborers. If a laborer defied a landowner he and his family could be evicted from their home, and the house might be destroyed. In 1971 the DMK government passed the Tamil Nadu Occupants and Kudiyiruppu (Conferment of Ownership) Act.[83] This act automatically gave laborers and agriculturalists (tenants and small owners) residing in *kudiyiruppu* dwellings ownership of the land and the structure. Thanjavur was the first district in the state to which the act applied. The DMK government also instituted a vigorous program to help laborers and tenants build improved housing on the sites they received. Both programs earned the Party widespread support in the Thanjavur labor community; CPI leader Manali Kandaswamy cited these programs as an important reason for his support of the DMK. The Party's success with its wage and housing policies emboldened it to begin building labor front organizations of its own in Thanjavur, which by 1975 had a significant following.[84] All of this was of course intended to widen the DMK's support in rural areas. One landlord put it well: "The ruling party always wants the confidence of the major number of voters who are always in bulk laborers."[85] Thus, the very logic of competitive party politics tended to disperse the mobilization of labor in Thanjavur into different party channels.

This is not to say that the Communists had been displaced as the dominant political force among laborers in the Zone 2 and 3 areas of Thanjavur. The identification established between laborers and, in some areas, poor tenants and the Communists over a twenty-

[83] *The Tamil Nadu Occupants and Kudiyiruppu (Conferment of Ownership) Act 1971 (Act No. 40 of 1971). With rules and Notifications up to 25-4-73* (Salem: Viyaya Pathippagam, 1973).

[84] *Hindu*, April 8, 1975.

[85] One of the replies to questionnaires mailed to about 125 members of two landowner associations, the Tamil Nadu Farmers' Forum and the East Thanjavur District Mirasdars' Association.

five-year period was too strong to be broken so easily. For instance, after four years of labor peace in Thanjavur the Communists still made a strong showing in the 1977 legislative assembly elections in the Zone 2 and 3 areas.[86] However, the Communists were themselves no longer a monolithic force. Fragmentation within the Communist camp contributed to the "pluralization" of the Thanjavur labor movement and, in spite of the militancy introduced by the competition between the CPI and the CPM, to its reformist trend.

The CPI-CPM split was, of course, a most important divisive force. To understand how this division developed in Thanjavur we must first examine ideological differences between the two parties on the agrarian question.[87] I have already noted that the CPM's search for a more revolutionary strategy caused it to look to the poor peasantry for support. The outbreak of the Naxalbari rebellion and the emergence of the CPI(M-L) accentuated this emphasis. While competition with the CPM together with the whole political environment of the late 1960s induced the CPI also to take a more militant approach, important tactical differences between the two parties persisted. The CPI's view of the role of the peasantry was still more influenced by Marx, emphasizing the difficulty of organizing the peasantry and thus continuing to give the urban proletariat the leading role in achieving socialism. The CPI therefore aimed at building a mass movement of laborers *and* poor peasants, *without* alienating the middle peasantry, as an instrument for bringing about a national democratic coalition. In other words, the CPI was not anxious to wage class war in the countryside and therefore was generally committed to peaceful mobilization of the peasantry.

The CPM, on the other hand, developed a Maoist strategy of revolution in which the rural proletariat had nearly equal importance with the urban working class, thereby adopting a militant, class-struggle tactical line of mobilizing the rural proletariat. Unlike the CPI, the CPM emphasized a sharp differentiation between the poor and the nonpoor peasant, thus giving greater importance to the agricultural laborer. A. K. Gopalan, a CPM leader long active in Communist agrarian affairs in South India, declared in 1968: "Agricultural labourers now constitute 25 to 40 percent of the population in most of the states and we have to make them the

[86] The CPI won easily in the Mannargudi and Tiruthuraipoondi constituencies, and the CPM squeezed out the DMK in Nagapattinam constituency. Together the CPI and CPM polled a majority of the votes in the Tiruvarur constituency, while the CPM came in a strong second in Poompuhar and Kuttalam constituencies.

[87] The following discussion is based on Sen Gupta, *Communism*, pp. 307-312.

hub of all our activity."[88] However, the CPM did believe it was necessary to move towards "creation of a single class of exploited peasantry" by gradually merging the struggle for wages and the struggle for land. Finally, although the CPM did not share the CPI (M-L) view that the Indian countryside was ripe for armed guerrilla warfare, it was more amenable than the CPI to the use of violence in building a mass movement of the poor against the nonpoor peasantry.

In some ways the activities of the CPI and the CPM in Thanjavur seem to reflect these ideological differences. But in other ways they demonstrate necessary adjustments to regional and local political and agro-economic realities. We saw previously (Table 85) that by 1970 the CPI and the CPM had developed geographically and agro-economically somewhat distinct support bases in Thanjavur. The CPI's stronghold was the Mannargudi area, in which Communist strength is correlated with both labor *and* tenancy, and the CPM's stronghold was the Nagapattinam area, in which Communist strength is correlated with labor only. Nagapattinam is also the area within Zones 2 and 3 where the agrarian structure is most sharply polarized and labor therefore most potentially radical.

Thus, consistent with its ideology the CPM focused its efforts on militant mobilization of labor. When we compare the correlations of CPI and CPM panchayat control with agro-economic characteristics (see Table 90) we find further evidence of this fact: CPI strength is correlated with Scheduled Caste population (labor *and* tenants); CPM strength is not. Furthermore, the correlation between CPM strength and agricultural labor remains significant *even* when we control for Scheduled Caste.[89] It is also interesting to note that CPM strength is positively correlated with agricultural development, and CPI strength is negatively correlated with land value. The former relationship probably reflects the especially negative impact of double cropping on landowner-laborer relations in Nagapattinam and the latter the CPI's support in areas of generalized agrarian poverty, encompassing *both* labor and poor tenants.

Support from agricultural labor of course underlay the strength of both parties. The difference in their support bases derived from

[88] Ibid., pp. 311-312.

[89] Hardgrave found in Kerala a clear distinction between CPI and CPM support bases. CPM support was greatest in districts with high percentages of agricultural laborers, while CPI support was greatest in the district with the lowest percentage of agricultural laborers in the state (Hardgrave, "Communist Parties of Kerala," p. 206).

TABLE 90

Agro-Economic Correlates of CPI and CPM Panchayat Control in
Zones 2 and 3

Agro-Economic Characteristics	N	Panchayat Control	
		CPI	CPM
Scheduled Caste, 1971	709	.335*	.006
Agricultural labor, 1971	709	.157*	.115*
Tenants, 1971	709	−.090**	−.064
Agricultural development rating, 1971	709	.026	.152*
Land value, 1961	705	−.164*	.000
Agrarian density, 1971	709	−.044	−.023
Isolation index, 1971	680	.059	.036
Overall development, 1971	709	−.068	.038
Controlling for scheduled caste			
Agricultural labor, 1971	706	−.022	.094*
Tenants, 1971	706	−.129*	−.071

* Significant at .001 level.
** Significant at .01 level.

the type of agrarian structure in which the agricultural labor force
was embedded, which of course had implications for the potential
militancy of the labor force. The two parties developed their bases
in areas whose structures were more suited to their tactics.

There were also some differences in the CPI's and the CPM's
approaches to the issues. They shared the fundamental wage issue,
although the militancy of their stand on it varied with other circumstances. The CPI disavowed the CPM's antitractor agitations
on these grounds, claiming that the tractor did not affect labor
adversely. Clearly the CPI took the more moderate stance of avoiding issues that might alienate landowners without resulting in any
direct benefit to labor. Furthermore, although the CPI was con-
centrating its efforts on agricultural labor, it continued through
the Agriculturalists' Association to appeal to small landowners on
the issues of crop prices, inputs, markets, et cetera (see Chapter
8). The CPM, on the other hand, focused its efforts entirely on
labor.

Whether there was a real difference between the CPI and the

CPM on the use of violence in Thanjavur is less clear. When I asked the secretary of the CPM Workers' Association what the difference between them and the CPI was, he replied: "They believe in talk, we believe only in violence." In the light of what we know about the CPM's activity in Thanjavur, this was clearly an exaggeration. However, at least after 1970 the CPM was more militant in its agitational tactics. For instance, in 1972 the CPI made its demand for a wage increase through a memo to the collector, while the CPM pressed the issue by organizing its followers to prevent farm work by outside laborers, a tactic that in the past had led directly to violence.[90]

Of course, in all these respects the CPI and CPM were forced to adapt their tactics to the agrarian situation in Thanjavur and to the political situation in the state. By 1967 the radical potential of tenancy in Thanjavur had been undercut by agro-economic change and agrarian reforms. Whatever radical potential still existed was derived from the situation of landless or largely landless labor. There were also serious constraints on the radical mobilization of labor in the district. First, the agro-climatic and agro-economic diversity of Thanjavur imposed a "structural quarantine" on the labor movement. The objective conditions most likely to foster "class action" were confined to certain areas. Even within Zones 2 and 3 structural conditions were not uniform or unchanging. For instance, polarization was greater in Nagapattinam than in Mannargudi or Tiruthuraipoondi. Second, the continuing salience of caste cleavages in Thanjavur's agrarian structure was a major obstacle to the sustained mobilization of both laborers and poor tenants. The predominance of Harijans in the labor force in Zones 2 and 3 was a facilitating factor in the rise of the movement in those areas but a limiting factor outside them.[91]

Similarly, the fact that by the late 1960s almost all laborers in Thanjavur were daily wage earners, with no direct attachment to the land, was both an opportunity and an obstacle. On the one hand, because laborers were now more independent of landowners and dependent solely on wage income it was easier to organize and mobilize them around the wage issue. On the other hand, it was harder to organize and mobilize them on other issues such as the

[90] *Ulavu Chelvam*, August 15, 1972, p. 2; *Indian Express*, August 2, 1972; *Hindu*, August 7 and 8, 1972.

[91] See Mythili Shivaraman, "Thanjavur: Rumblings of Class Struggle in Tamil Nadu," in *Imperialism and Revolution in South Asia*, ed. Kathleen Gough and Hari P. Sharma (New York and London: Monthly Review Press, 1973), p. 251.

ownership and control of land. Thus, for instance, the CPM would have found it very difficult to merge the struggle for wages and the struggle for land in Thanjavur. Any hope of accomplishing this was lessened further by the second wave of tenancy reforms.

Finally, changes in agricultural technology in the mid- and late-1960s in Thanjavur contributed in two ways to the realization of wage demands, thereby helping to defuse the conflict between land-owners and laborers. First, the increase in double cropping strengthened the bargaining position of labor. Second, increases in productivity made landowners more willing to pay higher wage rates.

The net result of these several internal characteristics and developments was reformism. In the late 1960s the agrarian structure of Zones 2 and 3 resembled in many ways what Paige terms the "plantation system." Paige finds that "reform labor movements" characterize plantation systems: a radical, class-conscious working force confronts an economically powerful upper class willing to make concessions and thus conflict focuses on the price of labor rather than the redistribution of property or the seizure of state.[92] This describes the Thanjavur situation quite well. But it is important to recognize that Paige's sharecropping system, which he finds leads to revolutionary socialist movements, and the plantation system have several characteristic in common. Sharecroppers resemble wage laborers in four respects: 1) weak ties to the land; 2) occupational homogeneity; 3) work group interdependence, and 4) a tendency to participate in workers' organizations and Communist parties.[93] This overlapping of the two systems certainly is characteristic of Thanjavur and helps to explain why radicalism has been an immanent but never yet fully realized characteristic of the agrarian system in eastern Thanjavur.

Paige argues that the critical difference between the sharecropping and plantation systems, and thus between reformist and revolutionary outcomes, lies in the nature of the upper class. In the sharecropping system a weak landed aristocracy rigidly committed to maintaining its position means that a direct attack on the agrarian system is the only way the work force can achieve economic gains. In other words, because the stakes are zero-sum rather than incremental, revolution is necessary. In the case of Thanjavur it is

[92] Jeffery M. Paige, *Agrarian Revolution: Social Movements and Export Agriculture in the Underdeveloped World* (New York: The Free Press, 1975), pp. 48-49.
[93] Ibid., pp. 58-61.

certainly true that the position of the landlords has made a difference in the character of agrarian conflict. The more powerful position and rigid stance of Thanjavur *mirasdars* in the 1940s resulted in greater militancy on the part of laborers and a higher level of violence than in the 1960s. By the later period landlords were both less able to resist and more willing to make concessions. The change was due largely to external economic and political forces. I have already mentioned the impact of new technology in making landowners both more vulnerable and more pliable. In addition, regulation of the agricultural economy of Thanjavur, such as price ceilings and restrictions on marketing, made agriculture less profitable, with the result that many Thanjavur landlords left agriculture for other more profitable occupations.

But more important, in my view, was the political isolation of Thanjavur landlords that accompanied the development of competitive party politics after Independence. Although repression was a significant element in the governmental response to agrarian radicalism in Thanjavur in both periods, accommodation of some of the laborers' and tenants' demands became the more important response. The beginnings of this shift were evident in the late 1940s, as the government intervened first by sponsoring negotiations and later by mandating settlements. The tenancy reform legislation of the 1950s was a further extension of this response, as when the Congress, facing elections in 1957, felt it was necessary to seek support among the numerous and politically active non-Brahmin tenants of Thanjavur. The DMK, seeking to widen its support in rural areas, continued the accommodation of tenants and went a step further, first supporting and then sponsoring pro-labor measures that largely satisfied, at least temporarily, the basically reformist demands inherent in the Thanjavur agrarian situation.

The impact of competitive party politics on Thanjavur is richly illustrated by the statements of large landowners whom I asked to describe what had happened to the relationship between landowners, tenants, and laborers and what should be done about it. Here are a few examples of their responses:

What happened?

> Due to the interference of the politicians, there is no harmony in the relationship.

As the tenants enjoy more privileges with the government, they don't care to pay the rent regularly.

Different laws of the government have very much affected the relationship between the owners and the laborers.

It is difficult to make a profit due to the interference of politicians.

Politicians always with an eye on the ballot box revel in creating disunity between owner, tenant and cultivator.

It is very difficult to make a profit because the agricultural costs have gone up. Irresponsible politicians have interfered and have made the situation worse.

The relationship has become worse with the interference by politicians and government.

They [laborers] always pose a hostile attitude towards landowners due to instigation by politicians.

What should be done?

Whenever the government brings changes in the agricultural sector it should consult the representatives of the landlords.

Government without party interest should rule.

There should be no government interference in the relationship between landowners and laborers.

No parties should be there. Laws should be promulgated to create a code of conduct for the different party leaders.

Laborers should be relieved from the clutches of leaders or politicians, and a sense of responsibility should be inculcated.

A partyless community must be established. Representatives who are also partyless must be chosen from *mirasdars*, laborers, and tenants, and the laws that pertain to agriculture should be laid down after consulting such representatives.

The problem will be solved and prosperity will usher in if and only when the various groups such as *mirasdars*, tenants, and laborers . . . relieve themselves from the clutches of the gambling politicians and live for the nation as a whole.

From the landowners' point of view the result of the widening politicization of agrarian relations in Thanjavur was destabilizing and threatening. But from another point of view the effect was "deradicalizing": the interest of the major parties in Tamil Nadu in attracting electoral support from an expanding population of politically conscious citizens was clearly a major force in turning the Thanjavur labor movement into reformist channels.

The other major political factor was of course the strategies and fortunes of the Communist parties. Because they alone provided leadership and organization for the mobilization of agricultural labor in Thanjavur the movement has been most active and militant at precisely those moments when the Communist parties have been most active and militant on the agrarian front. At the same time, the long-term reformist trend of the Thanjavur labor movement is in large part due to the long-term primacy of the "peaceful, parliamentary path" in Indian communism. Developments in Thanjavur have also been shaped by the Communist parties' organizational strengths and weaknesses and electoral fortunes. One result of the "political pluralization" of the Thanjavur labor movement might be that it will be less dependent on and affected by the Communist parties. Just how far that goes depends on many factors, such as the half-life of the Communist identification of Thanjavur laborers, further developments in Communist strategy and tactics, and the degree to which other parties are able to continue to be responsive to the Thanjavur situation.

While arguing that the mobilization of labor and thus the development of agrarian radicalism in Thanjavur District have been heavily influenced by external political factors, I do not wish to give the impression that I believe internal agro-economic conditions are either fixed or unimportant. In fact, as is evident from my study, it is my conclusion that the sources of agrarian radicalism (or reformism) in Thanjavur lie in *the interaction of economic and political factors, both internal and external.* I have argued that certain characteristics of the agrarian structure in Thanjavur are both sources of and obstacles to radical mobilization. Thus, the agrarian structure of Thanjavur represents a range of possible outcomes, different from others but in no sense determinant. The actual outcome depends on the combination of internal and external political factors.

CHAPTER 11

Conclusion: Modernization and Agrarian Society

"THE INDIAN VILLAGE," writes Gunnar Myrdal in *Asian Drama*, "is like a complex molecule among whose parts extreme tensions have been built up. Although the tensions crisscross in a manner that maintains equilibrium, it is conceivable that they may reorganize in a way that would explode the molecule. This would perhaps not happen spontaneously but as a result of forceful onslaught from outside."[1]

Myrdal's metaphor captures, perhaps a bit dramatically, the key issues I have addressed in this study. First, to continue the analogy, I have tried to discover what kind of organization, what internal structure, makes the molecule at least potentially explosive. Myrdal suggests that explosive potential is minimized where economic and social cleavages are crosscutting. Conversely, I have found that, at least in Thanjavur District, the potential for agrarian radicalism is greatest where the agrarian structure is relatively polarized.

Second, I have asked what causes the molecule to become polarized. Myrdal suggests that it must be due to external forces. Much of the literature on agrarian radicalism projects a similar view: that the structural sources of agrarian radicalism are the result of the impact of wider economic and social change. While it is certainly true that external forces are usually necessary to detonate an explosion, Stinchcombe, Zagoria, and Paige have argued that the structural conditions containing the explosive potential are as much a function of structural adaptation to agro-ecological conditions as of the impact of such forces as commercialization and the spread of state authority. While the limitations of this study have not allowed more than a superficial analysis of the historical role of such forces in Thanjavur, the evidence from other studies suggests that contemporary structural conditions in Thanjavur are not primarily the result of the breakdown of the "traditional peas-

---

[1] Quoted in Bhabani Sen Gupta, *Communism in Indian Politics* (New York: Columbia University Press, 1972), p. 288.

ant society" by the forces of modernization. What is made clear by the data presented in this study is that structural variations are closely associated with ecological variations. Thus, I am tempted to question the great importance attached to capitalism and imperialism as distant causes of agrarian radicalism.

Finally, I have examined how the explosion is detonated, or, more accurately in the case of Thanjavur, how the radical potential is mobilized, and what form the movement takes. Structural considerations are important here too; the form the movement takes reflects limitations inherent in the structure. But outside forces, particularly political forces, become very important at the mobilizational stage. The response of outside political forces to the radical potential in Thanjavur shaped and eventually transformed its political expression. The possibilities and limitations inherent in the constellation of political forces in a given society are a factor afforded too little attention in the literature on agrarian radicalism. In reviewing these issues in greater depth below I will attempt to relate the results of my analysis of Thanjavur District to the major arguments in the literature on agrarian radicalism.

Agrarian radicalism in Thanjavur is clearly associated with an agrarian structure that closely approximates Stinchcombe's and Zagoria's "family-size tenancy" and Paige's "decentralized sharecropping." This resemblance was greatest during the early phase of agrarian radicalism in Thanjavur before many of the *pannaiyals* and *varamdars* had been reduced to the status of daily laborers. The structure of Zones 2 and 3 was clearly dominated by a landed upper class that drew most of its income from the land and a lower class (poor tenants and laborers) that received most, if not all, of its income in wages. Because of the relatively poor soil and irrigation conditions in these areas, most production was carried out on large estates. It is likely that the relationship between the landlord and the sharecropper or laborer was strained somewhat by the growth of commercial markets for rice in the late-nineteenth and early-twentieth centuries.[2] The opportunity for commercial gain undoubtedly caused many landlords to try to extract more from the cultivators, especially because in a labor-intensive crop such as rice, production on large landed estates (where the quality of the labor input is poor) was less efficient than on small holdings. Thus, to gain an economic advantage large landowners had to rely on con-

[2] Kathleen Gough, "Colonial Economics in Southeast India," *Economic and Political Weekly* 12 (March 26, 1977): 546-548.

trol of a semiservile labor force. In Thanjavur this control was facilitated by sharp ethnic stratification between noncultivators and cultivators. Most of the *varamdars* and *pannaiyals* of the Zone 2 and 3 areas were Harijans (even in the nineteenth century), who were prevented by their caste status from owning land.[3]

Although commercialization may have contributed to tension in the relationship between landlords and sharecroppers and laborers in Thanjavur prior to 1940, it definitely did not bring about a breakdown of the agrarian structure, especially in the Zone 2 and 3 areas. This was mainly due to the fact that paddy cultivation was very difficult to capitalize; for instance, it could not be effectively mechanized. However, in the Zone 1 areas other modernizing forces did contribute to structural change. The urban occupational opportunities open to Brahmins drew many Brahmin landlords in Zone 1 from the land. In Zones 2 and 3, however, the predominantly non-Brahmin landlords tended to remain in agriculture, although many probably chose to live in the nearby towns. The departure of the Brahmins in Zone 1 provided some upward mobility to the cultivating class, who were, furthermore, less constrained by caste status. But in Zones 2 and 3 the avenues of upward mobility for sharecroppers and laborers were virtually nonexistent. The landlords remained close enough to exert control, while at the same time their departure to nearby towns weakened whatever reciprocal qualities their relationship to the cultivators might have had.

Thus, in the Zone 2 and 3 areas the situation of the landlord class prior to 1940 appears to be a humble example of Moore's principle of failed commercialization. The failure of the landed class to commercialize successfully, *or* to be otherwise modernized, allowed the agrarian structure of the premodern period to survive into the modern period in a weakened state. Furthermore, as Paige points out, the failure of the upper class to commercialize meant that the agricultural product was static and thus the issue between landlords, and cultivators zero-sum. Again, although there are no data to document this, we would expect that productivity was more sluggish in the relatively unfavorable ecological conditions of Zones 2 and 3 than in the more favorable conditions of Zone 1.

The agrarian structure of Thanjavur's Zones 2 and 3 also resem-

[3] Ibid., p. 548. See also Dharma Kumar, *Land and Caste in South India: Agricultural Labour in Madras Presidency in the Nineteenth Century* (Cambridge: Cambridge University Press, 1965), pp. 41-45.

bles the "family-size tenancy" and "decentralized sharecropping" systems in terms of the organization of the lower class, especially prior to 1940. First, there was relatively little internal stratification within the cultivating class. The two major cultivating groups were the sharecroppers and the attached laborers, and there was little difference between them. Both had weak ties to the land and were therefore more willing to take the risks involved in political organization. In Zone 1, on the other hand, there were relatively more small owners and fixed-rent tenants whose ties to the land were stronger and who were more likely to avoid the risk of involvement in radical political movements. In Moore's terms, property divisions in Zones 2 and 3 favored radical solidarity, and property divisions in Zone 1 favored conservative solidarity. Second, the predominance of wage earners in Zones 2 and 3 meant that there was greater occupational homogeneity and work-group interdependence in the cultivating community. This also facilitated the development of radical solidarity, whereas in Zone 1 the diversity of agro-economic statuses in the cultivating community inhibited it. Furthermore, economic homogeneity and heterogeneity were matched and reinforced by parallel caste homogeneity and heterogeneity.

The agrarian structure of Zones 2 and 3 favored the development of group solidarity and collective action. It is no accident, therefore, that the Communists' early organizational efforts in the area were successful. Nor is it surprising that when wartime price rises squeezed the area's sharecroppers and laborers they responded readily to the Communist calls for militant and often violent action. However, even in the 1940s the demands of the Thanjavur movement did not extend to land redistribution or overthrow of the state. Their demands were more the reformist demands of the plantation laborer; they sought changes in the distribution of the income from the land in the form of increased wages or decreased rents. This I attribute partly to the fact that the agrarian structure in eastern Thanjavur was in fact a blend of the sharecropping and plantation systems[4] and partly to the limited goals of the Communist lead-

[4] Paige emphasizes that his fourfold table by no means exhausts the possible types of agrarian systems. He points out that the sources of income for noncultivators and cultivators are continuous rather than dichotomous variables. Thus, it is logically possible to find almost unlimited local variability in agrarian structure. Given the role of highly variable ecological conditions in producing any agrarian structure, we should not be suprised to find many variations on Paige's four or five types. See Jeffery M. Paige, *Agrarian Revolution: Social Movements and Export Agriculture in the Underdeveloped World* (New York: The Free Press, 1975), pp. 10-12.

ership. The *pannaiyal's* ties to the land were even weaker than those of the sharecropper, and by this time the process of conversion of *pannaiyals* into daily laborers had begun. We would expect the laborers to be less amenable to demands for redistribution of property, especially when we remember strong sanctions against land-ownership by Harijans. In addition, we have seen that the ideology of the Communist leadership at this time was confused at best.

The structural distinctiveness of the Zone 2 and 3 areas of course also played a major role in the more recent phase of agrarian radicalism in Thanjavur. I have shown that the potential for radicalism and radical mobilization remained confined to these areas due to the persistent opposition between large landlords and poor tenants and laborers. The reforms of the 1950s served further to reinforce the structural sources of agrarian radicalism in Zones 2 and 3 and to undercut them in Zone 1. First, they virtually ended the *pannaiyal* system, creating a large daily labor force in its stead. Second, they offered an avenue of upward mobility to many tenants, especially those outside Zones 2 and 3 who were already relatively secure, and a promise of eventual improvement for many others. The combined effect of these changes was to deradicalize the tenancy issue and to concentrate the radical potential even more in labor and labor issues.

Furthermore, the character of the Thanjavur labor force changed quite dramatically after 1950. The *pannaiyal* system, in which the laborer was "attached" to a single landlord, helped to maintain a semiservile labor force. The almost complete displacement of the *pannaiyal* by daily, "free" labor had two consequences. First, the laborers were more independent of the landlords (in the sense that they no longer pledged loyalty to the landlord in exchange for security), and thus more amenable to organization in workers' associations. Second, the wage issue became even more important. Precisely because the relationship to the landlord no longer contained any sort of a security guarantee nor assured employment throughout the year wage *rates* were absolutely vital to labor. Laborers had to try to earn enough income for subsistence throughout the year during the peak periods when they knew they could get work. Thus, by the mid-1960s the composition and the economic orientation of the lower class in the Zone 2 and 3 areas resembled those of a plantation labor force.

At the same time important changes were also taking place at the upper end of the agrarian structure of eastern Thanjavur. More and more landowners were following in the footsteps of Zone 1 landowners and leaving the occupation of agriculture. While this did not immediately open up avenues of upward mobility for Zones 2 and 3 tenants and laborers who were economically and socially too depressed, unlike their Zone 1 counterparts, to move into the gap, it did tend to weaken the solidarity of the landowners and thus to reduce the rigidity of the confrontation between landowners and laborers. Second, technological change had two complementary effects: the increase in double cropping in the mid-1960s strengthened the bargaining position of laborers vis-à-vis landowners, making wage gains accessible through collective action (strikes) and collective bargaining (the tripartite agreements), and a few years later the introduction of high-yielding varieties led to increases in the productivity of land which in turn made landowners more willing to compromise on the wage issue. I am not of course arguing that the landowners of eastern Thanjavur had become like the commercial upper class of the plantation system; by and large paddy production remained resistant to capitalization. But because it had become less necessary and less possible for the landowners of Zones 2 and 3 to maintain economic advantage through control of the labor force, the conflict of the late 1960s was even more clearly focused on the economic issue of the price of labor.

Thus, the changing character of the agrarian conflict in eastern Thanjavur is explained in large part by changes in the agrarian structure. In Paige's terms the agrarian structure of the area became less like that of the sharecropping system and more like that of the plantation system, with the result that the radical potential of the earlier period was now sharply diverted into reformist channels. But the major structural characteristic of the Zone 2 and 3 areas, their relative agro-economic bipolarity, did not change. Paige points out that the sharecropping and plantation systems have in common a clear contradiction between the interests of noncultivators and cultivators and a relatively homogeneous and interdependent workforce. The fact that the reformist labor movement of the late 1960s did not spread to other areas of Thanjavur District demonstrates its dependence on these structural conditions.

My findings make clear that the emergence of a radical potential and the course of radical mobilization in Thanjavur District are closely related to agrarian structural conditions and change and thus lend support to those theories of agrarian radicalism that locate its sources at least as much within agrarian society as without. The case of agrarian radicalism in Thanjavur is further evidence against the classical Marxist view that class formation within the peasantry is not possible except as an extension of urban-industrial class conflict. Eric Wolf's argument that the middle peasantry must be the base for radical agrarian mobilization reflects this classical Marxist view. He bases his argument on two characteristics of the middle peasantry: 1) their exposure to urban-commercial influences; and 2) their economic independence.

In arguing that these characteristics are necessary to radical mobilization, Wolf overlooks alternative radicalizing conditions and mobilizational paths that are illustrated by the Thanjavur case. First, the radical potential may be primarily a function of tensions and contradictions within the agrarian structure rather than of exposure to the forces of wider economic and social change. This is likely to happen where the agrarian structure throws up a clear, uncompromisable conflict of vital interests between polarized and internally homogeneous groups, as in Thanjavur District. Second, Wolf fails to take account of the fact that the economic weakness of the peasantry may be offset by collective action. Now it is true that some measure of outside leadership and organizational initiative is usually necessary to bring about collective action. But it is not accurate to say, as does Migdal, that the development of class consciousness and class mobilization among the peasantry is solely a function of external organization. For instance, if the development of class consciousness and collective action were not conditioned by structural factors, we would be hard pressed to explain why the Communists have not been at all successful in mobilizing poor tenants and laborers in areas of Thanjavur District other than Zones 2 and 3.

The classical Marxist interpretation of agrarian radicalism rests, I believe, on an extremely undifferentiated view of "traditional" peasant society. According to this view, premodern peasant society was almost universally organized in one of two patterns: the "free-holding village," in which cultivation was carried out on small owner-cultivated holdings, and the "feudal village," in which cultivation of lands owned by a lord was carried out by peasants who received a share of the crop in return. The functioning of both systems was governed by the norms of subsistence and reciprocity. According to Marx and to several of the recent writers I have examined, it was the destruction of these traditional patterns by the forces of capitalism and imperialism (economic and political modernization in Moore's terms) that created the conditions out of which peasant radicalism and, where other conditions are met, rebellion and revolution have grown. As a very general statement this is hard to quarrel with. It is difficult to find any example of agrarian radicalism in which factors such as commercialization or the spread of state authority did not play some role. However, I would argue that most studies have not sufficiently taken into account variations in agrarian structure that predated the onset of modernization and how they mediated its impact.

Although the detailed historical analysis necessary to substantiate my claim is outside the scope of this study, it seems quite clear to me that Thanjavur is a case where local historical and ecological factors are at least as important in explaining structural variations as are the forces of the market and state power. First, most studies of the subject find little evidence of major change in Thanjavur's agrarian structure and economic system between the advent of British rule and 1940. Dharma Kumar has shown that Thanjavur possessed many large landed estates and a large landless labor force as early as 1800, a fact she attributes to the demands of irrigated paddy cultivation. Furthermore she argues convincingly that the impact of British rule and the concomitant commercialization of agriculture did not bring about any widespread change in the status of agricultural laborers in the district.[5]

Kumar's findings suggest that the twentieth-century agrarian structure of Thanjavur District was *not* the result of the impoverishment of peasant proprietors under British rule. In a separate study she offers evidence that 1) landownership was more unequally distributed in Thanjavur in the mid-nineteenth century than elsewhere in the Madras Presidency, but that 2) this inequality had not increased significantly by the mid-twentieth century. Similarly, David Washbrook was unable to find evidence of major economic change in Thanjavur prior to the Depression at the earliest. Finally, despite her overall argument to the contrary, Kathleen Gough is forced to admit that "despite its trade and emigration patterns, Tanjore's agrarian relations show extraordinary continuity during British rule."[6]

[5] Kumar, *Land and Caste*, pp. 18, 31, 186-193.
[6] Dharma Kumar, "Landownership and Inequality in Madras Presidency: 1953-54 to 1946-47," *The Indian Economic and Social History Review* 12 (July-September 1975): 229-261, and D. A. Washbrook, *The Emergence of Provincial Politics: The Madras Presidency, 1870-1920* (Cambridge: Cambridge University Press, 1976), pp. 85-90. See also Washbrook, "Political Change in a Stable Society: Tanjore District 1880 to 1920," in *South India: Political Institutions and Political Change, 1880-1940*, ed. C. J. Baker and D. A. Washbrook (New Delhi: The Macmillan Co., 1975), pp. 21-24, and Gough, "Colonial Economics," p. 549.

Thus, the available evidence suggests quite strongly that Thanjavur's agrarian structure was not the result of the impact of modernization on the "traditional" peasant society. It was instead largely the product of adaptation to local agro-ecological conditions and of local historical forces, such as the system of land grants that prevailed during the Chola and Vijaynagar periods.

This is not to say that wider economic conditions had *no* impact on Thanjavur. We have seen, for instance, that the availability of urban occupations and the stresses of the Depression caused many landlords to leave agriculture. However, these effects were mediated by Thanjavur's variable agrarian structure. Because of the differential access for different castes to nonagricultural occupations the withdrawal of landlords began much earlier in the Zone 1 area where Brahmins were dominant.

Thanjavur also felt the impact of growing population. Dharma Kumar has found that by the end of the nineteenth century increases in production were not keeping pace with the growth of population in the Madras Presidency. However, in Thanjavur the pressure of growing population was minimized in two ways. First, from about 1870 to about 1930 there were high rates of emigration of labor from Thanjavur and other Madras districts abroad (particularly to the plantations of Burma, Ceylon, and Malaya). Proximity to the port at Nagapattinam made it easier for Thanjavur laborers to emigrate than for laborers elsewhere in the Presidency. Second, we have good reasons to believe, as I have shown in Chapter 5, that increasing population was absorbed with less economic distress in the irrigated paddy areas of Thanjavur than in the predominantly dry districts. Thanjavur's relatively favored position is reflected in wage trends. According to Kumar, Thanjavur was the only one of seven districts she examined in which real wage rates increased between 1873 and 1900.[7]

If irrigated paddy cultivation played a role in softening the economic impact of population growth in Thanjavur, I would again suggest that the effect was not uniform throughout the district. We have seen that the superior ecological conditions in the Zone 1 area have allowed much greater intensification of cultivation than was possible in the Zone 2 and 3 areas. Once the demand for plantation labor began to decline in the 1930s, the Zone 2 and 3 areas would have begun to feel much more acutely the pressure of growing

[7] Kumar, *Land and Caste*, pp. 119, 128-143, 165-167.

population.[8] This is another illustration of the need to assess the impact of wider change in the context of local ecological and structural variability.

Another suggestion in the literature (Frankel and Griffin) has been that technological change contributes to radical mobilization by its polarizing effect on the agrarian structure. I have shown that technological change has not had this effect in Thanjavur. It would, of course, be unrealistic to expect such an effect within a short space of time, unless the technological change itself were very rapid and radical. That has not been the case in Thanjavur. Furthermore, the available evidence suggests that the technological changes introduced in Thanjavur have not tended to increase sharply or uniformly inequalities in income between large and small farmers, owners and tenants, cultivators and laborers, et cetera. The actual impact of new technology on income distribution has varied according to the type of technology and ecological conditions. There is considerable evidence that tenants have not been able to participate fully in the use of high-yielding varieties and fertilizer. But I would argue that the political effects of actual or expected changes in tenancy *rights* have far outweighed the political effects of any such changes in income. It is true that technological change (double cropping) contributed to the unrest of the late 1960s by strengthening the bargaining position of labor (note again that this effect was pronounced in the Zone 2 and 3 areas where the switch to double cropping interacted with ecological and structural conditions and made collective action by laborers possible). However, other technological changes (the varietal-fertilizer package) helped landowners absorb wage increases and thus softened the conflict. Under certain circumstances, as Paige proposes, technological change can be a deradicalizing force.

Barrington Moore suggests that one reason for the absence of widespread and effective peasant radicalism in India may be that "modernization has but barely begun in the Indian countryside."[9] I submit that the evidence from Thanjavur District is contrary to this interpretation. Thanjavur came under the influence of capitalist and imperialist forces at a relatively early date. The first British trading post was established in Thanjavur in 1749, and the district was annexed by the East India Company in 1799. Thanjavur's

---

[8] Gough, "Colonial Economics," p. 550.

[9] Barrington Moore, Jr., *Social Origins of Dictatorship and Democracy: Lord and Peasant in the Making of the Modern World* (Boston: Beacon Press, 1966), p. 460.

agriculture was integrated with domestic and international markets in the first half of the nineteenth century: by 1817 it monopolized the grain market in the Madras Presidency, and by 1841 it was exporting a quarter of its total paddy crop.[10] Revenue exactions began well before annexation in 1799, and, although the conversion of local land control systems into *ryotwari* (individual ownership) was gradual and not complete until 1890 the process began shortly after annexation.[11]

In spite of this early encounter with "modernizing" forces most observers agree that there was relatively little change in Thanjavur's agrarian system between 1800 and 1940. The evidence suggests that this was due to the peculiarities of Thanjavur's agrarian structure: the organization of production in large estates cultivated by landless laborers, and the high degrees of stratification and control that resulted from this mode of production. Washbrook argues that this structure insulated much of Thanjavur's agrarian population from the external forces of the market.[12] In a later period, the 1930s and 1940s, the impact of falling and then rising prices was again mediated by structural conditions. And finally, in the 1960s the effects of the technological change varied according to the type of agrarian structure that prevailed in a given area.

In each period the interaction of modernizing forces and local structural conditions had a different result. In the nineteenth and early twentieth centuries, when the mode of production was more uniform throughout the irrigated areas of the district, the agrarian structure limited the impact of modernization on the peasantry. In the 1930s and 1940s the interaction of economic change and a more variegated agrarian structure spawned agrarian radicalism in one area and inhibited it in another. In the 1960s the interaction of technological change and structural conditions had an overall deradicalizing effect, but for different reasons in different areas.

My general point here is of course that the impact of modernization is mediated by local ecological and structural conditions, and thus the political effects of modernization are not everywhere the

[10] Gough, "Colonial Economics," pp. 541, 545-546. According to Washbrook, Thanjavur paddy had been cultivated for the market for "centuries" before the British (Washbrook, *Emergence of Provincial Politics*, p. 86).

[11] Gough, "Colonial Economics," pp. 541-547. According to Gough, East India Company revenues amounted to 53 percent of Thanjavur's gross produce in 1800/1801.

[12] Washbrook, *Emergence of Provincial Politics*, p. 87; and Washbrook, "Political Change in a Stable Society," p. 23.

same. My analysis of Thanjavur District leads me to argue, therefore, that the limited spread and intensity of agrarian radicalism in India is not to be attributed to the weakness of modernizing forces per se, as suggested by Barrington Moore, but can be instead partly attributed to the nature of the interaction between modernizing forces and India's social structure.

Moore is thus much closer to the truth when he argues that Indian exceptionalism is due to the heterogeneity of Indian geography, economy, and culture, especially in the premodern period, and the resulting segmentation of Indian society. In such a system, concludes Moore, protest movements tend to form yet another segment and thus not to grow in intensity or to spread across space. If one expects that modernization would have an homogenizing and centralizing effect on Indian society, one can understand Moore's suggestion that the Indian case is explained by delayed modernization.

My own conclusion is that the diversity of Indian society has generally survived the modernization process, in fact still acts to bound and shape social and political responses to that process. This is true particularly in India's agrarian society, which closely reflects highly variable agro-ecological conditions. Thanjavur District is an excellent illustration of this principle: relatively fine ecological distinctions have given rise to different structural arrangements that in turn condition the political responses to economic conditions and change. In other words, political movements that develop as responses to the relations of agricultural production are especially likely to be "structurally quarantined." This tendency is much magnified in the Indian context.

However, I would certainly not claim this principle to be absolute. It can be overriden by events and forces. For instance, it takes more than the historical weight of centralized agrarian bureaucracy to explain the success of peasant revolution in China despite the obvious diversity of Chinese agrarian structure. The foremost example of such an overriding event is of course war, which is capable of bringing about a sudden and widespread breakdown of existing economic and social organization and a rapid fusion of society's elements along new economic and social lines. The powerful catalytic effect of war in bringing about agrarian revolutions, as in China, Yugoslavia, and Vietnam, has been noted by many scholars.

The other major overriding force is of course nationalism. Certainly one of the most important differences between the Chinese and the Indian situations, one that Barrington Moore seems to give little weight, was the success of the Chinese Communists in capturing the nationalist position (the success of which was owed to a combination of creative leadership and the opportunity presented by the Japanese invasion).[13] The isolation of the Indian Communists from the nationalist movement during World War II and in the immediate post-war period was a major reason for the eventual failure of the radical movements in Telengana and Thanjavur in the late 1940s.[14] That these movements found themselves opposed to a new national government at the moment of independence suggests they were doomed from the start. Furthermore, the fluctuations and divisions in Indian Communist ideology, leadership, and organization over the next twenty-five years, which hampered and bounded attempts at agrarian mobilization in Thanjavur and elsewhere, were the result of Communist efforts to come to terms with Indian nationalism. The reformist trend of these efforts was also reflected in the evolution of the Thanjavur movement.

However, it should be mentioned that in Thanjavur the Communist position on the periphery of the nationalist movement was not completely disadvantageous. In the 1940s this made it possible for the Communists to ally themselves with the growing Tamil regionalist movement, which undoubtedly contributed to their early support in Thanjavur.[15] However, by the late 1960s the Communists were in competition with the regionalist parties as well, and suffering from it.

The nationalist and regionalist ideologies appealed to social and political identities that transcended ecologically and structurally derived, and thus highly localized, agrarian class interests. Thus, as the nationalist and regionalist forces, seeking to broaden their mass support, incorporated the minimal economic demands of tenants and laborers in their programs the basis for radical mobilization in Thanjavur's agrarian system was progressively weakened.

[13] See Sen Gupta, *Communism*, pp. 426-427. The definitive statement of thesis is Chalmers A. Johnson, *Peasant Nationalism and Communist Power: The Emergence of Revolutionary China, 1937-1945* (Stanford, Ca.: Stanford University Press, 1962).

[14] One of the reasons for the early success of the Telengana rebellion was that, because it was initially directed against the government of the Nizam of Hyderabad, it drew strength from the nationalist upsurge at the time of independence. But when the Indian Army intervened it became a struggle against the new national government and lost strength quickly. See Hamza Alavi, "Peasants and Revolution," in *Imperialism and Revolution in South Asia*, ed. Kathleen Gough and Hari P. Sharma (New York and London: Monthly Review Press, 1973), pp. 325-328.

[15] See Andre Beteille, *Castes, Old and New: Essays in Social Structure and Social Stratification* (Bombay: Asia Publishing House, 1969), pp. 169-170.

Over the twenty-five years from Independence to 1972 competitive party politics resulted in a gradual widening of the circle of political mobilization in Thanjavur and in an incremental extension of agrarian reforms. Over the same period growth-oriented agricultural development policies combined with modest institutional change provided limited but crucial flexibility for compromise between the agrarian classes over the distribution of the agricultural product. The apparently stabilizing effects of these undramatic trends suggest that class-based political mobilization of the poor peasantry for radical change is not necessarily the only solution to the dilemma of India's political economy. The gradualist approach to transforming Indian society without revolutionary violence— Mahatma Gandhi's original vision—finds some support in the Thanjavur experience, provided of course that one can expect the political system and economic policy to continue to be responsive to growing political consciousness and economic expectations.

The sources and the limits of agrarian radicalism are defined by the interaction of complex agro-economic conditions and the wider political economy. It must be emphasized, however, that neither is static. For instance, the rapid growth of population in Thanjavur District threatens over the longer term to create a rural proletariat throughout the district. Between 1961 and 1971, for instance, the number of agricultural laborers in Zones 4 and 5 increased at a rate four to five times greater than that in Zones 1 through 3 (apparently due to massive immigration of laborers from Zones 2 and 3 seeking work). The beginnings of radical consciousness among laborers in Zone 5 revealed in my survey data could spread if this tendency to proletarianization is not checked. Furthermore, the responsiveness of the state and national political systems to the changing composition and needs of the agarian population cannot be extrapolated from the past. The future of agrarian radicalism in Thanjavur or elsewhere in India might be guessed, but it cannot be confidently predicted.

TABLE 91

Agricultural Workers in the Rural Population, 1961 and 1971

	1961			1971		
	Persons	Males	Females	Persons	Males	Females
Rural workers as % of total rural population						
All India	45.06	58.22	31.40	34.53	53.55	14.55
Tamil Nadu	45.57	59.74	31.28	39.21	58.37	19.88
Thanjavur	44.84	61.37	28.62	35.76	57.73	14.09
Rural cultivators as % of total rural workers						
All India	60.32	61.08	58.84	50.88	56.05	30.86
Tamil Nadu	50.97	53.14	47.35	39.91	45.77	22.53
Thanjavur	41.30	44.28	35.05	33.49	37.94	13.37
Rural agricultural laborers as % of total rural workers						
All India	18.87	15.77	24.84	29.98	24.92	49.55
Tamil Nadu	21.81	17.75	28.59	36.46	30.80	53.24
Thanjavur	37.02	30.37	51.03	48.26	41.36	70.53

SOURCES: *Census of India, 1971: Provisional Population Totals*, pp. 29-33; India, *District Census Handbook, 1971*, 1: 2-3; India, *District Census Handbook, 1961*, 2: 540-541.

TABLE 92

Work Force Participation Rates for Cultivators and Laborers in Rural Tamil Nadu: 1961 and 1971 Census Figures

Category and Sex	1961		1971
	Actual	Adjusted	
Cultivators			
Males	33.1	32.2	26.7
Females	17.6	15.6	3.9
Total	25.3	23.9	15.4
Agricultural laborers			
Males	11.0	10.8	18.1
Females	10.6	8.7	11.0
Total	10.8	9.9	14.6

SOURCE: *Census of India, 1971: Report of Re-Survey on Economic Questions—Some Results*, Paper 1 of 1974—Miscellaneous Studies (New Delhi: Office of the Registrar-General and Census Commissioner of India, 1974), p. 44.

TABLE 93

Decennial Population Growth Rates in New Delta Area and
Thanjavur District, 1931-1971

	New Delta:* % Increase in Total Population	Whole District: % Increase in Rural Population
1931-41	8.45	7.46
1941-51	32.97	12.52
1951-61	20.63	7.47
1961-71	26.11	18.12

SOURCES: All New Delta decennial growth rates and 1961-71 rates for the whole
district calculated by author from data in: Madras, *1951 Census Handbook, Tanjore
District*, p. 17; India, *District Census Handbook, 1961*, 1: 71; and India, *District Census
Handbook, 1971*, 1: 2-9. Whole district growth rates for 1931-41, 1941-51, and 1951-
61 from India, *District Census Handbook, 1961*, 1: 13.

NOTES: New Delta growth rates are for total population: whole district growth
rates are for rural population only. This discrepancy, necessitated by the lack of
comparable data for calculating the growth rates, is of little significance because the
New Delta population is almost entirely rural.

* The New Delta figures are for the taluk of Pattukottai in 1931, 1941, and 1951,
and for the combined taluks of Pattukottai and Orathanad in 1961 and 1971.

Agricultural Economics Research Centre, Department of Economics, University of Madras. *Sengipatti: A Re-Survey of a Dry Village in the Fertile Thanjavur District.* Madras, 1969.
"Study of High Yielding Varieties Programme in Thanjavur District: Rabi 1968-69." Typewritten. Madras, 1969.
———. "Study of High Yielding Varieties Programme in Thanjavur District, Tamil Nadu: Kharif 1968-69." Typewritten. Madras, 1969.
Agricultural Workers' Association. "East Thanjavur District Agricultural Workers' Problems: A Memorandum Placed Before the Judge of the Enquiry Commission on Behalf of the Agricultural Workers' Association, Thanjavur, March 11, 1969." Typewritten. Undated.
Alavi, Hamza. "Peasants and Revolution." In *Imperialism and Revolution in South Asia,* edited by Kathleen Gough and Hari P. Sharma, pp. 291-337. New York and London: Monthly Review Press, 1973.
Alexander, K. C. *Agrarian Tension in Thanjavur.* Hyderabad: National Institute of Community Development, 1975.
———. "Agrarian Unrest in Kuttanad, Kerala." *Behavioral Sciences and Community Development* 7 (1973): 1-16.
———. "Agricultural Labour Unions: A Study in Three South Indian States." National Institute of Rural Development, Occasional Monograph no. 1. Hyderabad: National Institute of Rural Development, 1978.
———. "Changing Labour-Cultivator Relations in South India." In *Changing Agrarian Relations in India: Papers and Proceedings of Seminar Held at the NICD, Hyderabad, April 5-6, 1974,* pp. 21-48. Hyderabad: National Institute of Community Development, 1975.
———. "Economic Status and Source of Agricultural Credit of Farmers in East Thanjavur." *Community Development and Panchayati Raj Digest* 5 (July 1973): 20-23.
———. "Emergence of Peasant Organisations in South India." *Economic and Political Weekly* 15 (June 28, 1980): A72-A84.
———. "Emerging Farmer-Labour Relations in Kuttanad." *Economic and Political Weekly* 8 (August 25, 1973): 1,551-1,560.
———. "Genesis of Agrarian Tension in Thanjavur: Findings of a Research Study." *Economic and Political Weekly* 10 (December 6, 1975): 1,881-1,886.
———. "Some Characteristics of the Agrarian Social Structure of Tamil Nadu." *Economic and Political Weekly* 10 (April 19, 1975): 664-672.
Archetti, Eduardo et al. "Agrarian Structure and Peasant Autonomy." *Journal of Peace Research* 3 (1970): 185-195.

Ayyar, K. N. Krishnaswami. *Statistical Appendix, Together With A Supplement to The District Gazetteer (1906) For Tanjore District.* Edited by T. G. Rutherford. Madras, 1933.

Badrinath. *A Report on the Implementation of the Tamilnadu Agricultural Lands Record of Tenancy Rights Act, 1969.* Madras, 1971.

Baker, Christopher John. *The Politics of South India, 1920-1937.* Cambridge: Cambridge University Press, 1976.

————, and Washbrook, D. A. *South India: Political Institutions and Political Change, 1880-1940.* New Delhi: The Macmillan Co., 1975.

Baliga, B. S. *Tanjore District Handbook.* Madras: Government Press, 1957.

Bardhan, Pranab. " 'Green Revolution' and Agricultural Labourers." *Economic and Political Weekly* 5 (July 1970): 1,239-1,246.

————. "Inequality of Farm Incomes: Study of Four Districts." *Economic and Political Weekly* 9 (February 1979): 301-307.

————. "Variations in Agricultural Wages." *Economic and Political Weekly* 8 (May 26, 1973): 947-950.

Barnett, Marguerite Ross. "Cultural Nationalist Electoral Politics in Tamil Nadu." In *Studies in Electoral Politics in the Indian States,* vol. 4, *Party Systems and Cleavages,* edited by Myron Weiner and John Osgood Field, pp. 70-106. New Delhi: Manohar Book Service, 1975.

————. *The Politics of Cultural Nationalism in South India.* Princeton, N.J.: Princeton University Press, 1976.

Beteille, Andre. "Agrarian Movements in India." Mimeographed. Undated.

————. *Caste, Class and Power: Changing Patterns of Stratification in a Tanjore Village.* Berkeley, Ca.: University of California Press, 1965.

————. *Castes, Old and New: Essays·in Social Structure and Social Stratification.* Bombay: Asia Publishing House, 1969.

————. *Studies in Agrarian Social Structure.* New Delhi: Oxford University Press, 1974.

Brass, Paul R. "Political Parties of the Radical Left in South Asian Politics." In *Radical Politics in South Asia,* edited by Paul R. Brass and Marcus F. Franda, pp. 3-116. Cambridge, Mass.: The M.I.T. Press, 1973.

————, and Franda, Marcus F., eds. *Radical Politics in South Asia.* Cambridge, Mass.: The M.I.T. Press, 1973.

Brown, Dorris D. *Agricultural Development in India's Districts.* Cambridge, Mass.: Harvard University Press, 1971.

Coimbatore Agricultural College, Agricultural Economics and Rural Sociology Wing. "An Economic Appraisal of the Owner-Operated and Tenant-Operated Farms in Thanjavur District." Mimeographed. Undated.

Das Gupta, Biplab. *The Naxalite Movement.* Centre for the Study of Developing Societies, Monograph no. 1. New Delhi: Allied Publishers, 1974.

————, and Morris-Jones, W. H. *Patterns and Trends in Indian Politics: An*

Ecological Analysis of Aggregate Data on Society and Elections. New Delhi: Allied Publishers, 1976.

Desai, A. R., ed. *Peasant Struggles in India.* Bombay: Oxford University Press, 1979.

Dharampal. *The Madras Panchayat System.* 2 vols. New Delhi: Impex India, 1972.

Dogan, Mattei. "Political Cleavage and Social Stratification in France and Italy." In *Party Systems and Voter Alignments: Cross-National Perspectives,* edited by Seymour M. Lipset and Stein Rokkan, pp. 129-195. New York: The Free Press, 1967.

————, and Rokkan, Stein, eds. *Quantitative Ecological Analysis in the Social Sciences.* Cambridge, Mass.: The M.I.T. Press, 1969.

Elkins, David J. *Electoral Participation in a South Indian Context.* Durham, N.C.: Carolina Academic Press, 1975.

Elliott, Carolyn M. "Decline of a Patrimonial Regime: The Telengana Rebellion in India, 1946-51." *Journal of Asian Studies* 34 (November 1974): 27-47.

Frankel, Francine R. *India's Green Revolution: Economic Gains and Political Costs.* Princeton, N.J.: Princeton University Press, 1971.

————. *India's Political Economy, 1947-1977: The Gradual Revolution.* Princeton, N.J.: Princeton University Press, 1978.

————. "The Politics of the Green Revolution: Shifting Patterns of Peasant Participation in India and Pakistan." In *Food, Population and Employment: The Impact of the Green Revolution,* edited by Thomas T. Poleman and Donald K. Freebairn, pp. 120-166. New York: Praeger Publishers for the Cornell University Program on Science, Technology, and Society, 1973.

————. "Problems of Correlating Electoral and Ecological Variables: An Analysis of Voting Behavior and Agrarian Modernization in Uttar Pradesh." In *Studies in Electoral Politics in the Indian States,* vol. 3, *The Impact of Modernization,* edited by Myron Weiner and John Osgood Field, pp. 149-193. New Delhi: Manohar Book Service, 1977.

Geertz, Clifford. *Agricultural Involution: The Processes of Ecological Change in Indonesia.* Berkeley, Ca.: University of California Press, 1963.

Ghazi, H. K. *Report on the Fifth General Elections in Tamil Nadu, 1971.* Madras: Government of Tamil Nadu, 1974.

Gough, Kathleen. "Agrarian Change in Thanjavur." In *Society and Change: Essays in Honour of Sachin Chaudhuri,* edited by K. S. Krishnaswamy et al., pp. 258-291. Published for Sameeksha Trust. Bombay: Oxford University Press, 1977.

————. "Caste in a Tanjore Village." In *Aspects of Caste in South India, Ceylon, and Northwest Pakistan,* edited by E. R. Leach, pp. 11-60. Cambridge: Cambridge University Press, 1971.

————. "Colonial Economics in Southeast India." *Economic and Political Weekly* 12 (March 26, 1977): 546-548.

————. "Harijans in Thanjavur." In *Imperialism and Revolution in South Asia,* edited by Kathleen Gough and Hari P. Sharma, pp. 222-245. New York and London: Monthly Review Press, 1973.

————. "Indian Peasant Uprisings." *Economic and Political Weekly* 9 (Special number, 1974): 1,391-1,412.

————. "Modes of Production of Southern India." *Economic and Political Weekly* 15 (Annual Number, 1980): 337-364.

————. "Peasant Resistance and Revolt in South India." *Pacific Affairs* 41 (Winter 1968-1969): 526-544.

————. "The Social Structure of a Tanjore Village." In *Village India: Studies in the Little Community,* edited by McKim Marriott, pp. 36-52. 1955. Reprint. Chicago: University of Chicago Press, Phoenix Books, 1969.

————, and Sharma, Hari P., eds. *Imperialism and Revolution in South Asia.* New York and London: Monthly Review Press, 1973.

Griffin, Keith. *The Political Economy of Agrarian Change: An Essay on the Green Revolution.* Cambridge, Mass.: Harvard University Press, 1974.

Hameed, N. D. Abdul. "Tenancy and Technological Progress in Thanjavur District Agriculture." In *Agricultural Development of India: A Study of the Intensive Agricultural District Programme,* edited by V. Shanmugasundaram, pp. 268-274. Madras University Publications, Economic Development Series no. 20. Madras: University of Madras, 1972.

Hardgrave, Robert L., Jr. "The Communist Parties of Kerala: An Electoral Profile." In *Studies in Electoral Politics in the Indian States,* vol. 4, *Party Systems and Cleavages,* edited by Myron Weiner and John Osgood Field, pp. 167-209. New Delhi: Manohar Book Service, 1975.

————. *The Dravidian Movement.* Bombay: Popular Prakashan, 1963.

————. "The Kerala Communists: Contradictions of Power." In *Radical Politics in South Asia,* edited by Paul R. Brass and Marcus F. Franda, pp. 119-180. Cambridge, Mass.: The M.I.T. Press, 1973.

Harriss, John. *Capitalism and Peasant Farming: A Study of Agricultural Change and Agrarian Structure in Northern Tamil Nadu.* School of Development Studies, University of East Anglia, Monograph in Development Studies no. 3. Norwich, Eng.: School óf Development Studies, University of East Anglia, 1979.

Harrison, James Q. "Agricultural Modernization and Income Distribution: An Economic Analysis of the Impact of New Seed Varieties on the Crop Production of Large and Small Farms in India." Ph.D. dissertation, Princeton University, 1972.

————. "Small Farmer Participation in Agricultural Modernization: Report on a Survey of Two IADP Districts (West Godavari and Thanjavur)." Mimeographed. Staff Document, The Ford Foundation. New Delhi, December 1970.

Haswell, M. R. *Economics of Development in Village India.* London: Routledge and Kegan Paul, 1967.

Hemingway, F. R. *Madras District Gazetteers*, pt. 1, *Tanjore*, edited by W. Francis. Madras, 1906.

Hindu (Madras), 1965-1973.

India. *Census of India, 1961*, vol. 9, *District Census Handbook, Thanjavur*. 2 vols. Madras: Superintendent of Census Operations, 1965.

——. *Census of India, 1961*, vol. 9, *Madras*, pt. 6, *Village Survey Monographs, 15, Kadambangudi*. Madras: Superintendent of Census Operations, 1965.

——. *Census of India, 1961*, vol. 9, *Madras*, pt. 6, *Village Survey Monographs, 11, Kunnalur*. Madras: Superintendent of Census Operations, 1964.

——. *Census of India, 1961*. vol. 9, *Madras*, pt. 6, *Village Survey Monographs, 25, Vilangulam*. Madras: Superintendent of Census Operations, 1966.

——. *Census of India, 1971: Provisional Population Totals*, Paper 1 of 1971—Supplement. New Delhi, 1971.

——. *Census of India, 1971*, ser. 19, *Tamil Nadu*, pt. X-B, *District Census Handbook: Village and Town Primary Census Abstract, Thanjavur*. 2 vols. Madras: Director of Census Operations, 1972.

——. Ministry of Agriculture and Irrigation. *All-India Report on Agricultural Census, 1970-71* by I. J. Naidu. New Delhi, 1975.

——. Ministry of Agriculture and Irrigation, Directorate of Economics and Statistics. *Studies in the Economics of Farm Management in Thanjavur District (Tamil Nadu): Report for the Year 1967-68* by V. Shanmugasundaram. New Delhi, 1974.

——. Ministry of Agriculture and Irrigation, Directorate of Economics and Statistics. *Studies in the Economics of Farm Management in Thanjavur District (Tamil Nadu): Report for the Year 1968-69* by V. Shanmugasundaram. New Delhi, 1974.

——. Ministry of Food, Agriculture, Community Development and Cooperation, Department of Agriculture, Expert Committee on Assessment and Evaluation. *Intensive Agricultural District Programme: Second Report (1960-65)*. New Delhi, undated.

——. Ministry of Food, Agriculture, Community Development and Cooperation, Department of Agriculture, Expert Commiittee on Assessment and Evaluation. *Intensive Agricultural District Programme: Third Report, 1965-66 and 1966-67*. New Delhi, undated.

——. Ministry of Food, Agriculture, Community Development and Cooperation, Department of Agriculture, Expert Committee on Assessment and Evaluation. *Modernising Indian Agriculture: Fourth Report on the Intensive Agricultural District Programme (1960-68)*, vol. 2, *District Chapters*. New Delhi, undated.

——. Planning Commission, Programme Evaluation Organisation. *Evaluation Study of the High Yielding Varieties Programme: Report for the Kharif, 1967*. August 1968.

——. Planning Commission, Programme Evaluation Organisation. *Evaluation Study of the High Yielding Varieties Programme: Report for the Rabi, 1968-69—Wheat, Paddy and Jowar*. November 1969.

Indian Express (Madras), 1965-1973.

Intensive Agricultural District Programme, Thanjavur. "A Case Study on The Linking of Credit with Marketing in Respect of Production Loans Issued by Multi-purpose Cooperative Societies in the Area of Operation on Mannargudi Cooperative Society During 1966-67." Typewritten. Undated.

———. "Farm Management Study of 114 Farms, 1962-63." Typewritten. 1965.

———. "Note on Fertilizer Use in Thanjavur District." Typewritten. Undated.

———. "A Note on Yield Trends of Paddy in Thanjavur District." Typewritten. Undated.

———. "Quick Study on the Causes for Not Converting The Entire Proposed Samba Lands into Double Crop Lands During 1967-68." Typewritten. Undated.

———. "A Quick Study on the Estimation of Marketable Surplus of Kuruvai Paddy in Thanjavur District During the Year 1971." Typewritten. Undated.

———. "Study of Awareness and Acceptance of the Package of Practices Recommended under the Intensive Agricultural District Programme, 1963-64." Operational Research Study no. 2. Typewritten. Undated.

———. "Study on the Assessment and Impact of Samba Conversion Programme." Typewritten. Undated.

———. "Study on the Cost of Cultivation of IR8 Paddy." Typewritten. Undated.

———. "Study on Impact of Package Programme, 1970-71." Typewritten. Undated.

———. "Study on Low Consumption of Phosphatic and Potassic Fertilizers." Typewritten. Undated.

———. *Study on Tenancy Patterns in Thanjavur District, 1969-70.* Madras: Government of Tamil Nadu, undated.

———. "Study on the Utilisation Aspect of Cooperative Crop Loans, 1969-70." Typewritten. Undated.

Irschick, Eugene F. *Politics and Social Conflict in South India: The Non-Brahman Movement and Tamil Separatism, 1916-1929.* Berkeley, Ca.: University of California Press, 1969.

Iyer, S. S. "A Case Study of Thanjavur District: Anatomy of Agrarian Unrest." *People's Action* 5 (New Delhi: May 1971): 23-26.

Johnson, Chalmers A. *Peasant Nationalism and Communist Power: The Emergence of Revolutionary China, 1937-1945.* Stanford, Ca.: Stanford University Press, 1962.

Kennedy, Richard. "Status and Control of Temples in Tamil Nadu." *The Indian Economic and Social History Review* 11 (June-September 1974): 260-290.

Khusro, A. M. *The Economics of Land Reform and Farm Size in India.* Institute of Economic Growth Studies in Economic Growth, no. 14. Madras: Macmillan, 1973.

Kumar, Dharma. *Land and Caste in South India: Agricultural Labour in Madras Presidency in the Nineteenth Century.* Cambridge: Cambridge University Press, 1965.

————. "Landownership and Inequality in Madras Presidency: 1853-54 to 1946-47." *The Indian Economic and Social History Review* 12 (July-September 1975): 229-261.

Kurien, C. T., and James, Josef. *Economic Change in Tamil Nadu: A Regionally and Functionally Disaggregated Analysis.* New Delhi: Allied Publishers, 1979.

Ladejinsky, Wolf. "Green Revolution in Bihar. The Kosi Area: A Field Trip." *Economic and Political Weekly* 4 (September 27, 1969): A147-A162.

————. "How Green is the Indian Green Revolution." *Economic and Political Weekly* 8 (December 29, 1973): A133-A144.

————. *A Study on Tenurial Conditions in Package Districts.* New Delhi: Government of India, Planning Commission, 1965.

Lewis, John Wilson, ed. *Peasant Rebellion and Communist Revolution in Asia.* Stanford, Ca.: Stanford University Press, 1974.

Linz, Juan J. "Patterns of Land Tenure, Division of Labor, and Voting Behavior in Europe." *Comparative Politics* 8 (April 1976): 365-430.

Madras. *1951 Census Handbook, Tanjore District.* Madras: Government Press, 1953.

————. Director of Statistics. *A Statistical Atlas of the Thanjavur District: Revised and Brought Up To The Decennium Ending Fasli 1360 (1950-51).* Madras, 1965.

————. Hindu Religious and Charitable Endowments (Administration) Department. *Administration Report for the Year from 1st April 1960 to 31st March 1961.* Madras, 1962.

————. The Land Revenue Reforms Committee. *First Report.* Madras: Government Press, 1951.

————. Legislative Assembly Department. *The Madras Agricultural Lands Record of Tenancy Rights Bill, 1968 (L.A. Bill No. 18 of 1968): Report and Proceedings of the Select Committee of the Tamil Nadu Legislative Assembly.* Madras, 1969.

Marx, Karl. *The Eighteenth Brumaire of Louis Bonaparte.* New York: International Publishers, 1963.

Mencher, Joan P. *Agriculture and Social Structure in Tamil Nadu: Past Origins, Present Transformations and Future Prospects.* New Delhi: Allied Publishers, 1978.

————. "Conflicts and Contradictions in the Green Revolution: The Case of Tamil Nadu." *Economic and Political Weekly* 9 (February 1974): 309-323.

————. "Land Ceilings in Tamil Nadu: Facts and Fictions." *Economic and Political Weekly* 10 (Annual number, 1975): 241-254.

————. "A Tamil Village: Changing Socio-Economic Structure in Madras State." In *Change and Continuity in India's Villages*, edited by K. Ishwaran, pp. 197-218. New York: Columbia University Press, 1970.

Migdal, Joel S. *Peasants, Politics, and Revolution: Pressures toward Political and Social Change in the Third World*. Princeton, N.J.: Princeton University Press, 1974.

Moore, Barrington, Jr. *Social Origins of Dictatorship and Democracy: Lord and Peasant in the Making of the Modern World*. Boston: Beacon Press, 1966.

Muehl, John Frederick. *Interview with India*. New York: The John Day Co., 1950.

Mukherjee, Nilamani. *The Ryotwari System in Madras, 1792-1827*. Calcutta: Firma K. L. Mukhopadhyay, 1962.

————, and Frykenberg, Robert Eric. "The Ryotwari System and Social Organization in the Madras Presidency." In *Land Control and Social Structure in Indian History*, edited by Robert Eric Frykenberg, pp. 217-226. Madison, Wis.: University of Wisconsin Press, 1969.

Muthiah, C. "The Agricultural Labour Problem in Thanjavur and the New Agricultural Strategy." *Indian Journal of Agricultural Economics* 25 (July-September 1970): 15-23.

————. "Development of Landless Labourers: Role of Group Bargaining Power." Paper presented to the Seminar on Weaker Sections held at the Indian Institute of Management at Ahmedabad, October 1972. Mimeographed.

————. "The Green Revolution—Participation by Small Versus Large Farmers." *Indian Journal of Agricultural Economics* 26 (January-March 1971): 53-66.

————. "Problems and Progress in Farm Mechanization in South India." Paper submitted for the Seminar on Farm Mechanization in Southeast Asia, November 27-December 2, 1972. Mimeographed.

Nicholas, Ralph W. "Structures of Politics in the Villages of Southern Asia." In *Structure and Change in Indian Society*, edited by Milton Singer and Bernard S. Cohn, pp. 243-284. Chicago: Aldine Publishing Co., 1968.

Nicholson, Norman K. *Panchayat Raj, Rural Development and the Political Economy of Village India*. South Asia Occasional Papers and Theses, no. 2. Ithaca: Cornell University Rural Development Committee and South Asia Program, 1973.

Paige, Jeffery M. *Agrarian Revolution: Social Movements and Export Agriculture in the Underdeveloped World*. New York: The Free Press, 1975.

Pavier, Barry. "The Telengana Armed Struggle." *Economic and Political Weekly* 9 (Special number, 1974): 1,413-1,420.

Peasant and Labor. Monthly Journal of the All-India Kisan Sabha. New Delhi, 1965-1973.

Pillai, Ganapathia. "Report of the Commission of Inquiry on the Agrarian Labour Problems of East Thanjavur District." Typewritten. [1969.]

Popkin, Samuel L. *The Rational Peasant: The Political Economy of Rural Society in Vietnam.* Berkeley, Ca.: University of California Press, 1979.

Rao, M.S.A., ed. *Social Movements in India,* vol. 1, *Peasant and Backward Classes Movements.* New Delhi: Manohar Publishers, 1978.

Ratnam, B. *Agricultural Development in Madras State Prior to 1900.* Madras: New Century Book House, 1966.

Riley, Parkes. "Poverty, Literacy and the Communist Vote in India." *Asian Survey* 15 (June 1975): 543-558.

Rosen, George. *Peasant Society in a Changing Economy: Comparative Development in Southeast Asia and India.* Urbana, Ill.: University of Illinois Press, 1975.

Rudolph, Lloyd I., and Rudolph, Susanne Hoeber. *The Modernity of Tradition: Political Development in India.* Chicago: University of Chicago Press, 1967.

Saini, G. R. "Farm Size, Productivity, and Returns to Scale." *Economic and Political Weekly* 4 (June 28, 1969): A119-A122.

———. "Green Revolution and the Distribution of Farm Incomes." *Economic and Political Weekly* 11 (March 27, 1976): A17-A21.

Sayana, V. V. *The Agrarian Problems of Madras Province.* Madras: The Business Week Press, 1949.

Scott, James C. "Exploitation in Rural Class Relations: A Victim's Perspective." *Comparative Politics* 7 (July 1975): 498-532.

———. *The Moral Economy of the Peasant: Rebellion and Subsistence in Southeast Asia.* New Haven: Yale University Press, 1976.

———. "Patron-Client Politics and Political Change in Southeast Asia." *American Political Science Review* 66 (March 1972): 91-113.

———. "Peasant Revolution: A Dismal Science." *Comparative Politics* 9 (January 1977): 225-249.

Sen, Bandhudas. *The Green Revolution in India: A Perspective.* New York: John Wiley & Sons, 1974.

———. "Opportunities in the Green Revolution." *Economic and Political Weekly* 4 (August 16, 1969): 1,345-1,347, and 5 (March 28, 1970): A33-A40.

Sen Gupta, Bhabani. *Communism in Indian Politics.* New York: Columbia University Press, 1972.

Shivaraman, Mythily. "Thanjavur: Rumblings of Class Struggle in Tamil Nadu." In *Imperialism and Revolution in South Asia,* edited by Kathleen Gough and Hari P. Sharma, pp. 246-264. New York and London: Monthly Review Press, 1973.

Sivaswamy, K. G. *The Madras Ryotwari Tenant.* Madras: South Indian Federation of Agricultural Workers' Unions, 1948.

Sivertsen, Dagfinn. *When Caste Barriers Fall: A Study of Social and Economic Change in a South Indian Village.* Oslo: Universitets Forlaget, 1963.

Sonachalam, K. S. *Benefit-Cost Evaluation of Cauvery-Mettur Project.* New Delhi: Planning Commission, Research Programmes Committee, undated.

———. *Land Reforms in Tamil Nadu: Evaluation of Implementation.* New Delhi: Oxford and IBH Publishing Co., 1970.

Srinivas, M. N. *Social Change in Modern India.* Berkeley, Ca.: University of California Press, 1967.

Stinchcombe, Arthur L. "Agricultural Enterprise and Rural Class Relations." In *Political Development and Social Change,* edited by Jason L. Finkle and Richard W. Gable, 2d ed., pp. 359-371. New York: John Wiley & Sons, 1971.

Swenson, Clyde Geoffrey. "The Effect of Increases in Rice Production on Employment and Income in Thanjavur District, South India." Ph.D. dissertation, Michigan State University, 1973.

Tamil Nadu. Directorate of Agriculture. *Report of the Backward Classes Commission, Tamil Nadu: 1970.* 2 vols. Madras, 1975.

———. Director of Agriculture. *World Agricultural Census, 1970-71 (Fasli 1380): Tamil Nadu.* 2 vols. Madras, 1974.

Thorner, Daniel. *The Agrarian Prospect in India: Five Lectures on Land Reform Delivered in 1955 at the Delhi School of Economics.* New Delhi: Delhi University Press, 1956.

———, and Thorner, Alice. *Land and Labour in India.* Bombay: Asia Publishing House, 1962.

Ulavu Chelvam (Madras), 1965-1972.

Venkataramani, G. *Land Reform in Tamil Nadu.* Madras: Sangam Publishers for the Madras Institute of Development Studies, 1973.

Vyas, V. S. "Structural Change in Agriculture and the Small Farm Sector." *Economic and Political Weekly* 11 (January 10, 1976): 24-32.

Washbrook, D. A. *The Emergence of Provincial Politics: The Madras Presidency, 1870-1920.* Cambridge: Cambridge University Press, 1976.

———. "Political Change in a Stable Society: Tanjore District 1880 to 1920." In *South India: Political Institutions and Political Change, 1880-1940,* edited by C. J. Baker and D. A. Washbrook, pp. 20-68. New Delhi: The Macmillan Co., 1975.

Wolf, Eric R. *Peasant Wars of the Twentieth Century.* New York: Harper & Row, 1969.

Yeshwanth, T. S. *Re-Survey of a Tanjore Village: Madigai.* Madras: University of Madras, Agricultural Economics Research Centre, 1966.

Zagoria, Donald S. "Asian Tenancy Systems and Communist Mobilization of the Peasantry." In *Peasant Rebellion and Communist Revolution in Asia,* edited by John Wilson Lewis, pp. 29-60. Stanford, Ca.: Stanford University Press, 1974.

———. "The Ecology of Peasant Communism in India." *American Political Science Review* 65 (March 1971): 144-160.

Zagoria, Donald S. "A Note on Landlessness, Literacy and Agrarian Communism in India." *European Journal of Sociology* 13 (1972): 326-334.

————. "Peasants and Revolution." *Comparative Politics* 8 (April 1976): 321-326.

————. "The Social Basis of Communism in Kerala and West Bengal: A Study in Contrast." *Problems of Communism* 12 (1973): 16-24.

Library of Congress Cataloging in Publication Data

Bouton, Marshall M., 1942-
  Agrarian radicalism in South India.

  Bibliography: p.
  Includes index.
  1. Peasantry—India—Thanjāvūr (District)—Political
activity. 2. Radicalism—India—Thanjāvūr (District)
3. Thanjāvūr (India : District)—Rural conditions.
4. Agriculture—Economic aspects—India—Thanjāvūr
(District) I. Title.
HD879.T47B68 1985   322′.2′095482   85-3411
ISBN 0-691-07686-3 (alk. paper)
                                            Rev

Marshall M. Bouton is Director of Public Affairs at
the Asia Society in New York City